TE

D1137885

JIM MANTHORPE has trekked in many of the world's mountainous regions from Patagonia to the Himalaya and Scandinavia to the Canadian Rockies. Since 1999 he has worked as a freelance travel writer, photographer and lecturer. He is the author of two other Trailblazer guidebooks, *Pembrokeshire Coast Path* and *South Downs Way*.

He has also researched and updated *West Highland Way*, *Cornwall Coast Path* and the *Coast to Coast Path* in the British Walking Guide series as well as *Trekking in Ladakh* and *Trek*

Following

Scotsman newspa

Knoydart, access

be contacted at

The

in

can

Scottish Highlands – The Hillwalking Guide
First edition: 2005; this second edition: August 2009

Publisher
Trailblazer Publications
The Old Manse, Tower Rd, Hindhead, Surrey, GU26 6SU, UK
Fax (+44) 01428-607571, info@trailblazer-guides.com
www.trailblazer-guides.com

British Library Cataloguing in Publication Data
A catalogue record for this book is available from the British Library

ISBN 978-1-905864-21-8

© **Jim Manthorpe 2005, 2009**
Text and photographs

The right of Jim Manthorpe to be identified as the author of this work has been
asserted by him in accordance with the Copyright, Designs and Patents Act 1988

Editor: Nicky Slade
Series editor: Patricia Major
Layout: Nick Hill
Proofreading: Anna Jacomb-Hood
Cartography: Nick Hill
Index: Anna Jacomb-Hood

Warning: mountain walking can be dangerous
Please read the notes on when to go (pp18-23) and mountain safety (pp303-8).
Every effort has been made by the author and publisher to ensure that the information
contained herein is as accurate and up to date as possible. However, they are unable
to accept responsibility for any inconvenience, loss or injury sustained by anyone
as a result of the advice and information given in this guide.

Printed on chlorine-free paper by
D2Print (☎ +65-6295 5598), Singapore

Tenbury Library

Borrowed Items 16/01/2018 16:34
XXXX8782

Item Title	Due Date
ridges of England, Wales and Ireland : scrambling, mountaineering and cl	06/02/2018
Scottish Highlands : the hillwalking guide	06/02/2018

Can't find a book to read?
Ask a member of staff for a recommendation

Don't forget to collect your reserved books before you leave the library

Scottish Highlands
THE HILLWALKING GUIDE

JIM MANTHORPE

TRAILBLAZER PUBLICATIONS

For Claire

Acknowledgements

For this second edition I would like to thank the good people at Trailblazer, particularly Bryn Thomas, Nicky Slade, Anna Jacomb-Hood, and Nick Hill; without them this book would not have been possible. Thanks are also due to the folk of Knoydart, particularly Tommy McManmon who helped update the Ullapool section and Angela Williams, Cath Curd and Mark Woombs.

Thank you to everyone who has helped by offering details on changes for this second edition, particularly the helpful folk at tourist information centres across the Highlands: Heather at Tarbert on the Isle of Harris, Rosie Morrison in Durness, Colin McRae in Tyndrum, Susan in Callander, Kath Whitford in Ullapool, Ian Colston in Lochinver, Nicola Robertson in Strontian, Diarmid MacAulay in Aviemore, Annette in Craignure, Linda Fleming in Pitlochry, Trish Wilson in Oban, Veronica in Balloch, Viona in Tarbet, Joyce Webb in Killin and the staff at Portree TIC and Fort William TIC. Thanks also to Ken MacLennan for the loan of his cottage in Stoer, Calum Smyth, and Nick Jeggo for information on route changes on Mull.

Finally, thank you to my brother Jack for the website (🖳 www.jimmanthorpe.com) and my Mum, Dad, Sam and Amy for their support.

Thank you also to Claire who has shared in so many recent hill days.

A request

The author and publisher have tried to ensure that this guide is as accurate and up to date as possible. Nevertheless things change. If you notice any changes or omissions that should be included in the next edition of this book, please write to Jim Manthorpe at Trailblazer (address on p2) or email him at jim.manthorpe@trailblazer-guides.com. A free copy of the next edition will be sent to persons making a significant contribution.

Updated information will shortly be available on the Internet at
www.trailblazer-guides.com

Front cover: Glen Hurich from Beinn Resipol © Jim Manthorpe

CONTENTS

INTRODUCTION

Munros and munro-bagging 9

PART 1: PLANNING YOUR WALK

Practical information for the hillwalker
Accommodation 10 – Food 13 – Drink 14 – Money 15 – Services 15
Access 15 – Walking companies 16 – Information for foreign visitors 16

When to go
Seasons 18 – Temperature 20 – Rainfall 20 – Daylight hours 21
Annual events, festivals and Highland games 22 – Estates & deer stalking 23

What to take
The pack on your back 24 – Footwear 24 – Clothes 25 – Toiletries 26
First-aid kit 27 – General items 27 – Sleeping kit 27 – Camping gear 28
Bivvy gear 28 – Maps 28 – Recommended reading 29

Getting to the Highlands
Getting to Scotland 31 – Getting around the Highlands 34

PART 2: MINIMUM IMPACT WALKING

Environmental impact 38 – Economic impact 42

Conservation
Scottish Natural Heritage 43 – National parks 44 – Other protected areas 45

PART 3: THE HIGHLANDS

Facts about the Highlands
Geography 46 – Geology 47 – History 48 – Language 50

Flora and fauna
Mammals 51 – Birds 53 – Trees 57 – Flowers and plants 58 – Lichens 59

PART 4: ROUTE GUIDES AND MAPS

Map keys 60

Using this guide 61

Loch Lomond and the Southern Highlands
The mountains: Ben Ledi 879m 64 – The Cobbler 884m 65 – Ben
Lomond 974m 68 – Ben Vorlich 943m 70 – Ben More 1174m & Stob
Binnein 1165m 72 – Beinn Dorain 1076m & Beinn an Dothaidh 1004m 74
Stob a' Choire Odhair 945m & Stob Ghabhar 1090m 77

Loch Lomond and the Southern Highlands *(cont'd)*

Towns and villages: Callander 81 – Arrochar 84 – Inverbeg 86
Rowardennan 86 – Ardlui 86 – Inverarnan 86 – Crianlarich 87
Tyndrum 88 – Bridge of Orchy 89

Glen Coe and Glen Nevis

The mountains: Buachaille Etive Mor (Stob Dearg 1021m & Stob
na Broige 956m) 90 – Aonach Eagach (Meall Dearg 953m & Sgorr
nam Fiannaidh 967m) 93 – Stob Coire Sgreamhach 1072m, Bidean
nam Bian 1150m & Stob Coire nan Lochan 1115m 97 – Ballachulish
Horseshoe (Sgorr Dhearg 1024m & Sgorr Dhonuill 1001m) 100
Stob Ban 999m & Mullach nan Coirean 939m 103 – Carn Mor
Dearg 1220m & Ben Nevis 1344m 106

Towns and villages: Kingshouse 110 – Glen Coe 111 – Glencoe
Village 111 – Ballachulish 113 – Glen Nevis 113 – Fort William 114

The Central Highlands

The mountains: Beinn Ghlas 1103m & Ben Lawers 1214m 118
Schiehallion 1083m 120 – Sgor Iutharn 1028m, Geal Charn 1132m
& Carn Dearg 1034m 122 – Ben Alder 1148m & Beinn
Bheoil 1019m 127 – Creag Dhubh 757m 129 – Creag Meagaidh 1128m 130
Stob Coire Easain 1115m & Stob a' Choire Mheadhoin 1105m 132

Towns and villages: Killin 138 – Dalwhinnie 140 – Laggan 140
Tulloch 141 – Roybridge 141 – Corrour 141

The Cairngorms and Eastern Highlands

The mountains: Ben Vrackie 841m 143 – Mayar 928m &
Driesh 947m 145 – Carn a' Choire Bhoidheach 1110m &
Lochnagar 1155m 147 – Derry Cairngorm 1155m, Ben Macdui 1309m
& Carn a' Mhaim 1037m 151 – Braeriach 1296m, Sgor an Lochain
Uaine 1258m, Cairn Toul 1291m & The Devil's Point 1004m 158
Cairn Gorm 1244m 164 – Meall a'Bhuachaille 810m 166

Towns and villages: Pitlochry 169 – Clova 171 – Braemar 172
Aviemore 173 – Glenmore 174

Sunart to Knoydart

The mountains: Beinn Resipol 845m 176 – Sgurr Ghiubhsachain 849m
& Sgorr Craobh a' Chaorainn 775m 178 – The Corryhully Horseshoe (Sgurr
nan Coireachan 956m & Sgurr Thuilm 963m) 182 – Beinn Bhuidhe
(Knoydart) 855m 185 – Ladhar Bheinn 1020m 189 – Sgurr a'
Mhaoraich 1027m 194

Towns and villages: Strontian 197 – Glenfinnan 198 – Mallaig 198
Inverie 200 – Tomdoun 201 – Kinlochhourn 201 – Barisdale 201

Glen Shiel to Torridon and Fisherfield
The mountains: Beinn Sgritheall 974m 203 – The Saddle 1010m &
Sgurr na Sgine 946m 206 – Sgurr na Lapaich 1036m, Mam Sodhail 1181m
& Carn Eige 1183m 209 – Beinn Damh 902m 213 – Beinn Alligin (Tom
na Gruagaich 922m & Sgurr Mhor 986m) 215 – Beinn Eighe (Spidean
Coire nan Clach 993m & Ruadh-stac Mor 1010m) 217 – Beinn an
Eoin 855m 220 – A' Mhaigdean 967m & Ruadh Stac Mor 918m 222
An Teallach (Bidean a' Ghlas Thuill 1062m & Sgurr Fiona 1060m) 227

Towns and villages: Glenelg 231 – Glen Shiel & Shiel Bridge 231
Tomich 232 – Torridon 232 – Kinlochewe 233 – Poolewe 233
Gairloch 234 – Dundonnell 234

The Far North
The mountains: Stac Pollaidh 613m 236 – Suilven (Caisteal
Liath 731m) 237 – Quinaig (Sail Gharbh 808m, Sail Gorm 776m &
Spidean Coinich 764m) 240 – Ben Stack 721m 242 – Arkle 787m 243
Ben Hope 927m 245 – Ben Loyal 764m 246

Towns and villages: Ullapool 249 – Lochinver 252 – Kylesku 253
Scourie 253 – Durness 253 – Tongue 254

The Islands
The mountains: Arran (Goatfell 874m 255) – Mull (Beinn
Talaidh 762m 258) – Rum (Ainshval 781m & Askival 812m 260)
Skye (Bla Bheinn 928m 265; Sgurr nan Gillean 964m 267;
Glamaig 775m 269; The Storr 719m 271) – South Uist (Beinn Mhor 620m,
Ben Corodale 527m & Hecla 606m 273) – Harris (Ceapabhal 365m 275;
Clisham 799m 278) – Lewis (Suaineabhal 429m 281)

Towns and villages: Arran (Brodick 283) – Oban (for Mull) 284
Mull (Craignure 286) – Rum (Kinloch 287) – Skye (Broadford 287;
Torrin 288; Sligachan 288; Portree 289; Uig 290)
South Uist (Tobha Mor 292) – Harris (An t-Ob 292, An Taobh Tuath 292;
Tarbert 293; Ardhasaig 294) – Lewis (Timsgearraidh 294)

The Big Treks
The Great Traverse – Corrour to Glen Nevis (via The Grey Corries,
  The Aonachs, Carn Mor Dearg & Ben Nevis), 2-3 days 295
Cairngorms – Aviemore to Linn of Dee, 2 days 298
Knoydart – Kinlochhourn to Inverie, 2 days 300
Fisherfield – Poolewe to Dundonnell, 2-3 days 301

APPENDICES
A: Mountain safety 303   C: Glossary 310
B: Gaelic 309   D: Mountain photography 311

INDEX 312

INTRODUCTION

'Thousands of tired, nerve-shaken, over-civilized people are beginning to find out that going to the mountain is going home; that wildness is a necessity'

John Muir, *Wild Wool*, 1875

The Highland region of Scotland is rightly considered to contain some of the most breathtaking landscapes in Europe. It is the largest upland area in the British Isles and, despite the modest height of the hills when compared to other European ranges, is home to some incredibly diverse mountain architecture from the high sub-Arctic plateau and deep corries of the Cairngorms to the knife-edged ridges of the Skye Cuillin. Add to this the tumbling burns and rivers, ancient Caledonian pine forests and the magnificent islands and sea lochs (fjords) along the west coast and you have a picture of what the Highlands have to offer.

It is perfectly possible to spend a lifetime walking these hills and many people do. Recreation in the mountains has become increasingly popular over the past ten to twenty years leading to the formation of a number of official long-distance paths, notably the West Highland Way and Great Glen Way. But to appreciate fully this diverse mountain region, the history, the wildlife and the ever-changing light there can be no better way than to don a pair of walking boots and climb to the tops.

A hugely popular activity among British hillwalkers is to 'bag' the munros (see box opposite), the 284 Scottish summits of 3000ft or more. To limit oneself to these mountains alone, however, is to miss out on some of the most beautiful peaks that Scotland has to offer.

Despite the popularity of the Highlands, it is still possible to walk for days in the mountains without seeing another soul, making this the premier mountain region in the UK when compared to the English Lake District or Welsh Snowdonia, which are altogether busier and much smaller in area.

The Scottish hills are certainly wild in character but they are far from untouched. Man has, over the centuries, upset the balance of nature in this fragile environment. The most notable change to the landscape has come through the loss of the ancient Caledonian pine forest that once filled many of the glens. Today around 1% of this woodland remains in vulnerable fragments. Efforts are being made to encourage natural regeneration but this is hampered by the grazing activities of the red deer that roam the hillsides. Their population has exploded following the eradication of the wolf by man around 300 years ago. The high peaks and ridges above the treeline, however, have changed little or not at all since the last Ice Age, some 10,000 years ago. A walk up there is the closest you can get in the British Isles to finding what some might call true wilderness.

The great wonder of the Highlands is how the mountains change in character over such a short distance. The tamest hills are in the south around beautiful Loch Lomond which spills out into the Lowlands. In the east, the massive high-altitude Cairngorm plateau cut with deep corries is home to arctic wildlife and semi-permanent snowfields, a marked contrast to the west coast which is a land of narrow ridges, pyramidal peaks and fjords. Even further west, the Isle of

Skye offers the most challenging and vicious-looking peaks in Britain in the shape of the Cuillin Hills, while the Outer Hebrides contain much smaller, rounded hills that look down on deserted white-sand beaches. Finally, in the far north, there is some of the remotest and wildest country, inselberg peaks rising as lonely sentinels from a vast lochan-studded floor.

The tops of many of these hills are relatively easy to attain while others require a certain level of ability, expertise and in some cases climbing experience. This book offers a selection of some of the best hill walks from each region of the Highlands. Some are straightforward walks of just a few hours while others are much longer and may involve a spot of scrambling or extra reserves of energy and fitness. The hills chosen for this book have been selected not just for their aesthetic quality but also to cover different levels of difficulty so that anyone with at least a little hillwalking experience will find some walks within these pages to suit their ability. Additionally, as anyone who enjoys the mountains should have an innate regard for the natural environment, most of the hills in this book are easily accessible by public transport, so you can leave your four wheels at home!

Munros and munro-bagging

Our propensity to list and categorise things is not just a modern trait. The Victorians started it. In 1891 Sir Hugh T Munro produced a list of all the Scottish mountains of 3000ft (914m) or higher. The number of mountains on the list has changed over the years, not due to sudden tectonic activity causing the collapse or growth of peaks, but because of the debate over when a peak is a peak in its own right or just an outlying top of a higher summit. Sir Hugh's desire to list all these peaks sparked the interest of like-minded people all over Scotland and beyond.

Today the popularity of 'bagging' all the summits on the list, which currently stands at 284, just grows and grows. In 1901, Rev A E Robertson kissed the top of Meall Dearg on the Aonach Eagach ridge to become the first munroist (someone who has completed 'the round'). It took 22 years for the achievement to be repeated (curiously by another member of the clergy, perhaps looking for heaven) and it was not until 1970 that the list reached 100 munroists. From then on the obsession really took off. Today over 4000 hillwalkers are on the list.

Munro-bagging certainly beats stamp collecting and to finish the round is a great personal achievement. It's important, however, to remember the real reason for climbing hills. It's easy to get so caught up in the ticking off of unpronounceable mountain names on a list that one forgets that being in the mountains is about appreciating the wind and the wild, the solitude and the ever-changing sky. Some munro-baggers even refuse to contemplate going up anything below that magical 3000ft mark so miss out on sweet gems such as Suilven, the Rum Cuillins and Ben Loyal, all of which are like foie gras to the mushy-pea munros that are Mount Keen and The Cairnwell.

The key is to keep a balance. The munro-bagging should not be the driving factor for a walk in the hills but an added pleasure. Enjoy the munro-bagging but above all else enjoy the hills. In this book there are munros, corbetts – mountains between 2500ft (762m) and 3000ft (914m) – and even unfashionable lumpy bits barely deserving of the title 'hill'. What they all have in common is a wild beauty and views that make the long climb more than worth the effort.

PART 1: PLANNING YOUR WALK

Practical information for the hillwalker

'I only went out for a walk and finally concluded to stay out till sundown, for going out, I found, was really going in'.
John Muir, From *John of the Mountains* edited by Linnie Marsh Wolfe, 1938

ACCOMMODATION

Most of the hills in this book are sufficiently close to villages to allow for overnight stays in a B&B (bed and breakfast) or hotel. These bastions of occasional luxury, however, are not for all tastes and budgets. Many of the more popular tourist haunts, such as Glen Coe and Skye, offer cheaper accommodation in the form of bunkhouses, hostels and campsites.

For each region in this book there is a list of villages and towns and a rundown of the accommodation that is on offer in the area, while each walk comes with an indication of the nearest gateway village or town. Bookings for all types of accommodation are strongly advised at Easter, on Bank Holiday weekends and between June and August.

A few of the walks are in very remote country and are reserved for the true outdoors person who is not afraid to rough it by sleeping under the stars, either with or without a tent.

Camping

There is no better way to get a real feel for the mountains and the outdoor life both day and night than to shun all mod-cons and camp. There are a number of campsites in the popular areas offering heated showers and washing facilities. Prices typically range from £5 to £8 per person per night.

Many campers baulk at the thought of pitching on a carefully mown field full of caravans, preferring instead to camp out in the wild. Wild camping (see p41) is a far more liberating experience than camping at an organised site and in some cases is the only choice for campers. The Scottish Outdoor Access Code (see box p40) states that responsible wild camping is allowed but you should not camp by roadsides or close to houses. It is also vital that you consider other land users. In the Highlands it is particularly important to avoid disturbing deer during the stalking season (see box p23).

Bivvying

The alternative to camping is to bivvy: the most natural way to spend a night. All that is needed is a sleeping bag, a sleeping mat and a bivvy bag (see Bivvy gear, p28) to keep everything, including you, dry. Bivvying is not everyone's idea of a night of luxury. Most people tend to prefer the shelter of a tent at the bare minimum, if not a roof and walls. The advantage of bivvying is the ability to sleep just about anywhere: on rocky beaches, among boulders on a grassy col or even on the top of a stony mountain. Add to this the chance to sleep directly beneath the stars, feel the wind on your face and wake to the sun climbing above the mountains and you have the ultimate way to pass the night in the outdoors.

If you are not familiar with the concept of bivvying start off gently by sleeping in a forest or somewhere not too far from civilisation in case things do not go according to plan. As you get to know the mountains and how the weather works you can start to take that bivvy bag to higher ground.

Bothies

Scotland is blessed with a number of bothies: simple mountain shelters, often restored from old, ruined crofts and typically located in beautifully remote spots. Bothies are unmanned and free for anyone to spend a night or two in but they are very basic shelters, usually consisting of a fireplace, dusty floor, some resident mice and, if you're lucky, a few chairs and a sleeping platform.

Their popularity has increased over the years and sadly a minority of people who use them show little respect for the bothy or their fellow bothiers. Litter, graffiti, wanton defecation and anti-social behaviour are growing problems that can lead to permanent closure by the estate owner.

Advertising the whereabouts of bothies is something of a faux pas, partly for the above reason and also to prevent overcrowding. It is commonly believed that to earn the right to stay in a bothy you should either stumble across it or hear about it by word of mouth from like-minded souls.

❏ The Bothy Code

Respect other users
● Please leave the bothy clean, tidy and with dry kindling for the next visitors.

Respect the bothy
● Guard against fire risk and don't cause vandalism or graffiti.
● Please take out all rubbish which you don't burn.
● Avoid burying rubbish: this pollutes the environment.
● Please don't leave perishable food, this encourages mice and rats.

Respect the surroundings
● Human waste must be buried carefully out of sight. Please use the spade provided.
● For health reasons never use the vicinity of the bothy as a toilet. Keep well away from the water supply.
● Conserve fuel. Never cut live wood.

Please note
● Bothies are available for short stays only. Permission should be obtained for longer visits. Unless the safety of the group requires the use of shelter in bad weather, bothies are not available for groups of six or more because of overcrowding and the lack of facilities such as toilets. For the same reasons groups are asked not to camp outside bothies. Groups wishing to use a bothy should seek permission from the estate owner.
● Finally, please ensure the fire is out and the door properly closed when you leave.

A night in a bothy can be a magical experience. Just remember to respect the surroundings, the other bothiers and the bothy itself (see the Bothy Code, box p11). And don't forget to pack a few candles, perhaps some dry wood for the fire, and of course a hip flask with a drop of your favourite malt. I have tried to avoid revealing the locations of many of the bothies for the reasons just mentioned, even though some of them are ideally situated for a number of the walks.

For more information contact the **Mountain Bothies Association** (🖳 www .mountainbothies.org.uk), the registered charity that is responsible for the maintenance of the majority of the bothies in the Highlands.

Hostels and bunkhouses

The standard of hostels and bunkhouses varies greatly but most charge between £10 and £16 a night. **Hostels**, such as those run by the Scottish Youth Hostels Association (☎ 01786-891400, 🖳 www.syha.org.uk) and independent hostels, usually have washing facilities, central heating, hot showers, and often a drying room for wet socks. The better ones also have a self-catering kitchen.

Bunkhouses usually offer more basic accommodation, often in dormitories, and you will need to bring your own sleeping bag. There are independently run bunkhouses all over the Highlands, and not just in the popular hillwalking centres such as Fort William and Aviemore. Many of them are perfectly positioned in some of the best hillwalking country.

Bed and breakfast

There are plenty of B&Bs across the Highlands, many of them situated conveniently for a day on the hill. B&Bs usually offer at least some rooms with en suite accommodation but most walkers are more concerned about getting just a good bed and a hot bath after a day's walking.

Rooms are usually designated as **singles** (one single bed), **doubles** (one double bed), **twins** (two single beds), and **family rooms** which comprise a double bed along with one or two singles. Single rooms are often hard to come by and the owner may choose to accommodate single guests in a double room only at quieter times and with a supplementary charge of between £5 and £10.

Rates can vary wildly depending on the luxuriousness, or lack thereof, of the establishment. The cheapest double or twin rooms are about £15 per person while places with a few more stars nailed to the wall will charge £35 or more per person. Most standard B&Bs, however, charge around £20 to £25 per person per night.

Guesthouses, hotels, pubs and inns

Guesthouses and **hotels** are a step up from B&Bs, usually offering an evening meal, a residents' lounge and sometimes room service. Accordingly, room rates are higher, with standard rates around £25 to £50 per person. The grander hotels may charge much more and may also sniff at the presence of a hillwalker treading bog-mud into the shag-pile. Nevertheless I have included some of these classier hotels in the accommodation sections of the guide for those who want to indulge in a little luxury whilst on their trip to the hills. Just remember to take your boots off before reaching reception.

Pubs and **inns** are great places to stay, not just for the bar downstairs, but also for the usually high standard of accommodation at a more affordable price than a hotel. Rates are typically around £20 to £30 per person. The only disadvantage is for those looking for an early night. There is always the potential for a disturbed evening from noisy drinkers below.

FOOD

While everyone knows Scotland to be the home of the finest single malt whiskies in the world, not so many are aware of its rich tradition in food. While many pubs and restaurants, sadly, insist on serving unimaginative, bog-standard pub-grub such as burger and chips, or microwaved lasagne, the Highlands is still the best place to find many of Scotland's national dishes; increasingly these are inspired by fresh, local produce. See p43 about farmers markets.

Look out for the **Taste of Scotland** signs (🖳 www.taste-of-scotland.com) for establishments that offer just that. Many of Scotland's traditional recipes are based on potatoes and other root vegetables that were commonly grown in crofting communities while fish and other seafood are also local specialities. Some of the best known, as well as lesser known, dishes are listed below. See pp305-6 for tips on what to eat when in the hills.

Some traditional dishes

For years tourist guides in Scotland have led many a gullible visitor to believe that the **haggis** (see box) is a small furry creature with legs shorter on one side to help it run along hillsides without falling over. Sadly, the haggis as a wild beast of the moors is about as real as Father Christmas.

The ubiquitous red deer that run rampant all over the hills have long been a source of food for native Highlanders. Today, **venison** is served in many forms from traditional steak to burgers and sausages.

Cullen skink is a haddock and potato broth originating from Cullen in north-east Scotland where it was made with Finnan haddock, and in

> ❏ **The native Scottish haggis**
>
> *Fair fa' yer honest, sonsie face,*
> *Great chieftain o' the pudden race!*
> **Robert Burns**, *Address to a Haggis*
>
> Haggis is minced lamb's or deer's liver and a collection of other meaty offal bits, mixed with oatmeal and boiled in a bag, traditionally a sheep's stomach bag. The result is a surprisingly tasty, peppery-flavoured dish. Haggis is usually served with neeps (swede) and tatties (potatoes). If the taste doesn't win you over, there is always the opportunity to enter the World Haggis Hurling Championships where the record stands at 180ft 10inches.

many cases, still is. **Cock-a-leekie** is a soup of chicken, leeks and onions. Some recipes for cock-a-leekie include prunes.

Salmon is big business and **Scotch salmon** is considered to be among the world's finest, finding its way onto dishes in classy restaurants worldwide. Consequently, many commercial fish farms have sprung up along the west coast of Scotland, although wild salmon is of superior quality. Commercial fish farming is a contentious issue, with opponents arguing that the metal cages are an eyesore in a beautiful landscape and that escaped captive-bred salmon are interbreeding with wild salmon, so threatening their very survival.

Crappit heids are haddock heads stuffed with lobster, and sometimes fish intestines, then boiled in fish stock, drained and served.

Nowadays **porridge** is eaten only for breakfast but crofters used to cook enough for a week and have it for both breakfast and lunch. Porridge is simply boiled oats and should, if you are a purist, be cooked and served with salt, not sugar as is often the case.

Clapshot may sound like something you need to visit a doctor for but it is in fact mashed turnip and potato. It is far tastier than plain old mashed potato and goes really well with haggis (see box p13).

Stovies are fried potatoes and onions mixed together with left-over meat and baked in an oven; a popular and filling dish.

Bannocks are oatcakes; oatcakes are made by frying oatmeal in melted fat and then baking the mixture in a hot oven. Bannocks/oatcakes are often served with cheese. **Bridies** are minced-beef pies.

Deep-fried Mars bars are a more contemporary choice. Fish and chip shops across the land began serving this most unlikely of delicacies around 1995 and continued to do so until the chocolate began to clog up their deep-fat friers. Suddenly they disappeared from the menu, but rumour has it that they are still out there, if you look hard enough.

DRINK

Whisky (and beer) galore!

Scotland is rightly famed as being the home of **whisky**. Whisky is made from malted barley, distilled in curiously pear-shaped stills, and is sold as either a single malt or a blend of more than one malt. At one time blends were supposed to be the tastier option, in the belief that two good malts thrown together were better than one, but that view has long since passed. Today single malts are the whisky of choice for the connoisseur.

There are literally hundreds of distilleries all over Scotland, each producing variations on their produce, usually distinguished by age. Those with a nose will be able to tell the difference between whiskies from different regions. Islay malts, for example, are usually considered to taste a bit peaty while Lowland malts have an altogether lighter touch. For the novice the best way of deciding which whisky to go for is to, well, try a few. And then a few more. Most pubs in the Highlands are blessed with a golden top shelf that could keep avid whisky fans merrily amused for nights on end. Some of these shelves sigh under the strain of over a hundred distinct bottles. For further information and education on discovering whisky contact the **Scotch Malt Whisky Society** (☎ 0131-554 3451, 🖳 www.smws.com), The Vaults, 87 Giles St, Edinburgh, EH6 6BZ.

For **real ale** drinkers, the Highlands of Scotland once had little to offer but this is changing. Brewers across the Highlands are producing a wonderful array of bitters. The contrast in flavours from one real ale to another is what makes the drinking of the brown stuff such a delight with brewers regularly bringing out new concoctions with enticingly romantic names. Ones to look out for on the beer pumps include Black Isle ales, Isle of Skye Cuillin ales, Orkney ale, Arran ale, Hebridean Gold ale, Hebridean Islander light ale, Glenfinnan ales, Caledonian ales, Inveralmond ale, Broughton ale, Aviemore ales and, for a real taste of the hills, Fraoch Heather ale.

To learn more about real ale contact the **Campaign for Real Ale** (**CAMRA**; ☎ 01727-867201, 🖳 www.camra.co.uk), 230 Hatfield Rd, St Albans, Hertfordshire, AL1 4LW.

MONEY

Banks are few and far between in the Highlands so it is wise to keep a good stash of cash on you at all times. Most shops, pubs and hotels accept credit and debit cards for payment but you should not rely on this, particularly in smaller guesthouses, B&Bs and local shops where cash is usually preferred.

If the nearest bank is miles away try the village post office, where customers of certain banks can now withdraw cash either with a chequebook and bankcard, or just with a debit card if you have a chip and pin number.

The town and village plans in Part 4 of this guide indicate if and where there is a bank, a post office, and/or an autoteller machine (ATM). Be aware that a charge is made for withdrawing money from some cash machines.

SERVICES

Many Highland villages have at least one small **shop** for groceries, along with a **post office**. Some of the larger ones may have a **bank**, **outdoor equipment shop**, **launderette**, **health centre**, **pharmacy**, **library**, **tourist information centre** (TIC) and, increasingly, **internet access** (if there is a library they usually offer this service for free).

ACCESS

In early 2005 new laws came into effect across Scotland that vastly improved the access rights for anyone who enjoys the outdoors. Essentially, everyone now has the right to roam freely, and camp, in most of the Scottish countryside.

The Scottish Outdoor Access Code (see box pp40-1) states that 'you can exercise these rights, provided you do so responsibly, over most land and inland water in Scotland, including mountains, moorland, woods and forests, grassland, margins of fields in which crops are growing, paths and tracks, rivers and lochs, the coast and most parks and open spaces.'

This new legislation is long overdue but now that it has come into effect walkers should not forget that most of Scotland is managed land. With the new right to roam comes added responsibility to respect both the land and those who work on it.

PLANNING YOUR WALK

WALKING COMPANIES

The following companies offer both tailor-made and independent walking holidays, covering everything from easy low-level treks to scrambling up the toughest of munros; ideal for those who have no time to organise a trip themselves.

- **North-West Frontiers** (☎ 01997-421474, 🖳 www.nwfrontiers.com), Viewfield, Strathpeffer, Ross-shire, IV14 9DS.
- **C-N-Do** (☎ 01786-445703, 🖳 www.cndoscotland.com), Unit 33, Stirling Enterprise Park, Springbank Rd, Stirling, FK7 7RP.
- **Walkabout Scotland** (☎ 0845-686 1344, 🖳 www.walkaboutscotland.com), 2F2, 70 Strathearn Rd, Edinburgh, EH9 2AF.
- **Scot-Trek** (☎ 0141-334 9232, 🖳 www.scot-trek.co.uk), 9 Lawrence St, Glasgow, G11 5HH.
- **Make Tracks Walking Holidays** (☎ 0131-229 6844, 🖳 www.maketracks .net), 26 Forbes Rd, Edinburgh, EH10 4ED.

❏ **Information for foreign visitors**

- **Currency** The UK has not adopted the euro and still uses pounds sterling (£). Pounds come in £100, £50, £20, £10 and £5 notes, and £2 and £1 coins. One pound is divided into 100 pence (or 'p') available in silver coins of 50p, 20p, 10p and 5p, and copper coins of 2p and 1p. Scotland circulates its own bank notes, including a £1 note, but English notes are also common. Scottish notes are sometimes refused in England despite being legal tender.
- **Rates of exchange** Check current rates at 🖳 www.xe.com/ucc.
- **Business hours** In the larger towns most **shops** open from 9am to 5.30pm Monday to Saturday; a few open on Sunday. **Post offices** close at 12.30pm on Saturdays. However, many of the villages in this book are very isolated and consequently opening hours (particularly of post offices) are often much shorter; they are frequently closed at the weekend and in the afternoon. **Banks** are generally open from 10am to 4pm Monday to Friday. Opening hours of Highland **pubs** are difficult to predict but they are usually open from 11am to 1am, closing earlier on Sundays. This is much later than most pubs south of the border thanks to more relaxed Scottish licensing laws.
- **National holidays** Most businesses are closed on January 1st and 2nd, Good Friday and Easter Monday (March/April), the first and last Mondays in May, the first Monday in August, December 25th and 26th. Expect a reduced or non-existent public transport service on these days.
- **School holidays** School holidays in Scotland are generally: a one-/two-week break mid-October, two weeks around Christmas and the New Year, a week mid-February, two to three weeks around Easter, and from late June/early July to mid-August.
- **Weights and measures** There is a certain degree of confusion with measurements in Britain. The younger generation is more familiar with the metric system while the older generation prefers imperial measurements. Both are readily used, with food generally sold in g and kg but also in pounds (lb: 1lb = 453g) and ounces (oz: 1oz = 28g). Most liquids are sold in litres except for milk and beer which are still measured in pints (1 pint = 568ml). Distances are in miles (1 mile = 1.6km), especially on road signs, but kilometres are growing in popularity when talking about walking distances.

● **Transcotland** (☎ 01887-820848, 🖳 www.transcotland.com), 5 Dunkeld Rd, Aberfeldy, Perthshire, PH15 2EB.
● **Bespoke Highland Tours** (☎ 01854-612628, 🖳 www.scotland-inverness.co .uk/bht-main.htm), Viewfield, Strathpeffer, Ross-shire, IV14 9DS.
● **Scottish Youth Hostels Association** (☎ 01786-891400, 🖳 www.syha.org .uk), 7 Glebe Crescent, Stirling, FK8 2JA.
● **HF Holidays** (☎ 020-8732 1220, 🖳 www.hfholidays.co.uk), Catalyst House, 720 Centennial Court, Elstree, Hertfordshire, WD6 3SY.
● **Wilderness Scotland** (☎ 0131-625 6635, 🖳 www.wildernessscotland.com), 3a St Vincent St, Edinburgh, EH3 6SW.
● **Experience Skye Mountain Guides** (☎ 01471-822018, 🖳 www.experience-skye.co.uk), Blaven Cottage, Torrin, Broadford, Isle of Skye, IV49 9BA.
● **Mountain Innovations** (☎ 01479-831331, 🖳 www.scotmountain.co.uk), Fraoch Lodge, Deshar Rd, Boat of Garten, PH24 3BN.
● **Scotpeak** (☎ 01343-545248, 🖳 www.scotpeak.co.uk), 8 Fleurs Place, Elgin, IV30 18T.

The height of hills is traditionally measured in feet (1ft = approx 0.3m) but metres are increasingly used, largely thanks to modern maps using the metric system. Many munro-baggers (see box p9) lament this change as the challenge of 'bagging' all the 3000ft mountains in Scotland has consequently become a less romantic pursuit of all the 914m peaks instead.

● **Time** During the winter, the whole of Britain is on Greenwich Mean Time (GMT). The clocks move forward one hour on the last Sunday in March, remaining on British Summer Time (BST) until the last Sunday in October.

● **Smoking** A ban on smoking in public places is now in force in Scotland. The ban relates not only to pubs and restaurants, but also to B&Bs, hostels and hotels. The latter have the right to designate one or more bedrooms where the occupants can smoke, but the ban is in force in all enclosed areas open to the public – even if they are in a private home such as a B&B. Should you be foolhardy enough to light up in a no-smoking area, which includes almost every indoor public place, you could be fined £50, but it's the owners of the premises who suffer most if they fail to stop you, with a potential fine of £2500.

● **Travel Insurance** The European Health Insurance Card (EHIC) entitles cardholders to any necessary medical treatment under the UK's National Health Service while on a temporary visit here; treatment is only given on production of the card so bring it with you. However, the EHIC is not a substitute for proper medical cover on your travel insurance, eg for getting you home should that be needed. Also consider cover for loss and theft of personal belongings, especially if you are camping or staying in hostels, as there may be times when you have to leave your luggage unattended.

● **Telephone** The international dialling code for Britain is +44 followed by the area code, minus the first 0, and then the required number. Calls are cheaper at weekends and after 6pm and before 8am on weekdays. Mobile phones do not work in the remoter regions of the Highlands. Relying on a mobile phone to get you out of trouble on a mountain is not recommended.

● **Emergency services** The police, ambulance, fire brigade, coast guard and mountain rescue can be reached by dialling ☎ 999.

Walking alone

'Only by going alone in silence, without baggage, can one truly get into the heart of the wilderness. All other travel is mere dust and hotels and baggage and chatter'.
John Muir, Letter to his wife 1888 (From *Life and letters of John Muir*, 1924)

Most people walking in the Highlands will either be with friends or with a group as part of a walking holiday (see pp16-17); few consider another option – walking alone – possibly because many books and armchair experts claim this is irresponsible and dangerous. However, these are probably the same people who have never dared walk alone in the hills because of their own inability to confront their fears. In our modern hectic lifestyle, people are rarely alone and have little time to stop, reflect and enjoy their own company. Such an existence is presumably why so many people are nervous and insecure about venturing into the hills alone. They are unfamiliar with it and feel unsafe in the way a lamb panics when the rest of the flock has disappeared.

Once you break through this irrational fear, walking alone in wild country suddenly becomes an utter joy. You see more, you hear more, you have time to think. At the end of the day you feel you have been a part of the world rather than a spectator. And far from being dangerous, walking alone instils a greater feeling of your own vulnerability and brings out an innate sense of self-preservation.

Having said that, walking alone is more dangerous if you do not prepare yourself for the additional risks. Always make sure someone knows where you are and what time you are due back. Be prepared for an unlikely accident by taking spare warm clothes, extra food and preferably a bivvy bag, along with the usual necessities of map and compass. But most of all, tread lightly and enjoy.

When to go

SEASONS

Scotland lies in a temperate zone which means summers are not particularly hot and winters not particularly cold. But it's not as simple as that. The British Isles sit with a continental landmass on one side and a big ocean on the other. Weather systems roll in from every direction, though most commonly from the south-west, and bring with them very varied weather. See also pp303-5.

In summer a westerly wind usually brings damp air from the sea resulting in rain and wind while an easterly drags in warm, dry continental air. Less frequently, weather fronts come down from the north drawing in cooler air which in winter results in snow showers down to sea level, particularly in the north and east, and even in summer can bring snow to the highest peaks. Generally speaking the west coast, in the firing line of the prevailing westerlies, is far wetter than the eastern Highlands.

It is not just weather, however, that dictates the best time for walking. Other big deciding factors are the midges and ticks (see box p26), and the fact that July and August are also the most popular months, so for solitude, and a better

❏ **Mountain guides**
As well as the walking holiday companies mentioned on pp16-17, mountain guides can be hired on a daily basis in some of the more popular regions: **Glen Coe and Glen Nevis** – Alan Kimber West Coast Mountain Guides (☎ 01397-700451, 🖳 www.westcoast-mountainguides.co.uk); **North-west** – Martin Moran Mountaineeering (☎ 01520-722361, 🖳 www.moran-mountain.co.uk); **Skye** – Experience Skye Mountain Guides (☎ 01471-822018, 🖳 www.experience-skye.co.uk). Some of these offer tuition and courses in both summer hillwalking and winter mountaineering. Rangers at the Cairngorms, and Loch Lomond and the Trossachs national parks, also provide a guiding service as do some of the National Trust for Scotland (see box p45) properties such as Kintail.

chance of booking a room, try to avoid the high season. Taking all these factors into account, the best months for hillwalking are May, June and September (winter is also very special but not the subject of this book, see box p20).

Spring (March to May)
Spring is a great time to be in the Highlands when the hills are decorated with patches of late snow. The midges are yet to appear and the temperature is perfect for walking. The days are getting longer after the gloom of winter and the weather is at its most stable, as the sea temperature comes to an equilibrium with the air temperature. It is not uncommon for the Highlands to be bathed in sunshine for weeks on end but don't rely on it. April, in particular, is notorious for blustery showers, and even a late burst of snow.

Summer (June to August)
The months of July and August are peak season in the Highlands but this is not necessarily the best time of year to visit. The midges are rampant, the roads are full of cars and the ridges alive with busy boots. The crowds make the hills feel somewhat less wild and untamed and the weather is mixed at best, with rainfall increasing as the season progresses. Nevertheless, the hills are at their greenest and in August the wild flowers and heather start to bloom, so when the sun does shine, there can be no better place to be than basking on a warm, rocky summit or jumping in a cool Highland burn.

Autumn (September to November)
After the chaos of summer, the hills are silent again. September brings the first night frosts and a subtle change of hue in the hills, green giving way to dusky brown with a low sun casting deep shadows across the mountainsides. In the glens birch trees turn golden and stags start to roar as the rut begins. Autumn often starts with more settled weather before the storms start in October and November. This is a magical time of year. Be prepared to encounter some snow and ice on the high ground towards the end of October.

Winter (December to February)
Winter in the Highlands brings rain, snow and ice and some severe storms. These can come one after another and then be followed by a period of settled

Winter hillwalking

The weather in Scotland is changeable and often surprising. I have sat at 1000 metres on Geal Charn in the Ben Alder Forest on mid-summer's day, sheltering behind an inadequate pile of rocks, as snow shower after snow shower slipped through from the north. This is not as unusual as it sounds but it is between November and April when true winter conditions descend upon the Highlands.

However, this guidebook should not be used for planning winter trips. Hillwalking in winter brings with it colder temperatures, fiercer winds, a greater wind-chill effect and fewer daylight hours. Most significantly of all, the conditions underfoot pose much greater risks with snow, ice and neve obliterating paths, making progress slow and certainly more challenging. There is also the avalanche risk to consider: in January 2009 nine climbers were caught in an avalanche on Buachaille Etive Mor, and were airlifted to hospital where three later died. The Scottish Avalanche Information Service website (🖥 www.sais.gov.uk/index.asp) had warned that the avalanche hazard for that day would be 'considerable'.

Anyone wishing to go winter hillwalking should always have an ice axe and crampons and, most importantly, know how to use them. Beginners should start off with an experienced friend or consider going on a winter skills course: Glenmore Lodge (see p175) near Aviemore is a good place for such courses.

There is no doubt that a day on the hills in winter is hard to beat. The mountains take on an almost alpine beauty and offer a real sense of isolation. The challenge is greater but so are the rewards. For inspiration, education and excellent advice try getting hold of Martin Moran's book, *Scotland's Winter Mountains* (see p29).

weather as high pressure builds. This is when the snow-covered mountains look their best. Periods of snow in the Highlands are commonly followed by milder interludes; this is known as a freeze-thaw cycle. During the thaw, snowfall is confined to the highest ground but a cold northerly or easterly blast can bring snow down to sea level for a time. The east, particularly the Cairngorms, is the snowiest and coldest part of the Highlands while the west coast remains relatively mild thanks to the Gulf Stream ocean current.

Walking in the mountains in winter is an altogether different proposition from walking at other times of year and is beyond the scope of this book (see box above).

TEMPERATURE

The bar charts (see opposite) indicate temperatures at sea level. In the hills the air temperature drops by roughly 1°C with every 100m to 150m of ascent so when the temperature in Fort William is 6°C, expect the summit of Ben Nevis, over 1300m higher, to be around -3°C or colder. Temperatures are generally a little higher on the west coast than the east.

RAINFALL

The west and north are much wetter than the eastern Highlands. Fort William enjoys 2m of rain each year compared with 90cm in Braemar in the Cairngorms.

❏ **Online weather forecasts**
There are some excellent websites that give regularly updated forecasts. For a general picture the two best sites are the **BBC Weather** site (🖳 www.bbc.co.uk/weather) and the **Met Office** site (🖳 www.met-office.gov.uk). Both give five-day forecasts for towns and villages across the UK and detailed surface pressure charts so that you can see what might be on the way. The Met Office site also gives a specific mountain forecast for the east and west Highlands and also has webcams for Loch Glascarnoch in the north and Aviemore in the east.

A more specific mountain forecast is given by the **Mountain Weather Information Service** (🖳 www.mwis.org.uk). The three-day forecast is updated daily and gives useful information such as temperatures at 900m, wind speed and its potential to disrupt walking, windchill, cloud base and the chance of cloud-free summits. In the winter months see 🖳 www.winterhighland.info for a similar forecast.

PLANNING YOUR WALK

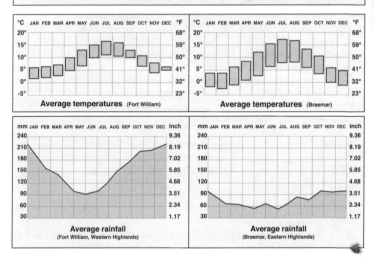

Average temperatures (Fort William)

Average temperatures (Braemar)

Average rainfall
(Fort William, Western Highlands)

Average rainfall
(Braemar, Eastern Highlands)

DAYLIGHT HOURS

During the summer it never gets properly dark, especially further north where the sun skims below the northern horizon for just a few hours. It's important to take into account the shorter days during the early spring and autumn when a headtorch is useful in case a walk takes longer than expected. This is even more important in winter when the sun only appears for around seven hours a day and stays low on the southern horizon.

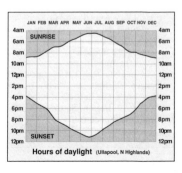

Hours of daylight (Ullapool, N Highlands)

ANNUAL EVENTS, FESTIVALS AND HIGHLAND GAMES

Throughout the year, but particularly in the summer, there is always something going on in some corner of the Highlands, from huge events such as the Braemar Highland Gathering (see below) to local community gala days. And then there are the music and food festivals showcasing Scotland's musical and culinary traditions. There are far too many events to name here; for an up-to-date listing contact Visit Scotland (☎ 0845-225 5121, 💻 www.visitscotland .com/guide/see-and-do/events.

Some of the best events to look out for are:

● **Fort William Mountain Film Festival** (March; 💻 www.mountainfilmfes tival.co.uk), Fort William. Lectures, exhibitions and films on mountains.

● **Aviemore Walking Festival** (May; 💻 www.aviemorewalking.com), Aviemore. Meet like-minded souls in the Cairngorms.

● **Angus Glens Walking Festival** (June; 💻 www.angusanddundee.co.uk/walk ingfestival), Kirriemuir near Glen Clova. Walking the hills of Glen Clova and Glen Prosen.

● **Highland Games** (June to August), across the Highlands. Check local libraries and noticeboards for details.

● **Hebridean Celtic Festival** (July; 💻 www.hebceltfest.com), Western Isles. Folk music and ceilidhs across the Western Isles.

● **The Hebridean Challenge** (July; 💻 www.hebrideanchallenge.com), Western Isles. Teams compete against each other as they run, cycle, swim and kayak the length of the Western Isles.

● **Braemar Highland Gathering** (first Saturday in September; 💻 www.brae margathering.org), Braemar. The most famous of all the Highland Games and a favourite of Billy Connolly, Robin Williams and Sean Connery, as well as the odd royal or two.

Traditional music

Folk music in Scotland is alive and well. Under the influence of artists such as Shetland fiddle player **Aly Bain**, a new generation of folk musicians helps to keep the tradition healthy. One of the great things about the traditional music scene is the intermingling of talents at folk music festivals, concerts and sessions at pubs and village halls across the Highlands.

During the summer keep an eye on local noticeboards for some of the smaller events, which are often the best, or just try the nearest pub. Some of the most active areas for live music are the west coast from Sunart to Kintail, the Isle of Skye, and parts of the Western Isles.

Names to look out for include fiddle players such as **Adam Sutherland**, **Duncan Chisholm** and **Jonny Hardie**, and bands such as **Blazin' Fiddles**, **Old Blind Dogs**, **The Battlefield Band**, **Deaf Shepherd**, **The Finlay MacDonald Band**, **Session A9**, **Daimh**, **Squashy Bag Dance Band** and **Harem-scarem**. Bands like **Wolfstone**, **Shooglenifty** and **The Peatbog Faeries** offer a modern style of folk music that usually has a bit of a rocky twang.

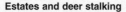

Estates and deer stalking

Unlike England and Wales, the Highlands of Scotland are home to a lot of wild land which is divided into large estates. There was a time when many of the estates were owned by rich, disinterested landowners who spent more time on the continent. Although that is still sometimes the case, many have now been bought by conservation bodies such as the John Muir Trust, the National Trust for Scotland, and Scottish Natural Heritage. And many others are passing into the hands of local communities: North Harris, Knoydart and Eigg to name but a few.

The way in which each estate is managed depends on who owns it but all of them practice deer stalking: a necessary conservation measure. Red deer in Scotland have no natural predator to perform this cull other than us; the last wolf was shot around 250 years ago. Consequently the deer population has rocketed. This has led to over-browsing of the fragile plant communities on the hills, a halt in native woodland regeneration and disease in the deer herd. The annual cull helps to maintain a healthy population of deer in balance with its habitat which in turn is of huge benefit to wildlife and people. Shooting wild animals is not to everyone's liking but it is important to bear these facts in mind before jumping to conclusions. It's also worth remembering that the deer that are shot are eaten, much of it locally. It is surely far more natural to hunt and eat a wild animal than it is to buy meat wrapped in plastic on a supermarket shelf that comes from an animal that has probably spent its life cooped up in a pen or cage far too small for it.

Even estates that are managed as nature reserves require a deer cull, in many cases to help aid natural regeneration of the forest that has disappeared due to overgrazing. Deer stalking also provides income for the estate and jobs for local people.

The stalking season runs from July 1st to October 20th for stags (the most important cull) and October 21st to February 15th for hinds. At this time many estates post notices indicating where they are stalking that day. Deer stalking does not take place on Sundays. On other days of the week call the estate office or a hillphone (see below) to check where stalking may be taking place.

More and more Highland estates are joining the hillphones scheme. During the main stag-stalking season call the hillphone number for a recorded message (updated by 8am daily) giving information on routes that are affected by stalking activity and a forecast for the following few days. New estate phone numbers are being added to the list each year. Look for the posters in outdoor shops and on noticeboards or check online at 🖳 www.snh.org.uk/hillphones. Current hillphone numbers relevant to the walks in this book are:

Grey Corries and Mamores	☎ 01397-732362
Glen Dochart and Glen Lochay	☎ 01567-820886
(Ben More and Stob Binnein)	
North Arran	☎ 01770-302363
Glen Shee	☎ 01250-885288
Callater and Clunie	☎ 01339-741997
Invercauld	☎ 01339-741911
Balmoral and Lochnagar	☎ 01339-755532

What to take

The amount of kit to squeeze into a rucksack is an important consideration. A heavy rucksack can turn a good walk into a painful slog. Obviously, more kit is needed for overnight treks when you will need to account for a sleeping bag, sleeping mat, stove, more food and possibly even a tent. Try to cut down on non-essentials. With experience it soon becomes clear that a lot of the things we take with us in our rucksacks never get used. There are certain items, however, that should live almost permanently in the depths of the sack. These include a first-aid kit (see p27), spare warm clothes, waterproofs, headtorch, spare food, water bottle/pouch, a relevant map, compass, whistle and preferably a bivvy bag. See also pp305-6.

THE PACK ON YOUR BACK

This is a very important piece of kit. Think of a rucksack as a reliable friend and treat it right. Firstly, make sure you buy a rucksack or daypack that has adjustable straps and, in the case of rucksacks, a hip belt. Then, make sure the straps are all adjusted so that when full the rucksack fits comfortably. Too many people forget to tighten up the hip and chest straps and this can make a great difference in the perceived weight of the burden on your back. The hip belt helps distribute the weight so that you are not carrying it all on your shoulders.

For a single day on the hill a 35-litre day pack is fine. It should be able to cope with all the essentials plus a few extras. For multi-day treks a larger rucksack of 65 to 75 litres should be enough. If the rucksack is too big you may be tempted to take too much.

FOOTWEAR

Do not scrimp on footwear. This is probably the most important piece of equipment. There are two main styles of **boots** for summer walking: leather boots and fabric boots. Leather boots are the preferred choice for hillwalking since they are better equipped to cope with rough terrain and sharp rocks. Fabric boots are fine on grassier hills but make sure they have a waterproof lining such as Gore-Tex. In addition to your boots, take a pair of **sandals** or **trail shoes**. If boots get wet it's useful to have some back-up footwear for pottering around in, in the evening.

Take two or three pairs of comfortable **socks**. A good pair will help prevent rubbing and blisters (see p306). There are all kinds on the market aimed at walkers but some of the best are the ones that have a high content of natural materials. Try socks made from merino wool which are comfortable, odourless and keep you warm when it's cold and cool when it's hot. Have you ever seen a sheep sweat or shiver? **Gaiters** provide added protection for the lower legs. They are not always needed but really come into their own in deep snow, wet heather and grass, bogs and on river crossings.

CLOTHES

Walking in Scotland can be a bit damp and cold so choosing the right type of clothing is essential to prevent, at best, shivers and at worst hypothermia (see p306) and death. Outdoor equipment manufacturers have developed a whole range of clothing that corresponds to what they call a base layer, a mid-layer and an outer layer.

Don't forget a spare set of regular clothes to reserve for evenings in pubs and restaurants, when the rest of the clientele would prefer the sweaty base layer to stay at home.

For the **base layer**, a thermal top, including one spare, that is tight-fitting and designed to wick moisture away from the skin is best. Avoid cotton garments which trap sweat and lead to shivering. Even on the coldest of days, the body generates a lot of heat. Just five minutes after starting a walk most walkers find themselves having to strip down to just the base layer. Try to avoid sweating too much because as soon as you stop walking, usually on top of a cold peak to admire the view, damp clothes cool down very quickly. This is when it is time to put on ...

... a **fleecy mid-layer**. This will help keep the chill off on those exposed summits. Take a spare in case the weather is harsher than expected and try to avoid getting it wet. Even if the rest of your clothing is damp with sweat at least you will have one warm and dry top to slip on for those lunch breaks and photo stops.

Lightweight, windproof and showerproof jackets are useful **outer layers** in drizzle and light showers but for real rain you need a real jacket. Even if the day starts off still with blue skies, shove the waterproofs in the rucksack. Showers can and do build up in the hills even on the unlikeliest of days. Good waterproof jackets and trousers should be breathable, to allow moisture to escape, and windproof, to limit the effect of windchill on the body. An extendable hood is useful for when the rain really starts to come down.

Thin, lightweight trousers that dry quickly and are not too tight are the most popular choice of **legwear**. Some now come with detachable calf sections, magically transforming them into a pair of shorts. Or you can just pack some **shorts**. **Thermal leggings** are useful for cold nights in tents and bothies and take a pair of waterproof trousers too. Never wear denim jeans which take days to dry once wet.

A woollen **hat** should be enough to maintain a snug head; a **cap** is useful on hot summer days. Consider taking a **balaclava** too for those really windy days and make sure your waterproof jacket has a hood. A **neck gaiter** or baffle is a good way of stopping cold draughts getting in, but is not essential.

Make sure your **gloves** are windproof. Taking two pairs, a thin liner and thicker over-gloves, is the best combination. You will only need those thick mit-

Midges and ticks

There are several species of **midge** in Scotland but it is the Highland midge, *Culicoides impunctatus*, endemic to Scotland, that is the most voracious of these biting insects. The uninitiated often wonder what all the fuss is about when they learn that the midge is no bigger than a fleck of coal dust. But, at their worst, midges can drive even the hardiest of outdoors folk to run, arms waving, spouting profanities to the nearest pub.

It is not the size of the midge but the number of them that is the problem. It is claimed that one hectare of boggy ground can contain around 25 million midge larvae. In summer, particularly on the west coast, clouds of them rise up to hunt out exposed flesh. It is the female midge that bites. She is not fond of bright sunlight, so is most active at dawn and dusk on still, muggy days and is attracted by dark clothing.

The best tactic for avoiding the little beasties is to climb to higher ground and hope for some wind. A gentle breeze is enough to disperse them. Insect repellents are not always reliable, but those that are said to have some effect include anything with the chemical DEET. DEET is said to be safe but it should be used sparingly. There have been claims that the chemical can cause skin irritation, rashes and even brain-cell damage. Some non-toxic repellents to consider include Eureka! and Neem. Avon's Skin-so-Soft moisturiser is also said to have remarkable midge-repelling qualities. More bizarrely, others have claimed that Marmite (thinly spread) will keep the little monsters at bay. Midge nets, available in many village shops and outdoor stores, are another wise investment.

Ticks are tiny parasitic mites common in long grass, bracken and heather in the summer. They usually feed on sheep and deer by burying their heads into the animal's skin. However, they are not fussy and will happily latch on to the bare legs and arms of hillwalkers. After a day on the hills, especially if you are wearing shorts, it is always a good idea to check yourself for ticks, or ask an intimate friend to enjoy the task.

Ticks are very small and do not cause any pain so are hard to detect, but it is extremely important to remove them quickly as they sometimes carry bacteria that cause Lyme disease which can be fatal. To remove a tick, use a pair of tweezers and gently, steadily and patiently twist and pull until the tick lets go. Do not pull too hard; you may leave the head in which can cause infection.

tens that are commonly available in outdoor shops for winter hillwalking and mountaineering.

TOILETRIES

The main items to take are **soap** (but don't use it in mountain streams), **toothbrush** and **toothpaste**. Also worth considering are: a **razor**, **deodorant**, **shampoo**, **tampons/sanitary towels**. In the summer, in particular, take high-factor **sunscreen** (see p305) and **after-sun moisturiser**, especially if you are not used to the prolonged exposure to the sun that comes with whole days in the hills, as well as **insect repellent**.

If you are spending any amount of time sleeping out rough or in bothies you will also need to pack **toilet paper** and a **lighter** to burn it (see p41).

FIRST-AID KIT

A first-aid kit is one of those pieces of equipment that sits in a rucksack and, hopefully, collects dust. However, never be tempted to do away with it on the grounds that it never gets used. It's there for an obvious reason.

A first-aid kit for the hills should include **plasters**, **painkillers**, **sterile dressings**, **antiseptic wipes** and **antiseptic cream**, **bandages**, **wound dressings**, **porous adhesive tape**, **safety pins**, **tweezers**, **scissors** and a **blister kit**. The best blister kits are **Moleskin**, **Compeed** and **Second Skin**. Use them as prevention rather than cure by putting one on at the first sign of any tenderness on the foot.

GENERAL ITEMS

Essentials are a **water bottle** that holds at least a litre, but preferably more, or a **pouch**. The advantage of a pouch is that it holds more water, fits snugly into a rucksack, and comes complete with a drinking tube that puts an end to rummaging for a bottle hidden at the bottom of the rucksack.

Pack a **compass** and know how to use it. A **GPS** device is also an excellent navigational tool but back it up with a compass in case the batteries die. A **whistle** is a good way of summoning help (six blasts repeated at one-minute intervals is the international distress signal) as is a **headtorch** which also helps in navigating off the hill when a walk takes longer than expected. A **bivvy bag** is a useful refuge whether planned or unplanned while degradable **plastic bags** are worth having for taking out rubbish or keeping clothes either dry or, if dirty, separate.

Trekking poles have become increasingly popular. Some folk see them as hill fashion or just another bit of paraphernalia that equipment manufacturers insist we need. However, they do help ease the strain on over-worked knees and make carrying a heavy rucksack much easier. They are also useful for river crossings and even as an impromptu 'monopod' for a camera.

Other items to consider include **sunglasses** (essential when snow is on the ground), a **penknife**, **flask** for hot drinks, **binoculars**, **notebook**, **camera** and **tripod**, a **watch** with **alarm**, and a good **book** to pass the time on bus and train journeys and for the evening if you are too tired to go out.

An **altimeter** is a good way of judging how much ascent is left to the summit and can aid navigation in poor visibility. Suunto and Silva both produce fancy watches that come with an altimeter. Depending on the watch these may also include a **barometer** (for predicting what the overall weather is doing) and even an **anemometer** for measuring wind speed and windchill temperatures.

Finally a **star chart** is great for those stellar nights, especially when bivvying or camping, although they usually lead to arguments about which one is the saucepan, or is it a frying pan?

SLEEPING KIT

Many hostels and bunkhouses provide bedding but check first. For bivvying, camping and bothying a good two-season **sleeping bag** should be adequate for the summer but for spring and autumn take a three-season bag or an extra liner. Almost as important as the bag is a **sleeping mat** or **inflatable mattress**. This is not just for comfort but to insulate from the cold ground. Inflatable mattresses, such as the ever-popular Thermarest, are much more comfortable than foam mats and often give a better night's sleep than some hostel beds.

CAMPING GEAR

A dome or ridge **tent** is fine. If it comes with a mesh netting this will help keep the midges at bay. The lighter the tent the better but be sure that it can withstand wet and windy conditions. In addition to a sleeping kit (see p27), campers will need: a **mug**, a couple of **cooking pots** with lids, **pan handle**, a **spoon**, maybe a **scrubbing brush** and a **stove** and **fuel**. The very popular MSR stoves which boil water in seconds, run best on petrol while the much slower Trangia stoves run on methylated spirit. These fuels are widely available in camping shops and petrol stations as are gas canisters for gas-based stoves (although Coleman fuel is a little scarce).

BIVVY GEAR

Bivvy bags come in all shapes and sizes and some include a hoop over the head that offers a little more space than the simple 'sack' design. Make sure the bivvy bag is waterproof and breathable and ensure you have a good two- or three-season sleeping bag to slip inside it. Waterproof, breathable bivvy bags cost around £150 but are hard-wearing and extremely light, making them a good alternative to a tent for hillwalkers who like to go that one step further and feel truly immersed among the mountains.

As well as the bivvy bag you will need the same kit as you would for camping (except a tent). For more on bivvying see pp10-11.

MAPS

The maps in this book are at a scale of 1:45,000 (approximately $1^1/_2$ inches = one mile; 2.2cm = 1km). On clear days these maps will help in navigating along the routes described but sadly the weather does not always oblige and walkers can lose their way. For this reason it is still necessary to carry an overall map of the area at a scale of at least 1:50,000 and preferably 1:25,000. Many of the walks in this book cross remote, featureless terrain where it can become necessary to navigate off distant landmarks. In mist you may need to take bearings using a map and compass.

The best maps for the Highlands are produced by **Harvey Maps** (☎ 01786-841202, 🖳 www.harveymaps.co.uk) who specialise in British walking maps at scales of 1:40,000 and 1:25,000, and **Ordnance Survey** (☎ 08456-050505, 🖳 www.ordsvy.gov.uk) who have a series of Landranger maps at a scale of 1:50,000 and more detailed Explorer maps at a scale of 1:25,000.

These maps are widely available in outdoor equipment shops throughout the Highlands and also in the following map shops: **Stanfords** (☎ 020-7836

1321, ⌨ www.stanfords.co.uk), 12-14 Long Acre, London, WC2E 9LP;
National Map Centre (☎ 020-7222 2466, ⌨ www.mapsnmc.co.uk), 22-24
Caxton St, London, SW1H 0QU; **The Map Shop** (☎ 01684-593146, ⌨ www.the
mapshop.co.uk), 15 High St, Upton-upon-Severn, Worcester, WR8 0HJ.

RECOMMENDED READING

Guidebooks on walking

The Munros, Donald J Bennett (SMC, 2006). Reference guide to all 284 of
Scotland's munros.

The Corbetts and Other Hills, D J Bennett et al (SMC, 2002). A reference guide
to the corbetts as well as some smaller hills which were too good to leave out.

The Book of the Bivvy, Ronald Turnbull (Cicerone, 2007). A quite brilliant little
read that does more than give the facts on sleeping rough in the wild; the heart-
felt writing would inspire even the softest of outdoor enthusiasts to abandon the
B&B for the bivvy bag.

Mountaincraft and Leadership, Eric Langmuir (Scottish Sports Council, 1995).
The bible for anyone who wants to take their mountaineering seriously and train
for a mountain-leader qualification. Covers everything you could possibly think
of related to walking and climbing in the hills.

Scotland's Winter Mountains, Martin Moran (David & Charles, 1998). A hugely educational book covering every aspect of walking and climbing in Scotland
in winter. Detailed coverage of mountain weather, snow conditions, equipment,
techniques and history, with some fascinating personal accounts of days on the
hill. Hard to find a copy of this book but your local library may have it.

Pocket First Aid and Wilderness Medicine, Jim Duff and Peter Gormley
(Cicerone, 2007). What to do should things go wrong when out in the sticks.

Walking in Scotland, Sandra Bardwell (Lonely Planet, 2007). General guide to
walks in the whole of the country.

West Highland Way, Charlie Loram (Trailblazer, 2008). If going up hills is getting too much try this famous national trail running 95 miles from Milngavie,
on the outskirts of Glasgow, to Fort William.

Literature on walking

Mountain Days and Bothy Nights, Dave Brown and Ian Mitchell (Luath Press,
2008). Widely considered a classic of Scottish mountaineering literature. The
authors take us through their years of exploring the hills, bothies and hoowfs of
the Highlands in a very entertaining read.

The Munros in Winter, Martin Moran (David & Charles, 1997). An epic account
of the author's completion of all the munros in one winter.

Scotland's Mountains before the Mountaineers, Ian Mitchell (Luath Press,
1998). A look at what the Highlands were like before they became so popular
as a leisure resource. Will change the way you look at the hills.

The Joy of Hillwalking, Ralph Storer (Luath Press, 2004). As the blurb goes
'this man has done more things in a sleeping bag than sleep'. A witty look at
why we are drawn to the hills.

General guidebooks

Scottish Highlands and Islands, Rob Humphreys and Donald Reid (Rough Guides, 2008). Comprehensive coverage of the region, places to stay and eat, and things to see and do.

Books on natural history

Scottish Birds, Valerie Thom (Collins, 2008). Pocket-sized guide covering over 180 birds to be found in Scotland; even includes their Gaelic names.
Where to Watch Birds in Scotland, Mike Madders (Christopher Helm, 2002). Highlights the best places to watch wild birds and also touches on where to watch other wildlife.
Scottish Wild Flowers, Michael Scott (Collins, 2008). Pocket-sized and comprehensive coverage of what you are likely to see at your feet.
Scotland's Nature in Trust, J Laughton Johnston (Poyser, 2002). A look at the National Trust's work conserving landscapes and wildlife of the Highlands, covering some of their properties including Torridon, Kintail and Glen Coe.

Magazines

The popularity of Scotland's hills has led to an explosion of related reading material on newsagents' shelves. Some to look out for are: *Scottish Mountaineer* (walking and climbing news and articles, from the Scottish Mountaineering Council); *Scotland Outdoors* (covers everything from hillwalking to kayaking and wildlife watching); *Trail* (a popular magazine geared particularly to hillwalking in Britain); *Country Walking* (usually concentrates on gentle walks of the canal towpath ilk but also covers more challenging hillwalks); *The Angry Corrie* (the first ever 'hillzine' and with articles such as '12 Great Mispronunciations of Scottish Hills' and '20 Differences between Glen Coe and Shakespeare' it has to be worth a pound of anyone's money. *The Angry Corrie* (TAC) is a labour of love written by walkers who know their stuff. Those who are not familiar with the Highlands may find much of the content bemusing while those in the know will appreciate the witty and knowledgeable approach that just can't be matched by the mainstream glossy magazines. It has limited distribution. Try any of the outdoor shops in the Highlands or visit TAC's website 🖳 www.bubl.ac.uk/org/tacit/tac.)

❏ **Organisations for walkers**
● **Mountaineering Council of Scotland** (☎ 01738-493942, 🖳 www.mcofs.org.uk), The Old Granary, West Mill St, Perth, PH1 5QP.
● **British Mountaineering Council** (☎ 0161-445 6111, 🖳 www.thebmc.co.uk), 177-179 Burton Rd, Manchester, M20 2BB.
● **Mountain Bothies Association** (🖳 www.mountainbothies.org.uk), c/o Henderson Black & Co, Edenbank House, 22 Crossgate, Cupar, Fife, KY15 5HW.
● **Backpackers' Club** (🖳 www.backpackersclub.co.uk)
● **Long Distance Walkers' Association** (🖳 www.ldwa.org.uk)
● **Ramblers' Association** (☎ 020-7339 8500, 🖳 www.ramblers.org.uk)
● **Walking World** (🖳 www.walkingworld.com)

Getting to the Highlands

Scotland's two biggest cities, Glasgow and Edinburgh, both have regular bus and train services to the main Highland towns of Fort William and Inverness and from either of these there are further buses and trains, as well as ferries, to the more remote locations (see pp34-6).

GETTING TO SCOTLAND

By air

Increasing numbers of airlines have services direct to Scotland, particularly from the rest of Europe and North America, but the majority still fly to London. The so-called budget airlines have made access to Scotland from London and the rest of Europe both cheap and easy. The two main carriers, Easyjet (🖳 www.easyjet.com) and Ryanair (🖳 www.ryanair.com), have regular flights from London and other major European cities to Glasgow and Edinburgh. Easyjet also run flights from London and Bristol to Inverness (which is useful for the north and north-west Highlands and the Cairngorms). Ryanair also fly to Inverness, from East Midlands Airport.

By train

Eurostar (🖳 www.eurostar.com) trains run from Paris and Brussels to London St Pancras which is a short walk from both Kings Cross and Euston stations (for trains to Scotland). For more information on rail travel from Europe contact your national rail company.

There are regular services from London and other major cities in England/Wales to Glasgow, Edinburgh, Inverness and Fort William. For fare, service and timetable information contact National Rail Enquiries (☎ 08457-484950, 🖳 www.nationalrail.co.uk) and for tickets contact the relevant rail company (Virgin Trains 🖳 www.virgintrains.co.uk; National Express East Coast 🖳 www.nationalexpresseastcoast.com), or try 🖳 www.the trainline.com or 🖳 www.qjump.co.uk.

❏ **Tourist information**
Local tourist information centres (TIC) stock a wealth of information on transport, things to see and do, and where to eat. Many also run an accommodation-booking service for a small fee. Contact details for individual TICs can be found in Part 4, under the corresponding village or town entry.

The Highlands of Scotland Tourist Board (☎ 0845-225 5121, 🖳 www.visithighlands.com) is based in Kingussie while the main Scottish Tourist Board, **Visit Scotland** (☎ 0845-225 5121, 🖳 www.visitscotland.com), is based in Edinburgh. Their excellent website answers just about any question you can think of on all matters Scottish.

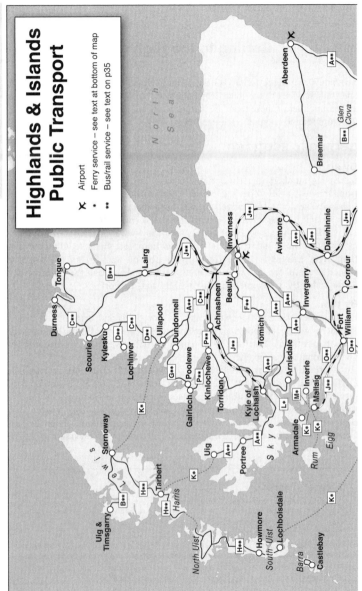

Highlands & Islands Public Transport

✗ Airport

* Ferry service – see text at bottom of map

** Bus/rail service – see text on p35

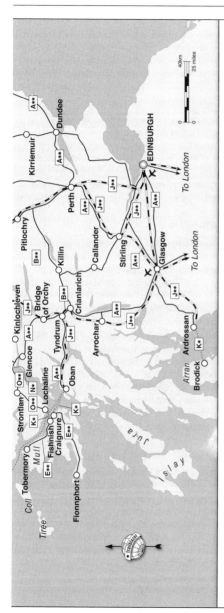

FERRY SERVICES

Note: details correct at time of writing. Check before travel.

K Caledonian MacBrayne (☎ 0800-066 5000, 🖵 www.calmac.co.uk)
- Ardrossan–Brodick (Arran), 4-6/day
- Lochaline–Fishnish (Mull) Mon-Sat 11-14/day, Sun 9/day
- Oban–Craignure (Mull), daily 5-6/day
- Oban–Lochboisdale (South Uist), Tue/Thu/Sat/Sun 1/day

K Caledonian MacBrayne *(cont'd)*
- Mallaig–Rum, Mon/Wed/Fri/Sat 1/day
- Mallaig–Armadale (Skye), daily 6-8/day
- Uig (Skye)–Tarbert (Harris), Mon-Sat 1-2/day
- Ullapool–Stornoway (Lewis), Mon-Sat 2-3/day

L Skye Ferry (🖵 www.skyeferry.com)
- Glenelg–Kylerhea (Skye), daily 3/hr Easter-end May & Sep-Oct 10am-6pm June-end Aug 10am-7pm

M Bruce Watt (office hours ☎ 01687-462320, 🖵 www.knoydart-ferry.co.uk)
- Mallaig–Inverie (Knoydart), Mon/Wed/Fri 2/day (also Tue/Thu mid May-mid Sep)

N Corran Ferry (☎ 01855-841243, 🖵 www.lochabertransport.org.uk/corranferry.html
- Nether Lochaber–Corran (Ardgour), daily 2-3/hr

Note: see box p35 for details of bus and rail services

PLANNING YOUR WALK

By coach

Eurolines (🖳 www.eurolines.com) is the major long-distance coach service in Europe. Coach services link all the major European cities with London. National Express (☎ 08717-818181, 🖳 www.nationalexpress.com) operates services from England and Wales to Scotland, as does Megabus (☎ 0900-160 0900, 🖳 www.megabus.com).

By car

Motorists can reach the UK from continental Europe by putting their car on the train and travelling via the Channel Tunnel on Eurotunnel (🖳 www.eurotunnel .com), or by taking a ferry. Along with the route between Calais and Dover there are also ferries linking Portsmouth with Bilbao and Rotterdam with Hull, among others. The two major carriers are P&O Ferries (🖳 www.poferries.com) and, for journeys between Dunkerque and Dover, Norfolk Line (🖳 www.norfolkline .com). A useful website for full details of services is 🖳 www.directferries.com.

GETTING AROUND THE HIGHLANDS

The route description for each mountain in Part 4 lists 'gateway' towns and villages; details about transport services between these gateways and the mountains or hills is given in the box opposite, or for ferries on the map on pp32-3, as well as in each town or village entry. This book has been designed with the environmentally friendly walker in mind. Most of the hills covered are easily accessible by public transport, so leave your car in the garage and discover that even the most far away of hills can be reached by train, bus or ferry.

If you are planning a long trip it is worth considering the **Freedom of Scotland Travelpass**. For £105 it allows travel by train, coach and ferry across Scotland for any four out of eight consecutive days, or £140 for any eight out of fifteen consecutive days. A cheaper option is the **Highland Rover** at £68 covering four out of eight consecutive days but valid only on specified routes in the Highlands. For further information contact First Scotrail (see opposite).

In addition to contacting the relevant operators (see box opposite) general timetable and fare information is available from **traveline** (☎ 0871-200 2233, 🖳 www.travelinescotland.com).

By train

The Highlands are quite well served by rail with lines running from Glasgow Queen St station up the west coast to Oban (for ferries to Mull and the Western Isles), Fort William and Mallaig (for ferries to Knoydart, Rum and Skye). From Edinburgh, which is linked to Glasgow through frequent daily trains, there is a line heading north via Stirling and Perth, through Aviemore to Inverness. From Inverness there is a very useful line running via Strathcarron to Kyle of Lochalsh (for links with buses over to Skye). One final route of interest to hill-walkers links Glasgow Central station with Ardrossan for the ferry to Arran.

The earlier you book a ticket the cheaper the fare. For fare and timetable information contact National Rail Enquiries (see p31) and for ticket sales contact First Scotrail (see opposite), 🖳 www.thetrainline.com or 🖳 www.qjump.co.uk.

❏ BUS AND RAIL SERVICES

Note: details correct at the time of writing, but check before travel.

Bus and coach services

A Scottish Citylink (☎ 08705-505050, 🖳 www.citylink.co.uk)
900 Glasgow–Edinburgh, daily 4/hour; **914/915/916** Glasgow–Fort William–Uig (Skye), daily 3-4/day; **917** Inverness–Portree (Skye), daily 2/day; **918** Oban–Fort William, Mon-Sat 2/day; **919** Inverness–Fort William, daily 2-5/day; **961** Inverness–Ullapool Mon-Sat 2/day; **976** Glasgow–Oban, daily 3/day; **M8/M9/M10/M11** Glasgow–Stirling–Perth daily 24/day; **M9/M11** Glasgow–Perth–Dundee–Aberdeen daily 13/day; **M91** Glasgow–Inverness 6/day

B Royal Mail Postbuses (🖳 www.postbus.royalmail.com)
025 Tyndrum–Crianlarich–Killin, Mon-Sat 1-2/day; **134** Tongue–Lairg, Mon-Sat 2/day; **220** Kirriemuir–(Glen) Clova–Glendoll, Mon-Sat 1-2/day; **242** (see also Maclennan Coaches below) Stornoway–Timsgarry, Mon-Sat 3/day

C Tim Dearman Coaches (☎ 01349-883585, 🖳 www.timdearmancoaches.co.uk)
Inverness–Ullapool–Scourie–Durness, May-Sep Mon-Sat 1/day, Jul-Aug daily 1/day

D Stagecoach (gen info ☎ 01463-239292, 🖳 www.stagecoachbus.com/highlands)
At the time of writing Rapsons' services (Ullapool to Lochinver, Glen Nevis Lower Falls to Fort William via Glen Nevis YH and Kinlochleven to Fort William via Glencoe Junction) had been taken over by Stagecoach; services may change so check Stagecoach's website for details or phone traveline, see opposite)

E Bowmans Coaches (☎ 01631-566809, 🖳 www.bowmanstours.co.uk)
495 Craignure–Salen–Tobermory, daily 4-6/day
496 Craignure–Fionnphort, daily 1-4/day

F Ross's Minibuses (☎ 01463-761250, ☎ 0780-1988491, 🖳 www.ross-minibuses.co.uk)
Inverness/Dingwall–Beauly–Tomich (Glen Affric), July-Sep Mon/Wed/Fri 1/day

G Westerbus (☎ 01445-712255)
Gairloch–Dundonnell–Inverness, Mon/Wed/Sat 1/day

H Hebridean Transport (☎ 01851-705050, 🖳 www.cne-siar.gov.uk/travel)
W10 Stornoway–Tarbert–Leverburgh, Mon-Sat 2-5/day
Western Isles Overland and Ferry route: a series of connecting buses and ferries from Lewis–Harris–North Uist–South Uist–Barra, Mon-Sat 4-5/day

I Maclennan Coaches (☎ 01851-702114, 🖳 www.cne-siar.gov.uk/travel)
W4 Stornoway–Timsgarry, Mon-Sat 1-2/day (school service on weekdays)

O Shiel Buses (☎ 01967-431272, 🖳 www.shielbuses.co.uk)
Fort William–Mallaig (Mon-Fri 2-4/day); Fort William to Lochaline (for Isle of Mull ferry; 1-2/day Tue/Thur/Fri, Sat 1/day summer only); Kilchoan to Fort William via Corran Ferry 1/day.

P Scotbus (☎ 01463-22410, 🖳 www.scotbus.co.uk)
708 Achnasheen (for the train station)–Kinlochewe–Gairloch–Poolewe–Inverewe Jun-Sep 3/day

Rail services

J First Scotrail (☎ 08457-550033, 🖳 www.scotrail.co.uk)

- Edinburgh–Perth–Aviemore–Inverness, 5+/day
- Edinburgh–Stirling–Perth, 5+/day
- Glasgow–Edinburgh, 5+/day
- Glasgow–Fort William–Mallaig, 4/day
- Glasgow–Crianlarich–Tyndrum–Oban, 3-4/day
- Inverness–Achnasheen–Kyle of Lochalsh, 1-4/day
- Inverness–Lairg, 1-3/day

By bus

Scottish Citylink (☎ 08705-505050, 🖥 www.citylink.co.uk) is the main coach carrier in Scotland. The company has regular departures from Glasgow to Campbeltown (for Arrochar), Oban, Glencoe, Fort William, Glen Shiel and Skye. Another service plies the A9 from Edinburgh to Inverness via Perth and Aviemore, continuing from Inverness to Ullapool (for ferries to Lewis). Other useful routes include the Edinburgh to Oban service via Stirling and Callander and the Great Glen route linking Inverness and Fort William. Megabus (see p34) also have services between Glasgow/Edinburgh and Inverness.

Scottish Citylink offer an **Explorer Pass** (£35 for three days out of five consecutive days, £59 for five days out of ten consecutive days and £79 for eight days out of sixteen consecutive days) for unlimited travel on all their services (as well as a 50% discount on Caledonian MacBrayne ferries, see below).

By Postbus

Many isolated communities in the Highlands can only be reached by single-track lanes where big Citylink coaches dare not roll. However, Royal Mail do send their little red vans down these lifelines and they don't just carry letters. They carry passengers for a small charge but they don't have much space so it is strongly recommended that you call ahead to reserve.

Visit the Postbus website (see box p35) for timetable and route information. Sadly, at the time of writing there were proposals to close many Highland post offices and Royal Mail services. As a result, many Postbus services are under threat so check the latest before travelling.

By ferry

The main ferry operator in Scotland is **Caledonian MacBrayne** (see map p33) often referred to as CalMac. They have regular ferry services from Ardrossan to Brodick (Arran); Oban to Craignure (Mull), Castlebay (Barra) and Lochboisdale (South Uist); Lochaline to Fishnish (Mull); Kilchoan to Tobermory (Mull); Mallaig to Armadale (Skye), Rum, Eigg, Canna and Muck; Uig (Skye) to Lochmaddy (North Uist) and Tarbert (Harris); Ullapool to Stornoway (Lewis) and services linking Barra, the Uists and Harris in the Western Isles.

For those planning on a number of ferry journeys it may be cheaper to buy an **Island Rover** ticket which allows unlimited travel per foot passenger for £53 over an eight-day period, or £76 over a fifteen-day period. Certain combinations of routes are cheaper when purchased as an **Island Hopscotch** ticket. For example it is possible to catch the three ferries from Mallaig to Skye, Skye to Harris and Lewis to Ullapool for just £25.30 which is much cheaper than buying three individual tickets.

Other operators include **Bruce Watt Ferries** (see map p33) for services from Mallaig to Inverie on Knoydart. **Skye Ferry** (see map p33) operates across the short stretch of water between Glenelg and Kylerhea between Easter and October and **Corran Ferry** (see map p33) makes trips (frequently between 6am and 9.30pm Mon-Sat, 8.45am-9.30pm Sun) across the short stretch of water between Nether Lochaber near Glen Coe and Corran for Ardgour and Ardnamurchan.

PART 2: MINIMUM IMPACT

There seems to be a steady change in attitude when it comes to the relationship between man and mountains. Where once it was a question of conquering peaks, and battling against nature, it is now about respect for the environment and feeling at home with the natural world. In heading for the hills we have a responsibility to limit any negative impact we may have on them while, at the same time, exercising that same respect for ourselves.

Getting out there

The last couple of decades have seen a huge explosion in the popularity of walking and outdoor activities. This can be explained by a number of factors. Many of us live in polluted, overcrowded cities. We rarely get a chance to breathe fresh air, view the stars, enjoy a cool breeze or watch mist rising from a lake. Instead, we spend our days enclosed, protected from whatever it is that may be outside. When we're not in the house, we're in the office. When we're not in the office, we're in the car. We're not designed for such an existence and as working hours get longer, and multimedia distractions compete for our time, more and more of us, possibly unconsciously at first, get the urge to escape, to leave the pursuit of money and things like the voyeuristic pleasures of talent-show TV for just a while.

In a bid to keep fit in a sedentary world, many throw some of their hard-earned cash into the local gym. But exercising for the sake of exercising in an indoor environment with central heating and artificial lighting – and paying for it – can hardly compare with walking for free in the hills.

People enjoy the hills for different reasons. Some go rock-climbing, some go for short walks, others climb the munros (see box p9) and others like watching wildlife. Some are after an adrenaline rush, a flirt with danger, some like to be alone and enjoy the peace while others appreciate the chance to be with friends. Whatever the reason, the over-riding inspiration must surely be the hills themselves, their very nature. That intangible quality of timelessness and beauty cannot be matched by even the smartest of Knightsbridge gyms.

Getting the most out of your walk

We don't always get as much as we could from the outdoor experience. It is very common to carry with us to the hills that restlessness and urgency that is part of everyday life. It usually takes a few days for these irritants to disappear but when they do, being in the mountains can feel more like home than anywhere else ever could.

The key to getting the most out of the mountains is to stop, think and slow down. Walking is not just about putting one foot in front of the other. If you do this you get to appreciate the handiwork of Footpath Repair Man rather than the handiwork of nature. It is about stopping and looking and allowing all the senses to take in the whole scene. Learn to use peripheral vision. Don't look directly at the view, rather allow everything in your range of sight to be drawn in.

Enjoying the outdoors is not just about turning up. As the person who gets out and walks benefits a lot more than the person who parks at the roadside to look out of the window, so the walker who consciously looks, listens, smells and touches all that is around him or her gets a lot more out of the experience than the walker who presses on head down at a pace that suggests there is an urgent meeting at the next col.

Respect for the environment

In Scotland, thousands of feet trample over the hills every year. Such an influx of people to so delicate an environment is bound to bring with it some problems. Littering, erosion and disturbance to wildlife are just a few. While it is encouraging that so many people are recognising the benefit of wild places and gaining so much pleasure and enlightenment from walking in them, it is unfortunate that our very enthusiasm for a place can often end up damaging it. It is vital that the mountains are not taken for granted. A little respect for them and some common sense measures are all that is needed. We can minimise our impact by not dropping litter, sticking to paths in popular areas, and leaving wildlife in peace.

It is not, however, the individual who is solely to blame. Damage inflicted by walkers is, at least, usually involuntary. Compare this to certain developers and groups who wilfully damage the environment through what is blindly perceived to offer further enjoyment of a region. 'Motorway' footpaths, unsightly metal bridges and inappropriate placing of signposts are just some of the blots on the landscape – and then there is the contentious issue of the Cairngorm Mountain Railway (see box p169), located in one of Scotland's most fragile mountain environments, given the go-ahead in an age when we are all supposed to be thinking in a shade of green. Sadly, such developments are often suggested by those ignorant of the real attraction of the mountains: the very absence of such paraphernalia. Or perhaps it is just about making money. A careful balance needs to be kept between promoting leisure activities and minimising the negative effect on the environment. The next section deals with some of these environmental issues in more detail.

ENVIRONMENTAL IMPACT

Walkers are often among the most knowledgeable when it comes to environmental issues, particularly their own impact on the immediate surroundings. The following are some commonly held attitudes to minimising any negative effect on the mountain environment.

Litter

Litter, which is not just unsightly but is a danger to wildlife, is easily dealt with by not dropping it in the first place. Very 'hill-friendly' types will even pick up the litter that others have left behind.

Everything that is taken into the hills must either be eaten or taken back out. It is worth considering just how long the lifecycle of litter is. Orange peel (see box below), for example, lasts for six months and, unless someone picks it up, an aluminium can will still be rotting on the ground well after the person who threw it there has completed his or her own lifecycle.

Erosion

Erosion is noticeably worse on the munros, which attract most of the walker traffic. The very presence of an eroded path on what would otherwise be a featureless ridge or plateau can aid navigation in mist. This is not necessarily a good thing as it leads to a false sense of security. It can become very easy to rely on such paths to such an extent that it comes as quite a shock to find, when on a more remote, less popular hill, that you need to work out how to get up the thing for yourself.

The issue of erosion, however, is not about whether it aids navigation or not. It is a question of its visual impact and the damage it does to fragile mountain habitats. There is some argument as to the best way of dealing with this. The general consensus is that, on the busiest hills, walkers should stick to designated paths to minimise pressure on the rest of the mountain and its wildlife. Many of us go to the mountains to get away from such restrictions but as we are all part of the problem, surely to keep to the path on just the most popular hills is a small price to pay while we can enjoy uninhibited access elsewhere. Concentrating everyone in one place, however, clearly leads to heavy pounding along a single line. Many landowners and conservation organisations such as the John Muir Trust and the Footpath Trust are helping by bringing in volunteers to construct well-drained, hard-wearing footpaths along popular mountain paths such as those on Schiehallion, Stac Pollaidh, and in Glen Coe. Nevertheless, even with footpath restoration, things can go awry. It could be argued that a neatly lain, gravel-strewn 'motorway' of a path is just as unsightly as an eroded trench and certainly does little to fit in with the surroundings. Footpaths that retain a little unevenness and are constructed of rock native to the area have to be preferred.

MINIMUM IMPACT WALKING

The Scottish mountain orange tree

Orange trees. All over the Highlands. Not one hillwalker has ever reported seeing one but the evidence of their existence is everywhere, usually on paths and tucked under rocks at summit cairns – orange peel!

Littering is apathetic and disrespectful. Anything dropped on the ground that does not naturally belong on the hill is litter, so that includes orange peel, banana skins and apple cores. To argue that these fruity deposits are biodegradable is a weak excuse to justify a lazy attitude.

Anyone who can carry a whole orange up a hill can carry a bit of one down it. Littering and hillwalking clearly do not go together and anyone who indulges in the former quite simply doesn't appreciate the latter. The majority of hillwalkers climb hills for the raw, natural essence of the mountains. As soon as that sense of wonder comes over you it becomes obvious why littering is so abhorrent.

Wildlife disturbance

If you see any wildlife, and the observant surely will, try not to disturb it by attempting to get nearer or making deliberate noises to attract its attention. Some of the best places to watch wildlife are at organised wildlife hides. There are many of these across the Highlands (see box p56) where you can watch wildlife such as ospreys, otters and red kites without them knowing you are there.

Never approach or touch young animals or birds. In many circumstances they are temporarily left alone by the parents and are not, as is often assumed, abandoned. Handling deer calves and fledgling birds may lead to abandonment by the parents.

Finally, leave wild flowers for others to enjoy and never cut live wood.

The code of the outdoor loo

It hardly needs saying that human waste is disturbing to our senses. It also contaminates the mountain streams that act as a drinking water supply to most walkers, and some local properties. The unwritten rule of defecating at least 30 metres away from any water source is there for a good reason. This distance

---

❏ **The Scottish Outdoor Access Code**

Take personal responsibility for your own actions. You can do this by:
● caring for your own safety by recognising that the outdoors is a working environment and by taking account of natural hazards;
● taking special care if you are responsible for children as a parent, teacher or guide to ensure that they enjoy the outdoors responsibly and safely.

Respect people's privacy and peace of mind. You can do this by:
● using a path or track, if there is one, when you are close to a house or garden;
● if there is no path or track, by keeping a sensible distance from houses and avoiding ground that overlooks them from close by;
● taking care not to act in ways which might annoy or alarm people living in a house; and
● at night, taking extra care by keeping away from buildings where people might not be expecting to see anyone and by following paths and tracks.

Help land managers and others to work safely and effectively. You can do this by:
● not hindering a land-management operation, by keeping a safe distance and following any reasonable advice from the land manager;
● following any precautions taken or reasonable recommendations made by the land manager, such as to avoid an area or route when hazardous operations, such as tree felling and crop spraying, are under way;
● checking to see what alternatives there are, such as neighbouring land, before entering a field of animals;
● never feeding farm animals;
● avoiding causing damage to crops by using paths or tracks, by going round the margins of the field, by going on any unsown ground or by considering alternative routes on neighbouring ground; and by
● leaving all gates as you find them.

should be increased to 200 metres around bothies and other popular overnight spots. If possible, use a public toilet. Clearly, this is not always practical, for example when straddling the Aonach Eagach ridge. When you feel the need, dig a small hole (much of the ground in the Highlands is soft and damp so kicking a heel in usually works, or carry a small trowel) and cover up with loose soil after the job is done. Toilet paper should not be buried since animals will be quick to dig it up. Instead pack it out in a plastic bag and dispose of it at the next public toilet, or burn it (taking care not to set fire to the hillside – heather is particularly flammable, even when the ground below is wet and boggy).

Wild camping

Not all campers are interested in pitching on a croquet lawn of a campsite with the caravanning club in residence, preferring instead to get out there and pitch away from everyone else. Until very recently wild campers were treated like second-class citizens. Thankfully, attitudes are changing, to the extent that the new access legislation that came into effect in 2005 (see box below) now allows campers to pitch on just about any wild land if it is well away from buildings. However, it is still important not to disturb any deer stalking; during the stalk-

Care for your environment. You can do this by:
● not intentionally or recklessly disturbing or destroying plants, birds and other animals, or geological features;
● following any voluntary agreements between land managers and recreation bodies;
● not damaging or disturbing cultural heritage sites;
● not causing any pollution and by taking all your litter away with you.

Keep your dog under proper control. You can do this by:
● never letting it worry or attack livestock;
● never taking it into a field where there are calves or lambs;
● keeping it on a short lead or under close control in fields where there are farm animals;
● if cattle react aggressively and move towards you, by keeping calm, letting the dog go and taking the shortest, safest route out of the field;
● keeping it on a short lead or under close control during the bird breeding season (usually April to July) in areas such as moorland, forests, grassland, loch shores and the seashore;
● picking up and removing any faeces if your dog defecates in a public open place.

Take extra care if you are organising an event or running a business. You can do this by:
● contacting the relevant land managers if you are organising an educational visit to a farm or estate;
● obtaining the permission of the relevant land managers if your event needs facilities or services, or is likely, to an unreasonable extent, to hinder land-management operations, interfere with other people enjoying the outdoors or affect the environment;
● talking to the land managers who are responsible for places that you use regularly or intensively.

MINIMUM IMPACT WALKING

ing season check where this is taking place (by calling the estate office or a hill-phone; see box p23) before making camp.

A few points to consider when wild camping: use a stove rather than lighting a fire; try to minimise disturbance to wildlife and other walkers by not staying too long and by positioning your tent out of sight if possible; follow the outdoor toilet technique described on pp40-1; don't use soap or detergent; and make sure there is no trace of your having been there once you leave.

ECONOMIC IMPACT

Scotland's tourism industry

By visiting the Highlands you are helping support Scotland's number one industry. In 2008 8% of the Scottish workforce worked in the tourism industry and its value stood at £4.8 billion per year. Without tourism modern-day Scotland would be a very different place: a much poorer place. It is a country that is known for its rich culture, architecture, music and proud traditions but the main draw for both visitors and Scots alike is, understandably, the scenery. Every year thousands come to admire the views, either from the safety of a car or, more sensibly, by getting out and walking, whether on a short stroll, a long-distance trek, such as the West Highland Way or Great Glen Way, or by walking and climbing in the mountains. The one thing they all have in common is that they spend money, which can only be a good thing for Scotland and its future prospects. However, there are certain ways that you can ensure your money goes to the right people and the best way is to buy local.

Buy local

It is a real shame that in a country that rightly prides itself on its heritage, tradition and history, most town centres are becoming duplicates of each other; characterless places centred around a familiar multi-national supermarket with few, if any, independent shops. Thankfully, many Highland villages still retain a lot of the individuality that, in the larger towns, has long since disappeared.

One way of helping the local economy is to buy local food and produce from locally run shops, whenever possible. Not only does this cut down on food miles, the transport of produce over huge distances by big polluting lorries, but the money that is spent stays within the community rather than disappearing to fat cats elsewhere. By buying local you also help the local job scene. A supermarket creates one job for every £250,000 spent compared to just £50,000 spent in a village shop. This is partly down to the huge costs involved for supermarkets in storing and transporting goods.

A great way to back local food producers is to buy directly from them. Some farmers run their business at a loss because their production costs exceed the price that supermarkets pay for their produce. There are a number of farmers' markets springing up across the Highlands where consumers can cut out the middle man and buy direct. This benefits not just the farmer but also the consumer who can enjoy much fresher food. Everything from meat and vegetables to beer and whisky can be bought locally in the Highlands. For the locations and dates of farmers' markets check the website of the **Scottish Association of Farmers' Markets** (🖳 www.scottishfarmersmarkets.co.uk). And it doesn't stop at shopping. When in restaurants always check the menu or ask if the food being served is fresh and local. If it is, it's better for the local community – and for your stomach.

Conservation

The natural habitats of the Highlands, and their associated species, are all under threat to greater or lesser degrees, be it through disturbance, loss of habitat, pollution and littering, illegal hunting or commercial and industrial development. There needs to be a careful balance between our land-use practices and the protection of these precious environments. We have a greater understanding, today more than ever, of how our everyday activities impact upon our world and more and more people recognise that we have a responsibility to conserve natural environments for their own sake and for ours.

There is a whole range of organisations that actively help in conserving Scotland's wildlife and landscape, all with a common goal of preserving and enhancing them for future generations. And, of course, we can all help as individuals by minimising our own personal impact when walking in the hills.

SCOTTISH NATURAL HERITAGE

Scottish Natural Heritage (SNH; ☎ 01463-725000, 🖳 www.snh.org.uk, Great Glen House, Leachkin Road, Inverness, IV3 8NW) is the government advisory body responsible for the conservation and enhancement of Scotland's wildlife, habitats and natural landscape. Their primary activity is the management of National Nature Reserves (NNR) and other protected sites. Since the first NNR was established at Beinn Eighe in 1951, SNH has gone on to set up a total of 55 NNRs across the country.

Along with managing NNRs they are also responsible for identifying private land that needs special protection, perhaps because there is a particularly rare species there or the habitat itself is unique. SNH has created a number of alternative categories for such areas. There are Sites of Special Scientific Interest (SSSI), Special Areas for Conservation (SAC), Special Protection Areas (SPA), Local Nature Reserves (LNR), Wetlands of International Importance (WII), National Scenic Areas (NSA) and now National Parks (see p44) too. SSSIs are probably the most significant of these designations. They are hugely important since they provide protection from changes in land use and other activities that may harm local species or the habitat itself. At present there are 1456 SSSIs, covering 12.9% of Scotland. It is encouraging that an organisation such as this exists but it is not enough to plaster the countryside with acronyms that give the suggestion of some level of protection, if the govern-

The concept of wilderness

The 'Last Wilderness in Europe' is a clichéd line that has been used by the tourist board to describe everywhere from Knoydart to Fisherfield and even the whole of the Highlands. The Polish forests and the mountains and tundra of Lapland must wonder what they have to do to merit the title. Everyone has a different idea of what wilderness is or should be. Research shows that to a deer-stalker the hills are a workplace, while to a city-dwelling hillwalker they are very much a wilderness. Most dictionaries include the words 'wild', 'uncultivated', and 'uninhabited apart from wild animals' in definitions of the word wilderness, so it's clear that it is not really the appropriate word for the Highlands.

To begin with, the hills are neither uninhabited nor uncultivated; indeed the population of the Highlands was, until the Clearances (see box p50), much greater than it is now. There are remains of agricultural workings, old stone houses and, in some cases, entire villages, in almost every glen. And there are modern-day developments too. Even in Knoydart and Fisherfield there are footpaths, 4WD tracks, fences, bridges, bothies and estate buildings. A true wilderness has none of these. Add to this large swathes of commercial forestry plantations, managed grouse moors and the clearing of just about all the native pinewoods and the true nature of the Highlands becomes clear. This is not really about the definition of the word 'wilderness'. It is about recognising how a landscape that at first appears to be untouched is, in fact, at least to a certain extent, man-made.

The Highlands are certainly more untouched than other parts of Britain and it could be argued that the Cairngorm plateau and other high mountain tops do constitute a wilderness. These high spots are, after all, if you ignore the occasional cairn or trig point, unchanged since the last Ice Age came to an end. Some would argue that a wilderness needs to be a vast area, much greater than the Cairngorm plateau. Others also argue that the global impact of human-induced carbon emissions precludes anywhere on Earth from being considered a true 'untouched' wilderness. One thing is for certain, in the Highlands there is plenty of wild land in the sense that much of it is remote, is left or managed in a natural state and, more often than not, is beautiful. But a wilderness? Perhaps not.

ment then overrides SNH's supposed authority. However, the creation of Scotland's first two national parks is a step in the right direction.

NATIONAL PARKS

After many years of debate **Loch Lomond and the Trossachs** became Scotland's first national park in 2002, quickly followed by the **Cairngorms** in 2003. According to the national park authorities, in both these areas 'the aims of national park status are to conserve and enhance the natural and cultural heritage, to promote the sustainable use of the natural resources of the area, to promote understanding and enjoyment of the special qualities of the area by the public and to promote sustainable social and economic development of the communities of the area'.

Significantly, the authorities have ensured that where conflict arises between any of these differing aims, preference will be given to the conservation of the natural and cultural heritage. This is welcome recognition of the fact that improving public access and facilities is not always in the best interests of the environment, or indeed of the public for whom such developments are aimed. It is also encouraging to see that SNH recognises the importance of the communities who live within the national park boundaries. Equal weight appears to be given to social, economic and cultural issues as well as to the conservation of the land and its wildlife.

OTHER PROTECTED AREAS

Apart from Scottish Natural Heritage there are a number of other organisations and charities who own and manage many of the Highland estates. Both the **Royal Society for the Protection of Birds (RSPB)** and the **Scottish Wildlife Trust (SWT)** manage nature reserves across the country with the protection of species and their habitat their primary concern, while the likes of the **John Muir Trust (JMT)** and the **National Trust for Scotland (NTS)** have the protection of wild land as their main aim (although the NTS also preserves historic sites and buildings).

Since its conception in 1983 the John Muir Trust, named after the Scotsborn conservationist and founder of the American national park movement, has purchased eight properties, nearly all of which feature in this book: Sandwood Bay, Quinaig, Schiehallion, part of Ladhar Bheinn in Knoydart, part of Ben Nevis, and three properties on Skye that include Bla Bheinn and Glamaig.

Like the JMT, the National Trust for Scotland can also lay claim to some of the most famous scenery Scotland has to offer with the likes of Ben Lawers, Glen Coe, Kintail, Torridon and the Mar Lodge estate all under their wing.

Countless other organisations are helping to protect the countryside that we come to enjoy. **Reforesting Scotland** and **Trees for Life** are very active in promoting the regeneration of the Caledonian pine forest while the Association for the Protection of Rural Scotland helps by pressuring the government to make informed decisions when it comes to matters of conservation.

❑ **Conservation organisations**
● **John Muir Trust** (☎ 0131-554 0114, 🖳 www.jmt.org), 41 Commercial St, Edinburgh, EH6 6JD.
● **National Trust for Scotland** (☎ 0131-243 9300, 🖳 www.nts.org.uk), Wemyss House, 28 Charlotte Square, Edinburgh, EH2 4ET.
● **Association for the Protection of Rural Scotland** (☎ 0131-225 7012, 🖳 www.ruralscotland.org), Gladstone's Land (3rd Floor), 483 Lawnmarket, Edinburgh, EH1 2NT.
● **RSPB Scotland** (☎ 0131-311 6500, 🖳 www.rspb.org.uk), Dunedin House, 25 Ravelston Terrace, Edinburgh, EH4 3TP.
● **Scottish Wildlife Trust** (☎ 0131-312 7765, 🖳 www.swt.org.uk), Cramond House, Kirk Cramond, Cramond Glebe Rd, Edinburgh, EH4 6NS.
● **Reforesting Scotland** (☎ 0131-220 2500, 🖳 www.reforestingscotland.org), 58 Shandwick Place, Edinburgh EH2 4RT.
● **Trees for Life** (☎ 01309-691292, 🖳 www.treesforlife.org.uk), The Park, Findhorn Bay, Forres, IV36 3TZ.

PART 3: THE HIGHLANDS

Facts about the Highlands

GEOGRAPHY

Scotland occupies the northern end of the British Isles and has three main **geographical regions**: the Southern Uplands, the Central Lowlands and the Highlands. The Highlands covers the north, west and north-east of the country. The two main Highland mountain ranges, which are kept apart by the Great Glen fault that almost bisects the country, are the Grampians and the North-west Highlands.

The Great Glen is a major landmark and an area of deep **glacial lochs**, the most famous of which is Loch Ness. Lochs are probably the most significant feature of the landscape after the mountains. While Loch Ness has the largest volume of water of any Scottish loch, it is not the deepest. That honour belongs to Loch Morar on the west coast which is over 1000 metres deep, a legacy of the power of the ice that scoured out these now flooded basins. Loch Lomond is probably the most popular loch for leisure activities, partly thanks to its natural beauty and its proximity to Glasgow, but many argue that the top prize for beauty goes to the island-studded Loch Maree in the north-west whose forested shores are protected on each side by the beautiful peaks of Slioch and Beinn Eighe.

Scotland's **hills** are small by global standards but, with most of them starting at sea level, they often appear bigger than they are. There are 284 mountains in Scotland of 3000ft (914 metres) or higher. Eight of these are at least 4000ft high with the highest, Ben Nevis, topping out at 4409ft (1344m).

Rivers in Scotland are quite short, especially along the west side of the country since the watershed is very close to the west coast. Rivers flowing to the east have further to go so they have a much greater catchment area. The likes of the Spey, Dee, Tay, Earn and Forth all originate deep in the mountains, ending their journeys on the North Sea coast.

There are four main **island groups** in Scotland and all of them have a distinctly Highland character, with few trees and plenty of windswept, grassy and rocky hills. The Shetland and Orkney Islands lie in the far north while the west coast is protected by two lines of islands: the Inner Hebrides, which include the mountainous islands of Skye, Rum and Mull, and the Western Isles (or Outer Hebrides) with their low hills, machair grassland and empty shell-sand beaches.

Scotland has a population of about five million **people**, the majority of whom live in the so-called central belt which includes Glasgow and Edinburgh. The Highlands are sparsely populated but in summer the roads, towns and some of the hills become very congested as the tourist season reaches its peak. The main centres of population are Inverness, the capital of the Highlands, which sits astride the River Ness at the northern end of the Great Glen, and Fort William at the southern end, in the shadow of Ben Nevis.

GEOLOGY

The character of the Scottish mountains varies considerably over short distances; the result of a fascinating geological story. This has been recognised on an international level with the designation of two UNESCO geoparks (areas recognised for their rich geology): Lochaber and North West Highlands.

The shape of the mountains is determined by a number of factors. The **rock type** affects the amount of weathering and therefore its physical appearance while it also affects the type of vegetation on the surface. Almost everywhere in the Highlands the bedrock is very close to the surface and often exposed, largely because of the climate and the effects of the last Ice Age. **Glaciation** has played a huge part in shaping present-day Scotland. Glaciers have gouged out once V-shaped river valleys and scoured the land, but to differing degrees. The Cairngorm plateau is the largest remnant of high ground that survived the ice while further west the mountains have been more heavily eroded. Here, on the west coast, the ridges are narrower and the U-shaped valleys deeper. In some areas further north, particularly Assynt, the ice only left behind inselberg peaks (islands of high ground standing defiantly amid a heavily eroded floor).

While thousands of years of glaciation have been responsible for shaping the topography, the actual map of the Highlands and the bedrock itself is influenced by three significant **fault lines** (breaks in the Earth's crust). These are not major fault lines like those on the edge of tectonic plates, which cause all the earthquakes, but much smaller fractures.

The first is the Highland Boundary Fault marking the change between the central lowlands and the Highlands. There is quite a marked contrast in the landscape upon crossing the Highland Boundary which is most obvious at the southern end of Loch Lomond and on the approach to the Trossachs, through Callander, where the fertile, sedimentary rocks of the Lowlands give way to the metamorphic rocks of the mountains. In places these metamorphic rocks are overlain by igneous intrusions, most famously at Ben Nevis and in the Cairngorms.

The second fault is the Great Glen fault, a strike-slip fault that has been exaggerated by the abrasion from glaciers, to form a massive part-flooded trench, part of which is Loch Ness. Over hundreds of millennia the land to the north of this fault has slowly been moving to the north-east while the land to the south has been moving in the opposite direction.

Further north there is another significant fault known as the Moine Thrust running from Loch Alsh to the Kyle of Durness. The corner of the Highlands to the north-west of this fault has some of the most varied geology in the country and hence some very diverse mountain landscapes. Most of the mountains contain a bedrock of Lewisian gneiss, as is the case in Fisherfield and Assynt, although the Torridonian sandstone peaks have a completely different look, with castellated towers, terraced slopes and bands of quartzite scree.

THE HIGHLANDS

Hillwalking is a joy but it is even more of an experience when you take time to appreciate the mind-boggling timescale of the processes that have shaped the mountains under your boots. Some of the rocks are over 400 million years old.

HISTORY

Until about 10,000 years ago Scotland was uninhabitable, largely thanks to the ice sheet that covered it. But as the ice retreated and the climate warmed the first settlers of the early **Stone Age** (Mesolithic period) arrived. Towards the end of the stone age (the Neolithic period) came the first man-made changes to the landscape as simple farming techniques and the domestication of animals took off. There is evidence of early settlements and human activity in many parts of the Highlands from this time, particularly on the Western and Northern Isles. On Orkney there are a number of incredibly well-preserved neolithic stone houses, such as the one at Skara Brae, while the Isle of Lewis has neolithic wheelhouses and the famous standing stones of Callanish.

Around the 12th century BC the **Celts** arrived in Scotland from mainland Europe. Along with the **Picts**, a little understood race, they asserted their culture and language on society, surviving well into the Iron Age. And then the Romans invaded in 79AD. The **Romans**, under Emperor Hadrian, built a wall marking their boundary with Scotland, in northern England; a wall that many today wrongly assume marked the northern limit of the Roman invasion. In fact there are earlier defensive fortifications further north, closer to the Highland boundary and they built another wall, the Antonine Wall, on a line between the Firth of Forth and Firth of Clyde. After the Romans, the people of Scotland continued to suffer a number of invasions. The **Irish** colonised much of the west, the **Anglo-Saxons** and later the **Normans** crept into the south from England and the **Vikings** came in from the north, all of which helped shape the people, language and culture in Scotland today.

Scotland's rather bloody history reached a peak around 1296 when the knight **William Wallace** led an uprising against the English, who continued to assert themselves in the lowlands. Wallace, widely regarded as a man of the people, won a famous victory at the Battle of Stirling Bridge and went on to inspire **Robert the Bruce**, who won the most famous battle of all at Bannockburn, near Stirling in 1314, but not before he had betrayed Wallace, in order to become King of Scotland. Consequently, Wallace was hung, drawn and quartered while Robert the Bruce went on to be crowned in 1306. The monument to William Wallace just outside Stirling and the statue of Robert the Bruce at Bannockburn are testament to their standing as Scottish folk heroes to this day. The story caught the attention of a certain actor/director, Mel Gibson, who gave Scottish history the popcorn treatment in his Hollywood epic *Braveheart*. The consequence of the Bannockburn victory, and Wallace's victory before that, was **independence** for Scotland in 1328. Attempts by the English to win back the country continued, most notably when **Mary Queen of Scots** inherited the Scottish throne as a baby. In a ploy to win control over Scotland, Henry VIII of England attempted to marry her off to his five-year-old son but failed when she married instead the French dauphin, Francis. Mary Queen of Scots eventually returned to Scotland when her father's cousin Elizabeth I sat on the English throne. Elizabeth had little time for catching up on family gossip and chose, instead, to lock Mary up for twenty odd years as a prelude to her beheading.

Upon her death, the Scottish crown was passed on to Mary's son **James VI** of Scotland and it is he who was responsible for the eventual **reunification** of Scotland and England. After inheriting the English crown to become James I of England he moved to London and the two crowns unified in 1603. The Scottish parliament was wound up some time later and a parliament for the unified nation was established in London.

The story doesn't end there, however. Attempts to wrest control of the British crown took place in earnest during the Jacobite uprisings. These began with the capture of Perth in 1715 under the guidance of **James Stewart**, the 'Old Pretender'. His success was short-lived and he ended up exiled in France. In 1745 his son, **Bonnie Prince Charlie**, the 'Young Pretender', in an effort to see his father installed as king, went back to Scotland from France to lead a number of successful battles that saw him and his clansmen march on as far south as central England. The early success did not last and they were forced back, tasting final defeat at the hands of the Hanoverian troops at the Battle of Culloden near Inverness.

Bonnie Prince Charlie went into exile the following year, hiding with his right-hand men in locations all over the Highlands before eventually fleeing back to France in 1746. A cairn marks his arrival and departure point on the shore of Loch nan Uamh near Arisaig, and all over the Highlands there are caves that are said to have sheltered him as he fled (these are often marked on Ordnance Survey maps for those interested in finding them). After the defeat at Culloden it became illegal for clansmen to wear tartan.

Far more damaging, however, was the law passed in 1756 which effectively gave wealthy landlords the right to evict their crofter tenants to make way for more productive forms of land-use, mainly sheep farming. These **Highland Clearances** resulted in death, annexation and mass emigration to Canada (see box p50).

The most recent chapter in Scotland's political history was a more peaceful affair. In 1999 **devolution** in Scotland led to the formation of a Scottish parliament in Edinburgh; a position that affords Scotland the right to govern the country's domestic affairs, under the guidance of the First Minister, at the time of writing, the Scottish National Party's Alex Salmond. However, overall control of international and defence matters continues to come from parliament in London.

Today, Scotland is a peaceful country. Some Scots still feel quite impassioned about the bloody history between the English and the Scots and opinion is divided on whether Scotland should ever be a fully independent nation again, but most rivalries between the two are friendly and usually confined to football and rugby pitches. This reflects an increasingly multi-cultural Scotland, particularly in the capital, Edinburgh, and in the largest city, Glasgow.

In recent years the demographics of the Highland population have also changed, particularly in the Highland capital, Inverness, but also in rural areas.

The Highland Clearances

The clan system, under which the people of a given area of the Highlands were controlled by a Clan Chief, survived until the Highland Clearances. This was a period during the agricultural revolution at the start of the 19th century when thousands of Highlanders were evicted from their homes to make way for large-scale sheep farming. The clearances led to migrations to Nova Scotia and Newfoundland for the lucky ones and starvation for the unlucky.

The subject still raises temperatures today. Descendants of those evicted live on the land which even today is still used for sheep-farming interests. It is easy to forget that many of those wild, empty glens once supported a flourishing population, but a closer look reveals the remains of the stone-built houses that were razed to the ground during the evictions. While most evidence suggests that many of these clearances were brutal affairs, other historians claim that it was simply a natural and sensible change in agricultural activity, even suggesting that many evictees left voluntarily. It is certainly a subject that sparks plenty of debate.

There has been a steady increase in non-Scots, particularly those from other parts of the UK, living and working in the mountains. Most of them work in the tourist industry and, probably without exception, were drawn to the Highlands by the scenery.

LANGUAGE

English is the dominant language of the Highlands but it is not the native language. That is Scots Gaelic which belongs to the same branch of Celtic languages as Irish Gaelic and Manx. It is important to note that Scots Gaelic was the language of the Gaels who lived in the Highlands, and not the language of southern Scotland, where Lowland Scots was the native tongue.

So-called minority languages are dying out throughout the world and Scots Gaelic has also suffered. Not many people in the Highlands speak Gaelic and very few have it as their mother tongue. The stronghold is the Western Isles where it's certainly not dead yet. The heavy promotion of the language in recent years, its continued presence on the school curriculum and the broadcasting of Gaelic-language television and radio programmes, suggests there is always hope of at least a partial recovery.

The other positive step is the Highland Council's decision to replace all the road signs with bilingual ones. For anyone with more than a passing interest in Gaelic, road signs are useful for seeing how the original words have been corrupted into their anglicised forms, and help to give some idea of how the original should be pronounced.

While it may not be the language of choice for many people there are a few Gaelic words that have found their way into the English language. Some are internationally understood: brogue, cairn, ceilidh, clan, glen, plaid, slogan, trousers and whisky, while others may only be familiar to the Scots: *'stravaig'* – a long walk, *'blether'* – to talk incessantly, and the great, and often needed, word *'dreich'* – cold, grey and drizzly weather. (See p309-10 for a fuller list.)

Flora and fauna

MAMMALS

If there is one animal that is synonymous with the Highlands it's the **red deer** (*Cervus elaphus*). There are few sights in the hills more impressive than that of a stag bellowing on the hillside during the October rutting season. Red deer are not difficult to spot as they roam the open hillsides in large herds (see also box p23).

Roe deer *(Capreolus capreolus)* are much smaller than red deer and prefer a bit more woodland cover. Look out for them crossing forest paths and in forest clearings. They have much gentler features than the red deer, with a black nose and a delicate, lithe frame. The male has short, spiky antlers.

The **reindeer** (*Rangifer tarandus*) hardly needs any introduction, apart from the introduction that took place in 1952, when some reindeer from Sarek in Arctic Sweden came over on a boat (not an act of volition of course) and were released near Aviemore. Today there are about 150 reindeer in the Cairngorms. They roam freely, living on the lichen but are still part-managed by Cairngorm Reindeer Centre (see box p169) who arrange trips to go and see them.

The **pine marten** (*Martes martes*) is a member of the weasel family but unlike its diminutive cousin, this beautiful creature with chocolate brown fur and a yellowish bib, is more at home in the treetops. The pine marten was once widespread throughout the British Isles and despite an upturn in numbers and an expanding distribution, it is still limited to the wilder corners of Scotland and northern England. They are elusive creatures but are sometimes spotted bounding across Highland roads at night. Other marten hotspots include the Beinn Eighe National Nature Reserve, Glen Affric and the oakwoods of Sunart, particularly Glen Cripesdale and Ariundle National Nature Reserves. There is also the quite brilliant Ardnamurchan Natural History Centre (see box p197) where you can view wild pine martens sleeping in a purpose-built den adjoining the centre.

The **otter** (*Lutra lutra*), like the pine marten, is related to the weasel but is more at home in water, be it freshwater rivers and lakes or in the sea. A good place to go otter-watching is along the shores of sea lochs, especially as the tide is coming in as this is when they tend to go in search of sand eels and other squidgy delights brought in by the tide. The best places to spot an otter are in the Western Isles, particularly the Uists, and also around Loch Sunart and parts of Skye.

The rarest of predatory mammals in the British Isles is the **wildcat** (*Felis sylvestris*), now limited to some remote areas of the Highlands. If the pine marten is a shy animal, the wildcat is downright anti-social, avoiding human interaction at all costs and leading a solitary life on the moors. Wildcats look like big, strong tabby cats but their survival is threatened through inter-breeding with the domestic cat.

THE HIGHLANDS

Much more common is the **fox** (*Vulpes vulpes*), loved and loathed in equal numbers. The fox is a successful species, feeling as much at home in the woods and on the moors as in a dirty city street. Although they are common they are harder to spot in the hills than in the city. The best chance is at dawn on the edges of fields and woodland where they hunt for mice and voles.

The **badger** (*Meles meles*) is present in the Highlands but not in the same numbers as in southern England. Badgers are related to martens and weasels but are much larger and have a distinctive black-and-white muzzle. They are generally nocturnal and spend their nights gorging themselves on earthworms and, in autumn, berries. A badger's sett is often vast and is passed down through generations. Watching them at their sett has become very popular but if you do, always avoid disturbing them and stay downwind.

Mountain hares (*Lepus timidus*) are limited to higher ground and prefer plateaus and rounded hills rather than narrow ridges. Good places to see them are Caenlochan National Nature Reserve on the Driesh and Mayar walk, the Cairngorm plateau and the Monadhliath mountains.

The Highlands is one of the last places in Britain where the **red squirrel** (*Sciurus vulgaris*) has not been replaced by the introduced North American **grey squirrel** (*Sciurus carolinensis*) although one grey, possibly a stowaway on a lorry, was reported close to Inverness in 2008. The colour is not the only difference between the two. Reds are smaller and tend to prefer coniferous forests, especially native Caledonian pine forest. Look out for them running from branch to branch and across the woodland floor in Abernethy Forest, Rothiemurchus, Glen Affric and any other wooded areas.

Feral goats (*Capra hircus*) in Scotland are descendants of domesticated animals, and have bred in the wild for generations, now roaming freely in the hills. They are quite varied in appearance but often have shaggy, black and

---

Beavering about

Following on from the successful reintroduction of native bird species, like the sea eagle and red kite, a native mammal has been reintroduced to the UK for the first time. The last of Britain's native **European beavers** (*Castor fiber*) was shot some time in the 16th century. There were further declines in population across the continent and by the 18th century the species was nearly wiped out across Europe. Thankfully, beavers have been reintroduced to 13 European countries and, after much campaigning and many setbacks the Scottish Executive finally gave the green light to a six-year trial reintroduction of this iconic species. The project is spearheaded by the Scottish Wildlife Trust and the Royal Zoological Society of Scotland who, in May 2009, released four beaver families, brought in from Norway, into the network of lakes at Knapdale Forest near Loṁchgilphead in Argyll. There is, of course, some opposition to the scheme; many people wrongly assume that beavers damage the environment. In fact the opposite is true; beavers are a 'keystone' species; they are of great benefit to the ecosystem as a whole as they create glades in woodland as well as pools, both of which are important habitats for other species. And then there are the potential economic benefits brought on by tourism.

You can learn more about the project at 🖥 www.scottishbeavers.org.uk.

white coats. Their range is limited to a few specific areas but where they do occur they are quite easy to see. Particularly good spots are the east coast of Loch Lomond, Kintail, Knoydart and the northern Fisherfield Forest. These non-native beasts can cause significant damage to fragile habitats already under pressure from the enormous numbers of red deer.

There are, of course, many other species including **stoats** (*Mustela erminea*), **weasels** (*Mustela nivalis*) and different species of **voles**, **mice** and **shrews**. It is rare to get a good view of such small speedy creatures. Most sightings come as a brief flash of brown shoots across the road.

BIRDS

On mountain tops and high plateaus

A number of tough bird species brave the cold and rain and make the high mountain tops their home. One fairly common sight is the **raven** (*Corvus corax*), a huge, glossy, black bird: the largest member of the crow family. It is so big that it is sometimes mistaken, at a distance, for a buzzard. Ravens are traditionally seen as portents of doom, which is a little unnerving when a couple of them start circling above you whilst you are inching your way across a narrow arête. Their deep, croaking call is one of the wildest sounds of the mountains.

Smaller and cuter than ravens are **snow buntings** (*Plectrophenax nivalis*), an arctic species about the size of a sparrow. They are mostly white but have some orange and brown tinges. In winter, snow buntings come to Scotland from their breeding grounds in Scandinavia, gathering in small flocks on mountain tops and plateaus. There are a few permanent residents breeding in the Cairngorms.

An arctic species that does stay all year is the **ptarmigan** (*Lagopus mutus*), a grouse-like bird seen quite frequently on high plateaus. In summer, ptarmigan are mottled grey but by winter they have turned white, a cunning ploy to blend in with the snow and avoid detection by eagles and buzzards. One has to wonder what the effect of climate change will have on them as lying snow becomes less common in the Highlands.

The **dotterel** (*Chardrius morinellus*), a member of the plover family, only comes to Scotland in summer when it breeds on the high exposed tops. Listen for a whistle, which is often the first indication that a dotterel is about. If you do hear and see one, try to give the bird a wide berth as you may be near the nest.

A close relation of the dotterel is the **golden plover** (*Pluvialis apricaria*), a much larger bird with majestic gold and black plumage. They also inhabit upland areas but may be seen on blanket bogs lower down.

Among the birds of prey that inhabit the mountains is the **peregrine** (*Falco peregrinus*), a master of fast, controlled flight and famed for its high-speed, stooping dives that can reach 180mph and knock a grouse clean out of the sky. Like many birds of prey, peregrines suffer from some unforgivable, and illegal, poisoning and snaring but conservationists are helping to keep the Scottish population reasonably healthy. Certainly their numbers have recovered since the 1960s, largely thanks to the banning of DDT, a chemical once used in farming.

THE HIGHLANDS

It entered the food chain and consequently caused the deaths of countless birds of prey.

The **golden eagle** (*Aquila chrysaetos*), a hugely enigmatic bird, is often top of people's lists of birds they would most like to see. There are around 440 pairs in Scotland and, while not as frequently spotted as buzzards, a patient observer should get some reward. They prefer remote spots and craggy open hillsides where they can feed and breed. Once you see one it is unmistakable: the two-metre wing span and slow, infrequent wing beats distinguish it from the buzzard.

Although the **white-tailed eagle** (*Haliaeetus albicilla*) is really a coastal species they are worth mentioning here since their range often encompasses coastal mountains. The presence of white-tailed eagles, or sea eagles, in Scotland is one of the great success stories of modern conservation. Like many native birds and mammals sea eagles were wiped out in Britain but a dedicated programme of reintroduction began in 1975 when the first birds were released on the Isle of Rum.

In 1985 the birds finally began breeding again on Scottish soil and by 2007 there were 42 breeding pairs. While Rum was the focus for the long-running release programme the eagles appear to have chosen the Isle of Mull and the Western Isles as their preferred haunts, although you may be lucky enough to see one anywhere along the west coast as their range expands. White-tailed eagles are easy to identify, partly thanks to their size; they have a wing span of almost two and a half metres, and partly because of their appearance – the clue is in the name.

On moorland

Of the many raptors that inhabit the moors and hills of Scotland the **buzzard** (*Buteo buteo*) is the commonest and most frequently seen, whether high above the mountains, in woodland or perched on a roadside telegraph pole. It looks much like a small eagle, is usually brown in colour and has a distinctive mewing cry. Buzzards have enjoyed a marked population explosion in recent years, so much so that it is thought they may have overtaken the kestrel as the most common bird of prey in Britain.

The **kestrel** (*Falco tinnunculus*), a small falcon with pointed wing tips, is also quite easy to see and is famous for its ability to hover in a fixed spot in even the strongest of winds. It's commonly seen above roadsides where it hunts for mice and voles in the grassy verges.

Another member of the falcon family is the **merlin** (*Falco columbarius*) which breeds on upland moorland. It is very similar to the kestrel but even smaller and not as common.

The entire UK population of the **red kite** (*Milvus milvus*) was until recently restricted to central Wales where a few pairs hung on to survival, but they have since been reintroduced to both England and Scotland. There were three release sites across Scotland. One of the best places to see them is on the Black Isle near Inverness, where they can often be seen above the road to Contin. They are very distinctive birds with a deeply forked tail, long pointed wings and a beautiful lilting flight.

The **red grouse** (*Lagopus lagopus*) shelters beneath the heather on upland moorland, often bursting out of cover at the last second as a walker inadvertently flushes it out. Shooting red grouse is a popular pastime in the Highlands and many estates manage their moorlands specifically with grouse shooting in mind. Much rarer is the **black grouse** (*Tetrao tetrix*), a protected species, and one that is very hard to track down. The black male has a distinctive red 'wattle' above each eye and a white tail.

Snipe (*Gallinago gallinago*) are also present on the moors, particularly where it is boggy and there are small pools where they can feed. They are quite plump waders with brown, streaky plumage and a sharp, straight bill. In a similar way to red grouse they often burst from cover at the last second as a walker approaches. Try not to linger as the nest may be near by.

The **curlew** (*Numenius arquata*) is another moorland wading bird. They are bigger and more slender than snipe, have much longer, spindly legs and a long, slightly curved bill. In winter they are confined to mudflats and estuaries along the coast but in summer listen for their haunting cries across wet upland moors, where they breed.

The **meadow pipit** (*Anthus pratensis*) is a fairly common bird of the small, brown variety. They are often seen flitting across moorland paths and perched on fenceposts. Like the meadow pipit, the **stonechat** (*Saxixola torquata*) is resident all year. The male is black and white with a striking flame-red breast and is easy to spot, often perching on the top of gorse bushes and other vantage points. The name comes from its call which is said to resemble the chink of two stones being knocked together. **Whinchats** (*Saxixola rubetra*) are very similar in appearance to stonechats but are summer visitors only and are more commonly seen around areas of rough grassland and bracken. Slightly less colourful summer visitors to look out for are **wheatears** (*Oenanthe oenanthe*) which have a bluish-grey back, a light orange belly and black wings. They are as comfortable breeding on moorland and grassland as they are on rocky ground.

Finally, the **skylark** (*Alauda arvensis*) is a sparrow-sized, ground-nesting bird, more often heard than seen. Often regarded as the sound of the summer, their incessant high-pitched warbles and whistles can be heard high above the moors as they rise ever upwards, eventually dropping quite suddenly back to the ground.

Around rivers and lochs

The **dipper** (*Cinclus cinclus*) is synonymous with fast-flowing mountain rivers. It's a chubby little dark bird with a white breast and is most commonly seen sitting on a rock in the middle of the river where it bobs up and down in a seemingly perpetual state of nervousness, before flying fast and low over the rushing water to the next rock. It is most famous for its ability to walk under water. The **grey wagtail** (*Motacilla cinerea*) occupies a similar niche to the dipper. It is a smaller and much more slender bird and, with its grey back, yellow breast and black wings, is far more colourful. Its name derives from its tail, which twitches interminably.

Not as common, but unmistakable when it does show itself, is the **goosander** (*Mergus merganser*), a black and white duck with a dark green head and red bill. They breed in hollows in trees next to fast-flowing upland rivers and streams.

Out on the open water of the lochs you may be lucky enough to see the rare **red-throated diver** (*Gavia stellata*) or the even-rarer **black-throated diver** (*Gavia arctica*). The red-throated diver is smaller than the black-throated but the obvious way to distinguish between the two is by the colour of their throat patches, which give them their names. Both of these summer visitors are designed with an aquatic lifestyle in mind, with their legs set so far back they can barely walk on land, only being forced to do so when they come ashore to breed on small undisturbed islands. In North America divers are known as loons.

In forest

The **capercaillie** (*Tetrao urogallus*) is an enormous grouse that lives in the native pinewoods of Scotland. The caper, as it is sometimes called, is a critical-

---

Where to watch wildlife

The following wildlife hides and reserves give the best opportunities of seeing some of the rarer Highland birds and mammals. There is no guarantee of seeing anything of course but a bit of patience and choosing the right time (usually dawn and dusk) and season (eg ospreys – April to August; badgers – May to July; red deer – all year but especially October since it is the rutting season; mountain hares – spring and autumn when their coats clash with their surroundings) increases your chances. This is just a selection of some of many nature reserves and wildlife hides across the Highlands. To discover more visit 🖥 www.nnr-scotland .org.uk, 🖥 www.swt.org.uk/Reserves and 🖥 www.rspb.org.uk/reserves.

● **Loch of the Lowes, nr Dunkeld** (🖥 www.swt.org.uk) – various aquatic birds and ospreys; see also box p138.

● **Caenlochan National Nature Reserve (NNR), nr Glen Clova** (🖥 www.nnr-scot land.org.uk) – mountain hares and golden eagles.

● **Craigellachie, Aviemore** (🖥 www.nnr-scotland.org.uk) – peregrine falcons.

● **Abernethy Forest and Loch Garten Osprey Centre, nr Boat of Garten** (🖥 www .rspb.org.uk) – ospreys, red squirrels, Scottish crossbills, crested tits and capercaillies; see also box p169.

● **Creag Meagaidh NNR, between Tulloch and Laggan** (🖥 www.nnr-scotland .org.uk) – ptarmigans, dotterels, golden eagles, pine martens and wildcats.

● **Ardnamurchan Natural History Centre, Sunart** (see box p197; 🖥 www.ardnamur channaturalhistorycentre.co.uk) – golden eagles, roe deer and pine martens.

● **Garbh Eilean hide, near Salen on Loch Sunart** (🖥 www.sunartoakwoods .org.uk) – grey seals, otters, buzzards, golden eagles and sea eagles.

● **Loch Frisa, Isle of Mull** (🖥 www.rspb.org.uk/brilliant/sites/mull/) – white-tailed eagles.

● **Kylerhea Otter Haven, Kylerhea, Skye** (🖥 www.forestry.gov.uk) – grey seals, otters, dolphins and porpoises.

● **Glen Affric NNR** (🖥 www.nnr-scotland.org.uk) – pine martens, capercaillies, Scottish crossbills, golden eagles and red-throated divers.

● **Torridon Countryside Centre, Torridon** (🖥 www.nts.org.uk) – red deer, pine martens, golden eagles and sea eagles.

● **Beinn Eighe NNR, nr Torridon and Kinlochewe** (🖥 www.nnr-scotland.org.uk) – golden eagles, pine martens and wildcats.

ly endangered species and despite their massive size they are very hard to see. A good place to look is at Abernethy Forest in Cairngorms National Park. At the other end of the size scale is the **crested tit** (*Parus cristatus*). Again, native pinewoods are their preferred habitat, where they feed on Scots pine seeds.

The most famous of the forest species is probably the **Scottish crossbill** (*Loxia scotica*). This small but stocky finch is found nowhere else in the world making it the only endemic bird in Scotland. The difference, however, between the Scottish crossbill and a **common crossbill** (*Loxia curviostra*) is minimal, making identification quite difficult.

The **siskin** (*Carduelis spinus*) inhabits both coniferous and deciduous woodland. It is a yellow finch that is sometimes seen high in the tops of the trees where it feeds on seeds and insects.

Associated as much with open water as with the forests where it breeds is the **osprey** (*Pandion haliaetus*), a beautiful bird of prey with black and white plumage. The osprey is essentially a fish-eating eagle. To watch this impressive bird swoop low over the water and hook a fish out of the loch is a sight you are unlikely to forget. You can see ospreys doing just this at various locations across Scotland, notably at the Loch of the Lowes reserve (see box p138) and on the Rothiemurchus estate. But the best place to see the birds on the nest is at what is probably the most famous nest in Britain, at Loch Garten (see box p169) where the RSPB have a hide.

TREES

The Caledonian pine forest is the most emblematic of Scotland's woodlands. Sadly 99% of it has been decimated. Caledonian forests are characterised, of course, by the **Scots pine** (*Pinus sylvestris*), a conifer distinguished by its pairs of dark green needles and a distinctive reddish bark that becomes very gnarled and flaky with old age. Scots pine trees can live for 500 years. These wonderfully crooked old trees are known as granny pines.

Also present in the Caledonian forest is **juniper** (*Juniperus communis*), an evergreen shrub from the cypress family. These sweet-smelling bushes grow very slowly and rarely reach more than five metres in height.

While the Caledonian forest represents the most dominant coniferous forests, the most widespread deciduous forests on the hills are those of birch which survives to much higher elevations than the Scots pine. There are two species in Scotland: the **silver birch** (*Betula pendula*) which prefers dry soil and the **downy birch** (*Betula pubescens*) preferring damp soil. There are some good examples of birch forest throughout the Highlands although much of the cover has become very fragmented and patchy.

The oakwoods of the Highlands are most commonly found in more sheltered lowland areas. Good remnants remain around the shores of Loch Lomond, in Glen Affric and on the shores of Loch Sunart. The two main species of oak are the **pedunculate oak** (*Quercus robur*) and the **sessile oak** (*Quercus petraea*), the latter tending to replace the former towards the north. Other species that are present in oak woodland include **elm** (*Ulmus glabra*), **hazel** (*Corylus avellana*), **ash**

Forests

The vast majority of forest in Scotland comes in the form of non-native commercial plantations managed by the **Forestry Commission Scotland** (☎ 0131-334 0303, 🖳 www.forestry.gov.uk/scotland, Silvan House, 231 Corstorphine Rd, Edinburgh EH12 7AT).

The predominant species is the **Sitka spruce** (*Picea sitchensis*), a native of North America which was planted across thousands of acres of the Highlands during the 1950s. The trees were often planted so close together that no other species was capable of getting established. After approximately 50 years the crop is harvested or 'clear-felled' and young trees are planted again.

While these plantations offer some benefits to certain species, such as crested tits, many of these forests are of limited benefit to native flora and fauna. Nevertheless, the Forestry Commission has certainly improved its methods over recent years, ensuring that riverbanks and other patches of land are left as open glades where wild flowers and butterflies can flourish, and planting more native species among the commercial product. This is all very positive but a truly native forest still has much greater biodiversity. A good place to see the difference is on the Meall a' Bhuachaille walk in the Cairngorms which begins in the ancient Caledonian pine forest and ends in the commercial plantations of the Queen's Forest. (The Caledonian Forest is the name given to the forests that once covered most of the Highland glens: Rothiemurchus, Abernethy, Glen Affric and the Beinn Eighe forests are all remnants of a once-much greater, country-wide forest). Aside from the benefits, or lack thereof, to wildlife, on a purely aesthetic level the natural beauty of the Caledonian forest, with its ground flora of heather, juniper and blaeberry, its gnarly old granny pines (Scots pines) and a natural forest edge that peters out slowly into the upland moorland, simply cannot be matched by a tightly packed monoculture of sitka spruce with hard forest edges that stop suddenly at a deer fence.

The Caledonian Forest is a hugely important habitat. Many forward-thinking organisations are going to great lengths to conserve what is left, and to encourage natural regeneration through planting and keeping the deer out. Those who need a break from climbing hills will find a walk in the Caledonian Forest a soothing alternative. The best places to enjoy a woodland walk are in Rothiemurchus Forest and Abernethy Forest in the Cairngorms National Park, Glen Affric and Beinn Eighe.

(*Fraxinus excelsior*) and **rowan** (*Sorbus aucuparia*), an elegant tree with small, narrow leaves and, towards the end of the summer, bright red berries. Rowan is also commonly seen growing alone on moorland, often by rivers or streams. This is also the best place to find **alder** (*Alnus glutinosa*).

FLOWERS AND PLANTS

Heather is everywhere in the highlands from the floors of the native pine forests to the high upland moors. Controlled burning of the heather on grouse moors helps to ensure it regenerates regularly. There are three species of heather in Scotland: **ling** (*Calluna vulgaris*) is the one most commonly associated with the grouse moors; **bell heather** (*Erica cinerea*) which has dark green leaves and deep purple flowers is most commonly associated with dry ground and is responsible for hillsides turning a spectacular shade of purple in August while

cross-leaved heath (*Erica tetralix*) is lighter in colour, with almost white flowers and pale green leaves, and prefers wetter, boggy areas.

Cloudberry (*Rubus chamaemorus*), **cowberry** (*Vaccinium vitis-idaea*) and **blaeberry** (*Vaccinium myrtilis*) are all common shrubs with edible berries, that are found on moorland and on forest floors. Blaeberry, with its rusty orange/green leaves, is particularly associated with decorating the Caledonian forest floor.

Both **whin**, or **gorse** (*Ulex europaeus*) with its prickly, dark-green spines, and **broom** (*Sarothamnus scoparius*), with thin, brush-like leaves, have striking yellow flowers in the summer. They are quite common species on dry, sandy soil.

The national flower of Scotland is the thistle, of which there are a number of species, the most distinctive of which is the **spear thistle** (*Cirsium vulgare*) which grows alongside other meadow species such as the **Scottish bluebell** or **harebell** (*Campanula rotundifolia*), **early purple orchid** (*Orchis mascula*) and **tormentil** (*Potentilla erecta*) which has small yellow flowers. It was once used for medicinal purposes and was said to 'torment' those who were prescribed it.

In boggier areas there are two insectivorous plants that stand out. The first is the **round-leaved sundew** (*Drosera rotundifolia*), a small, red-green plant with sticky hairs that trap insects which are then ingested. The other is the **butterwort** (*Pinguicula vulgaris*), an other-worldly-looking organism. Its bright green-yellow leaves hug the ground and trap insects in a similar way to the sundew. The pretty purple flowers emerge between May and July.

Other bog species of note include the **bog asphodel** (*Narthecium ossifragum*) which brightens up otherwise drab marshy areas with its bright yellow spiky flowers in July and August. **Bog cotton** (*Eriophorum angustifolium*) is most obvious in summer when the furry cotton heads dance in the wind.

On the high ground the predominant species are the grasses of which there are quite a variety. The most common is the **deer grass** (*Trichophorum cespitosum*) that turns a shade of golden brown in the autumn, transforming the hillsides. Finally, look out for the saxifrages that survive high up in cracks and crevices between rocks, hence the name which means rock-breaker. The **purple saxifrage** (*Saxifraga oppostifolia*) is the most common of a number of species of this alpine plant.

LICHENS

All over screes and bare rocks are hardy lichens, unique in that they consist of two distinct symbiotic partners: one an algae and the other a fungus. Lichens occur everywhere from churchyard headstones and tree trunks to rocky coastlines and mountain tops. There are literally thousands of distinct species of lichens with new ones being discovered every year. The ones most commonly associated with the Highlands include the feathery pale green lichens that grow on tree trunks and branches, often referred to as old men's beards because of their flowing, hairy appearance, and the lichens that cover exposed rocks at the tops of mountains. The abundance of lichens is widely considered to be an excellent indicator of clean air so it is good to see that the Highlands has plenty of them.

THE HIGHLANDS

Trail map key

Walking track	Cairn	Coniferous forest
Minor track	Trig. point	Deciduous forest
4WD track	Bridge	Building
Road	Fence	Accommodation
Slope	Stone wall	Campsite
Steep slope	Water	Church
Stile	Sand	Public toilet
Gate	Rocky ground	Public telephone
Track on ridge	River	Bus stop
Summit	Waterfall	Railway station
Subsidiary top	Cliffs	Car park
	Boggy ground	Map continuation

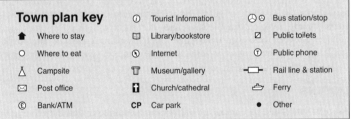

Town plan key

Where to stay	Tourist Information	Bus station/stop
Where to eat	Library/bookstore	Public toilets
Campsite	Internet	Public phone
Post office	Museum/gallery	Rail line & station
Bank/ATM	Church/cathedral	Ferry
	CP Car park	Other

PART 4: ROUTE GUIDES & MAPS

Using this guide

The mountains featured in this guide have been grouped into clear geographical areas. With the exception of the Big Treks (see pp295-302), and a few other routes, each walk can be completed in a day. For each entry there is a route description which includes vital information such as gradings of difficulty, timings, distance, total ascent and location of gateway villages or towns, as well as a route map and an ascent and distance profile. In addition to useful service information there are details about every place to stay and place to eat (at the time of writing) for smaller villages – a selection of these is given for larger villages and towns. To accompany the text there are also town and village plans for all but the smallest hamlets.

ROUTE MAPS

The sketch maps in this section are intended as an aid to navigation to the main routes described. However, while they are fine for using in clear weather, you should still carry with you a contour map of the whole area (Harveys and Ordnance Survey produce the best maps for walkers, see pp28-9). This is important, since even on a day that starts clear, the weather can deteriorate. In low cloud you will need to navigate with a map and compass and even in clear weather, if you lose your way you will need a map in order to navigate off distinct features to help you find your way to safety. Nevertheless, the sketch maps in this book include features and annotations that do not appear on the Harveys or Ordnance Survey maps making them a valuable tool to navigation.

❑ **Walk grades**
To help you decide which walks are within your capabilities each hillwalk has been graded for difficulty in four ways (where '▲' poses few difficulties and '▲▲▲▲▲' is for experienced hillwalkers only). The four grade categories are as follows:
● **Technical grade** indicates how much scrambling or climbing may be encountered.
● **Navigation grade** highlights how difficult it is to follow the route described. Where there is a clear path or obvious ridge(s) to follow the grading is low but a high grading suggests a walk with little or no path to follow and featureless terrain, maybe a plateau, where getting lost is very possible in low cloud.
● **Terrain grade** relates to the conditions underfoot. A high grade indicates awkward walking conditions such as bogs, river crossings, scree, boulder fields and cliffs.
● **Strenuousness** takes into account the amount of overall ascent and distance involved in the walk and also the nature of the terrain. Awkward walking can drain energy reserves much more quickly.

Scale and walking times

The scale of the sketch maps is 1:45,000 (approximately 1¹/₂ inches = one mile; 2.2cm = 1km). Along the side of each map there are time bars between significant points along the walk (indicated by black triangles). Arrows show the recommended direction of the walk. Everyone walks at a different speed and even individuals vary their pace from one day to another. It depends on all sorts of factors such as the current conditions, how fit you are and even whether you are alone or with friends/a group. Use the time bars to see how your speed relates to the guide and from that you should be able to judge how long each section will take. Do not think of the timings in the book as a judgment upon walking ability or an ideal speed to aim at.

Note: All times in this book refer only to the time spent walking. You will need to add 20-30% to allow for rests, photography, checking the map, drinking water etc.

Up or down?

The dashed line on the maps indicates the recommended route. At intervals along this line there are arrows indicating a steep slope. A double arrow highlights a very steep slope. The arrows point towards the higher ground so a walk between A at 50m and B at 100m would be shown as follows: A—>—B. Since walking in the mountains, by its very nature, involves going up and down a lot, only significant slopes are marked with these arrows.

Accommodation

All accommodation in the text also appears on the town or village plans, except for isolated places to stay. Where isolated B&Bs, hostels, hotels and campsites lie close to the walk, look on the route maps to find their location.

Accommodation prices vary greatly through the year but for the purposes of this guide the summer high-season price per person (/pp) is given, based on two people sharing a room in a B&B, guesthouse or hotel. Be aware that single occupancy of double rooms often involves a supplementary charge of between £5 and £10. There is contact information for each place to stay along with information on the number and type of rooms: S = single room, D = double room, T = twin room, F = family room (sleeps three or more). The rate quoted for a night in a youth hostel is for a member; non members pay an additional charge.

Other features

Features marked on the route maps are designed to aid navigation but not every fence, stream and boulder is marked as this would simply clutter the map.

❏ **Shelter cairns**
On the route maps there are features called shelter cairns, often situated on summits. The word 'shelter' here should be interpreted in its loosest possible form. More often than not these are simply piles of rocks laid out in a curve. At best they offer a little protection from the wind but not from the rain or cold.

Loch Lomond and the Southern Highlands

Loch Lomond and the Trossachs became Scotland's first national park in 2002 but even before that it was a hugely popular area for tourists and hillwalkers alike. Glasgow is barely an hour away with Edinburgh not much further. This is an area of high mountains and deep lochs typified by Ben Lomond, the most southerly munro, towering over the largest expanse of freshwater in the British Isles, Loch Lomond. Stretching from its narrow glaciated trough in the north, Loch Lomond spills into the lowlands in the south where forested islands decorate its waters. Despite the region's popularity there are still some surprisingly quiet, undiscovered glens and peaks for those wishing to escape the crowds that are drawn to the popular tourist hotspots along Loch Lomondside and Strath Fillan to the north.

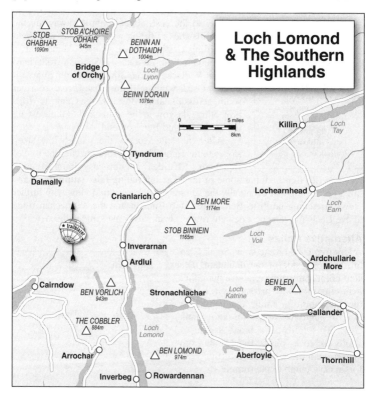

BEN LEDI (879m/2885ft) [MAP 1]

Overview

This distinctive and popular hill, on the edge of the Loch Lomond and Trossachs National Park, is visible from as far as the Forth Road Bridge near Edinburgh. It is an easy climb and a great introduction to the Highlands, sitting on the Highland fault line with expansive views towards the Central Belt of Scotland and the Campsie and Ochil Hills.

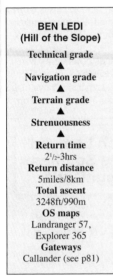

**BEN LEDI
(Hill of the Slope)**

Technical grade
▲
Navigation grade
▲
Terrain grade
▲
Strenuousness
▲
Return time
2¹/₂-3hrs
Return distance
5miles/8km
Total ascent
3248ft/990m
OS maps
Landranger 57,
Explorer 365
Gateways
Callander (see p81)

Route

The car park and start of the mountain path is a three-mile walk from Callander. Just follow the old railway path through the Pass of Leny. From the **car park**, a way-marked trail climbs through commercial forestry to arrive at a **stile** on the open hill. From here the way-marking stops but the path is still a good one.

The views start as soon as you leave the forest. Directly to the east, about 15 miles away are the Ochil Hills above Stirling where you can just about see Stirling Castle and the Wallace Monument, a tower erected in honour of Scottish folk hero William Wallace, famous for his Australian accent in the Oscar-winning film, *Braveheart*. Further south, across Flanders Moss, are the Campsie Hills, protecting Glasgow to the south, and to the west are the Trossachs and Ben Lomond.

After the stile, follow the path below steep slopes to the right. The path soon reaches the foot of Ben Ledi's SE ridge. It is an easy climb, in good weather, but Ben Ledi has some of the most infuriating **false summits** of any hill so persevere and eventually the summit cairn comes into view with further views stretching north to Ben More, Stob Binnein and the Tarmachan ridge above Loch Tay. The best descent route is back down the same path.

Alternative routes

A less frequented route is via Stank Glen on the north side of the mountain. The start point is the same as above but rather than climb the way-marked path, follow the track north for a mile and then take a trail through the forest up into Stank Glen. This leads to a broad saddle of knolls and rocky bluffs. Head south from here to gain the north ridge of Ben Ledi for an easy climb to the summit.

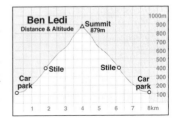

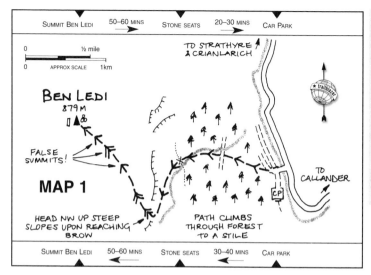

Within the map:

SUMMIT BEN LEDI   50–60 MINS →   STONE SEATS   20–30 MINS →   CAR PARK

0   ½ mile
0   APPROX SCALE   1km

TO STRATHYRE & CRIANLARICH

BEN LEDI
879M

FALSE SUMMITS!

MAP 1

HEAD NW UP STEEP SLOPES UPON REACHING BROW

PATH CLIMBS THROUGH FOREST TO A STILE

TO CALLANDER

CP

★ trailblazer

SUMMIT BEN LEDI   50–60 MINS ←   STONE SEATS   30–40 MINS ←   CAR PARK

THE COBBLER (884m/2900ft)   [MAP 2, p67]

Overview

This jagged little peak, with its fearsome-looking rocky towers dominating each end of the summit ridge, is rightly considered a classic Scottish mountain. Its modest height makes a mockery of the belief that bigger is better as it easily outclasses the neighbouring munros. Access to the summit ridge is straightforward enough but the actual summit is a five-metre rocky tower that involves a short but exposed scramble to an airy platform.

Route

A **car park** near the head of Loch Long (GR294049) marks the start of The Cobbler path. Cross the road and follow the sign-posted trail that winds gradually through commercial forestry to a forest track where a **radio mast** marks the continuation of the path as it climbs through the forest. At 300m above sea level the forest ends and the path passes a **small dam** on the left. Once out of the forest there are some great views along the length of Loch Long but it is the view ahead, of the eastern corrie, that really cries for attention. The teeth of The

THE COBBLER (Ben Arthur)
Technical grade
▲ (▲▲▲▲ to the summit rock)
Navigation grade
▲
Terrain grade
▲▲
Strenuousness
▲▲
Return time
3–4½hrs
Return distance
5½miles/9km
Total ascent
2920ft/890m
OS maps
Landranger 56, Explorer 364
Gateways
Arrochar (see p84)

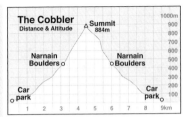

The Cobbler
Distance & Altitude

Summit
884m

1000m
900
800
700
600
500
400
300
200
100

Narnain
Boulders o

Narnain
o Boulders

Car
o park

Car
park o

1 2 3 4 5 6 7 8 9km

Cobbler point skywards and a good eye can pick out the summit rock towards the SW end of the ridge.

The gradient eases as it climbs into the corrie and past the massive **Narnain Boulders**, two house-sized rocks next to the path. The trail soon splits with the right-hand fork leading towards the munros of Beinn Narnain and Beinn Ime and the left-hand fork continuing over a stream before climbing sharply up the face of the eastern corrie. The path is steep in places but is easy to follow as it winds between a series of **short cliffs**. Finally the path tops out at a large cairn on the ridge just below the impressive cliffs of The Cobbler's NE top. The summit, however, is to the SW. Follow the path that stays below the actual line of the ridge, instead keeping to the northern slopes climbing slowly to the flat ground just short of the summit rock.

Those of a vertiginous nature or with no scrambling experience may like to consider admiring the summit rock from the safety of the flat ground below it. However, the **true summit** is at the top of the rock. Despite appearances the scramble to the top is relatively easy but very exposed. Clamber through the hole between two large rocks and turn left across a narrow ledge above a precipitous drop. From here it is a short scramble on to the top of the rock.

The descent is either a reverse of the ascent or, to make a satisfyingly circular walk, by way of the SE ridge; a path drops down below the south side of the summit rock and winds between large boulders to a short ridge. Directly ahead is the formidable face of the large fortress-like SE peak. The path appears to aim directly for the foot of this impenetrable cliff but this is in fact an approach route for climbers looking for routes on the rock. Walkers will find an easy path that drops sharply off the short ridge to the right. Continue along the path as it contours around the foot of the tower over more boulders and on to the broad undulating SE ridge. At the col below a final rise in the ridge turn left over shallow boggy ground to return to the main path at the Narnain Boulders and follow the path back through the forest to the car park.

Alternative routes

There are two more approach routes to The Cobbler, both of which start from the A83. The first begins near Ardgarten and follows the SE ridge to the summit. The second begins further up Glen Croe and follows the stream in the small glen to the north of the mountain. The best path, however, despite its popularity, is the one described.

❏ **Important note – walking times**
All times in this book refer only to the time spent walking. You will need to add 20-30% to allow for rests, photography, checking the map, drinking water etc.

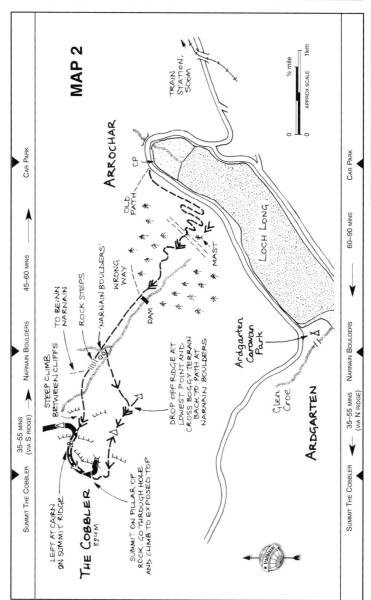

MAP 2

ARROCHAR

CP

OLD PATH

LOCH LONG

TRAIN STATION, 500m

0   ½ mile   1km
0   APPROX SCALE

TO BEINN NARNAIN

ROCK STEPS

NARNAIN BOULDERS

STEEP CLIMB BETWEEN CLIFFS

WRONG WAY

MAST

DAM

Ardgarten Caravan Park

DROP OFF RIDGE AT LOWEST POINT AND CROSS BOGGY TERRAIN BACK TO PATH AT NARNAIN BOULDERS

Glen Croe

ARDGARTEN

LEFT AT CAIRN ON SUMMIT RIDGE

THE COBBLER 884M

SUMMIT ON PILLAR OF ROCK. GO THROUGH HOLE AND CLIMB TO EXPOSED TOP

trailblazer

SUMMIT THE COBBLER ▶ 35-55 MINS (VIA S RIDGE) ▶ NARNAIN BOULDERS ▶ 45-60 MINS ▶ CAR PARK

SUMMIT THE COBBLER ◀ 35-55 MINS (VIA N RIDGE) ◀ NARNAIN BOULDERS ◀ 60-90 MINS ◀ CAR PARK

BEN LOMOND (974m/3195ft) [MAP 3]

Overview

The most southerly munro in Scotland, Ben Lomond, is something of a centre-piece in the national park. There are no other peaks of notable stature in the vicinity giving Ben Lomond a touch of individuality as it looms over its namesake loch. The view over the island-studded southern expanse of the loch is well-worth the somewhat laboured climb to the top. Access is easy. Two popular and well-managed paths lead to the summit from Rowardennan.

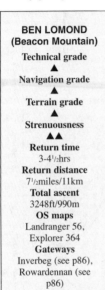

**BEN LOMOND
(Beacon Mountain)**

Technical grade
▲

Navigation grade
▲

Terrain grade
▲

Strenuousness
▲▲

Return time
3-4½hrs

Return distance
7½miles/11km

Total ascent
3248ft/990m

OS maps
Landranger 56,
Explorer 364

Gateways
Inverbeg (see p86),
Rowardennan (see p86)

Route

The Ben Lomond path starts at the wooded car park, a couple of minutes north of **Rowardennan Hotel**. Aim for the Ben Lomond shelter (where you will find information displays and toilets) and follow the wide path as it winds upwards through the spruce forest. After crossing a forest track, the trail continues to climb steadily through the trees eventually coming to a **gate** on the edge of the forest. After passing through the gate the trail swings northwards and begins its steady climb over exposed moorland to a **second gate**.

Being such a popular mountain the path is well-trodden and easy to follow all the way to the summit. The gradient is easy until the path reaches the steeper upper slopes of the mountain where it **zigzags** sharply upwards to gain the eastern end of the summit ridge. Follow the path as it skirts just below the line of the ridge to reach the summit. The steep northern corrie wall that eats into the summit cone comes as something of a surprise as there is no indication of it from the south side.

Rather than descend by the same path continue onwards from the summit and follow the alternative path that drops steeply for 150m down the NW ridge. At the 800m contour interval the trail bears left to follow the wide **Ptarmigan ridge** in a SW direction. Stepping stones ease the way over the boggier patches. The ridge begins to point in a southerly direction and drops away quite suddenly. Take time to look ahead to admire further fine views of the islands of Loch Lomond. There is a brief respite in the steep gradient before it drops away again. Look over your shoulder just

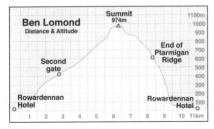

Ben Lomond
Distance & Altitude

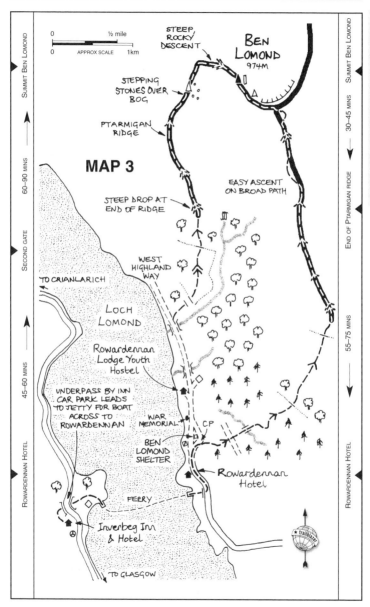

after passing through the gate here as there is a tumbling **waterfall** above on the wooded crag. Another gate leads the way into the woodland on the lower flanks of the mountain before one last gate brings the path out onto a wide track by a bridge. This is part of the West Highland Way. Follow it in a southerly direction through the loch-side woodland, past Rowardennan Youth Hostel and back to the car park and Rowardennan Hotel. Look out for the **war memorial** on the wooded shore just before the car park.

Alternative routes
Access to Ben Lomond is possible from Inversnaid in the north but this involves a very long approach over boggy ground to reach the mountain's north ridge. The route described above is a much better choice and can be reversed so that the ascent is by way of the more interesting Ptarmigan ridge.

BEN VORLICH (943m/3095ft)   [MAP 4]

Overview
The rocky bluffs and convoluted ridges of Ben Vorlich sit high above the narrow northern reaches of Loch Lomond. The hidden ridges are less popular than Ben Lomond across the water but the views are no less impressive.

Route
From Ardlui follow the main road south. There is no pavement so take extra care on this busy stretch. Head past the underpass to the train station and walk through the **second underpass**. Follow the trail through the field (watch out for the Highland cows!) passing through patches of bracken in a SSW direction. At the top of the field cross over the **stile** and continue up steep ground to a stream. The going gets a bit boggier after crossing the burn but the gradient eases. Continue heading into the wide corrie to a **small dam**. A few metres past the dam look out for a small cairn marking a faint trail on the right; it is just before a **second small dam**. Climb over more boggy ground keeping the stream to your left and head up an old peat track to the **col** at 560m.

The path is much more solid from here, beginning by skirting around a rocky bluff and heading directly up the ridge in a SSW direction. The path negotiates a number of knolls and rocky bluffs on this slightly confusing ridge but is relatively easy to follow.

On approaching the **summit ridge** there is a choice of routes. The first heads over the northern top of the mountain while a second path bypasses this peak and instead contours below the east side of the peak before descending a few metres to a col.

BEN VORLICH (Mountain of the Bay)
Technical grade ▲
Navigation grade ▲▲
Terrain grade ▲▲
Strenuousness ▲▲
Return time 3-4¹/₂hrs
Return distance 5¹/₂miles/9km
Total ascent 3018ft/920m
OS maps Landranger 56, Explorer 364
Gateways Ardlui (see p86), Inverarnan (see p86)

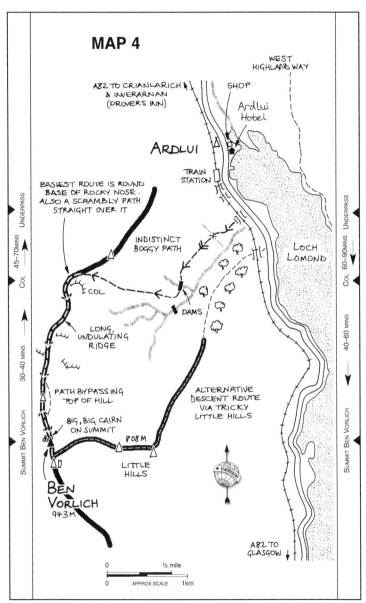

MAP 4

A82 TO CRIANLARICH & INVERARNAN (DROVERS INN)

WEST HIGHLAND WAY

SHOP

Ardlui Hotel

ARDLUI

TRAIN STATION

LOCH LOMOND

EASIEST ROUTE IS ROUND BASE OF ROCKY NOSE. ALSO A SCRAMBLY PATH STRAIGHT OVER IT

INDISTINCT BOGGY PATH

COL

DAMS

LONG, UNDULATING RIDGE

PATH BYPASSING TOP OF HILL

BIG, BIG CAIRN ON SUMMIT

808 M

LITTLE HILLS

ALTERNATIVE DESCENT ROUTE VIA TRICKY LITTLE HILLS

BEN VORLICH 943M

★ trailblazer

A82 TO GLASGOW

0   ½ mile
0   APPROX SCALE   1km

UNDERPASS — 45–70MINS — COL — 30–40 MINS — SUMMIT BEN VORLICH

UNDERPASS — 60–90MINS — COL — 40–60 MINS — SUMMIT BEN VORLICH

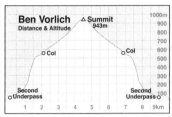

From here it is a short climb up an easy ridge to the **summit cairn**, perched on a rocky shelf.

Below is the dammed Loch Sloy while to the south are the rest of the Arrochar Alps. Looking east the view takes in the Crianlarich hills of Beinn Chabhair and An Caisteal while to the north are the munros of Ben Lui, Ben Oss and Beinn Dubhcraig. The easiest route of descent is to return the same way, but see below.

Alternative routes

There is an interesting route of ascent (or descent) over the complicated eastern ridge known as the Little Hills. The access point is at Stuckendroin where a railway underpass leads onto the steep lower slopes of the ridge. Climb in a SSW direction to the first of the Little Hills and then continue west to the summit.

BEN MORE (1174m/3850ft)   [MAP 5]
STOB BINNEIN (*'Stop Bin-yen'*, 1165m/3820ft)

Overview

Ben More is a mighty hulk of a hill, towering above Glen Dochart and drawing the eye of everyone who passes through Crianlarich. Despite appearances, it does not take long to climb which means there is plenty of time to take in the neighbouring peak of Stob Binnein. Apart from some steep ground they pose few difficulties and those who are not put off by their imposing nature are sure to enjoy the wide-ranging views from these, the highest of the Crianlarich hills.

Route

The route described here climbs the relentlessly steep NW shoulder of Ben More. This type of ascent is not to everyone's liking so alternative routes are suggested on p74.

From Crianlarich follow the A85 for two miles eastwards through Glen Dochart. A signpost by the **roadside**, some 100m on from Benmore Farm, indicates the start of the Ben More path. A **stile** in the hedgerow leads onto a farm track that winds upwards into Benmore Glen. Pass through a **gate** where the track levels out and continue for 50m to a tiny **cairn** on the left.

A very indistinct trail leaves the farm track here to climb the steep grassy slopes of Ben More's NW

BEN MORE
(Big Mountain)

STOB BINNEIN
(Anvil Peak)

Technical grade
▲

Navigation grade
▲

Terrain grade
▲▲

Strenuousness
▲▲▲

Return time
4-5¹⁄₂hrs

Return distance
5¹⁄₂miles/9km

Total ascent
4265ft/1300m

OS maps
Landranger 51,
Explorer 365

Gateways
Crianlarich (see p87)

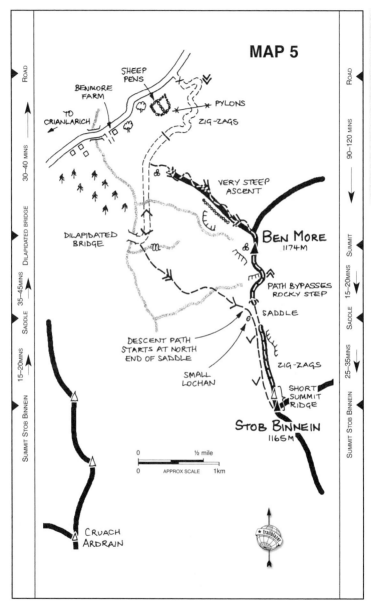

MAP 5

ROAD

30-40 MINS

DILAPIDATED BRIDGE

35-45MINS

SADDLE

15-20MINS

SUMMIT STOB BINNEIN

ROAD

90-120 MINS

SUMMIT

15-20MINS

SADDLE

25-35MINS

SUMMIT STOB BINNEIN

BENMORE FARM

SHEEP PENS

TO CRIANLARICH

PYLONS

ZIG-ZAGS

VERY STEEP ASCENT

DILAPIDATED BRIDGE

BEN MORE 1174M

PATH BYPASSES ROCKY STEP

SADDLE

DESCENT PATH STARTS AT NORTH END OF SADDLE

SMALL LOCHAN

ZIG-ZAGS

SHORT SUMMIT RIDGE

STOB BINNEIN 1165M

CRUACH ARDRAIN

0 ½ mile
0 APPROX SCALE 1km

trailblazer

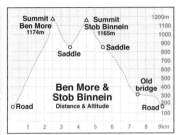

shoulder. The going can be quite soggy and the trail hard to distinguish until a collapsed stone wall appears about halfway up the mountain. The path is more obvious from here as it climbs parallel to the line of stones on the right. As the gradient finally begins to ease near the summit, bear south to reach the **summit cairn** on a rocky ledge. There is a useful cleft right next to the cairn that provides notional shelter in windy weather. In clear weather there are great views along the length of Strath Fillan and west to Cruach Ardrain. Head initially SSE from the summit and follow the path down the south ridge. There is one short step over a rocky shelf that is easily avoided to the left. From the broad **saddle** climb the uniform ridge on its long sweep to the summit of **Stob Binnein**.

Return to the saddle for the descent into Benmore Glen. Note that the descent path leaves the saddle at its northern end and not in the middle as one would expect. Instead the path contours the slopes of the mountain in a NW direction to a **stream**. Descend steeply on the south bank of this burn to reach the end of the farm track next to an **old**, **dilapidated bridge**. Follow the farm track back to the main road in Glen Dochart.

Alternative routes

A less-punishing ascent route follows the less-steep NE ridge. Start by the bridge over the Allt Coire Chaorach and follow the path through the coniferous forest before heading west to reach the lower slopes of the ridge.

Another way to avoid the steep NW shoulder of Ben More is to continue along the Benmore Glen track and up to the col. From here both peaks can be tackled before returning back down the glen.

BEINN DORAIN (*'Bayn Door-en'*, 1076m/3530ft)
BEINN AN DOTHAIDH (*'Bayn an Doy-ee'*, 1004m/3295ft)   [MAP 6]

Overview

From the south the sweeping profile of Beinn Dorain is unmistakable and to reach the summit appears at first sight to be a bit of a slog. However, the path into the western corrie of the mountain makes an ascent of these two peaks a relatively straightforward affair. The views take in the vastness of Rannoch Moor and

BEINN DORAIN
(Little Stream
Mountain)

BEINN AN
DOTHAIDH
(Scorching Mountain)

Technical grade
▲

Navigation grade
▲

Terrain grade
▲

Strenuousness
▲▲

Return time
4½-6½hrs

Return distance
8miles/13km

Total ascent
3904ft/1190m

OS maps
Landranger 50,
Explorer 377

Gateways
Br of Orchy (see p89)
Tyndrum (see p88)

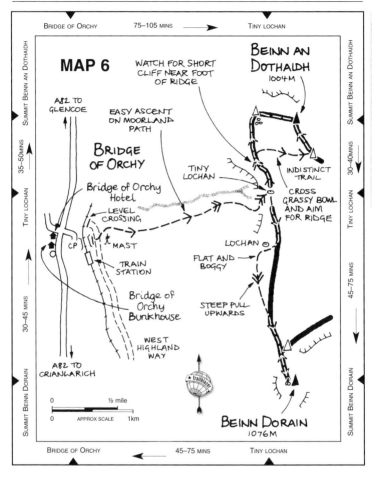

the Black Mount hills as well as the Tyndrum hills to the south. There are few difficulties to face, although navigation on the wide grassy slopes of each peak can be testing when the mist is down.

Route

The path to Beinn Dorain starts rather conveniently by **Bridge of Orchy** train station. Go through the **underpass** below the tracks, then through a **gate** and cross the West Highland Way to join the clear path to the left of the mobile phone mast. Continue in an easterly direction as the path follows the Allt Coire an Dothaidh into its namesake corrie.

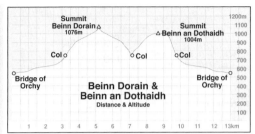

Early thoughts of what a nicely drained path it is soon evaporate as it trips and squelches through a series of spongy peat bogs. After enjoying the slurping sounds of soggy peat trying to suck your boots off, the path finally regains solid ground as it climbs steeply over a wide lip into the upper corrie. From here it is a short push to the **col** between the two peaks, 1¼ to 1¾ hours from Bridge of Orchy.

For Beinn Dorain, the summit of which is not visible until near the end of the ascent, head south over the immediate ribs of rock. The ridge is quite broad and can be confusing if the mist comes in. A path leads the way upwards and takes a sharp right to avoid the peat bogs ahead. At the small **lochan** continue once again in a southerly direction to gain a steep climb of 100m. Here the ridge becomes less narrow and leads quickly to a large cairn on what appears to be the summit. Drop down from this **false summit** to a small col and climb the final 20m to the **true summit**.

It is well-worth walking on a short way from here to fully appreciate the views. **Beinn Dorain** is known for its relentless western and southern slopes, possibly the longest such uniform slopes anywhere in the Highlands. The uninterrupted views straight down into the glen are perhaps unmatched in this part of the Highlands.

Follow the same route back to the col and, if tired legs permit, follow the path in a north-easterly direction. The path starts well but begins to fade as it crosses boggy ground. The best course of action is to follow a bearing of 45° to reach the ridge between the summit of **Beinn an Dothaidh** and its south-easterly top. A faint path follows the ridge northwards to the cairn atop the summit. In good visibility the peaks of Glen Coe, the Mamores, Ben Nevis and the Grey Corries can be seen across Rannoch Moor. Fit, experienced hillwalkers may well be tempted by the ridges of Beinn Achaladair and Beinn a' Chreachain that wind northwards.

Rather than follow the same route back to the col it is worth making the short 10-minute detour westwards from the summit to the cairn on the north-western top of the mountain. There are further spectacular views across Rannoch Moor as well as Stob Ghabhar and the Black Mount hills across Loch Tulla.

From this top head south to rejoin the path back to the col taking care to avoid the cliff directly to the north of the col. The descent route is by way of the same path used for the ascent.

Alternative routes

The route described is the only sensible choice but the walk can be extended to take in the munros of Beinn Achaladair and Beinn a' Chreachain to the north. Note that this more than doubles the length of the walk and involves a lengthy hike back down the glen to the starting point.

STOB A' CHOIRE ODHAIR (*Stop a Chor-ee-ow-er'*, 945m/3100ft)
STOB GHABHAR (*'Stop Gow-er'*, 1090m/3575ft)
[MAP 7a, p78; MAP 7b, p80]

Overview

Towering above Loch Tulla on one side and the vastness of Rannoch Moor on the other this complicated mountain massif offers varied views across the Western and Southern Highlands and some fine ridge walking. A section of steep scrambling to gain the spine of the Aonach Eagach ridge followed by a short but exposed narrow ridge traverse are the main obstacles.

Route

Those travelling by car should head straight for the road end at Victoria Bridge on the short A8005. Those without their own transport have a little more work to do, unless they can blag a lift from the afore-mentioned four-wheeled friends.

If walking from **Bridge of Orchy** cross the road bridge below the hotel and follow the omnipresent West Highland Way through the conifer plantation and over a low ridge. It is less than an hour to the road and the historic **Inveroran Hotel**, a useful coffee stop, and a further 15 minutes to the road end at Victoria Bridge. Motorists should park in the car park just before the bridge. There are good views across Loch Tulla, with its lonely crannog, and the Black Mount estate buildings, half hidden by pine forests on the north shore.

No combustion engines from here on. Just feet. After crossing Victoria Bridge take the next left and follow the track to the small green corrugated **JMCS hut**. Stob Ghabhar looms to the north-west while the zigzagging path up the southern shoulder of Stob a' Choire Odhair can be seen to the north.

A few steps after the JMCS hut take a right and follow the well-trodden path up the east bank of the Allt Toaig. Approximately one hour later a **stream** crosses the path at the 430m contour. After crossing

---

STOB A' CHOIRE ODHAIR
(Peak of the Dun-coloured Corrie)

STOB GHABHAR
(Peak of the Goats)

Technical grade
▲▲▲

Navigation grade
▲▲

Terrain grade
▲▲▲

Strenuousness
▲▲▲

Return time
From Bridge of Orchy
6-8³/₄hrs
From Victoria Bridge
4¹/₂-6¹/₂hrs

Return distance
From Bridge of Orchy
17miles/28km
From Victoria Bridge
11miles/18km

Total ascent
From Bridge of Orchy
1525m/5003ft
From Victoria Bridge
1200m/3937ft

OS maps
Landranger 50,
Explorer 377

Gateways
Bridge of Orchy (see p89)

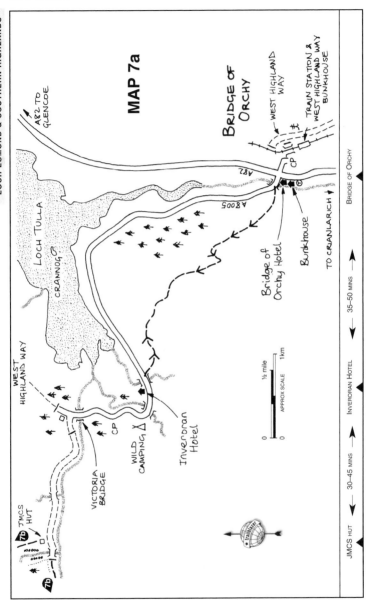

MAP 7a

BRIDGE OF ORCHY

A82 TO GLENCOE

WEST HIGHLAND WAY

TRAIN STATION & WEST HIGHLAND WAY BUNKHOUSE

CP

A82

A8005

LOCH TULLA

CRANNOG

Bridge of Orchy Hotel

Bunkhouse

TO CRIANLARICH

BRIDGE OF ORCHY

WEST HIGHLAND WAY

CP

WILD CAMPING

Inveroran Hotel

VICTORIA BRIDGE

JMCS HUT

7b

7b

½ mile   1km

0   APPROX SCALE

0

JMCS HUT   ◄— 30–45 MINS —►   INVERORAN HOTEL   ◄—— 35–50 MINS ——►   BRIDGE OF ORCHY

trailblazer

the stream look out for the smaller path branching off to the right. Follow this as it climbs in a series of **zigzags** northwards to the summit of **Stob a' Choire Odhair**. The views across the lochan-studded expanse of Rannoch Moor come as a pleasant surprise, as does Coire Ba, said to be the largest corrie in Scotland, to the north. The descent to the **col**

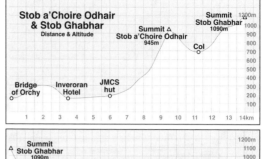

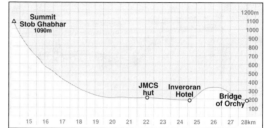

at 660m is by way of the broad western ridge. Be careful with the route finding in misty conditions. Those not intending to climb Stob Ghabhar should head south-east from the col to rejoin the ascent path and follow the same route back.

Continuing on to Stob Ghabhar, a faint path leads west from the col to climb on to a low shoulder. There are stunning views of the small **lochan** in Coirein Lochain to the north. The gullies in the steep back-walls of this corrie, which rise to the summit of Stob Ghabhar, hold snow well into the summer. Enjoy the view while you can because all eyes now need to be on the ascent. The path swings sharply to the south, ascending steeply for 300m to gain the lower end of the **Aonach Eagach ridge (not to be confused with the more famous ridge of the same name in Glen Coe)**. Take care on the loose scree that has been eroded on this section.

Follow the Aonach Eagach ridge past a small **cairn** on a bearing of 255° for 500m. The ridge passes a small col and narrows quite suddenly. Where it begins to widen again, continue on a bearing of 320° for 600m to gain the summit of **Stob Ghabhar**. In good weather the peaks of the Black Mount stretch out to the north. The massif to the west is Ben Starav while the pointed summit of Ben Cruachan can be seen further south.

The best route of descent is to continue WNW for 600m before following the ridge west between two deep corries for a further 600m. Head south across wide grassy slopes, taking care to avoid the cliffs of Coire Ghabhar to the east, and descend to the saddle of Mam nan Sac. Before reaching the saddle look out for the **stalkers' path** and follow this eastwards where it hugs the

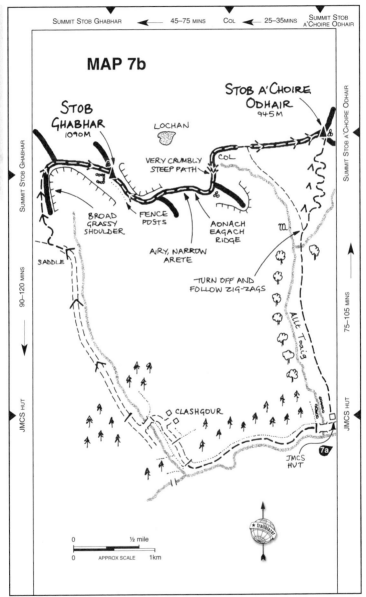

SUMMIT STOB GHABHAR ← 45–75 MINS COL ← 25–35MINS SUMMIT STOB A'CHOIRE ODHAIR

MAP 7b

STOB GHABHAR 1090M

LOCHAN

STOB A'CHOIRE ODHAIR 945M

SUMMIT STOB GHABHAR

SUMMIT STOB A'CHOIRE ODHAIR

VERY CRUMBLY STEEP PATH

COL

BROAD GRASSY SHOULDER

FENCE POSTS

AONACH EAGACH RIDGE

AIRY, NARROW ARETE

TURN OFF AND FOLLOW ZIG-ZAGS

SADDLE

90–120 MINS

75–105 MINS

Allt Toaig

CLASHGOUR

JMCS HUT

JMCS HUT

JMCS HUT

7a

0 ½ mile
0 APPROX SCALE 1km

★ trailblazer

west bank of the Allt Ghabhar to the farm buildings at Clashgour. A **farm track** just before the farmyard leads through the conifer plantation to join a path on the north bank of the river. Continue eastwards along this path to rejoin the track by the JMCS hut and on to Victoria Bridge and Bridge of Orchy.

Alternative routes

It is not obligatory to climb both these mountains in one round; the col between the two is an ideal escape route, enabling an early descent of Stob a' Choire Odhair or alternatively a quicker ascent route of Stob Ghabhar.

❏ **Other hills in the area**

● **Ben Lui (*'Ben Loo-ee'*, 1130m/3705ft)** A peak that makes many a motorist's head turn on the drive up the A82. An imposing mountain with a long walk-in but a surprisingly simple ascent for such a beast of a hill.

● **Ben Cruachan (*'Ben Croo-er-chen'*, 1126m/3695ft)** Combined with its sister peak, Stob Diamh, these finely sculpted high tops above Loch Awe make for a grand high-level day out.

LOCH LOMOND & SOUTHERN HIGHLANDS – TOWNS & VILLAGES

CALLANDER [see map p82]

Callander sits right on the edge of the Highlands and takes full advantage of its position as a gateway to the mountains. The main high street is unashamedly geared to tourism with twee gift shops selling fudge, shortbread and stuffed Rob Roy MacGregors. If you can stand such naffness Callander is an ideal base for exploring the Trossachs or just for stocking up on supplies.

Services

Citylink **buses** pass through the town on their way south to Stirling and Edinburgh and north to Crianlarich and beyond. There are also more regular local buses running between the town and Stirling which is on the national rail network. See also pp32-6.

The **TIC** (☎ 01877-330 342, 🖥 www .incallander.co.uk) is in an old church in a square halfway along the main street. It is a substantial place with local history displays and an accommodation-booking service. Also on the main street there are **banks** with ATMs, two **post offices** and a **chemist**. There are two **supermarkets** at either

end of the main street and also the **CCW Outdoor Shop** which mainly deals in outdoor clothing but also has other outdoor paraphernalia.

Where to stay

In keeping with a town that markets itself so well for tourism, Callander is awash with places to stay, most of them strung out along the main street.

Starting at the western end is a cluster of B&Bs including **Lenymede B&B** (☎ 01877-330952, 🖥 www.lenymede.com, 3D) charging from £22.50 per person, and **Lubnaig House** (☎ 01877-330376, 🖥 www .lubnaighotel.co.uk, 6D/4T), on Leny Feus, offering beds from £36/pp.

At **Westerton B&B** (☎ 01877-330147, 🖥 www.westerton.co.uk, 3D) the rooms cost from £42.50/pp while **Riverview Guest House** (☎ 01877-330635, 1S/2D/2T) is a little cheaper at £27.50/pp. Next door is **Poppies Hotel** (☎ 01877-330329, 🖥 www .poppieshotel.com, 5D/1T/3F) which has reasonable rooms from £35, while opposite is a modern bungalow, **Almardon Guest**

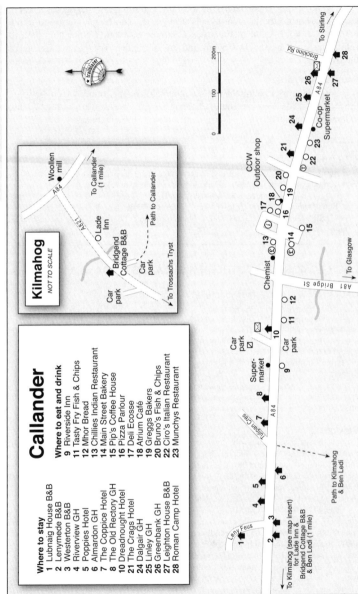

Kilmahog
NOT TO SCALE

Callander

Where to stay
1 Lubnaig House B&B
2 Lenymede B&B
3 Westerton B&B
4 Riverview GH
5 Poppies Hotel
6 Almardon GH
7 The Coppice Hotel
8 The Old Rectory GH
10 Dreadnought Hotel
21 The Crags Hotel
24 Dalgair GH
25 Linley GH
26 Greenbank GH
27 Leighton House B&B
28 Roman Camp Hotel

Where to eat and drink
9 Riverside Inn
11 Tasty Fry Fish & Chips
12 Mhor Bread
13 Chillies Indian Restaurant
14 Main Street Bakery
15 Pip's Coffee House
16 Pizza Parlour
17 Deli Ecosse
18 Atrium Café
19 Greggs Bakers
20 Bruno's Fish & Chips
22 Ciro's Italian Restaurant
23 Munchys Restaurant

House (01877-331597, 1D/1T), with beds from £25/pp.

Closer to the town centre near the big supermarket is *The Coppice Hotel* (☎ 01877-330188, 🖳 www.thecoppicehotel .co.uk, 3D/1T/1F), which has beds from £30. If this is full try *The Old Rectory Guest House* (☎ 01877-339215, 🖳 www .theoldrectoryincallander.co.uk; 1S/2D/2F) which costs £25/pp or £30 for the single.

Continuing into town the imposing *Dreadnought Hotel* (☎ 01877-330184) stands on the left. It has 61 rooms with prices starting at £25. There's a handful of places to stay at the eastern end of the main street including: *Crags Hotel* (☎ 01877-330257, 🖳 www.cragshotel.co.uk, 3D/1T/2F en suite), an elegant hotel with rooms from £25 to £35/pp, *Dalgair Guest House* (☎ 01877-330283, 🖳 www.dalgair-house-hotel.co.uk, 8 rooms), with B&B from £32.50, *Linley Guest House* (☎ 01877-330087, 🖳 www.incallander.co.uk/linley cal, 3D/1T), which has cheap and simple but comfortable rooms from just £21/pp, *Greenbank Guest House* (☎ 01877-330296, 1S/3D/ 1T), from £20/pp, and *Leighton House* (☎ 01877-330291, 1D/1T) with simple, clean rooms from £22/pp.

For something grander head for *Roman Camp Hotel* (☎ 01877-330003, 🖳 www .roman-camp-hotel.co.uk, 9D/5T), a sensitively decorated 17th-century hunting lodge with oak-panelling and big log fires. A room here will set you back from £67.50/pp (£85/pp for single occupancy).

Finally, about a mile out of town in **Kilmahog**, a small hamlet at the junction of the A821 and A84, *Bridgend Cottage* (☎ 01877-330385, 2D/1F) is an immaculate stone-built old gamekeeper's cottage on the banks of the River Leny and offers B&B from £25/pp. About a mile further west, just off the A821 is *Trossachs Tryst* (☎ 01877-331200, 🖳 www.scottish-hostel .com) a modern hostel with single rooms and beds in small dormitories as well as family rooms. The overnight charge of £17.50 is excellent value considering the rooms are all en suite and breakfast is included.

Where to eat and drink

There is no shortage of teashops and cafés in Callander. One of the best is *Atrium Café* (☎ 01877-331610) above CCW Outdoor Shop. This modern, spacious café serves some very original and tasty concoctions including the Ben Ledi: fried eggy bread dipped in mozarella.

For a more traditional style try *Pip's Coffee House* (☎ 01877-330470) opposite the TIC, which has sandwiches from £1.95.

The *Riverside Inn* (☎ 01877-331536) is a stylish restaurant with some traditional dishes. Try the steak and ale pie for £8.95. There's also *Ciro's Italian Restaurant* (☎ 01877-331070) at the east end of the town and next to it, *Munchy's Restaurant* where you can enjoy steak, pie and chips for £6.95.

The obligatory town curryhouse, with a typically lengthy menu including chicken madras for £6.95, is *Chillies Indian Restaurant* (☎ 01877-339111) near the TIC. Just around the corner is the *Deli Ecosse* (☎ 01877-331220), where you can get a very wholesome soup and baguette for £2.95 or a packed lunch for £5.

All the bakeries on the main street (*Mhor Bread*, *Main Street Bakery* and *Gregg's Bakery*) have a good choice of potential lunchbox items. For a quick bite, *Pizza Parlour* has pizzas from around £5 and there are two good chippies: *Tasty Fry Fish and Chips* and *Bruno's Fish and Chips*.

At **Kilmahog** (see map opposite), one mile west of Callander, is the quite brilliant *Lade Inn* (☎ 01877-330152, 🖳 www .theladeinn.com); everything a pub should be. There is regular live folk music and they produce their own house ales. The results – their Way Lade, Lade Back and Lade Out ales – are all available from the bar. There is also a restaurant serving up excellent dishes such as baked Trossachs trout for £12.75 and haggis, neeps and tatties for £8.50.

❑ **Rainy days**
● **Cruachan Power Station** Bored with going up the mountains? Try going inside one instead. Guided tours of this underground hydro-electric power station in the 'hollow mountain' of Ben Cruachan, on the A85 halfway between Tyndrum and Oban, cost £5.50 (Easter-Oct 9.30am-5pm daily; Nov-mid Dec and Feb-Mar 10am-4pm Mon-Fri; mid Dec-Jan closed; ☎ 01866-822618; 🖳 www.visitcruachan.co.uk).
● **Drovers' Inn pub walk** This is a short, easy stroll through old oak woodland with stunning views down the length of Loch Lomond. From Ardlui catch the ferry (see p86) to the opposite side of the loch and walk two miles north along the West Highland Way to the **Drovers Inn** (see p87) for a pint before staggering back.

ARROCHAR

The village of Arrochar sits on the western side of an isthmus that separates freshwater Loch Lomond from the salt waters of Loch Long. The village consists of a line of white-washed buildings on the waterfront at the head of Loch Long, commanding magnificent views across the water to the Arrochar Alps with The Cobbler taking centre-stage.

Services

The isthmus between the two lochs is just over a mile wide. On the Loch Lomond side in the village of **Tarbet** (Gaelic for isthmus) there is a tiny **TIC** (☎ 01880-820429). The **train station** is halfway between the two villages and is the place to catch trains to Glasgow, Edinburgh, Fort William and Oban. These destinations are also served by the Citylink **buses** that pass through nearby Tarbet, while the Campbeltown bus from Glasgow stops at Arrochar. See also pp32-6.

There is a **bank** and there are a few small grocery **shops** in the village, the most central one incorporating a **post office**. The **petrol station** has a **cash machine** and there is a **bank** (without cash machine) open Tue and Thu, 10am-1pm.

Where to stay

Arrochar can be divided into two distinct sections: the southern shore and the northern, separated by the main road junction. Most of the B&Bs are along this combined stretch of loch shore but there are also a few along the main road to Tarbet including **Ballyhennan Old Toll House** (☎ 01301-

702203, 🖳 www.oldtollhouse.co.uk, 1D/1T/1F) by the train station, which has B&B from £18 to £25/pp, and **Dalkusha House** (☎ 01301-702234, 🖳 dalkusha@aol.com, 1D/1T/2F) nearer the road junction, with beds starting at £30/pp. Also by this junction is **Rowantree Bank B&B** (☎ 01301-702318, 🖳 www.rowantreebank.co.uk, 1S/1D/1T/2F), a small centrally located cottage charging from £27.50/pp, and **Arrochar Hotel** (☎ 01301-702484, 🖹 01301-702599). This grand white-washed building holds almost 80 rooms, some costing from £29/pp.

There's a handful of affordable places to rest your head along the **northern shore** starting with **Argyll View** (☎ 01301-702932, 🖳 www.argyllview.com, 1S/1D/1F en suite). B&B in this small cottage is £30/pp. Also worth a look are **Rowantree Cottage** (☎ 01301-702540, 🖳 www.rowan treecottage.com, 1S/1D/1F) with B&B from £27 to £36/pp, **Lochside Guest House** (☎ 01301-702467, 🖳 lochsideGH7@aol .com, 1S/3D/1T/1F), a sizeable place with B&B from £23, and the similarly priced **Greenbank Guest House and Restaurant** (☎ 01301-702305, 🖳 www.greenbank restaurant.co.uk), which is almost suffocating in vegetation.

There is a large campsite, with over 200 pitches (£9-13.70 per two-person pitch), two miles west along the A83 at **Ardgarten Caravan Park** (see Map 2, p67; ☎ 01301-702293; open Mar-Jan).

The selection of B&Bs on the **southern shore** is limited. **Cruachan B&B** (☎ 01301-702521, 🖳 www.cruachanscotland .co.uk, 1D) is a good choice. It has a self-contained en suite room and lounge upstairs where the whirlpool bath makes the £35/pp charge worth every penny. **Burnbrae B&B** (☎/🖷 01301-702988, 🖳 www.scotland2000 .com/burnbrae/, 1D/1T en suite) next to the pub, has equally luxurious pine-clad rooms with uninterrupted views of the Arrochar Alps. B&B is £30-35/pp. There is also the excellent **Village Inn** (☎ 01301-702279, 🖳 www.maclay.com/village-inn-arrochar .html, 13D/1T en suite) where B&B costs between £37.50 and £45.

Where to eat and drink
The **Village Inn** (see above) is the best place to eat, serving traditional fare such as ploughmans (£8.95) and breaded haddock (£7.50) in classy yet historical surroundings. Also on the southern shore, but a far cry from the haute cuisine of the Village Inn, is the **Pitstop Diner**, the place for burgers and chips.

Moving into the main village, on the northern shore, look for **Annabel's Café** (☎ 01301-702552) which has scones, sandwiches and baked potatoes.

Further up the road, the steak and kidney pie (£6.95) at **Greenbank Guest House and Restaurant** (see Where to stay) is delicious. Next door is **Ben Arthur's Bothy** (☎ 01301-702347), a no-frills bar with cheap pub grub such as burger and chips for £3.95. At the northern end of the village there are cheap sandwiches and cakes at **Craigard Tearoom** (☎ 01301-702672). Fast food is available from the **fish and chip shop** and from the **burger van** by the petrol station.

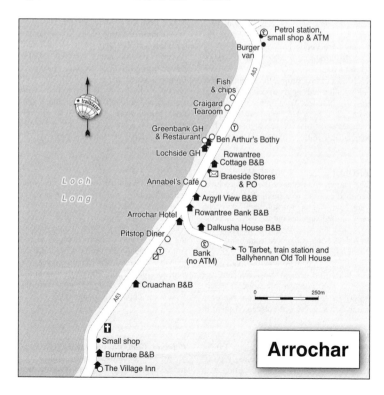

LOCH LOMOND & SOUTHERN HIGHLANDS

INVERBEG [SEE MAP 3, p69]

Inverbeg consists of nothing more than a large roadside hotel, a bus stop and a ferry to Rowardennan. **Buses** stop by the hotel on their way to and from Glasgow, Fort William and Skye. The **ferry** from Inverbeg to Rowardennan (for Ben Lomond) departs from the jetty below the hotel at 10.30am, 2.30pm and 6pm (Easter-Sept, £4 single, £6 return + 50p per rucksack).

If you do need a bed here, *Inverbeg Inn* (☎ 01436-860678, 🖳 www.inverbeg inn.co.uk, 14D/4T/2F) offers B&B from £25 to £75 per person. Their adjoining Mister C's fish and whisky bar is the place for food. It is very good and much of it is local fishy stuff such as Loch Fyne oysters (£7.95 for half a dozen) and fish curry (£10.95).

ROWARDENNAN [SEE MAP 3, p69]

Rowardennan sits on the eastern shore of Loch Lomond, accessible by **ferry** from Inverbeg on the other side of the loch (☎ 01360-870273, departs Rowardennan 10am, 2pm and 5.30pm Easter-Sept, fares as above) or by the road from Drymen that ends here at Rowardennan.

This is the most convenient starting point for an ascent of Ben Lomond (see p68) and, despite its lack of size, has places to stay for all budgets.

Rowardennan Lodge Youth Hostel (☎ 01360-870259, Mar-Oct, 75 beds, £13.50-15.50), has a tiny **shop** at the reception desk selling a limited supply of packet foods and tins. The National Trust for Scotland has set aside an area where **campers** can pitch their tents for free for one night only. It is located just north of the youth hostel in a

woodland clearing. *Rowardennan Hotel* (☎ 01360-870273, 🖳 www.rowardennan hotel.co.uk, 18 rooms all with private facilities) charges from £55/pp. Within the hotel are the cosy confines of the Clansman Bar, the best place to ease those post-hike aches and pains by sampling a beer or two or trying one of their tasty specialities such as haggis from the Highlands for £7.95.

If there are no beds at Rowardennan try *Passfoot Cottage* (☎ 01360-870324, 🖳 www.passfoot.com, Apr-Sep, 1D/1T, £28.50/pp) which is in the village of Balmaha about six miles down the road. Halfway between Rowardennan and **Balmaha** is another cosy bed and breakfast: *Anchorage Cottage* (☎ 01360-870394, 🖳 www.anchoragecottage.co.uk, Apr-Sep, 1D/1T en suite, £37/pp).

ARDLUI [SEE MAP 4, p71]

The hamlet of Ardlui at the head of Loch Lomond consists of a small **shop** (Mon-Fri 9am-2pm, 4-6pm, Sat-Sun 9am-6pm) with only limited supplies but plenty of newspapers and the three-star *Ardlui Hotel* (☎ 01301-704243, 🖳 www.ardlui.co.uk, 1S/ 2T/4D/3F) with beds from £47.50/pp. There is also a **campsite** by the road; ask in the hotel for details. Non-residents can have a full Scottish breakfast (8.30am-noon) in their *Terrace Restaurant* or a much better value and substantial meal in

the friendly main bar (noon-9.15pm) while the stuffed Highland cow's head peers over your dinner table.

Below the hotel is Ardlui Marina, where a small **ferry** carries walkers across the northern end of Loch Lomond to and from the abandoned crofts of Ardleish on the West Highland Way (£3, on request Apr, Sep, Oct 9am-7pm; May-Aug 9am-8pm). **Buses** and **trains** (see pp32-6) serving the west coast stop regularly in Ardlui.

INVERARNAN

Just north of Ardlui is the roadside hamlet of Inverarnan which has a limited yet varied range of accommodation starting with

Beinglas Campsite (☎ 01301-704281, 🖳 www.beinglascampsite.co.uk) with pitches for £6/pp and cosy wigwam **bunkhouses**

for £12-25/pp (for 1-4 people). They also do **B&B** in four chalets (2D/2F) for £30-55/pp and there is a well-stocked **shop** (8-10am, noon-7.30pm) and a **bar** serving evening meals. Just down the road is *Rose Cottage* (☎ 01301-704255, 🖳 fletcher.j3 @talk21.com, 1T/1D/1F) offering a step up in comfort with beds costing from £20/pp and *Clisham Cottage* (☎ 01301-704339, 🖳 www.clishamcottage.com, 2T in house and 3D/1T in static caravan) which offers B&B for £24-27.50/pp.

Inverarnan is rightly famous for *The Drovers Inn* (☎ 01301-704234, 🖳 www .thedroversinn.co.uk, 2S/1T/6D/2F) which has been a stop-off point for travellers for centuries. It barely seems to have changed through all that time; a wonderful tumble-down building with creaking floorboards, candles on the tables and ancient stuffed animals growling in the hallway. And of course there is plenty of good food such as steak and Guinness pie for £8.95 (served 11am-8pm), real ales and a good top shelf of malt whiskies. Double rooms start at £34/pp. Opposite the Drovers Inn is the altogether more contemporary *Drovers Lodge* which is owned and managed by the same folk as those at the Drovers Inn so the contact details and room rates are the same as for the Inn.

Citylink **buses** (see pp32-6) between Glasgow, Fort William and Skye can be hailed from outside the Drovers Inn. The nearest train station is two miles south at Ardlui.

CRIANLARICH

Positioned at the junction of Strath Fillan, Glen Falloch and Glen Dochart, the small, rather plain-looking village of Crianlarich is a useful base for the surrounding hills and a good spot for local services. This is a major Highland transport hub with **trains** serving Glasgow, Fort William and Oban. **Buses** serve the same places along with Stirling, Perth, Edinburgh and Skye (see pp32-6). The **shop** (Mon-Sat 8am-6pm, Sun 9am-5pm), which incorporates a **post office**, has a good supply of foodstuffs including fresh fruit.

The best budget beds can be found at *Crianlarich Youth Hostel* (☎ 01838-300260, Feb-Oct, 72 beds, £13-15.25/pp). The most convenient places for B&B are along the Glen Dochart main road, namely *Craigbank B&B* (☎ 01838-300279, 1D/3T/2F, Mar-Oct) charging £21/pp (at the time of research this property was up for sale so check before turning up) and next door, *Glenardran Guest House* (☎ 01838-300236, 1S/1D/1T/2F) offering homely accommodation close to the village centre for £27.50/pp. About a mile east of the village, near the start of the Ben More path, is *Inverardran House* (☎ 01838-300240, 🖳 www.inverardran.demon .co.uk, 3D/1T), a beautiful red and white former shooting lodge offering B&B from £20/pp.

In the opposite direction, a little way out of the village on the way to Tyndrum is

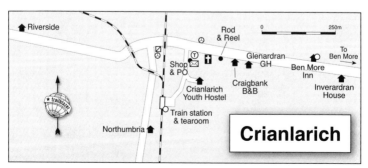

Crianlarich

Riverside (☎ 01838-300235, 🖳 www.river sideguesthouse.co.uk, 1S/2D/1T/2F) with B&B from £25/pp.

There is also a cheap B&B on the Glenfalloch road, just up the hill from the bridge, called *Northumbria* (☎ 01838-300253, 🖳 anderson@northumbria9.fsnet .co.uk, 2D/1T). B&B in this modern home will set you back a mere £20-22.50/pp.

Ben More Inn (☎ 01838-300210, 🖳 www.ben-more.co.uk, 9D/2F) has beds in Swiss-style cabins (from £33/pp) and also does good food (daily noon-2.30pm & 6-9.30pm) in the cosy bar, including chicken curry (£8.95) and lamb shank (£10.95). There is live music most weekends. Pub grub is also available at the central *Rod and Reel* (☎ 01838-300271) and there's an as-simple-as-they-come **tearoom** (open from 7.30am) on the station platform. There are also **left-luggage** facilities here.

TYNDRUM

Tyndrum has long been a stop-off point for motorists needing to fill up on the busy A82 and A85. There is a **TIC** (☎ 08707-200626, daily 10am-6pm Jul-Aug, 10.30am-5pm Sep-Oct, 10am-5pm Apr-Jun) which includes a bookshop and **internet access** (£1/12mins) as well as two **train** stations. The lower station is for trains to Oban and the upper one for Fort William. There are also frequent Citylink **buses** (see pp32-6) plying the busy A82 between Glasgow and Fort William and the A85 to Oban.

Most folk who stop here head straight for the **Green Welly Stop** a filling station and wannabe supermarket. Next door is the **Outdoor Shop** (☎ 01301-702080, daily 8.30am-5pm), useful for all those outdoor essentials, and a modern souvenir shop selling other essential kit for a trip to the Highlands: shortbread, tartan berets and

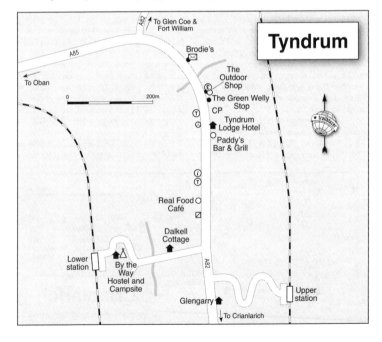

sprigs of heather. Within the complex is a **cash machine** and a self-service **café** (daily 8.30am-5pm, sandwiches from £2.60) but better sandwiches can be found around the corner in **Brodie's shop**, a family-run store which also houses the **post office**.

Head south from the hive of activity at the Green Welly for *Tyndrum Lodge Hotel* (☎ 01838-400219, 🖳 www.glhotels.co.uk /tyndrumhotel.html, 5S/4D/8T/4F) for the best beds (from £33 for B&B) and their adjoining *Paddy's Bar and Grill* a run of the mill bar with pub grub from £7.95. Further down the road, by the TIC, the *Real Food Café* is a modern sit-in fast-food place, open Sun-Thu 10am-10pm and Fri-Sat 8.30am-10pm, with burgers and pies from £3.25 and fish and chips for £4.95.

BRIDGE OF ORCHY [SEE MAP 7a, p78]

Bridge of Orchy consists of little more than a **train station** and the plush *Bridge of Orchy Hotel* (☎ 01838-400208, 🖳 www .bridgeoforchy.co.uk, 3T/6D/2F), all tiled floors and bar staff in shirts and ties. If £90 for a double room (£60 single) is too expensive there is always the adjoining **bunkhouse** with space for 46 in rooms of six, four and two beds (£13/pp). Cunningly, there are no self-catering facilities forcing guests to eat in the Caley Bar in the hotel. The food, served from noon to 9pm, is of a very high standard; the menu includes

Other than the hotel the best places to hunt out a bed are *Dalkell Cottage* (☎ 01838-400285, 🖳 www.dalkell.com, 1S/ 5T or D) with B&B from £26/pp and *Glengarry Guest House* (☎ 01838-400224, 🖳 www.glengarryhouse.co.uk, 1D/1T/1F) which does B&B for £27.50/pp.

Campers can find relative luxury for £6 at the *By The Way Hostel and Campsite* (☎ 01838-400333, 🖳 www.tyndrumbythe way.com), near the lower station. The hostel includes four twin rooms (£17.50/pp) and dormitory rooms (£14/pp). Their slightly more upmarket trekker huts sleep 2-6 people and cost £9-14/pp. Be warned that this site is often busy with West Highland Way walkers.

such mouth-watering dishes as rump of lamb for £13.50 and mixed bean casserole for £8.50.

Another budget option is the *West Highland Way Sleeper Bunkhouse* (☎ 01838-400548, 🖳 www.westhighlandway sleeper.co.uk) on the station platform. Beds here cost £13.50/pp and this includes use of self-catering facilities. There is a lovely spot for **wild camping** across the River Orchy by the old 18th century bridge.

Trains and Citylink **buses** call here (see pp32-6).

Glen Coe and Glen Nevis

Heading north across Rannoch Moor the A82 enters the upper reaches of Glen Coe, a brooding glacial valley bordered on one side by the serrated Aonach Eagach ridge and on the other by the Three Sisters of Glen Coe. Famous as the site of a bloody massacre in 1692, it is also the unofficial home of Scottish mountaineering.

Further north is a region of high peaks centred around Glen Nevis. On the south side of the glen is the Mamores Range, an intricate series of ridges including ten munros, and on the north side the Grey Corries, an equally fascinating ridge containing even loftier summits that lead to the highest mountain in the British Isles, Ben Nevis. This is a true mountain playground capable of providing hungry hillwalkers with countless expeditions.

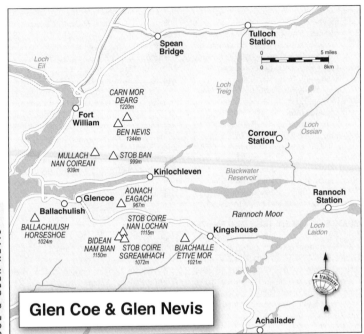

Glen Coe & Glen Nevis

BUACHAILLE ETIVE MOR *'Boo-achul-a Etif Mor'* [MAP 8, p92]
STOB DEARG (*'Stop Jyerrack'*, 1021m/3350ft)
STOB NA BROIGE (*'Stop na Pro-yck-ya*, 956m/3135ft)

Overview

This picture-postcard mountain is up there with the best Scotland has to offer. No matter how many times one heads north up the A82, Buachaille Etive Mor never fails to draw an expletive of awe from the most saintly of folk. The summit provides stunning views across lonely Rannoch Moor and despite appearances is easily accessible. While the sheer gullies and towers on its east face offer some of Scotland's most famous climbing routes, for walkers there is a back door that opens out on to the mountain's two-mile spine.

Route

Buachaille Etive Mor is a popular mountain for walkers and climbers alike. In summer the lay-by at **Altnafeadh**, the main access point to the mountain, resembles a car showroom. Leave the cars behind and cross the bridge over the River Coupall. The path passes the **mountain-rescue point** at Lagangarbh and climbs into the mouth of **Coire na Tulaich**, a deep enclosed corrie characterised by scree and shattered boulders. Being the main access route to the mountain, the path is easy to make out and in places is quite heavily eroded.

The going gets steeper and steeper as the path reaches the back-wall of the corrie. The final 100m is a laboured scramble over, at first, a band of **scree** of almost liquid consistency and, second, a stretch of light scrambling over a big rocky staircase.

Once on the flat back of the mountain bear east over rocky slabs to gain the summit of **Stob Dearg**. There are a number of false summits along the ridge but the true summit is obvious as it looms over Rannoch Moor.

It is worth continuing a short way from the summit to get a view over the top of the mountain's east face, which falls away dramatically to the moor some 700m below. Climbers are drawn to this magnificent face by such classic routes as Curved Ridge, Crowberry Ridge and Deep Gully Buttress. Return to the top of Coire na Tulaich and continue along the wide ridge. At first it rises briefly to a cairn. Bear SW along a level ridge for just over half a mile (1km). It is about a 100-metre climb to the cairn at the summit of **Stob na Doire**.

Be sure to descend by the correct ridge in a WSW direction. At the grassy **col** continue SW to reach the shoulder of Stob Coire Altruim and continue climbing to this top. It is then just over half a mile (1km) along a fairly level ridge to the summit of **Stob na Broige**. This marks the end of the Buachaille Etive Mor ridge and is a great vantage point from which to appreciate the U-shaped Glen Etive stretching away to Ben Starav.

Return to Stob Coire Altruim and descend back to the flat shoulder just above the grassy col. There is no need to return to this col. A **well-worn path** drops away from the shoulder into Coire Altruim reaching the Lairig Gartain below in around 40 minutes. This path can be a little awkward to negotiate in places, particularly in wet weather. About halfway down it crosses over some rocky bluffs that require a bit of concentration particularly if fatigue is setting in.

BUACHAILLE ETIVE MOR (Great Shepherd of Etive)
Technical grade ▲▲
Navigation grade ▲▲
Terrain grade ▲▲▲▲
Strenuousness ▲▲▲
Return time 4¼-6hrs
Return distance 8miles/13km
Total ascent 3642ft/1110m
OS maps Landranger 41, Explorer 384
Gateways Kingshouse (see p110) Glen Coe (see p111) Glencoe Village (p111)

GLEN COE & GLEN NEVIS

Cross the **river** in the Lairig Gartain and follow the moorland path for 1¼ miles (2km) back to the busy A82. This is a dangerous stretch of

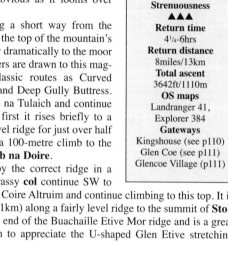

Buachaille Etive Mor
Distance & Altitude

Summit Stob Dearg 1021m △
Summit Stob na Doire △
Summit Stob na Broige 956m △
Top of descent path
River crossing
Altnafeadh
Altnafeadh

1200m 1100 1000 900 800 700 600 500 400 300

1 2 3 4 5 6 7 8 9 10 11 12 13 14km

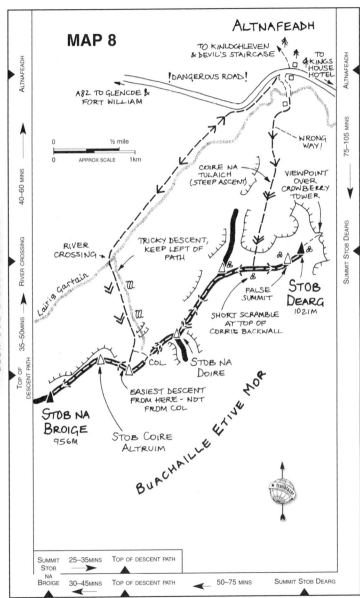

MAP 8

ALTNAFEADH

TO KINLOCHLEVEN & DEVIL'S STAIRCASE

TO KINGS HOUSE HOTEL

!DANGEROUS ROAD!

A82 TO GLENCOE & FORT WILLIAM

WRONG WAY!

0   ½ mile

0   APPROX SCALE   1km

COIRE NA TULAICH (STEEP ASCENT)

VIEWPOINT OVER CROWBERRY TOWER

RIVER CROSSING

TRICKY DESCENT, KEEP LEFT OF PATH

Lairig Gartain

FALSE SUMMIT

STOB DEARG 1021M

SHORT SCRAMBLE AT TOP OF CORRIE BACKWALL

COL

STOB NA DOIRE

EASIEST DESCENT FROM HERE - NOT FROM COL

STOB NA BROIGE 956M

STOB COIRE ALTRUIM

BUACHAILLE ETIVE MOR

trailblazer

ALTNAFEADH

40–60 MINS

RIVER CROSSING

35–50MINS

TOP OF DESCENT PATH

GLEN COE & GLEN NEVIS

ALTNAFEADH

75–105 MINS

SUMMIT STOB DEARG

SUMMIT STOB NA BROIGE	25–35MINS →	TOP OF DESCENT PATH	
	30–45MINS ←	TOP OF DESCENT PATH ←	50–75 MINS SUMMIT STOB DEARG

Cairns
Cairns are small piles of rocks that are traditionally used to mark the summits and tops of mountains and to indicate routes through barren, otherwise featureless, terrain. In this sense they are useful navigational aids but in some areas the propensity to construct cairns has got out of hand. There is a fine line between the occasional lonely cairn that acts as a sensitive landmark, even complementing the wild feel of a mountain, and a plethora of small piles of stones that serve no purpose and detract from the natural beauty of an area.

road so take care on the return to the start point at Altnafeadh. It is much safer to cross the trackless heathery ground below the road rather than risk the cars, coaches and supermarket delivery lorries speeding along the tarmac.

Alternative routes
The walk can be shortened by leaving out the second or third peaks. Early descents can be made via the route of ascent or via Coire Altruim.

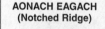

AONACH EAGACH *'Urn-uch Eg-kuch'* [MAP 9a, p94; MAP 9b, p96]
MEALL DEARG (*'Me-yowl Jyerrack'*, 953m/3125ft)
SGORR NAM FIANNAIDH (*'Skor nam Fee-a-nee'*, 967m/3175ft)
Overview
The infamous Aonach Eagach is one of the most entertaining ridges on the Scottish mainland. Strung between two munros on the north side of Glen Coe, this 'Notched Ridge' is aptly named and should only be attempted by those with plenty of experience on such terrain. In places the scrambling turns into exposed climbing (graded 'easy') as the ridge is, at times, very narrow with significant precipices on each side. Some people choose to take a rope.

Route
The favoured route of ascent begins at the **car park** on the A82 Glen Coe road (GR173568). A well-trodden path ascends grassy slopes and then begins to climb sharply in a series of tight zigzags up the SE shoulder of Am Bodach. In places a little light scrambling is necessary but this is nothing compared to what is to come. The path soon levels out as it approaches the top of **Am Bodach**, the first peak on the ridge. Follow the flat ridge in a WNW direction to reach, after a few minutes, the first of many down-climbs. It is a drop of about 20m but the holds are good. About halfway down move over to the left (when facing west) for the easiest descent to the small col.

AONACH EAGACH (Notched Ridge)
Technical grade
▲▲▲▲▲
Navigation grade
▲
Terrain grade
▲▲▲▲▲
Strenuousness
▲▲▲
Time
3½-5hrs
Distance
4½miles/7km
Total ascent
3610ft/1100m
OS maps
Landranger 41, Explorer 384
Gateways
Glen Coe (see p111)
Glencoe Village (p111)

GLEN COE & GLEN NEVIS

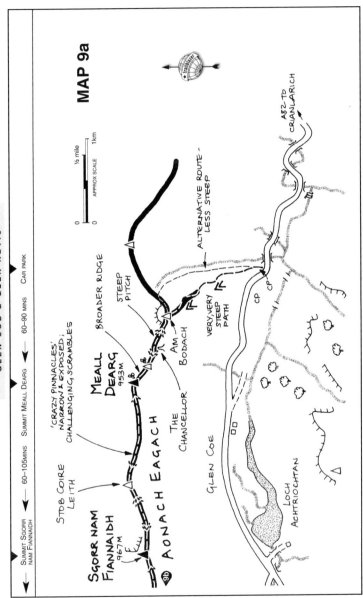

SUMMIT SGORR
NAM FIANNAIDH
← 60–105MINS → STOB COIRE LEITH → SUMMIT MEALL DEARG → 60–90 MINS → CAR PARK

MAP 9a

APPROX SCALE
0 ½ mile
0 1km

A82 TO CRIANLARICH

ALTERNATIVE ROUTE – LESS STEEP

BROADER RIDGE

STEEP PITCH

VERY, VERY STEEP PATH

CP

CP

AM BODACH

MEALL DEARG
953M

'CRAZY PINNACLES' NARROW & EXPOSED; CHALLENGING SCRAMBLES

THE CHANCELLOR

STOB COIRE LEITH

AONACH EAGACH

SGORR NAM FIANNAIDH
967M

9b

GLEN COE

LOCH ACHTRIOCHTAN

The first of many stunning views across Glen Coe begin to appear. One particularly interesting detour is to venture on to the rocky tower, on the south side of the ridge, known as **The Chancellor**, as it offers one of the best views of the glen below.

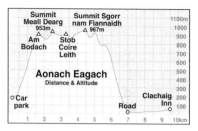

Continue along the main ridge which climbs again to reach the summit of the first munro, **Meall Dearg** (953m). Continuing from here the ridge really begins to show why it is held in such high regard. For the next half mile or so (1km) the crest becomes more and more convoluted and very narrow with precipitous drops on both sides for much of the way. With this being such a popular traverse the well-worn path makes route-finding relatively easy.

There are a number of steep climbs and down-climbs along this section with two particularly interesting obstacles worthy of note: the ascent of a 15m chimney followed later on by the aptly named '**Crazy Pinnacles**'. These three pillars of rock sit on a particularly exposed section of the ridge. The main pinnacle of the three is the craziest of them all, involving a careful scramble around its exposed northern side with a view directly down to the corrie floor some 300m below.

Some more exposed scrambling follows the pinnacles before the ridge begins to rise to the peak of **Stob Coire Leith**. West of here the ridge narrows one more time but is relatively easy to negotiate. The tough stuff is over and it is now an easy walk up the ridge to the summit of the second munro, **Sgorr nam Fiannaidh**.

To find the Clachaig Gully descent path head west for about 500m to a cairn at a col. From the col a path traverses SW across the rocky slopes at the top of a shallow corrie to gain the exceedingly steep descent path that follows the western side of the Clachaig Gully. The **Clachaig Gully** is a vicious gash in the mountainside that stretches all the way to the floor of the glen. Take care if descending from here. It is a notoriously dangerous path with plenty of loose scree and some rocky shelves that need to be negotiated. Accidents do happen here, often from falling rocks dislodged by other walkers and climbers, whilst others have fallen into the gully. However, competent walkers should have no problems if they take the descent at a steady pace. A longer but easier descent route is described in the alternative routes section below.

Once at the lane the final part of the walk is to cross the **road** and head straight through the door of the Boots Bar at **Clachaig Inn** (see p111) to complete what some might call the finest pub walk in Scotland.

Alternative routes

An alternative, and less steep, ascent path begins at the same point described above but branches off to follow the stream into Coire an Ruigh, eventually reaching the col NE of Am Bodach's summit.

GLEN COE & GLEN NEVIS

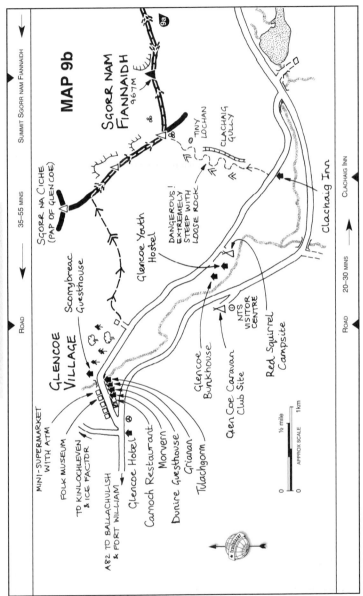

SUMMIT SGORR NAM FIANNAIDH

ROAD

35-55 MINS

MAP 9b

SGORR NAM FIANNAIDH
967M

Sgorr na Ciche
(PAP OF GLENCOE)

Scorrybreac
Guesthouse

GLENCOE
VILLAGE

TINY
LOCHAN

CLACHAIG
GULLY

DANGEROUS!
EXTREMELY
STEEP WITH
LOOSE ROCK

Glencoe Youth
Hostel

MINI-SUPERMARKET
WITH ATM

FOLK MUSEUM

TO KINLOCHLEVEN
& ICE FACTOR

A82 TO BALLACHULISH
& FORT WILLIAM

Glencoe Hotel

Cannoch Restaurant

Morvern

Dunire Guesthouse

Grianan

Tulachgorm

Glencoe Bunkhouse

Glen Coe Caravan
Club Site

NTS
VISITOR
CENTRE

Red Squirrel
Campsite

Clachaig Inn

ROAD

20-30 MINS

CLACHAIG INN

½ mile

1km

APPROX SCALE

0

0

trailblazer

Aonach Eagach can be tackled in either direction although most people favour east to west, partly because the ascent is easier and begins at a higher elevation and partly because the walk finishes at the pub. Another advantage of starting in the east is that the path is easier to follow. If starting at the Clachaig end it is much easier to miss the path, find yourself at a dead-end on a rocky spur and have to backtrack to locate the correct route. Nevertheless, those who have already crossed the ridge on a previous occasion will find that it throws up a whole new set of challenges when tackled in the opposite direction.

At the western end the Clachaig Gully path is considered by many to be a poor route choice; a relentlessly steep path of loose scree that does not let up for 800m. Some scrambling is necessary in places. If this sounds a little unpleasant for descending or ascending there is an alternative path over easier slopes but it adds about a mile and a half to the walk. If tackling the ridge east to west continue along the ridge from Sgorr nam Fiannaidh to the saddle below the Pap of Glencoe and follow the slopes down to a point just north of Glencoe Youth Hostel, being sure to avoid the private, fenced farmland near the bottom. It is about a mile along the lane to Clachaig Inn (see p111) for a well-deserved drink or two.

STOB COIRE SGREAMHACH (*'Stop Corry Skre-hach'*, 1072m/3515ft)
BIDEAN NAM BIAN (*'Bidyen nam Bee-yan'*, 1150m/3775ft)
STOB COIRE NAN LOCHAN (*'Stop-Corry-nan-Loch-un'*, 1115m/3660ft)

[MAP 10, p98]

Overview
Standing as the unrivalled king of Glen Coe this mountain massif, the largest in the area, is a fascinating maze of long ridges, pointed peaks and deep corries. There are a number of possible outings to enjoy. The route described here takes in the three main peaks as well as the two most beautiful corries.

Route
On summer days the car parks on the Glen Coe road are packed to overflowing as people are drawn to the magnificent views of the 'Three Sisters of Glen Coe': the three prominent ridges of the Bidean massif that end abruptly on the south side of Glen Coe.

Beginning at any of these **car parks**, follow the path that leads towards Coire Gabhail, otherwise known as 'The Lost Valley' for reasons that soon become apparent. The Lost Valley is the left-hand corrie as you face the Three Sisters. The path cross-

---

STOB COIRE SGREAMHACH
(Peak of the Dreadful Corrie)

BIDEAN NAM BIAN
(Pinnacle of the Animal Hides)

STOB COIRE NAN LOCHAN
(Lochan Corrie Peak)

Technical grade
▲▲▲
Navigation grade
▲▲▲
Terrain grade
▲▲▲
Strenuousness
▲▲▲
Return time
4-6hrs
Return distance
7miles/11km
Total ascent
4094ft/1250m
OS maps
Landranger 41,
Explorer 384
Gateways
Glen Coe (see p111)
Glencoe Village
(see p111)

GLEN COE & GLEN NEVIS

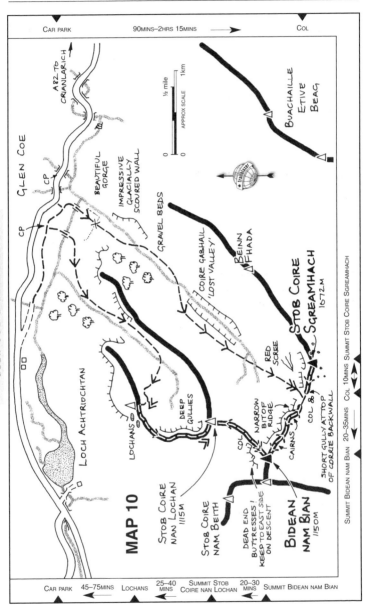

MAP 10

GLEN COE & GLEN NEVIS

CAR PARK — 90MINS–2HRS 15MINS ⟶ COL

CAR PARK

A82 TO CRIANLARICH

GLEN COE

CP

CP

BEAUTIFUL GORGE

IMPRESSIVE GLACIALLY SCOURED WALL

GRAVEL BEDS

COIRE GABHAIL 'LOST VALLEY'

BEINN FHADA

STOB COIRE SGREAMHACH 1672M

RED SCREE

COL 80?

NARROW BIT OF RIDGE

CAIRNS

SHORT GULLY AT TOP OF CORRIE BACKWALL

BUACHAILLE ETIVE BEAG

COL

½ mile   1km
APPROX SCALE
0   0
* Trailblazer

DEEP GULLIES

LOCHANS

LOCH ACHTRIOCHTAN

COL

STOB COIRE NAN LOCHAN 1115M

STOB COIRE NAM BEITH

DEAD END BUTTRESSES! KEEP TO EAST SIDE ON DESCENT

BIDEAN NAM BIAN 1150M

Summit Bidean nam Bian 20–35MINS   Col 10MINS   Summit Stob Coire Sgreamhach

CAR PARK — 45–75MINS — LOCHANS — 25–40 MINS — Summit Stob Coire nan Lochan — 20–30 MINS — Summit Bidean nam Bian es the River Coe by way of a **bridge** and climbs steeply through deciduous woodland, soon emerging from the trees and continuing upwards into the corrie. This is a beautiful part of the walk. The native woodland is tucked into a narrow defile with a haphazard river tumbling urgently over rocks in a narrow gorge below.

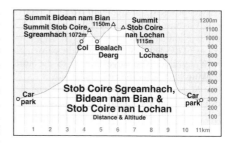

Above to the left is a good example of glacial scouring; the cliffs are polished and smooth and patterned by dancing trails of water. Quite suddenly and spectacularly the corrie opens out to reveal a wide alluvial plain, '**The Lost Valley**'. At the time of the Glen Coe massacre (see box p112) of 1692 some of the MacDonald clan took refuge in this hidden glen as the King's men hunted them down.

Bloody massacres aside, it is a stunning location from which to admire two of Bidean's most prominent peaks: Stob Coire Sgreamhach ahead to the left and the pointed summit of Bidean nam Bian to the right. Aim for the col between the two: the **Bealach Dearg**. A clear path crosses the alluvial plains and begins to climb to the back of the corrie. There is a lower path and an upper path, both on the western side of the stream and both reaching the same point at a junction of streams. Ignore the path that branches off to the right and instead continue ahead in a SW direction. The path gets steeper and steeper as it climbs over rocks towards the col, passing a buttress on the right. Keep to the left of the fan of scree for the firmest ground. The final 20m of ascent to the col are very steep but there is an easy route through a small gully between the rocks to reach the **col** and a small cairn. The summit of **Stob Coire Sgreamhach** involves a short detour up the rocky ridge to the left (30 mins return, 130m ascent). Back at the **Bealach Dearg** follow the obvious ridge to the summit cairn atop Bidean nam Bian. There are a couple of **false summits** on the way up and care should be taken to avoid the gullies that cut into the ridge.

The summit of **Bidean nam Bian** offers magnificent views in all directions. Highlights include Ben Starav and Ben Cruachan across Glen Etive to the south, the Aonach Eagach ridge, Mamores, Grey Corries and Ben Nevis to the north and the great Loch Linnhe and the Ardgour hills to the west.

The third and final peak of the day is Stob Coire nan Lochan to the north. Descend by way of the NE ridge, which is steep and precipitous in places. Try to keep to the faint path that follows the safest route down on the eastern flank of the ridge and be sure to avoid the dead-end ridge that leads onto a **buttress** and a long drop. A brief scramble near the bottom leads quickly to the col. It is possible to descend from here, either to the left through Coire nam Beith or to the right for the return through the Lost Valley. If time allows, however, it is only a further 100m ascent up an easy rocky ridge to the summit of **Stob Coire nan Lochan** for more exceptional views. These include a look back at the two peaks climbed earlier and an interesting perspective looking down on to the backs of the Three Sisters. From the cairn at the top descend the SW ridge over rocky ground. The ridge swings to the north and passes some frightening-looking gullies on the right-hand side which hold snow for much of the year. The ridge leads towards Aonach Dubh, one of the Three Sisters. At the **col** south of this top there is a pair of small **lochans**. A faint path leads SE from the two lochans down a sharp incline to a shallow bowl. Aim for the gap between two rocky outcrops and follow the southern bank of a small stream that drops sharply to join a solid path in the bottom of the corrie.

Follow this path on the southern side of the river all the way to the mouth of the corrie and back into Glen Coe. The path crosses a **bridge** over the River Coe and climbs back up to the car park on the other side of the glen.

Alternative routes

There are too many route possibilities on 'Bidean' to mention them all here. One good alternative is to continue along the NW ridge from the summit of Bidean nam Bian to the outlying peak of Stob Coire nam Beith. From this peak a descent route can be found by continuing along its NW ridge and descending through Coire nam Beith to Loch Achtriochtan in Glen Coe.

For a shorter day the col between Bidean nam Bian and Stob Coire nan Lochan is useful as either an ascent route or descent route from either Coire nam Beith or Coire Gabhail (The Lost Valley).

One final route of ascent worth mentioning starts just east of the Pass of Glen Coe by a perfectly formed roadside cairn at GR188563. Follow the path in a SW direction before climbing the very steep NE slopes of Beinn Fhada. Follow the Beinn Fhada ridge as it rises spectacularly to the summit of Stob Coire Sgreamhach.

BALLACHULISH HORSESHOE ('*Bala-<u>hoo</u>-lish*') [MAP 11, p102]
SGORR DHEARG ('*Skor <u>Jyerrack</u>*', 1024m/3360ft)
SGORR DHONUILL ('*Skor <u>Don</u>-nul*', 1001m/3285ft)

Overview

The twin peaks of Beinn a' Bheithir ('*Bayn a Vayhar*', better known as the Ballachulish Horseshoe) dominate the view above the mouth of Loch Leven and provide extensive views along Loch Linnhe and Glen Coe. The east ridge of the mountain offers fairly tricky scrambling that makes an otherwise uncomplicated hillwalk a little more testing. Alternative routes that avoid this section are suggested below.

Route

Take the lane past the primary school at the southern end of **Ballachulish** village and pass through a series of gates. A track continues across grazing land to a **final gate** which leads onto open moorland. On the right-hand side a faint path climbs away from the track. Follow this, at times, boggy trail climbing the increasingly steep lower slopes of the mountain. The path becomes more defined on the approach to an easy **step**, the first obstacle on the ridge. A little further on, things get more interesting. The ridge is interrupted by a series of rocky shelves that cannot be avoided. The first of these is the most exposed and difficult. In places the rock is a little loose so make sure you find firm holds. Once past these obstacles it is a short distance to the top of the ridge. Continue SW from this top to a small **col** before climbing again to the summit of the first peak, **Sgorr Dhearg**. It is a fairly long descent, in a SW direction, to the **col** between the peaks. The remains of a rusty fence mark the low point of the col. Continue west climbing the grassy ridge towards a dog-leg just below the steep cliffs of **Sgorr Dhonuill**. Climb the rocky back of the summit ridge to reach the cairn at the top. The descent is back the way you came to the col between the two main peaks. From the col a path descends sharply to the north into a boggy, grassy bowl where the gradient shallows. Keep to the right of the fence ahead as the path leads down into the coniferous forestry plantation. The path emerges onto a **forestry track** marked by a cairn. Turn left here and follow the track round to a junction. Keep to the right and follow the track down the glen. As it approaches Loch Leven ahead, it swings round the bottom of the north ridge of Sgorr Dhearg. Turn right at the main road where it is a short walk back to Ballachulish.

BALLACHULISH HORSESHOE
Technical grade
▲▲▲▲ (via E ridge)
▲▲ (via alternative routes of ascent)
Navigation grade
▲▲
Terrain grade
▲▲▲▲ (via E ridge)
▲▲ (via alternative routes of ascent)
Strenuousness
▲▲▲
Return time
4½-7hrs
Return distance
9miles/14km
Total ascent
3884ft/1185m
OS maps
Landranger 41, Explorer 384
Gateways
Ballachulish (see p113) Glencoe Village (see p111)

GLEN COE & GLEN NEVIS

Alternative routes

The east ridge has some fairly serious scrambling including a tricky 5m climb up an exposed rocky step. Inexperienced scramblers should ascend via the described descent route or via the NE ridge to avoid these difficulties. To gain the NE ridge follow the lane past the school and then the track as far as the final gate. From here cross the wooded corrie and ascend heathery slopes to reach the spine of the NE ridge.

To complete the true 'horseshoe' continue from the summit of Sgorr Dhonuill along the wide ridge, heading at first W and then NW and N. There

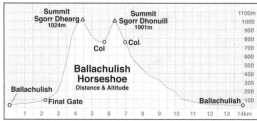

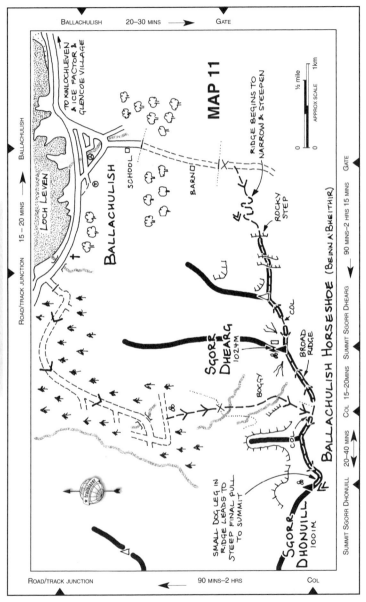

Mountain or hill?
The dictionary defines a hill as being 'smaller than a mountain' and a mountain as being 'greater than a hill'. Since there is no clear point when a hill becomes a mountain most people tend to use both. The dictionary definitions, however, are beset with problems. Is a Himalayan valley floor at 3000m considered a mountain while the summit of Ben Nevis at 1344m considered a hill? It's best to look at each case on a local level. In the Highlands it is perfectly logical to refer to the peaks as mountains to distinguish them from the even lowlier 'hills' in Scotland such as the Ochils and Pentlands. Nevertheless, most hillwalkers refer to the Scottish mountains generically as 'the hill'. Throughout this book the terms mountain and hill are used in equal measure.

are two descent routes, from this ridge, into the confusing mass of conifers in Gleann a' Chaolais. The first is at GR025564 and the later one is at GR033572. Navigating through the forest from these points can prove a little challenging. The descent described for the main route (see p101) is much easier.

STOB BAN ('_Stop Ban_', 999m/3280ft)   [MAP 12, p105]
MULLACH NAN COIREAN ('_Moo-lach nan Coor-yan_', 939m/3080ft)

Overview
A long and easy ridge links these two peaks, lying at the western end of the Mamores range above Glen Nevis. Each hill is unique in character with the sharp peak and grey scree of Stob Ban contrasting greatly with the plateau-like top of its red-stoned neighbour. There are few obstacles on the circuit although there is a steep pull up the back of Stob Ban's summit cone and a short exposed section halfway along the linking ridge.

Route
By the Lower Falls at **Polldubh** in the dog-leg of Glen Nevis follow the farm track between the two bridges. The track soon peters out to become a heavily trodden trail as it heads south into the sparsely wooded Coire a' Mhusgain. The ascent is a gratifyingly gradual one as the path eases its way upwards high above the east side of the river. Just past a rocky buttress the path suddenly climbs in a series of sharp **zigzags** before continuing on an easier gradient to reach another shorter steep section and eventually the upper bowl of the corrie.

To the SW are the menacing cliffs of Stob Ban's eastern corrie, particularly impressive when winter snow is still clinging to the gullies and ledges. The path swings to the right and then to the left to reach the **col** at 760m. At the col turn right and climb a short sharp grassy incline which tops out on the lower end of Stob Ban's east ridge.

The ridge cuts away sharply on the north side in a series of spectacular cliffs and gullies while the other side is a steep and sweeping slope of white rock, hence the mountain's name.

GLEN COE & GLEN NEVIS

**STOB BAN
(White Peak)**

**MULLACH NAN
COIREAN
(Top of the Corries)**

Technical grade
▲▲

Navigation grade
▲▲▲

Terrain grade
▲▲

Strenuousness
▲▲▲

Return time
3¹/₂-5hrs

Return distance
8miles/13km

Total ascent
3757ft/1145m

OS maps
Landranger 41,
Explorer 392

Gateways
Glen Nevis (see p113)
Fort William
(see p114)

Negotiating this ridge is not as frightening as it first appears. A path leads upwards over rocky steps and ledges and continues on to the high southern side of the mountain before swinging north to reach the cairn on the summit of **Stob Ban**. There is a good view down the north ridge into Glen Nevis and the huge hulk of Ben Nevis's less attractive backside. To the east is the rest of the Mamores range dominated by Sgurr a' Mhaim immediately opposite across Coire a' Mhusgain.

From the summit descend the NW ridge which swings to the west and climbs briefly to a small top complete with a little cairn. There is little drop in height from here to Mullach nan Coirean but the ridge does narrow about halfway along. Two precarious-looking **pinnacles** just below the ridge mark the end of this exposed section that lasts all of five minutes.

After admiring the pinnacles the ridge drops over rocky ground and suddenly becomes much wider and grassier. Follow this ridge past another top with a cairn and on to **Mullach nan Coirean**. This flat-topped mountain with sheer cliffs on its eastern rim contrasts markedly with the white scree of Stob Ban.

Take time to enjoy the view down Loch Linnhe before descending back to Polldubh along the NE ridge. Begin by following the ridge northwards. After a few minutes the ridge splits. To avoid accidentally following the N ridge keep to the right-hand side and follow the NE ridge as it descends steeply and then swings back towards a NNE direction.

A faint path leads to a deer fence. Continue along this path keeping the fence and the commercial forest to the right. Very steep slopes of heather lead down to a **stile** over the fence.

Cross into the forest and follow the path through the trees to a forest track and a small **cairn**. Turn right and follow the track which drops very gradually as it contours the hillside. Take the left-hand track where it forks to reach a sharp hairpin. There is a path leading from this bend back to the road in Glen Nevis from where it is a five-minute walk to **Polldubh**.

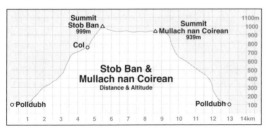

Stob Ban &
Mullach nan Coirean
Distance & Altitude

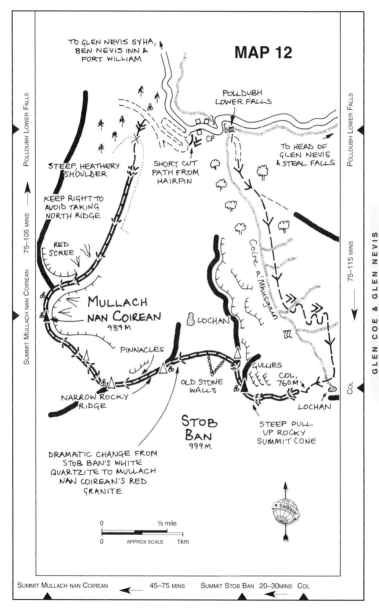

MAP 12

TO GLEN NEVIS SYHA,
BEN NEVIS INN &
FORT WILLIAM

POLLDUBH
LOWER FALLS

CP

TO HEAD OF
GLEN NEVIS
& STEAL FALLS

POLLDUBH LOWER FALLS

POLLDUBH LOWER FALLS

STEEP, HEATHERY
SHOULDER

SHORT CUT
PATH FROM
HAIRPIN

KEEP RIGHT TO
AVOID TAKING
NORTH RIDGE

RED
SCREE

75–105 MINS

75–115 MINS

Coire a' Mhusgain

GLEN COE & GLEN NEVIS

SUMMIT MULLACH NAN COIREAN

MULLACH
NAN COIREAN
939M

LOCHAN

PINNACLES

GULLIES

COL
760M

OLD STONE
WALLS

COL

NARROW ROCKY
RIDGE

STOB
BAN
999M

LOCHAN

STEEP PULL
UP ROCKY
SUMMIT CONE

DRAMATIC CHANGE FROM
STOB BAN'S WHITE
QUARTZITE TO MULLACH
NAN COIREAN'S RED
GRANITE

0   ½ mile

0   APPROX SCALE   1km

★ trailblazer

SUMMIT MULLACH NAN COIREAN   ◄   45–75 MINS   SUMMIT STOB BAN   20–30 MINS   COL   ◄

Alternative routes

The only other possibility of note is a long approach from Kinlochleven that would include Sgorr an Iubhair. From Sgorr an Iubhair descend to the col below Stob Ban and follow the above-mentioned route. From Mullach nan Coirean head SW to the outlying top of Meall a' Chaorainn. Descend by way of its broad south ridge, veering to the SE before reaching the end to gain the track at Lairigmor in the glen below. From Lairigmor it is a further 4 miles (6.5km) along a broad track to Kinlochleven.

CARN MOR DEARG (*'Carn mor Jyerrack'*, 1220m/4005ft)
BEN NEVIS (*'Ben Nev-is'*, 1344m/4410ft) [MAP 13a]

Overview

The magnificent North Face of Ben Nevis dominates the view on the traverse of the Carn Mor Dearg arête as it sweeps spectacularly towards the summit dome of Scotland's highest peak. This challenging route gives a real sense of the alpine nature of Ben Nevis that is all but completely lost to those ascending the easier tourist path.

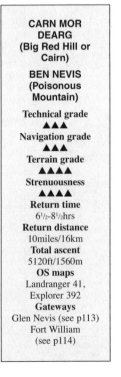

CARN MOR DEARG
(Big Red Hill or Cairn)

BEN NEVIS
(Poisonous Mountain)

Technical grade
▲▲▲
Navigation grade
▲▲▲
Terrain grade
▲▲▲▲
Strenuousness
▲▲▲▲
Return time
6¹/₂-8¹/₂hrs
Return distance
10miles/16km
Total ascent
5120ft/1560m
OS maps
Landranger 41,
Explorer 392
Gateways
Glen Nevis (see p113)
Fort William
(see p114)

Route

Beginning in Glen Nevis there are **two access points** to the tourist path, one at **Ben Nevis Inn** and another opposite Glen Nevis Youth Hostel. Navigation is not difficult at these lower elevations. Follow the crowds up the old pony-cart track that has been transformed into a well-constructed path as it climbs the lower flanks of Meall an t-Suidhe. It continues up the west bank of the **Red Burn** to emerge at a path junction near **Lochan Meall an t-Suidhe** (*'Myowl an t-Aya'*). Ignore the tourist path which continues to the right and follow instead the path bearing north. The trail follows the 600m contour into Coire Leis below the fearsome cliffs of Carn Dearg. Do not follow the path all the way to the **CIC hut** but cross the stream below and aim directly for the scree slopes of Carn Dearg Meadhonach. Ascend these slopes to gain the ridge that leads SSE to the summit of **Carn Mor Dearg**.

Ahead, the spectacular sweep of the Carn Mor Dearg arête draws the eye to the high summit of Ben Nevis and the savage North Face, site of a number of famous climbing routes. The arête is rightly considered one of the finest ridges in the Highlands and is just one of the reasons why this mountain is held in such high regard in Scottish mountaineering circles. Those who climb the

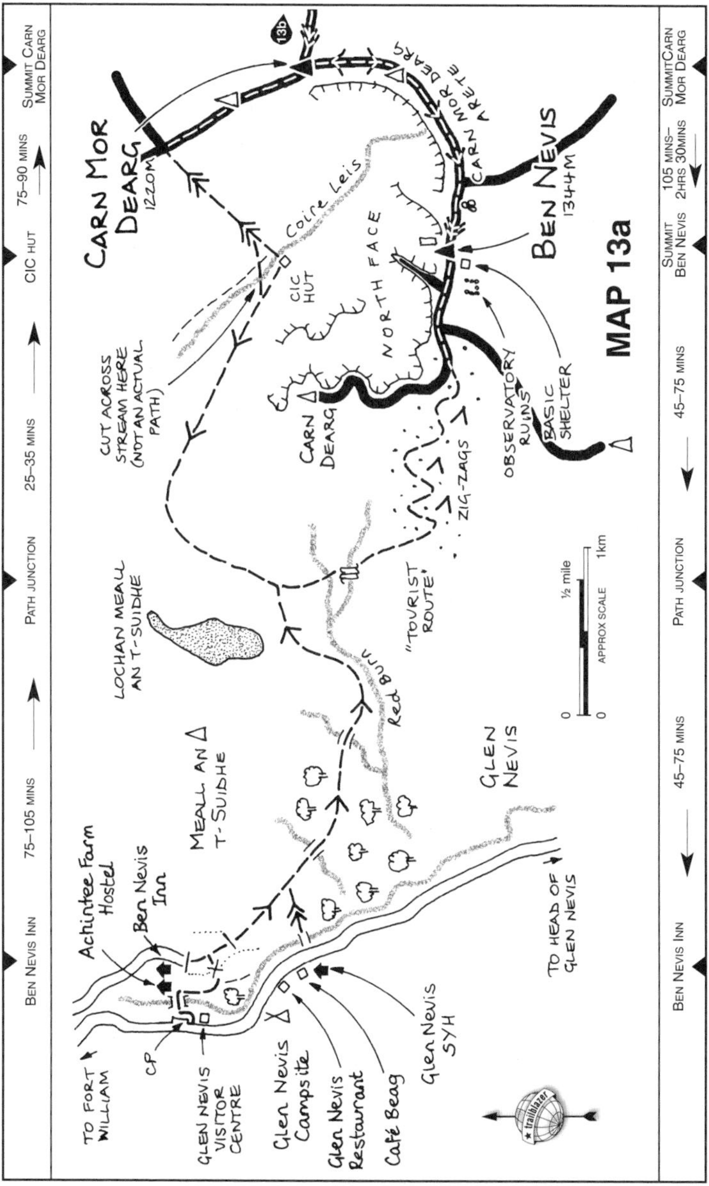

MAP 13a

SUMMIT CARN MOR DEARG

75–90 MINS

CIC HUT

25–35 MINS

PATH JUNCTION

75–105 MINS

BEN NEVIS INN

CARN MOR DEARG 1220m

CARN MOR DEARG ARETE

BEN NEVIS 1344m

Coire Leis

CIC HUT

NORTH FACE

Carn Dearg

CUT ACROSS STREAM HERE (NOT AN ACTUAL PATH)

LOCHAN MEALL AN T-SUIDHE

MEALL AN T-SUIDHE

OBSERVATORY RUINS

BASIC SHELTER

ZIG-ZAGS

"TOURIST ROUTE"

Red Burn

Achintee Farm Hostel

Ben Nevis Inn

CP

TO FORT WILLIAM

GLEN NEVIS VISITOR CENTRE

Glen Nevis Campsite

Glen Nevis Restaurant

Café Beag

Glen Nevis SYH

GLEN NEVIS

TO HEAD OF GLEN NEVIS

SUMMIT CARN MOR DEARG

105 MINS– 2HRS 30MINS

SUMMIT BEN NEVIS

45–75 MINS

PATH JUNCTION

45–75 MINS

BEN NEVIS INN

0   ½ mile   1km

APPROX SCALE

trailblazer

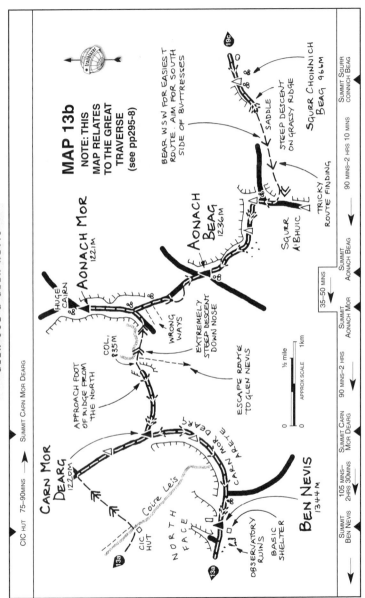

GLEN COE & GLEN NEVIS

MAP 13b

NOTE: THIS MAP RELATES TO THE GREAT TRAVERSE (see pp295-8)

BEAR WSW FOR EASIEST ROUTE. AIM FOR SOUTH SIDE OF BUTTRESSES

AONACH MOR 1221M

AONACH BEAG 1236M

STEEP DESCENT ON GRASSY RIDGE

SADDLE

SGURR CHOINNICH BEAG 966M

19c

TRICKY ROUTE FINDING

SGURR A'BHUIC

HUGE CAIRN

WRONG WAYS

COL, 835M

EXTREMELY STEEP DESCENT DOWN NOSE

APPROACH FOOT OF RIDGE FROM THE NORTH

ESCAPE ROUTE TO GLEN NEVIS

½ mile   1km

0   APPROX SCALE   0

CARN MOR DEARG 1220M

CARN MOR DEARG ARETE

Coire Leis

CIC HUT

NORTH FACE

13b

BEN NEVIS 1344M

OBSERVATORY RUINS

BASIC SHELTER

13a

CIC HUT 75-90MINS → ▶ SUMMIT CARN MOR DEARG

◀ ▶ SUMMIT BEN NEVIS

105 MINS-2HRS 30MINS
↓

SUMMIT CARN MOR DEARG

90 MINS-2 HRS
↓

SUMMIT AONACH MOR

35-50 MINS

SUMMIT AONACH BEAG

90 MINS-2 HRS 10 MINS
↓

SUMMIT SGURR COINNICH BEAG

mountain by way of the aptly named tourist path on the other side would be surprised to see just how spectacular this peak can be.

Although not technically difficult, the **arête** is a long and narrow ridge with one or two sections of light scrambling. After passing over a small top midway along, descend briefly to a low point. On the north side of the ridge there is a dangerous escape route down steep slopes into Coire Leis where there is an emergency shelter and, further down the corrie, the CIC climbers' hut. This escape route should only be used as a last resort.

Continue up to the top of the **abseil posts** on the north side of the ridge at 1150m. This is where the arête finishes and the broad whaleback slopes of 'the Ben' begin. The ascent, on a bearing of 305° from the abseil posts, climbs over steep rocky terrain for nearly 200m to the summit where there is a mounted trig point, an emergency shelter and the ruins of the Victorian observatory (see box p110).

On most days of the year, whatever the weather, there will be a crowd of hillwalkers as well as poorly decked-out tourists wearing jeans and trainers. Around 125,000 people visit the **summit of Ben Nevis** every year. On a clear day they can enjoy fantastic views across the western seaboard. To the west the view sometimes stretches as far as the Outer Hebrides while the Aonachs and Grey Corries peaks wind away to the east.

The **tourist path** makes a very useful descent route. On many days the way is obvious as plenty of other people pass back and forth. But the top of Ben Nevis is in the cloud more often than not and can be a distinctly inhospitable place with strong winds and snow possible on any day of the year. With the added problem of the summit sitting on a featureless plateau, with the North Face cliffs just a few metres from the trig point, it is important not to underestimate the mountain, no matter how much company there is at the top. The standard bearings to follow from the summit to gain the tourist path are as follows: 231° for 150m followed by a bearing of 282°.

The tourist path then **zigzags** its way down wide boulder fields before contouring to the north to reach the path junction above Lochan Meall an t-Suidhe. Continue down the wide trail above the **Red Burn** into Glen Nevis. There is a sign-posted junction at around 150m above sea level. Anyone staying at the youth hostel or campsite should take the steep left-hand branch. For the visitor centre, Ben Nevis Inn and the quickest way into Fort William continue straight ahead.

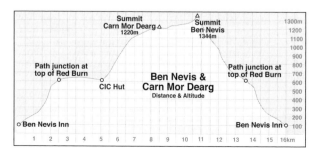

Ben Nevis observatory
At the summit of Ben Nevis are the remains of a Victorian observatory where meteorological data was collected continuously for 20 years. The figures reveal that, during that time, the average annual temperature was just 0.3°C, the mean annual rainfall was over four metres and the lowest recorded temperature was -17.4°C. The observatory was finally closed in October 1904 as maintenance costs grew too high but the rubble remains.

Alternative routes

The so-called tourist path is by far the most popular and easiest of routes to the top but is also the least interesting. It follows the descent route described on p109.

For the Carn Mor Dearg arête route an alternative starting point is next to the Ben Nevis distillery just north of Fort William; this avoids the congested tourist path. The path climbs steadily into Coire Leis to join the route described on p109.

❑ **Other hills in the area**
● Ben Starav (*'Ben Sta-raf'*, **1078m/3535ft**) An enormous hill dominating the head of Loch Etive. The ascent is not difficult but it involves a sea-level start so it is quite strenuous. The rewards are views across the western seaboard.
● Ring of Steall – Sgurr a' Mhaim (*'Skor-a-Vaym'*, **1099m/3605ft**) A very popular horseshoe ridge in the Mamores range taking in four munros, of which Sgurr a' Mhaim and its narrow 'Devil's Ridge' is the highest.

GLEN COE & GLEN NEVIS – TOWNS & VILLAGES

KINGSHOUSE   [OFF MAP 8, p92]
The white-washed *Kingshouse Hotel* (☎ 01855-851259, 🖳 www.kingy.com, 5S/ 8D/4T/5F), sitting alone on the western edge of bleak Rannoch Moor, has been a drovers' inn since the 17th century. The hotel's name stems from 1745 when George III stationed his troops here after the Battle of Culloden. Today it provides welcome shelter for walkers on the West Highland Way and for hillwalkers and climbers exploring the Glen Coe peaks. Accommodation is available from £27.50/pp with breakfast an extra £5-7. You can also **wild camp** at no charge on the flat ground over the bridge from the hotel. There are, however, no facilities, which can

prove problematic when nature calls in the morning. Ankle-high heather provides little privacy to a crouching camper.

The hotel has two bars, the public bar for squeaky-clean guests and the rather pokey Boots Bar for smelly walkers. The latter, with its flagstone floor, climbing pictures hanging from the walls, and large jar of dead midges, has more character than the former. Food is served in each bar and they usually have a couple of real ales on tap.

Citylink **buses** (see pp32-6) run through Glen Coe on the nearby A82 heading for Glasgow, Edinburgh, Fort William and Skye.

GLEN COE   [SEE MAP 9b, p96]

At the western end of Glen Coe is the **NTS Visitor Centre** (☎ 01855-811307/729, 💻 www.glencoe-nts.org.uk, end Mar-end Aug 9.30am-5.30pm daily; Sep-Oct 10am-5pm daily; Nov-mid Dec & Jan-Feb, 10am-4pm Thu-Sun; mid to end Dec & Mar 10am-4pm daily) which was rather sensibly transplanted from its previous position slap-bang in the middle of the glen. Back then it did little more than detract from the view of one of Scotland's most beautiful glens and certainly its most historic. Thankfully, the land has been restored and the new visitor centre is hidden behind a screen of trees. For £5 you can wander around the exhibition. There are displays on the wildlife, mountains and history of the area and an audio-visual insight into the infamous Glen Coe massacre (see box p112) of 1692 when Highland troops, by order of the crown, slew their MacDonald hosts in cold blood.

Next to the visitor centre is **Glen Coe Caravan Club Site** (☎ 01855-811397, Mar-Oct) which has tent pitches for £5.05-6.95/pp. It's a large site and you'll be sharing it with lots of shiny white caravans. A more aesthetic spot for camping is at the smaller **Red Squirrel Campsite** (☎ 01855-811256, 💻 www.redsquirrelcampsite .com, open all year) situated on farmland by the River Coe, on the Clachaig road. Pitches are £7/pp. Close by is **Glencoe Youth Hostel** (☎ 01855-811219, 💻 glencoe@syha.org.uk, 56 beds, £13-16.50) and almost next door are the more informal and cheaper **Glencoe Hostel and Bunkhouses** (☎ 01855-811906, 💻 www .glencoehostel.co.uk), comprising a hostel (£10-13/pp), bunkhouse (£9.50/pp), static caravans (£16-20/pp) and log cabin (£16/pp).

Further east along this road in an enviable position below the heady peaks of Glen Coe is the infamous **Clachaig Inn** (☎ 01855-811252, 💻 www.clachaig.com, 2S/7T/5D/5F) which has been providing hospitality for passing travellers for centuries. Unmuddied hillwalkers might like to sup a pint and dine in the convivial surroundings of the Bidean Lounge. The real fun, however, is in the more raucous Boots Bar, a cavernous drinking den with a big stove, a shelf sagging beneath 120 malt whiskies, real ales galore, live music at the weekends and a crush of exhausted hillwalkers and climbers recounting their epic days on the hill. Food is served from noon to 9pm daily (extensive menu including burgers from £8.95 and venison casserole for £11.95) while B&B accommodation is available from £39 to £42/pp. They also have **internet access** for £1 per 20 minutes.

GLENCOE VILLAGE   [SEE MAP 9b, p96]

The small **Spar general store** (daily 8am-8pm) has most essential groceries and is also the location of the only **cash machine** for miles.

For good-value meals try the **Carnoch Restaurant** (☎ 01855-811140, open daily 11am-4pm and 5-9pm) in the small bungalow in the centre of the village. The menu changes frequently but the food is tasty and wholesome and usually includes pasta dishes and a good old-meat-and-two-veg dish for around £8.

There are lots of B&Bs, the best of which is **Scorrybreac Guest House** (☎ 01855-811354, 💻 www.scorrybreac.co.uk, 3D/2T/1F) just outside the village over the bridge. B&B is from £25 to £30/pp. In the heart of the village is **Dunire Guest House** (☎ 01855-811305, 3D/2T en suite) with beds from £22 to £27/pp. For a similar price and on the same stretch of road are a number of other B&Bs and guest houses including **Grianan** (☎ 01855-811322, 1D/1F), **Tulachgorm** (☎ 01855-811391, 1D/1T) and **Morvern** (☎ 01855-811544, 1D/1T), all charging around £20-25/pp. On the main A82 road, opposite the village road junction, is the **Glencoe Hotel**. At the time of research the hotel had closed down. It is due to reopen in 2010 under new management (see 💻 www.crerarhotels.com/ourho tels/glencoe_hotel).

GLEN COE & GLEN NEVIS

Rainy days

● **Glen Nevis waterfalls** Waterfalls are always best when it's raining so head up Glen Nevis to the Lower Falls of Polldubh and then continue to the end of the road for the short stroll through a fantastic wooded gorge, jumbled full of water-carved rocks. Once in the upper glen a three-wire bridge leads across the river to the spectacular Steall Falls tumbling out of the high corrie above. Take care on the three-wire bridge; people have slipped into the swollen river and drowned.

● **Ice Factor** Perfect for outdoor folk who don't like the wet. Ice Factor (☎ 01855-831100; 💻 www.ice-factor.co.uk; Mon 9am-7pm, Tue-Thu 9am-10pm, Fri-Sun 9am-7pm), in Kinlochleven, is probably the most significant indoor climbing centre in the UK, housing both climbing and ice walls, as well as a climbing shop and a lecture theatre which holds regular talks by leading mountaineers and outdoor luminaries.

● **Treasures of the Earth** Small but interesting exhibition (☎ 01397-772283; 9.30am-7pm summer, 10am-5pm winter) of geological delights: crystals and gemstones galore. On the A830 in Corpach, just west of Fort William.

● **Ben Nevis distillery** Tours of the distillery (☎ 01397-702476; 💻 www.bennevis distillery.com; Jul-Aug Mon-Fri 9am-6pm, Sat 10am-4pm, Sun noon-4pm; Easter-Sept Sat only 10am-4pm; Sep-Jun Mon-Fri 9am-5pm), one of the oldest in Scotland, cost £2.

Glen Coe massacre

Long before it became associated with a red-headed clown promoting French fries to kids the name MacDonald was synonymous with Glen Coe, for this was the domain of the Clan MacDonald who, in 1692, were the victims of the famous Glen Coe Massacre. Following the failure of the Jacobite uprisings the newly installed king, William III, offered a pardon to the clan chiefs of the Highlands and ordered them to swear an oath of allegiance to the crown by 1 January 1692. The clan chief of the MacDonalds of Glen Coe, Alastair MacIain, failed to meet the deadline after leaving it till the last minute. The consequences were bloody.

The government decided to make an example of the MacDonalds and sent the following order to Captain Robert Campbell:

'You are hereby ordered to fall upon the rebels, the M'Donalds of Glencoe and putt all to the sword under seventy. You are to have special care that the old fox and his sons doe upon no account escape your hands …This is by the King's special command, for the good of the country, that these miscreants be cutt off root and branch.'

In February 1692 Captain Robert Campbell led 200 men to Glen Coe where they were welcomed by the MacDonalds and given food and shelter and invited to play cards. Despite this show of hospitality, in the early hours of 13 February 1692, the government troops woke silently and carried out their gruesome orders. Thirty-eight members of the clan were slain in cold blood either in their homes or as they fled into the hills.

To this day there remains a certain degree of animosity between the MacDonalds and Campbells. Just look at the tongue-in-cheek sign above the Clachaig Inn doorway: 'No Hawkers or Campbells'.

BALLACHULISH

This compact village, beside a now-disused slate quarry, is an excellent base for excursions on the Ballachulish horseshoe as well as the other Glen Coe peaks.

Services

Buses (see pp32-6) serving Glasgow, Edinburgh, Fort William and Skye leave from the bus stop by Chisholm's garage.

The **TIC** (☎ 01855-811866; summer daily 9am-6pm; winter Mon-Sat 9am-5pm, Sun 10am-5pm) is full of free information and also incorporates a gift shop and **tearoom**, selling filled rolls. There is also **internet** access here for £1 per hour.

Opposite the TIC is a hardware store with **camping supplies**, including fuel and stoves, while the small **supermarket** (daily, till 8pm), which incorporates a **post office**, is well stocked. Unfortunately, the Bank of Scotland next door does not have a cash machine; the nearest one is at the general store (see p111) in Glencoe village.

Where to stay

There is a good choice of accommodation in Ballachulish. *Strathassynt Guest House* (☎ 01855-811261, 🖳 www.strathassynt.com) by the TIC, is the most centrally located option and is particularly walker friendly. B&B is between £20 and £27 per person. Continuing up past the park from the supermarket is *Fern Villa* (☎ 01855-811393, 🖳 www.fernvilla.org.uk, 3D/2T en suite) offering tasty local food for residents

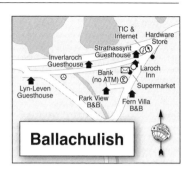

and beds from £20 to £27/pp. In the centre of the village near the river is *Park View B&B* (☎ 01855-811560, 🖳 www.glencoeparkview.co.uk, 1S/2D/1T) which has beds from £22.50 to £25/pp.

In the opposite direction, on the road leading west from The Laroch Inn, is *Inverlaroch Guest House* (☎ 01855-811726, 🖳 www.scotland2000.com/inverlaroch, 3F en suite) with beds from £25 to £28/pp and, at the end of this road, *Lyn-Leven Guest House* (☎ 01855-811392, 🖳 www.lynleven.co.uk, 1S/3D/2T/2F) where B&B is £29/pp.

Where to eat and drink

The only place for food is *The Laroch Inn* (☎ 01855-811900, food served 12.30-2.30pm and 5.30-9.30pm). Thankfully, it is a good pub with tasty food and friendly and efficient service. The restaurant is bright and modern with peach and orange walls.

GLEN NEVIS   [SEE MAP 13a, p107]

Glen Nevis with its patches of native deciduous woodland, rushing river and Highland cattle grazing in meadows of buttercups is quite simply entrancing. It does get very busy in summer but even the cars plying the single-track road and the shrieks of kids playing in the water cannot detract from such a delectable place. The climax of the glen is where it passes through a narrow defile at its upper reaches. The river violently squeezes through a short gorge of jumbled, shattered rocks under the trees. Beyond this point the glen opens out

below the Steall Falls. This part of the glen is happily undeveloped by tourist amenities, unlike the mouth of the glen which is where you will find beds, beer and food. You will also find the **Glen Nevis Visitor Centre** (☎ 01397-705922, 🖳 glen.nevis @highland.gov.uk, open all year 9am-5pm daily) which has some interesting displays on local history and wildlife and helpful staff.

A little further up the glen is the busy *Glen Nevis Youth Hostel* (☎ 01397-702336, 88 beds, £12-16) while *Ben Nevis*

Inn (☎ 01397-701227, 🖥 www.ben-nevis-inn.co.uk) is at Achintee Farm, at the end of Achintee Rd. This is a lovely pub, fashioned out of an old stone byre, with a cheap but crammed bunkhouse (£12.50-14/pp) sleeping 24 in a partitioned room. There is also a drying room and self-catering kitchen. If this is full try *Achintee Farm Guest House and Hostel* (☎ 01397-702240, 🖥 www.achinteefarm.com) between the inn and the river. The guest house has an en suite double or twin for £35/pp while the hostel has kitchen facilities and dormitory beds for £13/pp and twin rooms from £15/pp.

Campers will find *Glen Nevis Caravan and Camping Site* (☎ 01397-702191, 🖥 www.glen-nevis.co.uk, Mar-Oct) by the main glen road just before the youth hostel. It's hard to miss, filling up quite a large swathe of the lower glen with lots of caravans, but they have done quite well hiding them by planting some carefully positioned trees. The site includes a good **shop** for essential supplies and a **laundry**. Camping prices depend on the number of campers per tent but it works out at £4.40-6.50/pp.

FORT WILLIAM

It is a shame that those responsible for designing the Highland town of Fort William could not have drawn some inspiration from the magnificent natural surroundings which include Ben Nevis, Glen Nevis and the gulping depths of Loch Linnhe. There have been some moderately successful attempts to beautify this urban-sprawl-in-the-mountains, particularly along the High St and the Parade, but Fort William remains a place to stock up on mountain supplies, fill your stomach and maybe lay your head for a night before moving on.

Services

The **TIC** (☎ 0845-225 5121, Mon-Sat 9am-6pm, Sun 9.30am-5pm) is a well-organised affair with an accommodation-booking service and **internet** access. It is right in the centre of town, halfway down the High St.

The best place for **food** is *The Ben Nevis Inn* (see column opposite), cunningly situated right at the foot of the tourist path. Consequently, this old converted barn with its big log fire is often abuzz with exhausted-looking folk drinking celebratory pints and tucking in to the healthy portions from the menu: for example fresh Mallaig haddock for £8.90 and Ben Nevis burger for £7.60 – made from fresh ingredients. A good time to be here is on Thursday or Saturday night when there is usually a spot of live folk music.

Alternative places to eat include *Café Beag* and *Glen Nevis Restaurant* (☎ 01397-705459) both between the campsite and the youth hostel. The former is pleasant enough and serves light lunches of the baked potato and sandwich ilk, while the latter is a bit characterless. The menu consists of standard pub grub but at least much of it is from local sources.

If Stagecoach (see p35) doesn't continue the summer **bus** service Rapson's used to operate from Fort William along Glen Nevis call one of Fort William's **taxi companies**: Al's (☎ 01397-700700) and Linnhe Taxis (☎ 01397-700000).

The **supermarket** by the train station seems to have the monopoly on food shopping in town but there is another on the High St.

The **train** station, for services south to Glasgow and west to Mallaig, is reached via an underpass at the north end of the High St. There are **left-luggage** lockers at the station. The **bus** station is next door, just past the supermarket car park. Citylink coaches (see pp32-6) leave from here for Glen Shiel and Skye, Inverness, and on the A82 route south to Glasgow.

The High St is the place to go for **banks**, the **post office** and the **library**. Fort William is brimming with **outdoor equipment stores** including the omnipresent Nevisport at the north end of the High St, Blacks on the High St and, on Belford Rd, next to the station, Ellis Brigham.

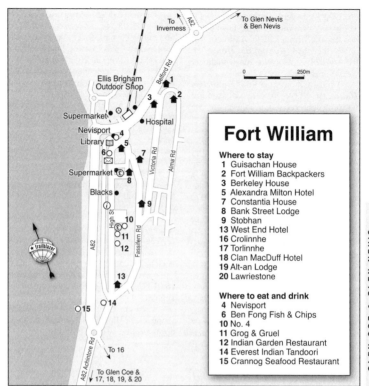

Fort William

Where to stay
1 Guisachan House
2 Fort William Backpackers
3 Berkeley House
5 Alexandra Milton Hotel
7 Constantia House
8 Bank Street Lodge
9 Stobhan
13 West End Hotel
16 Crolinnhe
17 Torlinnhe
18 Clan MacDuff Hotel
19 Alt-an Lodge
20 Lawriestone

Where to eat and drink
4 Nevisport
6 Ben Fong Fish & Chips
10 No. 4
11 Grog & Gruel
12 Indian Garden Restaurant
14 Everest Indian Tandoori
15 Crannog Seafood Restaurant

GLEN COE & GLEN NEVIS

Where to stay

Approaching Fort William from the south, Achintore Rd is lined with waterfront B&Bs and guesthouses and there are even more once you get into the town itself.

The best budget beds are at one of the bunkhouses: **Bank Street Lodge** (☎ 01397-700070, 🖳 www.bankstreetlodge.co.uk) has dormitory beds from £14 and a self-catering kitchen or en suite doubles, twins and family rooms from £16.25 to £22.50/pp; on Alma Rd **Fort William Backpackers** (☎ 01397-700711, 🖳 www.fortwilliamback packers.com) has dorm beds for £13.50/pp and twin rooms for £20/pp.

The aforementioned Achintore Rd is a bit of a walk but you will find plenty of

B&Bs here, including **Alt-an Lodge** (☎ 01397-704546, 🖳 www.bedandbreakfast fortwilliam.co.uk, 1S/1D/1T) from £23 to £27/pp (single room £30-40pp) and the old Victorian guesthouse of **Lawriestone** (☎ 01397-700777, 🖳 www.lawriestone.co.uk, 3D/1T) from £30 to £40/pp. Meanwhile, **Torlinnhe** (☎ 01397-702583, 🖳 www.tor linnhe.co.uk, 1S/2D/1T/2F) charges £25-33.50/pp. At the other end of town, heading towards Glen Nevis, on Belford Rd is **Berkeley House** (☎ 01397-701185, 🖳 ber keleyhouse67@hotmail.com, 2D/1T/1F en suite), a family-run B&B charging from £30 to £35/pp.

Another good place to try is Fassifern Rd, just off the High St. **Stobhan** (☎ 01397-

702790, ✉ boggi@supanet.com, 2D/1T/1F) is very convenient for the town centre and has B&B from £20/pp. A little further down the road **Constantia House** (☎ 01397-702893, ✉ www.constantiahouse.co.uk) offers beds from £20/pp.

Up the hill on Alma Rd is **Guisachan House** (☎ 01397-703797, ✉ www.fortwilliamholidays.co.uk), a large place with 17 en suite bedrooms, set in its own quiet grounds with views across the loch, a residents' bar and B&B from £26 to £31/pp.

For that little bit of extra comfort try **Crolinnhe** (☎ 01397-702709, ✉ www.crolinnhe.co.uk, 2D/1T) on Grange Rd; a beautiful Victorian guesthouse with a roaring open fire. B&B here is from £47.50 to £62.50/pp.

Also worth a look are **Clan MacDuff Hotel** (☎ 01397-702341, 🖷 01397-706174, ✉ www.clanmacduff.co.uk, 36 rooms) which has reasonably priced B&B from £24/pp and **West End Hotel** (☎ 01397-702614, ✉ www.westend-hotel.co.uk; 50 rooms) with similarly priced accommodation: both are on Achintore Rd.

Finally, in the centre of town on The Parade is the elegant **Alexandra Milton** (☎ 01397-702241, ✉ www.strathmorehotels.com/alex_site/, 93 rooms) where B&B is from £30/pp.

Where to eat and drink

The choice of eateries in Fort William is surprisingly good. Starting on the pier is **Crannog Seafood Restaurant** (☎ 01397-705589, ✉ www.oceanandoak.co.uk) with local langoustines and seafood platters as well as non-seafood dishes.

On the High St is **Grog and Gruel** (☎ 01397-705078, ✉ www.grogandgruel.co.uk) run by the same folk as those responsible for Glen Coe's Clachaig Inn (see p111). A wide range of real Highland ales and a good bar menu, including steak and ale pie for £7.45, make this a great place to wind down after a day in the hills.

At the top end of the High St is **Nevisport** (☎ 01397-704921, ✉ www.nevisport.co.uk), the outdoor store which incorporates a self-service restaurant upstairs and a cosy climbers' bar with burgers and chips downstairs.

At **No 4 Restaurant** (☎ 01397-704222, ✉ www.no4fortwilliam.com), on the High St, the menu boasts a range of local produce.

For a good curry try **Indian Garden Restaurant** (☎ 01397-705011, noon-2pm, & 5.30-11pm), which claims Hollywood stars among its clientele. The eat-all-you-want buffet costs £8.95. Alternatively, there is the **Everest Indian Tandoori Restaurant** (☎ 01397-700919). Both of these are on the High St.

There are also a couple of fish and chip shops on the High St including **Ben Fong**, down an alley, near the post office.

Call this climbing?

Climbing and walking are very different pursuits; a fact not lost on either of the two groups. So what is climbing a mountain? Climbers argue that climbing a mountain means hands and feet, climbing up rock, with ropes, karabiners and other jangly bits. Walkers also use the word climb to describe the act of walking up a mountain, much to the chagrin of the climbing fraternity who don't want the phrase belittled by lowly walkers with their trekking poles and gaiters. Unfortunately for climbers, the truth is that the dictionary definition suggests that climbing involves the use of hands and feet, or only feet.

The Central Highlands

The mountains may not be as dramatic as in other areas but the sense of isolation on the mountains of the Central Highlands can be great. The vast tract of land that centres around the Ben Alder Forest contains some very remote and beautiful mountains but you have to work to get there.

If long walks-in are not your thing there are some easily reached roadside hills to enjoy too. Wherever you walk in the Central Highlands one thing the mountains have in common is a wide-ranging view stretching almost from coast to coast.

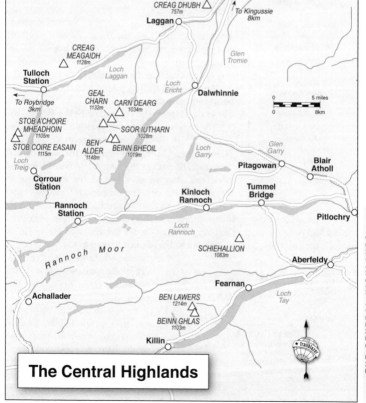

The Central Highlands

BEINN GHLAS (1103m/3620ft)   [MAP 14]
BEN LAWERS (1214m/3985ft)

Overview

An easy ascent of the biggest grassy hill in the region with views stretching across the southern and central Highlands. Be prepared to share the hill with others as this is something of a honey-pot. A minor road leading to the NTS visitor centre means nearly half the ascent can be negotiated on four wheels at 40mph. It is the final half of the ascent on two legs at two mph, however, that proves to be the more enjoyable stretch.

BEINN GHLAS
(Grey Mountain)
BEN LAWERS
(Hoofed Mountain)
Technical grade
▲
Navigation grade
▲
Terrain grade
▲
Strenuousness
▲▲
Return time
2-3hrs
Return distance
6miles/10km
Total ascent
2920ft/890m
OS maps
Landranger 51,
Explorer 378
Gateways
Killin (see p138)

Route

It is hard to go wrong on this hill. Simply park at the **visitor centre** and follow the path through a **couple of gates** and climb up the west bank and then the east bank of the burn. The area you are walking through is a National Nature Reserve, notable for its mountain flora. These fenced-off lower slopes have been replanted with birch, a fast-growing native tree which is gradually transforming the approach to the mountain.

Pass through the top gate to leave the fenced-off area and take the right-hand fork in the path to climb the ridge to the summit of **Beinn Ghlas**.

The mighty pyramidal peak of Ben Lawers looms ahead. Drop down the easy NE ridge of Beinn Ghlas to a **col** marked by some small lochans. The path to the summit of **Ben Lawers** is wide and obvious as it begins the initially steep ascent from the col. The path and ridge wing round to the ENE and soon reach the **summit cairn** perched above the steep southern slopes of the mountain. To descend, return to the col and once there take the path WSW below the north side of Beinn Ghlas to reach the col below Meall Corranaich. This avoids having to re-ascend Beinn Ghlas and also adds a bit of variety to the walk with fine views north to Glen Lyon and the Cairn Gorm massif.

A path descends from the col into Coire Odhar. Follow this south until it joins the ascent path, just above the gate, and follow that back to the car park.

THE CENTRAL HIGHLANDS

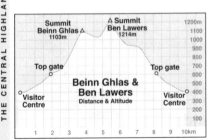

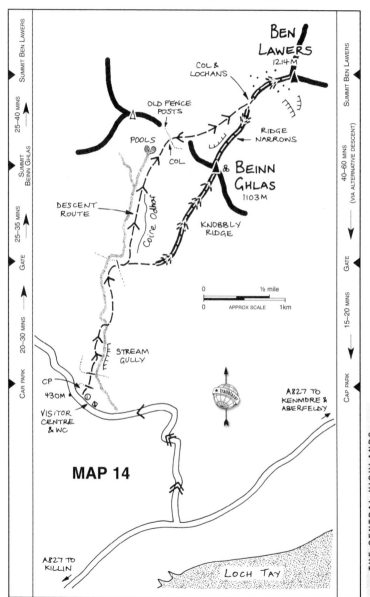

Alternative routes
During the long summer days it is well-worth making the most of the light by continuing north from the summit of Ben Lawers for the long traverse of the neighbouring peaks – the munros of An Stuc, Meall Garbh and Meall Greigh. The going is easy but the distance is great and after dropping off the final hill you will find yourself on the main road a long way from the car. Hitching or walking along the road is the only way back and remember you will have to climb back up the lane to the car park at 400 odd metres.

SCHIEHALLION ('*Shee-hal-y-en*', 1083m/3555ft)   [MAP 15]

Overview
Queen Victoria was a fan of the Scottish hills, although she was never spotted with boots or a rucksack, preferring to admire them from a distance. Schiehallion was one of her favourites and remains a hugely popular peak thanks to its striking appearance, towering above the rather dumpy hills around it. The hill also has a place in scientific history. In 1774 experiments were conducted on Schiehallion to determine the mass of the earth. More importantly, for hillwalkers, this is where the idea of mapping terrain with contour lines was first envisaged. Despite a lot of these lines appearing on maps of Schiehallion, the ascent is quick and easy.

**SCHIEHALLION
(Fairy Hill of the
Caledonians)**

Technical grade
▲
Navigation grade
▲
Terrain grade
▲
Strenuousness
▲
Return time
2½-3½hrs
Return distance
5½miles/9km
Total ascent
2495ft/760m
OS maps
Landranger 42,
Explorer 386
Gateways
Pitlochry (see p169)

Route
Schiehallion is about half an hour's drive west from Pitlochry. The path to the summit, constructed by the John Muir Trust (see p45) who own much of Schiehallion, begins at the Braes of Foss **car park**, on Schiehallion Road, a minor road leading from the B846 Tummel Bridge to Aberfeldy road.

From the car park the easy-to-follow path crosses a **footbridge** and then the moorland at the foot of the mountain. After ten minutes there is an old **stone-walled sheep pen** marking the point where the gradient steepens sharply. The path, however, makes the initial climb very straightforward.

There is some argument as to the wisdom of constructing such obvious, flag-stoned paths up mountains. The thinking behind them, of course, is to combat erosion on popular hills. Schiehallion is certainly a popular hill, as is obvious from the car park on summer weekends when vehicles overflow onto the road verges, but many argue that such a 'motorway' of a path gives the false impression that the hill is an easy one. This might explain the glut of badly decked-out tourists shivering at the top in summer.

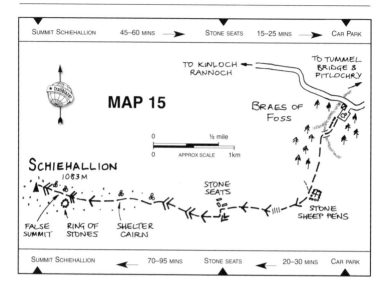

SUMMIT SCHIEHALLION 45–60 MINS ⟶ STONE SEATS 15–25 MINS ⟶ CAR PARK

TO KINLOCH ← RANNOCH

TO TUMMEL BRIDGE & PITLOCHRY

MAP 15

BRAES OF FOSS

trailblazer

0 ½ mile
0 APPROX SCALE 1km

SCHIEHALLION
1083M

STONE SEATS

STONE SHEEP PENS

FALSE SUMMIT | RING OF STONES | SHELTER CAIRN

SUMMIT SCHIEHALLION ← 70–95 MINS STONE SEATS ← 20–30 MINS CAR PARK

Continue upwards past some **stone seats** and begin the climb of the lower end of Schiehallion's long ridge. There are a couple of steep sections and with increasing altitude the terrain changes from heather to shattered rock making the going more awkward. After a couple of **false summits** the **true summit** is finally reached, marked by rocky outcrops.

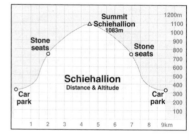

Being in such a central location the views are wide-ranging, taking in the central Highlands, Ben Vrackie, directly east, Glen Coe to the west and the Carn Mairg group to the south. The only sensible way to return to the car park is by following the same path back down the mountain.

Alternative routes
The route described is the only logical route to the summit.

❏ **Important note – walking times**
All times in this book refer only to the time spent walking. You will need to add 20-30% to allow for rests, photography, checking the map, drinking water etc.

THE CENTRAL HIGHLANDS

SGOR IUTHARN ('*Skor Yew-harn*', 1028m/3373ft)
GEAL CHARN ('*Gyal Harn*', 1132m/3714ft)
CARN DEARG ('*Carn Jyerrack*', 1034m/3392ft)
[MAP 16a; MAP 16b, p124; MAP 16c, p125]

Overview
This trio of high peaks, all above 1000m, provides a stunning outing in remote country. This is a walk of contrasts starting with the highlight of the day, Sgor Iutharn's east ridge. This short, knife-edged arête known as the Lancet Edge offers wonderful views across the raised bog below.

The walk continues over the high sub-arctic plateau of Geal Charn and culminates on the broad rocky spine of Carn Dearg.

Route
The most straightforward access is from Dalwhinnie on the main A9 road where there is a bus stop and train station. Many walkers wisely cover the initial nine miles of forest track to Culra by bike. It is also worth considering an overnight stop at Culra (in a tent or the bothy) and schedule in an extra day for the ascent of Ben Alder (see p127) across the glen.

From Dalwhinnie train station (Map 16a) cross the level crossing and follow the forest track, along the west shore of Loch Ericht, for five miles to **Ben Alder Lodge** (Map 16b). Turn right at the grand gateway to the lodge and follow the track uphill onto the open moorland. The track bears west towards Loch Pattack, a kettle-hole lake formed by a remnant block of glacial ice at the dying end of the last Ice Age. Take the path that leaves the track by a **lock-up store** and follow it towards Culra. The path crosses a large raised bog that, in summer, is coloured by an array of flowering plants: bog cotton, creeping buttercup and bog asphodel. Look out too for red deer. Just before Culra (Map 16c) a side path leads to a precarious **suspension bridge** across the river. Continue along the west bank of the river, past **Culra**, and towards the Lancet Edge which looms ahead.

Leave the riverside path where the stream that flows from Loch an Sgoir joins the main river. Climb the shallow slopes of heather and aim for the far (northern) side of the rocky bluff guarding the lower slopes of Sgor Iutharn. This is where the steep climb begins. Head directly up the grassy slopes to reach a short cliff. A faint

SGOR IUTHARN (Hell's Peak)
GEAL CHARN (White Hill or Cairn)
CARN DEARG (Red Hill or Cairn)
Technical grade ▲▲▲
Navigation grade ▲▲▲
Terrain grade ▲▲▲
Strenuousness ▲▲
Return time 3¹/₂-5hrs from Culra (Dalwhinnie to Culra 3-3¹/₂hrs)
Return distance 7miles/12km from Culra (Dalwhinnie to Culra 9miles/15km)
Total ascent 3018ft/920m from Culra (Dalwhinnie to Culra 328ft/100m)
OS maps Landranger 42, Explorer 393
Gateways Dalwhinnie (see p140)

THE CENTRAL HIGHLANDS

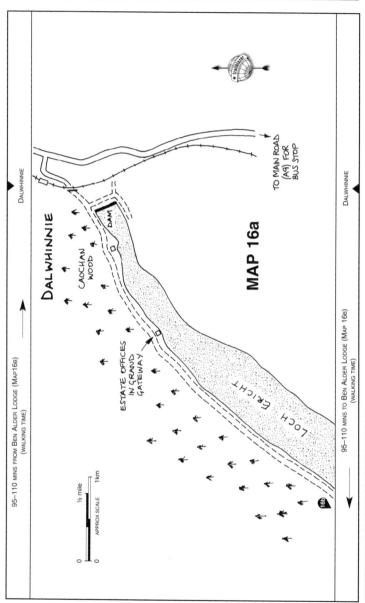

95–110 MINS FROM BEN ALDER LODGE (MAP16B) (WALKING TIME)

95–110 MINS TO BEN ALDER LODGE (MAP 16B) (WALKING TIME)

DALWHINNIE

DALWHINNIE

DALWHINNIE

MAP 16a

TO MAIN ROAD (A9) FOR BUS STOP

CAOCHAN WOOD

DAM

ESTATE OFFICES IN GRAND GATEWAY

LOCH ERICHT

16B

½ mile   1km
APPROX SCALE
0   0

THE CENTRAL HIGHLANDS

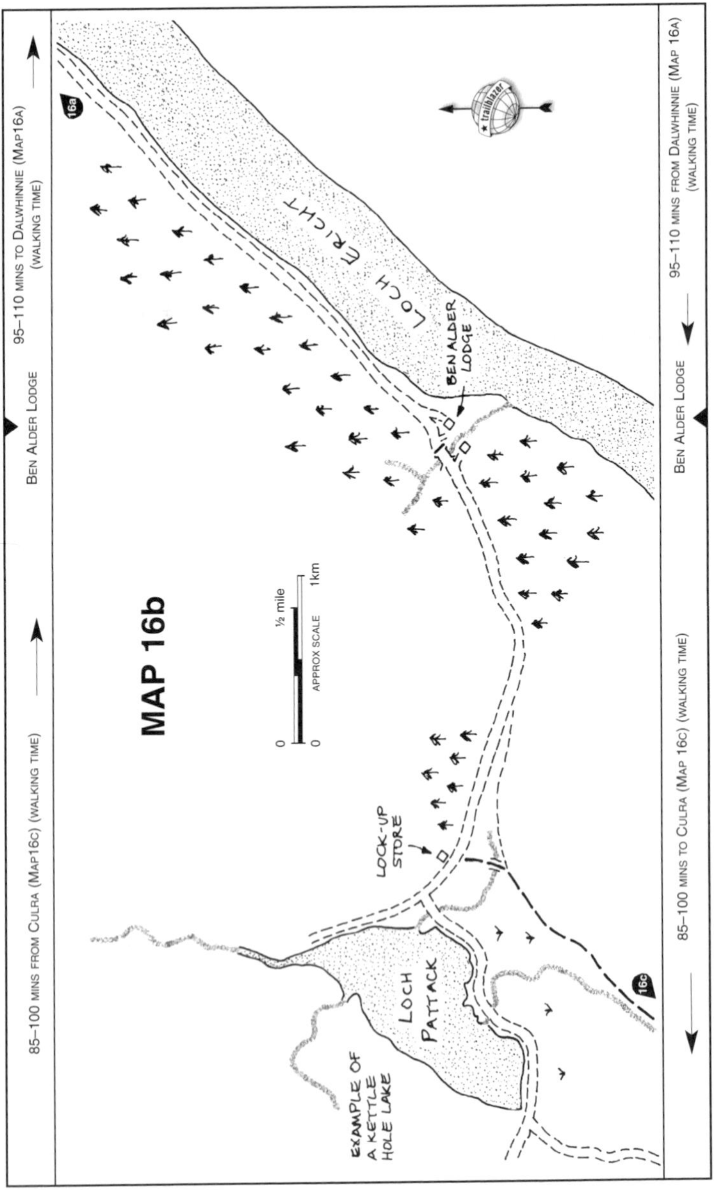

MAP 16b

95–110 MINS TO DALWHINNIE (MAP16A) (WALKING TIME)

BEN ALDER LODGE

85–100 MINS FROM CULRA (MAP16C) (WALKING TIME)

95–110 MINS FROM DALWHINNIE (MAP 16A) (WALKING TIME)

BEN ALDER LODGE

85–100 MINS TO CULRA (MAP 16C) (WALKING TIME)

LOCH ERICHT

BEN ALDER LODGE

½ mile
1km
APPROX SCALE
0
0

LOCK-UP STORE

LOCH PATTACK

EXAMPLE OF A KETTLE HOLE LAKE

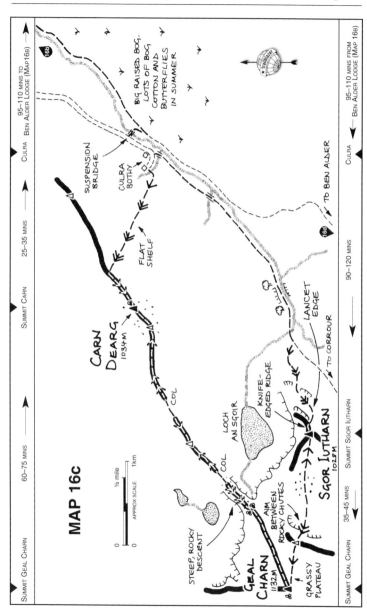

MAP 16c

½ mile

0   1km

APPROX SCALE

SUMMIT GEAL CHARN

60–75 MINS

SUMMIT CARN

25–35 MINS

CULRA   BEN ALDER LODGE (MAP 16b)

95–110 MINS TO

16b

BIG RAISED BOG,
LOTS OF BOG
COTTON AND
BUTTERFLIES
IN SUMMER

SUSPENSION
BRIDGE

CULRA
BOTHY

FLAT
SHELF

CARN
DEARG
1034+M

COL

LOCH
AN SGOIR

KNIFE-
EDGED RIDGE

STEEP, ROCKY DESCENT

COL

GEAL
CHARN
1132M

GRASSY
PLATEAU

AIM
BETWEEN
ROCKY CHUTES

SGOR IUTHARN
1011M

LANCET
EDGE

TO BEN ALDER

TO CORROUR

16a

90–120 MINS

CULRA   BEN ALDER LODGE (MAP 16b)

95–110 MINS FROM

SUMMIT GEAL CHARN

35–45 MINS

SUMMIT SGOR IUTHARN

90–120 MINS

SUMMIT SGOR IUTHARN

SUMMIT CARN

60–75 MINS

THE CENTRAL HIGHLANDS

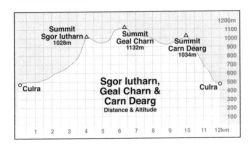

path appears below this rocky interruption and bears left to climb sharply but easily on to the narrow crest of the **Lancet Edge**.

The scrambling is easy but there is a real sense of exposure with each side of the mountain dropping away suddenly.

Once at the summit of **Sgor Iutharn** continue west along much broader slopes scattered with boulders to a wide saddle below the summit slopes of Geal Charn. The best route to the summit is to head WNW and climb the slopes to the left of a small cliff. From the top of the slope continue in the same direction across a high **plateau** of neat grass that could almost pass as a bowling green or cricket pitch. In misty conditions be sure to take a compass bearing to the summit of **Geal Charn** where there is a cairn. In clear weather the views stretch to Buachaille Etive Mor in Glen Coe to the south-west, the Grey Corries and Ben Nevis to the west, and Schiehallion to the south. Directly north is the massive hulk of Creag Meagaidh, its impressive corrie sadly hidden from view.

Leave the summit in an ENE direction and cross the plateau. After just over half a mile (1km) a precipitous cliff appears on the left. The descent path to the col below is further to the right, indicated by a pair of small cairns. Despite initial appearances the path that picks its way steeply down to the col is quite straightforward although it is often covered by a cornice well into April and May. On each side of this descending ridge are deep corries filled by lonely lochans and backed by sheer cliffs; textbook examples of glacial mountain architecture.

The going becomes easier from the col passing over a long hump before climbing again over easy grassy slopes to the boulder field that marks the final pull to the summit ridge. The rocky tor at the SW end of this short ridge should not be mistaken for the summit of **Carn Dearg** which lies at the NE end and is marked by a shelter cairn.

The return begins by following the summit ridge to the NE and then dropping first down a fairly steep slope to a heathery shelf and then down through the heather to Culra. From Culra take the forest track back to Dalwhinnie.

Alternative routes
The route described is the most logical. If time does not allow for the ascent of Carn Dearg, descend from the col above Loch an Sgoir.

❏ **Important note – walking times**
All times in this book refer only to the time spent walking. You will need to add 20-30% to allow for rests, photography, checking the map, drinking water etc.

BEN ALDER (1148m/3765ft)
BEINN BHEOIL (*'Bayn Vy-owl'*, 1019m/3345ft)
[MAP 16a, p123; MAP 16b, p124; MAP 16c, p125; MAP 16d, p128]

Overview
Bulky Ben Alder with its sweeping ridges is the jewel of the central Highlands but getting there involves some effort as it lies ten miles from any road. Neighbouring Beinn Bheoil acts as the perfect viewpoint from which to admire the cliffs and corries.

Route
For the route description from Dalwhinnie to Culra see p122. Keep on the east side of the river on the way past **Culra** and follow the stalkers' path into the wide corrie ahead (Map 16c).

After half an hour leave the path, **cross the river** (Map 16d), and head straight for the **Long Leachas ridge** ahead (the neighbouring and more difficult Short Leachas ridge to the south is another option). The ridge leads directly to the summit plateau and involves, in places, some tricky scrambling. Once on the plateau head south to the summit of **Ben Alder**. On a good day it is possible to see all the way down the spine of the Grey Corries to Ben Nevis and beyond.

The walk continues south around the rim of the eastern corries before swinging round to the east and a subsidiary top. Beyond this the mountain falls away sharply.

Descend carefully to the **saddle** below. An easy and broad ridge leads at first E and then NE to an outlying top that marks the beginning of Beinn Bheoil's long spine. If anything the views from **Beinn Bheoil's summit**, taking in the length of Loch Ericht and Ben Alder's striking corries, are even greater than those of its bigger neighbour.

The descent from here is easy. Continue north along the ridge for five to ten minutes to a col.

Drop west down the steep slope to the **outflow of the loch** below and follow the stalkers' path back to Culra.

**BEN ALDER
(Rock-water
Mountain)**

**BEINN BHEOIL
(Mouth Mountain)**

Technical grade
▲▲▲
Navigation grade
▲▲▲
Terrain grade
▲▲▲
Strenuousness
▲▲▲
Return time
4-5 hrs from Culra
(Dalwhinnie to Culra
3-3¹/₂hrs)
Return distance
7¹/₂miles/12km from
Culra (Dalwhinnie to
Culra 9miles/15km)
Total ascent
3020ft/920m from
Culra (Dalwhinnie to
Culra 328ft/100m)
OS maps
Landranger 42,
Explorer 393
Gateways
Dalwhinnie (see p140)

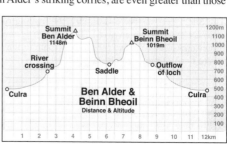

Ben Alder &
Beinn Bheoil
Distance & Altitude

THE CENTRAL HIGHLANDS

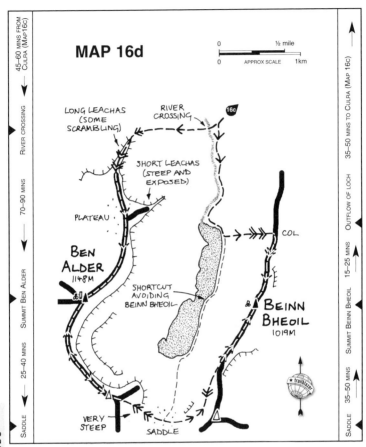

MAP 16d

0 ———— ½ mile

0 ———— APPROX SCALE ———— 1km

45–60 MINS FROM CULRA (MAP16c)

RIVER CROSSING

70–90 MINS

SUMMIT BEN ALDER

25–40 MINS

SADDLE

LONG LEACHAS (SOME SCRAMBLING)

RIVER CROSSING

16c

SHORT LEACHAS (STEEP AND EXPOSED)

PLATEAU

BEN ALDER 1148M

SHORTCUT AVOIDING BEINN BHEOIL

COL

BEINN BHEOIL 1019M

VERY STEEP

SADDLE

35–50 MINS TO CULRA (MAP 16c)

OUTFLOW OF LOCH

15–25 MINS

SUMMIT BEINN BHEOIL

35–50 MINS

SADDLE

Alternative routes

The Short Leachas ridge is a more challenging route to the summit with more exposed scrambling involved. To avoid any scrambling ignore both Leachas ridges and follow instead the stalkers' path to the saddle beyond the loch, from where both summits can be tackled.

> ❏ **Important note – walking times**
> All times in this book refer only to the time spent walking. You will need to add 20-30% to allow for rests, photography, checking the map, drinking water etc.

THE CENTRAL HIGHLANDS

CREAG DHUBH (*'Crayk <u>Doo</u>'*, 757m/2485ft)   [MAP 17]

Overview

A relatively low but shapely peak standing in isolation at the head of mighty Strath Spey. The ascent is not difficult and, from an early point, views of the Cairngorms, Monadhliath and Creag Meagaidh open up.

Route

The walk begins halfway between Laggan and Newtonmore at the **lay-bys** opposite a small lochan on the A86. Once over the stile turn right and climb gradually through the birch forest to a steep slope of boulders. To avoid the cliff above head north and follow the fence that marks the edge of a conifer plantation. The ground here is very steep and leads into a **heathery bowl**. Continue to the back of this bowl and climb even steeper ground to the lip of this small corrie. There is no path and the heather in places is quite deep.

At the lip of the corrie climb over the **stile** and join the clear path that leads up the lower rocky slopes of the ridge to the NE. Navigation should not be a problem here. The path is clear and the ridge well-defined. Continue over another fence to a **false summit**, marked by a cairn. A short, sharp drop is followed by a further short climb to the **true sum-**

CREAG DHUBH (Black Rock)
Technical grade
▲▲
Navigation grade
▲
Terrain grade
▲▲
Strenuousness
▲
Return time
2-3hrs
Return distance
3miles/5km
Total ascent
1640ft/500m
OS maps
Landranger 35, Explorer 402
Gateways
Laggan (see p140)

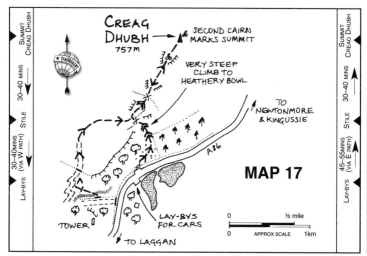

mit marked by a second cairn. The huge mass of Creag Meagaidh dominates the view to the west while Strath Spey stretches away to the north-east.

Descend back down the ridge to the stile at the lip of the corrie. To vary the descent a little continue west across the moorland to join a four-wheel drive track that drops down into a shallow glen. Leave the track before crossing the stream and return through the birch woodland to the road where it is five minutes back to the start point.

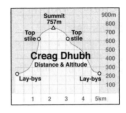

Alternative routes

To avoid the extremely steep slopes of heather at the start of this walk use the above descent route for the ascent as well.

CREAG MEAGAIDH ('*Crayk May-gee*', 1128m/3700ft) [MAP 18]

Overview

The great cliffs of Coire Ardair that eat into this massive plateaued giant of a mountain are the main feature of Creag Meagaidh. Formed by thousands of years of erosion by the glacier that once filled the corrie, the resulting 400m craggy face offers plenty of gullies and chimneys for Himalayan mountaineers to practise on. There are a number of easier routes to the summit, however, for plucky hillwalkers.

Route

Creag Meagaidh is a National Nature Reserve managed by Scottish Natural Heritage, who are doing an excellent job in encouraging the natural regeneration of the native montane birch woodland in the lower reaches of Coire Ardair.

Start at the nature reserve **car park** on the A86, halfway between Tulloch and Laggan, and follow the path, past the **SNH buildings**. The path begins to climb up and into the mouth of Coire Ardair and through the **native birch forest**. The gradient soon eases as the path swings round into the corrie where the massive cliffs slowly come into view. Follow the path to the **lochan** at the foot of the cliffs (where there is a mountain rescue kit at GR436879, which you will hopefully not need) and begin the climb towards the obvious narrow col on the skyline known as **'The Window'**. The going gets trickier here with lots of jumbled boulders. At The Window head south up the rocky slope that faces you. This is the steepest part of the day's walk and climbs

CREAG MEAGAIDH (Rock of the Boggy Place)

Technical grade
▲▲▲
Navigation grade
▲▲▲▲
Terrain grade
▲▲▲
Strenuousness
▲▲▲
Return time
4¹/₂-6¹/₂hrs
Return distance
10miles/16km
Total ascent
3133ft/955m
OS maps
Landranger 42,
Explorer 401
Gateways
Tulloch (see p141)
Laggan (see p140)

THE CENTRAL HIGHLANDS

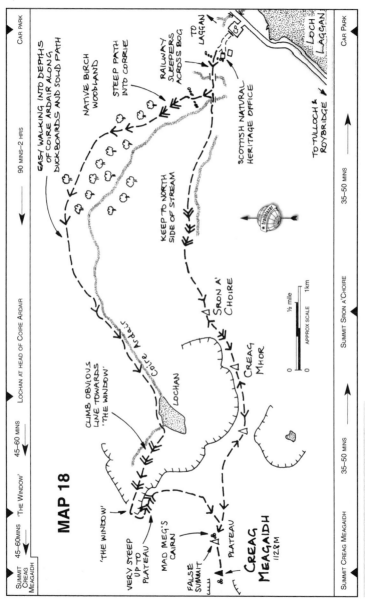

MAP 18

SUMMIT CREAG MEAGAIDH — 'THE WINDOW' 45-60MINS — 'THE WINDOW' 45-60 MINS — LOCHAN AT HEAD OF COIRE ARDAIR 45-60 MINS — 90 MINS-2 HRS — CAR PARK

EASY WALKING INTO DEPTHS OF COIRE ARDAIR ALONG DUCKBOARDS AND SOLID PATH

NATIVE BIRCH WOODLAND

STEEP PATH INTO CORRIE

RAILWAY SLEEPERS ACROSS BOG

TO LAGGAN

LOCH LAGGAN

SCOTTISH NATURAL HERITAGE OFFICE

TO TULLOCH & ROYBRIDGE

CAR PARK

KEEP TO NORTH SIDE OF STREAM

CLIMB OBVIOUS LINE TOWARDS 'THE WINDOW'

COIRE ARDAIR

LOCHAN

SRON A' CHOIRE

CREAG MHOR

APPROX SCALE
0 — ½ mile
0 — 1km

'THE WINDOW'

VERY STEEP UP TO PLATEAU

MAD MEG'S CAIRN

FALSE SUMMIT

PLATEAU

CREAG MEAGAIDH 1128M

SUMMIT CREAG MEAGAIDH — 35-50 MINS — 35-50 MINS — SUMMIT SRON A'CHOIRE — 35-50 MINS — CAR PARK

relentlessly for about 150m to the plateau of Creag Meagaidh. Continue south for about 500m before turning to the west for the walk to the summit. Look out for **Mad Meg's Cairn**, a huge pile of rocks that has led many an innocent munro-bagger to sit down with their thermos and sandwiches, wrongly assuming they have reached the summit. The true summit of **Creag Meagaidh** is about 500m further west.

For the descent, return E for just over half a mile (1km) and then follow a bearing ESE for about the same distance. In mist you will need a compass and know how to use it. This is a featureless plateau on which even competent hillwalkers and climbers have become hopelessly lost and found themselves in danger of stepping over the cliffs that mark the edge of the plateau.

As you approach a slightly narrower section of the plateau head E, then NE to the top of **Sron a' Choire**. Continue east and descend via the shallow corrie, keeping to the left of the burn. The knee-crunching descent eventually leads to a bridge over the Allt Coire Ardair and back past the SNH buildings to the car park.

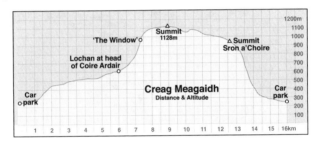

Alternative routes

The route above can be reversed but this means you will be walking away from, rather than towards, the Coire Ardair cliffs on the way out. Unless you are adept at walking backwards you would have less time to appreciate the view. There are a number of other less-frequented ascent routes on Creag Meagaidh's southern ridges but these miss out Coire Ardair altogether, which is undoubtedly the main reason for exploring the mountain. A very long outing continues on from 'The Window' to the north and east taking in the munros of Stob Poite Coire Ardair and Carn Liath.

STOB COIRE EASAIN (*'Stop Corr-a Ay-sen'*, 1115m/3660ft)
STOB A' CHOIRE MHEADHOIN (*'Stop a Horr-a Viyan'*, 1105m/3625ft)
[MAP 19a, p134; MAP 19b, p135]

Overview

These attractive twin peaks overlooking the dark depths of Loch Treig may be a little hard to reach but once there they provide a straightforward and enjoyable walk. The views of the Mamores and Grey Corries, with Ben Nevis looming in the distance, are stunning. To the north and east are the huge masses of Creag

Meagaidh and Ben Alder while the Glen Coe peaks can also be picked out to the south. There are no major difficulties to be found on this route except for one short, sharp descent from Stob Coire Easain.

Route

Those coming by public transport are best off catching a train to Corrour (see p141 and Map 19a). From the station it is a 7^1/$_2$-mile (12km) walk (3^1/$_2$-4^1/$_2$hrs) to Lairig Leacach. First cross the tracks to gain the path on the west side of the railway line, then follow this quagmire of a trail in a roughly north-westerly direction keeping the tracks to the right. The going can be a bit slow since it is necessary to negotiate a route through the peaty bog. In places railway sleepers and old fence posts have been laid down to ease the way but some of them float rather than provide a solid footing. Tread with care!

Conditions improve once the trail passes a large **railway bridge**. Keep on the same side of the train lines and follow the jeep track as it descends to the shores of **Loch Treig**. Follow the track around the southern shore of Loch Treig, over a couple of streams and cross the high bridge over the Abhainn Rath. On the other side is Creaguaineach Lodge, a private house with 'Beware of the Dogs' signs. Beware of them by following the path to the left of the stand of pine trees and continue across the peat hags to some sheep pens and enclosures.

Once through the **sheep pens** (Map 19b) a trail leads through a short and pretty gorge and along the southern bank of the Allt na Lairige. The path climbs slowly but steadily up the glen to the watershed of Lairig Leacach where there is a small hut. From **Lairig Leacach** ford the river onto the east side of the glen (easier to do at a point north of where the Allt a' Chuil Choirean joins the main river) and follow the stalkers' path south for about ten minutes. When the steep heathery slopes on the left begin to ease, leave the path and ascend at an angle on a bearing of roughly 100°. There are no trails to follow so it becomes a bit of a trudge as the heather snaps at your ankles.

Cross the wide but shallow dip in the hillside where a series of streams thread their way through heather and grassy bog. On the other side of this dip is a sheep trail climbing steeply up onto slopes that lead to the field of scree above. Follow this trail and then head directly up the slopes to a point just

---

**STOB COIRE EASAIN
(Peak of the Little Waterfall Corrie)**

**STOB A' CHOIRE MHEADHOIN
(Peak of the Middle Corrie)**

**Technical grade
▲▲**

**Navigation grade
▲▲**

**Terrain grade
▲▲▲**

**Strenuousness
▲▲**

Return time
3-5hrs from Lairig Leacach
6^1/$_2$-9^1/$_2$ hrs from Corrour

Return distance
5^1/$_2$miles/9km from Lairig Leacach
13 miles/21km from Corrour

Total ascent
3104ft/936m from Lairig Leacach
3857ft/1176m from Corrour

OS maps
Landranger 41, Explorer 392

Gateways
Corrour (see p141)
Tulloch (see p141)

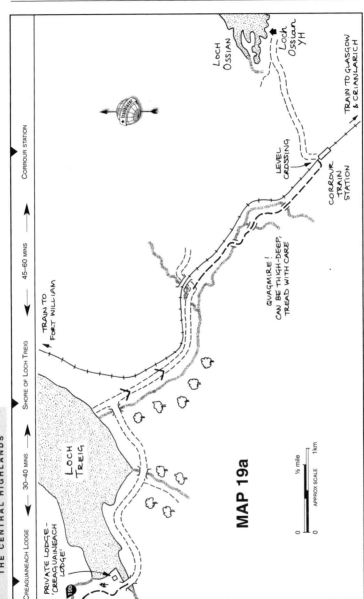

THE CENTRAL HIGHLANDS

CREAGUAINEACH LODGE ◀ 30–40 MINS ▶ SHORE OF LOCH TREIG ◀ 45–60 MINS ▶ CORROUR STATION

LOCH OSSIAN

Loch Ossian YH

TRAIN TO GLASGOW & CRIANLARICH

LEVEL CROSSING

CORROUR TRAIN STATION

QUAGMIRE! CAN BE THIGH-DEEP, TREAD WITH CARE

TRAIN TO FORT WILLIAM

LOCH TREIG

PRIVATE LODGE – 'CREAGUAINEACH LODGE'

19b

MAP 19a

½ mile

0 — APPROX SCALE — 1km

0

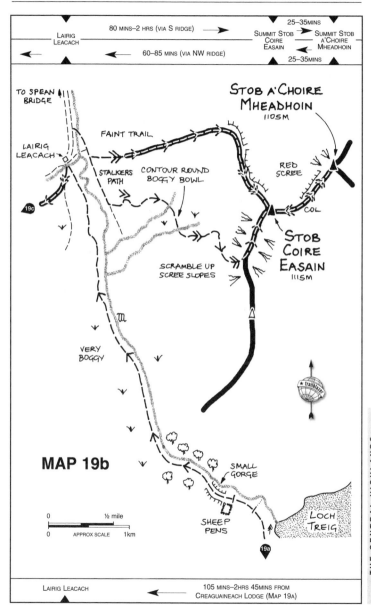

LAIRIG LEACACH — 80 MINS–2 HRS (VIA S RIDGE) → — 25–35MINS → SUMMIT STOB COIRE EASAIN — SUMMIT STOB a'CHOIRE MHEADHOIN

← ← 60–85 MINS (VIA NW RIDGE) — 25–35MINS

TO SPEAN BRIDGE

LAIRIG LEACACH →

19c

FAINT TRAIL

STALKERS PATH

CONTOUR ROUND BOGGY BOWL

SCRAMBLE UP SCREE SLOPES

STOB a'CHOIRE MHEADHOIN 1105M

RED SCREE

COL

STOB COIRE EASAIN 1115M

VERY BOGGY

MAP 19b

trailblazer

SMALL GORGE

0 ½ mile
0 APPROX SCALE 1km

SHEEP PENS

19a

LOCH TREIG

LAIRIG LEACACH ← 105 MINS–2HRS 45MINS FROM CREAGUAINEACH LODGE (MAP 19A)

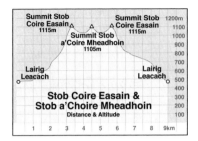

below the scree.

The most direct route from here is to climb the frighteningly steep north-west ridge but it is a good idea to contour south below the fans of scree and then climb the 100m or so that remain to gain the south-west ridge. This is an attractive ridge and well worth the small detour. Follow it as it climbs gently to the cairned summit of **Stob Coire Easain**.

From the summit take time to admire the steep gully and cliffs that drop into the deep northern corrie of the mountain along with the bands of red scree on the other side of this gulf. A path drops steeply away to the east to reach the **col** between the two peaks and then it is a case of heading north-east up a broad ridge to the summit of **Stob a' Choire Mheadhoin** which boasts a relatively large acreage of rocky summit plateau. In contrast now, the more shapely point of Stob Coire Easain stands out in pyramid form across the corrie. On a good day the huge massif of Creag Meagaidh dominates the view to the north-east with the equally imposing Ben Alder holding firm to the east.

To return to Lairig Leacach climb back to the summit of the first peak and descend by way of a path that drops suddenly and steeply off the north-west ridge over some loose scree. To find the path take a bearing of 310° from the summit cairn. At the bottom of the scree the ridge shallows and broadens significantly. Continue on the same bearing for about 350m. There is one short steep section where a path eases between rocky slabs before bearing directly west and following the broad hummocky ridge back to the point of ascent and the Lairig Leacach.

Alternative routes

To return to Lairig Leacach without reascending Stob Coire Easain it is possible to pick a less than obvious route through the bowl of the corrie, over scree and shelves of rock to gain the lower end of Stob Coire Easain's NW ridge. However there is no defined path and good route finding is needed to avoid hitting dead ends.

An alternative route to Lairig Leacach for the start of the climb is the 5$\frac{1}{2}$-mile (9km) trudge along the long track from Corriechoille (GR250806) to the north but this can only be reached with your own car.

Finally, the usual and most direct route of ascent is by the very long NE ridge of Stob a' Choire Mheadhoin reached by a 4$\frac{3}{4}$ mile (6km) walk from the village of Fersit (GR352782). Again there is no public transport at Fersit, although there is a train station at Tulloch (see p141) 1$\frac{1}{2}$ miles (2.5km) still further north.

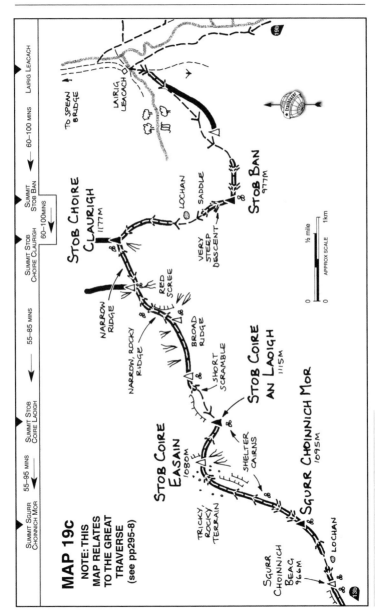

MAP 19c

NOTE: THIS
MAP RELATES
TO THE GREAT
TRAVERSE
(see pp295-8)

SUMMIT SGURR
CHOINNICH MOR
← 55-95 MINS →
SUMMIT STOB
COIRE LAOIGH
← 55-85 MINS →
SUMMIT STOB
CHOIRE CLAURIGH
← 60-100MINS →
SUMMIT
STOB BAN
← 60-100 MINS →
LAIRIG LEACACH

TO SPEAN
BRIDGE

LAIRIG
LEACACH

19b

STOB CHOIRE
CLAURIGH
1177M

LOCHAN

SADDLE

STOB BAN
977M

VERY STEEP
DESCENT

NARROW
RIDGE

RED
SCREE

BROAD
RIDGE

NARROW, ROCKY
RIDGE

SHORT
SCRAMBLE

STOB COIRE
AN LAOIGH
1115M

STOB COIRE
EASAIN
1080M

SHELTER
CAIRNS

SGURR CHOINNICH MOR
1095M

TRICKY,
ROCKY
TERRAIN

SGURR
CHOINNICH
BEAG,
966M

LOCHAN

13b

½ mile
APPROX SCALE
0   1km

THE CENTRAL HIGHLANDS

❏ **Other hills in the area**

● **Beinn a' Ghlo (1121m/3680ft)** A distinctive and massive hill near the village of Blair Atholl on the A9. From the road the mountain is impressive enough but it is only on closer inspection that it reveals its true beauty.

● **A' Chailleach ('A Ha-yuch', 930m/3050ft)** This isolated and lonely peak, deep in the bleak Monadhliath range, is best reached from the A86 near Newtonmore.

CENTRAL HIGHLANDS – TOWNS & VILLAGES

KILLIN

The delightful wee village of Killin sits on the wooded banks of the River Dochart at the western extreme of Loch Tay. It is surrounded by high mountains and makes an ideal base for a walk up Ben Lawers.

Services

Local **buses** between Stirling and Killin are infrequent but the more regular Citylink service from Edinburgh stops at the Lix Toll road junction about two miles west of the village.

There is a **post office**, a **TIC** (☎ 01567-820254; Apr-Oct, daily 10am-5pm), and a couple of small **supermarkets**.

For essential outdoor supplies, such as maps and hiking socks, look out for **Killin Outdoor Centre and Mountain Shop** (☎ 01567-820652, 💻 www.killinoutdoor.co .uk) on the main street.

Where to stay

Killin is a linear village, running north–south between the rivers Dochart and Lochay. Starting at the southern end by the falls is the well-kept *Falls of Dochart Inn* (☎ 01567-820159, 💻 www.falls-of-doch art-inn.co.uk, 8 rooms) with B&B from £40/pp. If the noise from the bar is too much try *Breadalbane House* (☎ 01567-820134, 💻 www.breadalbanehouse.com, 1D/1T/3F) halfway up the main street, which has well-presented rooms from £30/pp. Opposite this are *Craigard Hotel* (☎ 01567-820285, 💻 www.craigard-hotel .co.uk, 2S/3D/1T/2F en suite) with B&B from £28/pp and *Fairview House* (☎ 01567-820667, 💻 www.fairview-killin.co .uk, 1S/2D/2T/1F mostly en suite) which has a big open fire and beds from £25/pp.

At the northern end of the main part of the village there is B&B from £30/pp (the

❏ **Rainy days**

● **Falls of Dochart** By the bridge in Killin, the broad, crashing rapids of the Falls of Dochart look best after heavy rain. If it is still raining after you have finished admiring them you can spend the rest of the day enjoying the great pubs in the village, the best of which, **The Falls of Dochart Inn** (see above and opposite), is just a few steps away.

● **Ospreys at Loch of the Lowes, Dunkeld** Watch the ospreys on their nest from the observation hides at this Scottish Wildlife Trust reserve, just east of the A9 at Dunkeld (☎ 01350-727337, 💻 swt.org.uk, Apr-Sep 10am-5pm, mid-Jul to mid-Aug 10am-6pm, £3).

● **Distilleries Dalwhinnie** (☎ 01540-672219) runs tours.

● **Laggan Wolftrax Mountain Bike Trails** This fairly new development of mountain-bike trails in Strathmashie Forest, one mile west of Laggan on the A84, certainly gets the adrenalin streaming. There are lots of downhill trails with a blue run for beginners and black runs for nutters. If you don't have a bike, just hire one for £16 per day. Contact ☎ 01528-544780, 💻 www.basecampmtb.com.

THE CENTRAL HIGHLANDS

four-poster room costs £35/pp) at *Craigbuie House* (☎ 01567-820439, 🖳 www.craig buie.com, 4D/3F). There is another four-poster bed at *Killin Hotel* (☎ 01567-820296, 🖳 www.killin-hotel.com, 5S/12D/9T/6F), the big, white, former coaching inn on the bend, where prices start at £40/pp. The beautiful *Dall Lodge Country House* (☎ 01567-820217, 🖳 www.dalllodgehotel .co.uk, 1S/5D/2T/2F) overlooking the river has beds from £25 to £38/pp. Nearby, standing in the middle of an immaculate lawn with views of Ben Lawers, is the attractive stone-built former manse *Invertay Guest House* (☎ 01567-820492, 🖳 www.invertay house.co.uk, 4D/2T) which has rooms from £55/pp (includes dinner and breakfast).

Further on still, looking across the length of Loch Tay, are *Dunlochay B&B* (☎ 01567-820257, 1T/1F en suite), with beds for £25/pp, and *Ardlochay Lodge* (☎ 01567-820962, 🖳 www.ardlochaylodge .co.uk) with beds for £27/pp and beyond these the *Bridge of Lochay Hotel* (☎ 01567-820272, 🖳 www.bridgeoflochay .com) which offers B&B for £35/pp.

Braveheart Backpackers (☎ 01567-829089, 12 beds) with dorm rooms for £15-20/pp and twins for £20/pp offers the cheapest beds. It is next to Killin Hotel.

Where to eat and drink

For food and drink you cannot go too wrong in Killin which is blessed with a number of enticing old inns. Next to the rumbling river is the *Falls of Dochart Inn* (see Where to stay), a traditional hostelry with granite flagstones and a vast fireplace covering the end wall. The adjoining restaurant is the place for such niceties as cullen skink, haddock and chips and steaks. *Killin Hotel* (see above) also does food for non-residents while *Shutters Restaurant* (☎ 01567-820314) is a good choice for all-day breakfasts (£5.95) or something healthier such as cheese and broccoli pasta (£6.95). Also worth a look is *Capercaillie Restaurant* (☎ 01567-820355) which serves good traditional food. The best place for snacks is *The Wee Bake Shop* on the main street. **Fish and chips** can be sniffed out at the chip van by the village hall.

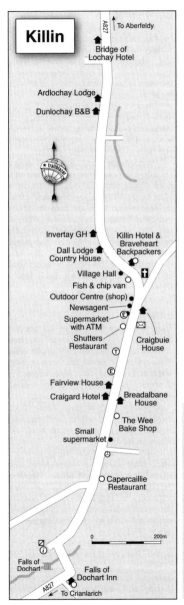

THE CENTRAL HIGHLANDS

DALWHINNIE

Dalwhinnie is Scotland's highest village but has little else to be proud of, except the **whisky distillery** (see box p138) of course. The village, a collection of rundown buildings within earshot of the busy A9 road, is the main access point for the remote country of the Ben Alder Forest.

Buses to and from Inverness, Glasgow and Edinburgh stop on the main road by the village turn-off and there are frequent **train** services for Inverness and the main transport hubs to the south. See pp32-6

Services are limited to a small **shop** at the filling station. There is also *The Inn at Loch Ericht* (☎ 01528-522257, 🖹 01528-522270, 11D/13T/2F) a few paces down the road where there are beds for £30/pp and cheap bar food such as steak and onion pie. They also have **internet** access. The only other accommodation is *Balsporran Cottages* (01528-522389, 🖳 www.balsporran.com, 1S/1D/1T), four miles south of Dalwhinnie, on the A9. B&B here is £30/pp.

LAGGAN

Some will know Laggan, on the banks of the River Spey, as 'Glenbogle', the fictitious village in the BBC TV drama series *Monarch of the Glen*, last aired in 2005. Much of the filming was done here and on the nearby Ardverikie estate. The community website (🖳 www.laggan.com) is a good place to find out more about the village. With its star credentials, Laggan is a popular spot for tourists so book any accommodation in advance.

In the centre of the village there is a small **shop** (Mon-Sat 9am-6.30pm, Sun 10am-6.30pm) and **post office** (Mon-Wed 9am-1pm & 2.30-5.30pm, Sat 9am-5.30pm, Sun 11am-noon, closed Thursday afternoon) with a fairly good stock of foodstuffs, and there is a doctor's **surgery** (☎ 01528-544225) too.

Over the river from the village centre at the *Pottery Bunkhouse* (☎ 01528-544231, 🖳 www.potterybunkhouse.co.uk) there is space for 34 weary walkers (£11/pp) and a kitchen. They even have an

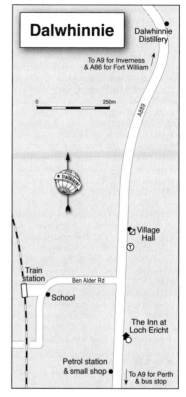

outdoor hot tub to help ease those aches away after a day on the hill. And they run a lovely coffee shop with homemade cheese scones and carrot cake.

Nearby, *Monadhliath Hotel* (☎ 01528-544276, 🖳 www.lagganbridge.com, 7D/1T) is a traditional Highland lodging with eight rooms. B&B is £30-35/pp.

In the village is *The Rumblie* (☎ 01528-544766, 🖳 www.rumblie.com, 3D en suite), a small but very homely B&B; £25-32.50/pp.

Finally, worth a mention is the *Base Camp Café* (☎ 01528-544786) at the **Wolftrax Mountain Bike Centre** (see box p138), where you can eat paninis whilst reading about mountain biking.

TULLOCH

The **train station** at Tulloch serves a small collection of houses including *Station Lodge Bunkhouse* (☎ 01397-732333, 🖳 www.stationlodge.co.uk), a clean, modern independent hostel in the old station building. There is space for 24 folk and it has all a walker might need, including drying room, hot showers and an open fire in the lounge. Dormitory beds are £14/pp and twin rooms are £15/pp. Residents can also have breakfast (from £3), a packed lunch (£4) and/or dinner (£8).

ROYBRIDGE

At Roybridge, eight miles west of Tulloch on the A86, there is a **train station**, a small **shop** and **post office**, and a greater spread of accommodation including *Bunroy Campsite* (☎ 01397-712332, 🖳 www.bunroycamping.co.uk) with pitches for £5.50/pp.

Homagen B&B (☎ 01397-712411, 🖳 www.homagen.co.uk) is centrally located and does B&B for £23/pp. Opposite is *Roy Bridge Hotel* (☎ 01397-712236, 🖳 www.roybridgehotel.co.uk) offering B&B for £25/pp. Aside from the main hotel they also have a **hostel** upstairs with dorm beds and the neighbouring *Grey Corrie Lodge*, which has 28 beds. Both the hostel and bunkhouse cost £12.50/pp. The food in the hotel is cheap and filling.

Stronlossit Inn (☎ 01397-712253, 🖳 www.stronlossit.co.uk, 1S/7D/2T) is a short walk away; it's a well-run place with rates starting at £42.50/pp. The bar is the place to try a malt whisky or two by the open fire and the excellent **restaurant** has an enticing and varied menu. The sizeable leg of Lochaber lamb at £9.25 is not for the sheepish. Look out for their infamous

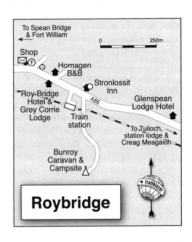

Roybridge

ceilidh nights too. A couple of miles east of the village is the grand and rather expensive *Glenspean Lodge Hotel* (☎ 01397-712223, 🖳 www.glenspeanlodge.co.uk, 6D/4T/1S/1F), a traditional granite structure run by the Best Western chain. The cheapest beds are £60-85/pp.

CORROUR   [SEE MAP 19a, p134]

Catching the **train** to Corrour is a great way of getting into a remote spot without walking a step. This is the start point for the 'Great Traverse' trek to the Lairig Leacach and Grey Corries as described on pp295-8. There are no roads here but the West Highland railway line from Glasgow to Fort William passes right through (see public transport map pp32-3). Film buffs might recognise the station as the location for a scene in the film *Trainspotting*, where Ewan McGregor's character, and his drug-

addled friends, briefly consider climbing the hill, Leum Uilleum.

There are no shops or places to eat but a short walk from the station, sitting in an enviable spot among a lonely scattering of trees at the head of Loch Ossian, is *Loch Ossian Youth Hostel* (☎ 01397-732207, 20 beds, £10.50), a little green hut, powered by wind and solar power, famous for the friendly red deer that come to the door to be fed. Beds should be booked in advance.

The Cairngorms and Eastern Highlands

The Cairngorms is the most important mountain area in the British Isles on many levels. It is the largest area of sub-arctic plateau and is an extremely valuable area for much of Britain's endangered wildlife. As well as the seemingly barren plateau, home to mountain hares and ptarmigan, there are also large areas of Caledonian pine forest in the glens and on the lower slopes. Here you will find capercaillie, pine marten and crested tit.

This is a land shaped by ice. On the edge of the high plateau deep cirques, or corries, drop away dramatically where the higher reaches of glaciers have plucked away at the rock. Longer and more powerful glaciers carved out the gaping trenches of the Loch Avon and Loch Einich basins and the Lairig Ghru.

The weather here can be harsh at any time of year and semi-permanent snow patches pattern the corries' back-walls well into high summer. This has long been a popular recreation area for skiers, hillwalkers, climbers and outdoor enthusiasts of every ilk and in 2003 was given national park status. Let's hope this means that the Cairngorms are preserved as they are for generations to come.

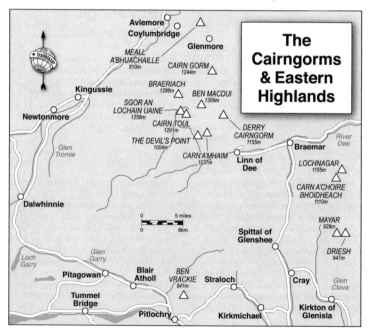

BEN VRACKIE (841m/2760ft) [MAP 20, p144]

Overview
Ben Vrackie is a distinctive pyramidal peak standing alone above the village of Pitlochry in Glen Garry. The summit is easy to reach thanks to a well-crafted footpath that climbs gradually through the heather. The rewards for such an easy climb are outstanding views along the length of Loch Tummel and north to the heathery peaks of Glen Shee.

Route
From Pitlochry take the road north to the adjoining village of Moulin. Turn left up the lane next to Moulin Hotel, which is well worth stumbling into on the way back, and follow the lane to a **car park** in the woodland. From here it is hard to go wrong. A very well-constructed path leaves the car park next to a large information board detailing various other ambles in the area. The path climbs steadily through some lovely mixed woodland, crosses a track and then joins it a little further up, follows it briefly and then continues up the path to a **gate** at the edge of the forest. From here continue climbing gradually over the expansive moorland, through **another gate**, eventually passing below and around a small rocky bluff to reach the **lochan** that sits below the mountain's steep upper slopes. Cross the **small dam** at the eastern end of the lochan and begin the steep climb up Ben Vrackie's SE slopes.

BEN VRACKIE (Speckled Mountain)
Technical grade
▲
Navigation grade
▲
Terrain grade
▲
Strenuousness
▲
Return time
2-3hrs
Return distance
5miles/8km
Total ascent
2100ft/640m
OS maps
Landranger 43 and 52, Explorer 386
Gateways
Pitlochry (see p169)

The going is fairly steep but the path, even at this high altitude, is clear and easy to follow. About 100m below the summit, the gradient eases and the trail swings round to the west, quickly reaching the summit. The top is marked by an old OS trig point and a circular **indicator dial** showing the names of all the mountains that can be seen on a clear day. Directly west is the long glen holding Loch Tummel and Loch Rannoch, and above it the unmistakably pointed peak of Schiehallion, a mountain famous for appearing on countless calendars and postcards. To the north are the heathery hulks of Beinn a'Ghlo and the high tops around Glen Shee, contrasting greatly with the fertile green fields that can be seen in the distance further south.

The best route of descent is to retrace your steps with a detour through the heavy door of Moulin Hotel (see p171) where the staff at the bar will gladly suggest ways of replacing the calories that you lost on the hill.

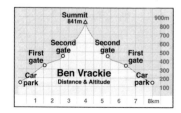

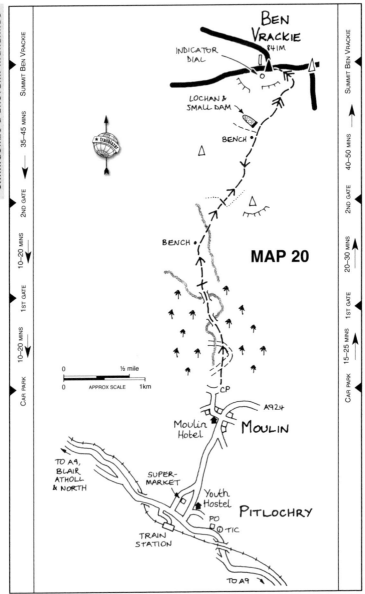

SUMMIT BEN VRACKIE — 35-45 MINS — 2ND GATE — 10-20 MINS — 1ST GATE — 10-20 MINS — CAR PARK

BEN VRACKIE 841M

INDICATOR DIAL

LOCHAN & SMALL DAM

BENCH

BENCH

MAP 20

SUMMIT BEN VRACKIE — 40-50 MINS — 2ND GATE — 20-30 MINS — 1ST GATE — 15-25 MINS — CAR PARK

CP

A924

Moulin Hotel

MOULIN

TO A9, BLAIR ATHOLL & NORTH

SUPER-MARKET

Youth Hostel

PO TIC

PITLOCHRY

TRAIN STATION

TO A9

0 ½ mile
0 APPROX SCALE 1km

Alternative routes

A less explored route of ascent starts at Killiekrankie via the mountain's western slopes. To avoid retracing your steps you could combine the two routes to make one linear walk, finishing off with a hitch or bus ride back up the A9.

MAYAR (928m/3045ft) & DRIESH ('_Drey-esh_', 947m/3105ft) [MAP 21, p146]

Overview

These flat-topped hills on the edge of the Mounth plateau, a vast expanse of high tundra where you may see mountain hares and snow buntings, are easily reached from the head of Glen Clova where it leads into Glen Doll. The glens themselves, steep-sided and gouged with cavernous corries, offer beautiful low-level walks but the high vantage points of Mayar and Driesh give an altogether different perspective over these deep troughs.

Route

A **car park** at the road end of Glen Clova, which has followed the recent trend of installing a pay-and-display machine, marks the start of the walk. Follow the forest track, past the estate buildings and the now ex-youth hostel, for about 1¼ miles (2km) along the north side of the river.

Ignore the 'Jock's Road' path branching off and continue downhill to a **bridge**. Follow this main track, which turns into a narrow trail through the trees, to a **gate** where the forest abruptly ends and the Caenlochan National Nature Reserve begins.

Coire Fee comes, dramatically, into view once past this woodland threshold. The path continues towards the back of the corrie to begin a steep ascent to the left of the burn, which tumbles down the corrie wall in a crashing waterfall. After climbing the **zig-zagging path** for about 150m the path reaches a higher, grassy **corrie**. The path becomes

> **MAYAR**
> (High Plateau)
>
> **DRIESH**
> (The Thorn Bush)
>
> **Technical grade**
> ▲
> **Navigation grade**
> ▲▲▲
> **Terrain grade**
> ▲▲
> **Strenuousness**
> ▲▲
> **Return time**
> 3-4hrs
> **Return distance**
> 8½miles/14km
> **Total ascent**
> 2790ft/850m
> **OS maps**
> Landranger 44,
> Explorer 388
> **Gateways**
> Clova (see p171)

much fainter as it climbs south out of this corrie onto the plateau. After a steady climb over shallow slopes the small summit cairn of **Mayar** comes into view, from where there are far-reaching views south into Glen Prosen and north to Lochnagar.

Head briefly NE from the summit to avoid some steep ground and then follow the path east across the grassy turf. After a brief drop the walking is easy across flat ground; a good area for mountain hares. Continue past a thoughtlessly placed metal signpost that would look better on a residential estate than a windswept hill, and follow a fence-line NE to a narrower section of the hill. Make note of this point, as this marks the descent route for later.

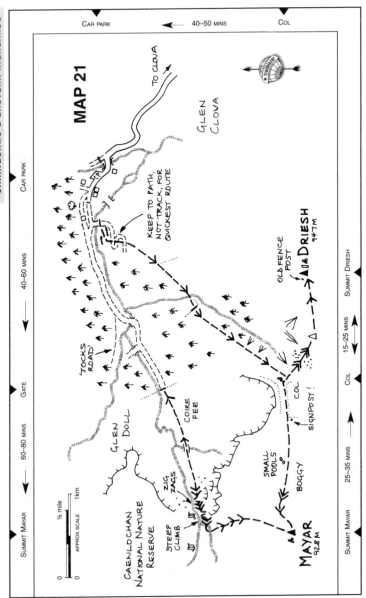

For now, turn 90° to the SE and drop down the ridge to a wide **col** from where it is a fairly steep ascent over easy ground to an outlying spur of the mountain. Cross this, briefly,

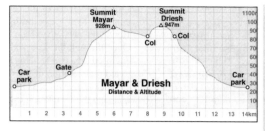

level ground and then climb the easy slope to the summit of **Driesh**. In poor visibility the shelter cairn on the summit can be quite hard to find. In clear weather it is a great vantage point from which to admire the carefully sculpted Glen Doll and Glen Clova.

Retrace your steps to the col and follow the path at the far end of it. This leads down the flanks of a ridge known as the Shank of Drumfollow, just one of the many odd hill names in this area: Clinking Cauldron, Craigie Thieves, Long Goat, Benty Roads and Manywee are just a few of the other quirky mountain monikers to be seen on the local map. The path drops down into the forest below and crosses the forest track twice before reaching a bridge over the river which leads back to the car park.

Alternative routes

The walk can be shortened by missing out either of the two peaks or extended by approaching Mayar from the north across 2½ miles (4km) of featureless high moorland (not recommended in mist). For this route follow the 'Jock's Road' path (an ancient byway linking Glen Clova with Braemar) as far as an old shelter at GR232778. From here aim south for approximately 1¾ miles (3km) and then SE for just over half a mile (1km).

CARN A' CHOIRE BHOIDHEACH (*'Carn a Horr-a Voy-eech'*, 1110m/3640ft)
LOCHNAGAR (1155m/3790ft)   [MAP 22a, p149; MAP 22b, p150]

Overview

With its sweeping plateau and mighty curves, Lochnagar is unmistakably Cairngorm in character but lies detached from the main Cairngorm massif, south of the Dee, giving it a haughty air of independence. Add to this its Royal endorsements and you have a proud mountain of magnificent beauty.

Route

The first couple of miles of this walk are through some beautiful Caledonian pine forest, typical of the Eastern Highland glens. Begin at **Invercauld Bridge** over the River Dee, three miles east of Braemar on the A93 (GR186909). After crossing the pretty stone **Bridge of Dee** (Map 22a) turn left and follow the wide track through the pine forest. At the fork take the rising path straight ahead.

**CARN A' CHOIRE
BHOIDHEACH
(Beautiful Corrie
Hill or Cairn)**

**LOCHNAGAR
(Noisy Loch or
Laughter Loch)**

Technical grade
▲▲

Navigation grade
▲▲▲▲

Terrain grade
▲▲▲

Strenuousness
▲▲

Return time
4¹/₂-6¹/₂hrs

Return distance
13miles/21km

Total ascent
3084ft/940m

OS maps
Landranger 43 and 44,
Explorer 388

Gateways
Braemar (see p172)

Ignore the paths to the left and right and instead continue over a footbridge to the next junction. Here you need to take a right through the **gate**. Once through the gate you find yourself in a large enclosed area that is being kept free of deer in order to aid regeneration of the Caledonian forest.

Stick to this track as it climbs through the forest, ignoring the temptation to follow the two left-hand forks that lead to bridges over the Feindallacher Burn. Another gate at the tree-line marks the end of the enclosure and the track continues along the west bank of the burn over open grouse moorland and past a small, and unmistakably ugly, corrugated shelter. Just past this shed cross the small footbridge over the burn (Map 22b) and begin the climb up the broad heathery **ridge**. It is an easy climb up an easy-to-follow path which emerges just above the col to the east of Carn an t-Sagairt Mor. This rounded lump is a munro and is only a short detour for those who want to tick it off.

For the continuation to Lochnagar aim ENE skirting just below the summit of **Carn an t-Sagairt Beag** across a band of boulders to reach the start of the plateau. There is a great view of Lochnagar's summit from here. Drop down briefly to a wide saddle and begin the climb up along the edge of a dramatic north-facing corrie. The munro of Carn a' Choire Bhoidheach is ten minutes' walk SSE from the top of the cliffs, across the plateau.

From this summit bear NE to gain a worn track. After crossing the saddle the gradient steepens before emerging on the summit ridge and the false summit of **Cac Carn Mor** with its huge cairn. Take a few minutes to appreciate the stunning corrie immediately to the east before continuing north to the true summit of Lochnagar: **Cac Carn Beag**. The names of these two peaks are unusual not just for their curious translations but also for the fact that the one named 'beag' (small) is higher than the one named 'mor' (big).

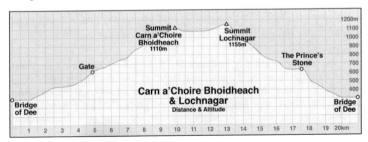

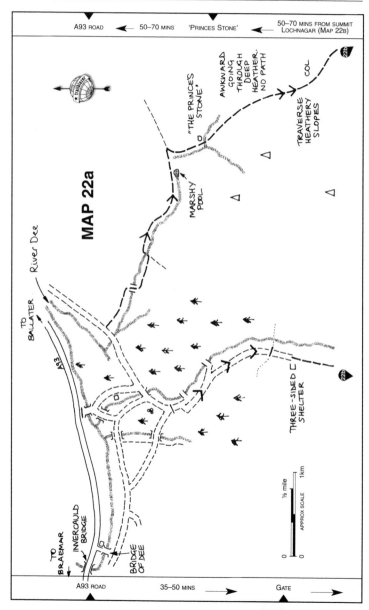

CAIRNGORMS & EASTERN HIGHLANDS

A93 ROAD ← 50–70 MINS 'PRINCES STONE' ← 50–70 MINS FROM SUMMIT LOCHNAGAR (MAP 22B)

22b

AWKWARD GOING THROUGH DEEP HEATHER- NO PATH

COL

TRAVERSE HEATHERY SLOPES

"THE PRINCE'S STONE"

MAP 22a

River Dee

TO BALLATER

A93

MARSHY POOL

THREE-SIDED SHELTER

22b

TO BRAEMAR

INVERCAULD BRIDGE

BRIDGE OF DEE

A93 ROAD   35–50 MINS →   GATE →

½ mile   1km

APPROX SCALE

0   0

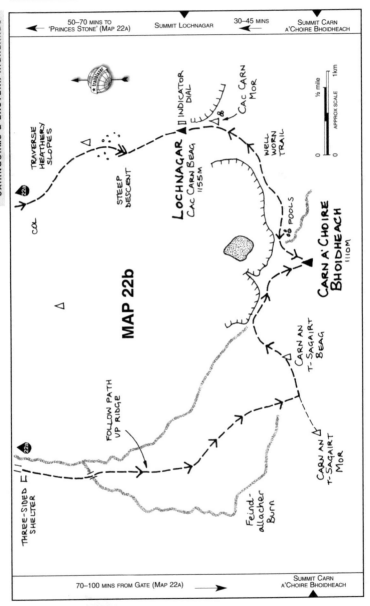

50–70 MINS TO ◄— 'PRINCES STONE' (MAP 22A)

SUMMIT LOCHNAGAR

30–45 MINS ◄—

SUMMIT CARN A'CHOIRE BHOIDHEACH

TRAVERSE HEATHERY SLOPES

COL

STEEP DESCENT

MAP 22b

INDICATOR DIAL

CAC CARN MOR

LOCHNAGAR CAC CARN BEAG 1155M

WELL WORN TRAIL

POOLS

CARN A'CHOIRE BHOIDHEACH 1110M

CARN AN T-SAGAIRT BEAG

FOLLOW PATH UP RIDGE

CARN AN T-SAGAIRT MOR

THREE-SIDED SHELTER

Feind-allacher Burn

½ mile 1km
APPROX SCALE

70–100 MINS FROM GATE (MAP 22A) —►

SUMMIT CARN A'CHOIRE BHOIDHEACH

An indicator dial next to the trig point will help resolve arguments about which hill is which in the beautiful views all around. Most notable of all is the Cairngorm massif and Beinn a' Bhuird to the north-west.

For the descent, head NW down rocky slopes to a point where the gradient steepens markedly. From here bear NNE down steep, bouldery slopes to a **col** below the peak of Meall Coire na Saobhaidhe. This hill can be avoided by following the deer trails that contour its western flanks to gain the broad heathery saddle to the NW. Descend into the wide bowl to the north (Map 22a), crossing through tussocky heather that tugs rather annoyingly at your ankles.

At the confluence of two burns is '**The Prince's Stone**', an upright rock with a faded engraving that reads 'Here HRH The Prince Consort slept on the night of the 5 Oct 1857 in a wooden hut'. He may well have been one of the first ever bothiers. Let's hope he remembered the bottle of malt.

From the stone a welcome path appears. Follow this down by the stream gully and cross the stream at the bottom where it joins another, better, path. Take this trail west back into the ancient pine forest then follow the trail that parallels the burn down to a wide forest track. Turn left here and follow the track west to a **footbridge**. On the other side turn right down the hill and cross another footbridge. From here it's a straightforward walk along the south side of the River Dee back to Invercauld Bridge.

Alternative routes

There are countless possibilities on Lochnagar. The most popular approach for the car-driving fraternity is from Spittal of Glenmuick at the end of a long minor road running south from Ballater. From the car park follow the track to the col below Meikle Pap. This approach is the easiest of the ascents and despite the initial drudgery of the walk it does take in the spectacular northern corrie of the mountain. Descend by the Glas Allt corrie for a return along the north shore of Loch Muick.

Fit and experienced hillwalkers might like to try the full round of Loch Muick, starting at Spittal of Glenmuick, taking in five munros: Broad Cairn, Cairn Bannoch, Carn an t-Sagairt Mor, Carn a' Choire Bhoidheach and Lochnagar. This is a massive walk across a remote sub-Arctic plateau that does not drop below the 900m contour for most of the day; only for those who know what they are doing.

DERRY CAIRNGORM (1155m/3790ft)
BEN MACDUI (1309m/4295ft)
CARN A' MHAIM ('*Carn a Vaym*', 1037m/3400ft)
[MAP 23a, p154; MAP 23b, p155; MAP 23c, p156]

Overview

A very long day on the high Cairngorm plateau taking in mighty Ben Macdui. This, the second highest peak in the British Isles, is reputedly haunted by a Grey Man but you are more likely to spot ptarmigan, reindeer and snow bunting than you are colourless phantoms.

**DERRY CAIRNGORM
(Blue Hill or Cairn of Derry)**

**BEN MACDUI
(MacDuff's Mountain)**

**CARN A' MHAIM
(Cairn of the Round Hill)**

Technical grade
▲▲▲

Navigation grade
▲▲▲▲▲

Terrain grade
▲▲

Strenuousness
▲▲▲▲▲

Return time
6¹/₂-9hrs from Linn of Dee
(4¹/₂-6hrs from Derry Lodge)

Return distance
19miles/30km from Linn of Dee
(12¹/₂miles/20km from Derry Lodge)

Total ascent
4396ft/1340m from Linn of Dee
(4232ft/1290m from Derry Lodge)

OS maps
Landranger 43, Explorer 403

Gateways
Braemar (see p172)

Throughout the walk the views are unlike any others in Scotland. This is true sub-arctic terrain. The scale, remoteness and lack of navigational features on the vast plateau make any trip into the Cairngorms one that should not be taken lightly. To say that the weather changes quickly in the mountains is clichéd but true and always worth remembering, particularly in the Cairngorms where it is less easy to make a hasty retreat.

This is a very long walk but there are ways to ease the strain. Competent hillwalkers who are familiar both with the area and with the inside of a bivvy bag (see p28) can cover the route suggested in two days by bivvying on the plateau between Derry Cairngorm and Macdui.

If the weather closes in there is the famous Shelter Stone hoowf (bivvy site), a short detour from the route at the head of Loch Avon. Those with little experience of, or little inclination for, such basic sleeping practices might prefer to keep the walk to one day. If so, it is a good idea to save precious walking hours by cycling the three miles in and out to Derry Lodge along the estate track from the Mar Lodge car park (pay-and-display) at Linn of Dee.

Route

The route, whether walking or cycling (see above) from Linn of Dee (Map 23a) to the abandoned estate buildings at **Derry Lodge** is straightforward. From there continue past the lock-up shed, cross the **footbridge** (Map 23b) and follow the path straight ahead through the pine trees to begin the steep climb up the lower slopes of Creag Bad an t-Seabhaig.

A well-worn path follows the broad shallow ridge towards Carn Crom. The path bypasses the highest point of this subsidiary top contouring instead around the eastern side above a precipitous drop above Glen Derry.

Drop briefly for a few metres to the exposed **col** and continue northwards along the rather drawn-out open ridge. The rocky peak ahead is, unfortunately, not the summit. The path skirts to the east of this top before climbing onto the back of the ridge for the final pull over hefty boulders to the true summit of **Derry Cairngorm** (Map 23c), marked by a tapered cairn. A second cairn to the north marks the descent across more boulder fields to a col 150m below the summit.

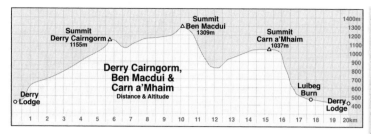

A good path leaves the boulders behind and crosses the grassy plateau slightly to the west of the top of **Creagan a' Choire Etchachan** ('Craigan a Horra Etch-hachan'). Navigation here is tricky if the cloud is down. (An escape route into Glen Derry can be found to the east of Loch Etchachan. Ben Macdui is in the opposite direction.) Before the ground begins to drop away to the north head roughly WSW to pick up the well-worn path across the plateau above the back-wall of Coire Sputan Dearg. There is a melt-water pool ahead and above this some **semi-permanent snow patches** in a shallow stream gully. The path climbs sharply to the left of this gully before swinging to the west for the final shallow climb over the featureless expanse of the plateau.

In good visibility a ruined shelter, complete with chimney stack, is visible on the horizon. The summit of **Ben Macdui** is about 100m further on from this ruin and is marked by a trig point on a raised cairn. In bad weather do not mistake the summit for any of the numerous smaller cairns scattered around the plateau.

The views from Ben Macdui give a real sense of the grandeur of the Cairngorms. These mountains are unlike any others in Britain. The high plateau is more characteristic of Northern Scandinavia than Scotland. You are likely to see ptarmigan, dotterel and maybe even some of the reindeer introduced from Sweden in the 1950s.

On a geomorphological level there are no more spectacular displays of the power of glaciation than when standing on Ben Macdui. The bowl that houses Loch Etchachan is a text-book example of a hanging valley. Below it, the deeper glacial trough of Glen Avon cuts a swathe through the mountains while directly west, the Lairig Ghru, the best example of a glacial breach in the Highlands, divides the Cairngorm plateau from the Braeriach plateau. Taking a huge chunk out of this high ground is Garbh Coire, one of the largest corries in Scotland and commonly believed to be the most likely spot for glaciers to reappear in the Highlands should the climate ever take a turn for the colder.

Looking south is the relatively narrow ridge of Carn a' Mhaim. Arêtes such as these are not particularly common in the Cairngorms. Before you think about this next summit, concentrate first on the descent. Bear ESE from the summit of Macdui, for around 800m, to a stream. Cross the stream and head at first S and then SW down a broad bouldery shoulder, keeping the stream gully far to the right. A descent of around 400m brings you to a broad grassy col. Head SSE

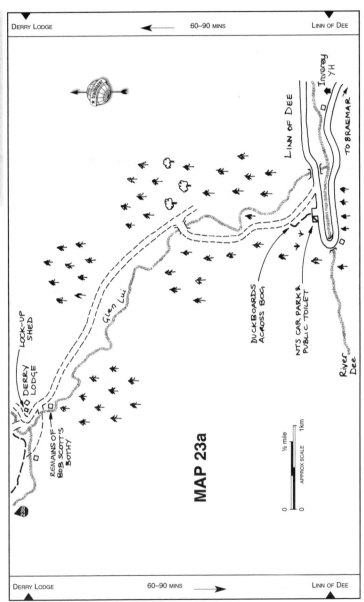

DERRY LODGE   ← 60–90 MINS   LINN OF DEE

LINN OF DEE

Inverey YH

TO BRAEMAR

DUCKBOARDS ACROSS BOG

NTS CAR PARK & PUBLIC TOILET

River Dee

Glen Lui

LOCK-UP SHED

DERRY LODGE

REMAINS OF BOB SCOTT'S BOTHY

23b

MAP 23a

½ mile   1km

APPROX SCALE

0   0

DERRY LODGE   60–90 MINS →   LINN OF DEE

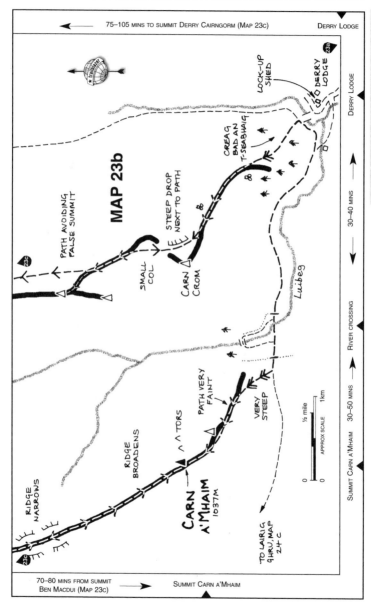

← 75–105 MINS TO SUMMIT DERRY CAIRNGORM (MAP 23c)

DERRY LODGE

LOCK-UP SHED

DERRY LODGE

CREAG BAD AN T-SEABHAIG

DERRY LODGE

30–40 MINS

MAP 23b

PATH AVOIDING FALSE SUMMIT

STEEP DROP NEXT TO PATH

SMALL COL

CARN CROM

Luibeg

RIVER CROSSING

PATH VERY FAINT

VERY STEEP

30–50 MINS

1km
½ mile
0   APPROX SCALE   1

RIDGE NARROWS

RIDGE BROADENS

TORS

CARN A'MHAIM
1037M

SUMMIT CARN A'MHAIM

TO LAIRIG GHRU, MAP 24c

70–80 MINS FROM SUMMIT BEN MACDUI (MAP 23c) →

SUMMIT CARN A'MHAIM

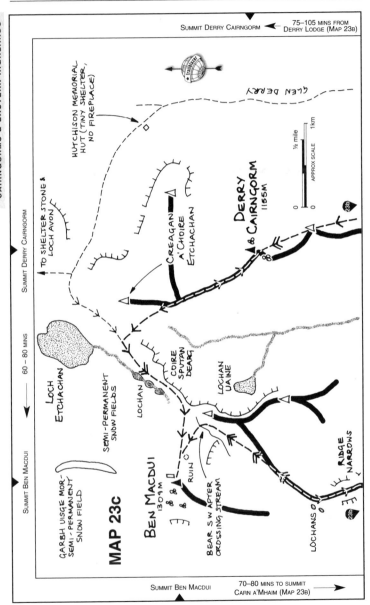

SUMMIT DERRY CAIRNGORM ← 75–105 MINS FROM DERRY LODGE (MAP 23B)

HUTCHISON MEMORIAL HUT (TINY SHELTER, NO FIREPLACE)

GLEN DERRY

TO SHELTER STONE & LOCH AVON

CREAGAN A'CHOIRE ETCHACHAN

DERRY CAIRNGORM 1155M

APPROX SCALE
½ mile
1km

23B

SUMMIT DERRY CAIRNGORM

60 – 80 MINS

LOCH ETCHACHAN

SEMI-PERMANENT SNOW FIELDS

LOCHAN

COIRE SPUTAN DEARG

LOCHAN UAINE

SUMMIT BEN MACDUI

GARBH UISGE MOR– SEMI-PERMANENT SNOW FIELD

MAP 23c

BEN MACDUI 1309M

RUIN

BEAR SWAPTER CROSSING STREAM

RIDGE NARROWS

LOCHANS

23B

SUMMIT BEN MACDUI

70–80 MINS TO SUMMIT CARN A'MHAIM (MAP 23B) →

CAIRNGORMS & EASTERN HIGHLANDS

along the long ridge to Carn a' Mhaim (Map 23b). After a couple of fairly short sharp climbs, the ridge narrows before levelling out again and widening on approach to the summit.

Carn a' Mhaim offers a good perspective of the great hulk of Ben Macdui and is also a great spot from which to appreciate the Lairig Ghru glacial breach. On the far side of this trough are the beautifully sculpted peaks of Braeriach, Sgor an Lochan Uaine, Cairn Toul and smallest but possibly most spectacular of all, the chiselled edges of the Devil's Point at the mouth of the glen.

Head briefly SSE from the summit to join the descent path that swings round to the SE across rocky ground. A steep drop of 150m leads over heathery ground to the main path in the glen below. Follow this path east to the **Luibeg Burn**. This can easily be forded but if the river is in spate cross via the footbridge a short way up the glen. The path continues through patches of Caledonian pine forest, home to crested tits, pine martens and crossbills, to the bridge at Derry Lodge where it is about one hour's walk back to the car park at Linn of Dee.

Alternative routes
The walk can be shortened in a number of ways: descend Derry Cairngorm via Coire Etchachan and Glen Derry or descend Ben Macdui via the south ridge called Sron Riach and out along the Luibeg Burn.

The Big Grey Man of Macdui
Forget green monsters in Loch Ness, the Big Grey Man of Macdui, *Am Fear Liath Mor*, is far more terrifying. This ghostly apparition is said to send walkers mad with fear, driving them to jump to their deaths over the cliffs. And it's not just crackpots who have reported sinister goings-on on Macdui. The earliest report of a presence came from respected Scottish scientist and climber, Professor Norman Collie, who in 1891 reported a strange 'crunch, and then another crunch as if someone was walking after me but taking steps three or four times the length of my own'. Collie fled, terrified, down the mountainside but the stories didn't stop there and further tales of irrational fear and visions of a ten-foot Yeti-like creature have come from walkers and climbers not just on Macdui but occasionally on other hills too.

❏ Important note – walking times
All times in this book refer only to the time spent walking. You will need to add 20-30% to allow for rests, photography, checking the map, drinking water etc.

BRAERIACH
(Greyish Upper Slope)

SGOR AN LOCHAIN UAINE
(Peak of the Green Lochan)

CAIRN TOUL
(Barn Hill or Cairn)

DEVIL'S POINT

Technical grade
▲▲▲

Navigation grade
▲▲▲▲▲

Terrain grade
▲▲

Strenuousness
▲▲▲▲▲

Return time
10-13hrs in total
(6-8hrs Coylumbridge to
Corrour via Braeriach,
4-5hrs Corrour to
Coylumbridge via
Lairig Ghru)

Return distance
26miles/42km in total
(15miles/24km
Coylumbridge to Corrour
via Braeriach,
11miles/18km Corrour
to Coylumbridge via
Lairig Ghru)

Total ascent
6010ft/1830m in total
(5120ft/1560m C'bridge
to Corrour via Braeriach,
890ft/270m Corrour to
Coylumbridge via
Lairig Ghru)

OS maps
Landranger 36 and 43,
Explorer 403

Gateways
Aviemore (see p173)
Coylumbridge (see p174)

BRAERIACH (*'Bray-ree-ach'*, 1296m/4250ft)
SGOR AN LOCHAIN UAINE
   (*'Skor an Loch-an Ony-er'*, 1258m/4125ft)
CAIRN TOUL (*'Carn Tool'*, 1291m/4235ft)
THE DEVIL'S POINT (1004m/3295ft)
        [MAP 24a; MAP 24b, p160; MAP 24c, p162]

Overview

This substantial hike involves a long walk-in
through the beautiful Rothiemurchus Forest followed by exposed walking over the vast Braeriach
plateau, eaten away on its eastern side by gaping
corries. The walk home through the Lairig Ghru is
almost as long and might persuade some to take
two days over the journey, stopping off at the tiny
Corrour Bothy (which is often bursting at the seams
in summer, so carrying a tent as back-up is wise)
below the Devil's Point.

The length, isolation and exposure on the high
plateau make this a serious undertaking that should
only be considered by those who are confident in
their ability to cope with the strenuous nature of the
walk. Throw in the potential for some nasty sub-
arctic weather and you have the ingredients for
quite a challenging little expedition.

Route

From Aviemore catch Stagecoach's Cairn Gorm
mountain bus and jump off by the Rothiemurchus
campsite in Coylumbridge (Map 24a). A way-marker indicates the path that leads to the Lairig Ghru.

The path is wide and firm and passes through a
couple of gates to take you deep into the primeval
Caledonian pine forest. Be sure to appreciate this
magnificent woodland. This is natural history in its
truest sense, representing one of the finest remnants
of a forest that once covered much of the
Highlands, as well as more southerly parts of
Britain. The gnarly trunks, deep beds of heather and
the sticky sweet smell of pine resin create an almost
Narnian atmosphere. If you are very lucky you may
see a pine marten or even the very rare capercaillie
(see pp56-7).

Take the left fork where the path splits and follow this through a gate to the **Cairngorm Club**

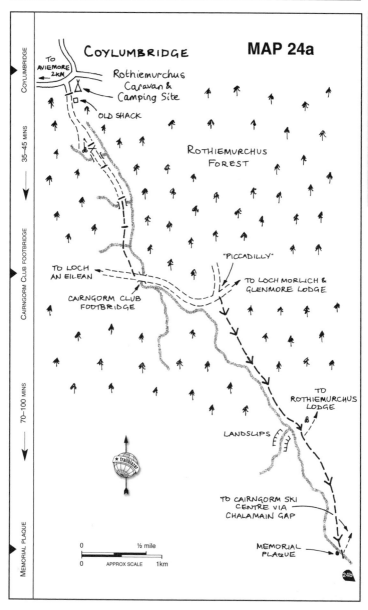

COYLUMBRIDGE

MAP 24a

TO AVIEMORE 2KM

Rothiemurchus Caravan & Camping Site

OLD SHACK

ROTHIEMURCHUS FOREST

"PICCADILLY"

TO LOCH AN EILEAN

TO LOCH MORLICH & GLENMORE LODGE

CAIRNGORM CLUB FOOTBRIDGE

TO ROTHIEMURCHUS LODGE

LANDSLIPS

TO CAIRNGORM SKI CENTRE VIA CHALAMAIN GAP

MEMORIAL PLAQUE

24b

★ trailblazer

0   ½ mile
0   APPROX SCALE   1km

COYLUMBRIDGE

35–45 MINS

CAIRNGORM CLUB FOOTBRIDGE

70–100 MINS

MEMORIAL PLAQUE

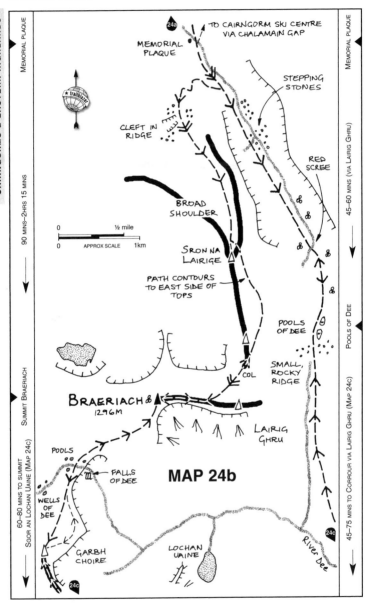

MEMORIAL PLAQUE

90 MINS–2HRS 15 MINS

SUMMIT BRAERIACH

60–80 MINS TO SUMMIT

SGOR AN LOCHAIN UAINE (MAP 24C)

MEMORIAL PLAQUE

45–60 MINS (VIA LAIRIG GHRU)

POOLS OF DEE

45–75 MINS TO CORROUR VIA LAIRIG GHRU (MAP 24C)

TO CAIRNGORM SKI CENTRE
VIA CHALAMAIN GAP

24a

MEMORIAL
PLAQUE

STEPPING
STONES

CLEFT IN
RIDGE

RED
SCREE

BROAD
SHOULDER

SRON NA
LAIRIGE

PATH CONTOURS
TO EAST SIDE OF
TOPS

POOLS
OF DEE

COL

SMALL,
ROCKY
RIDGE

BRAERIACH
1296M

LAIRIG
GHRU

POOLS

FALLS
OF DEE

MAP 24b

WELLS
OF
DEE

GARBH
CHOIRE

LOCHAN
UAINE

River Dee

24c

24c

0   ½ mile
0   APPROX SCALE   1km

Footbridge. Cross the river and continue along the path with the river on your right.

The path begins to swing to the left and then crosses through a long clearing before rising slightly back into the forest to reach a four-way path junction with the tongue-in-cheek nickname '**Piccadilly**'. A sign helpfully points out the path on the right that climbs to the Lairig Ghru. The trees begin to thin out as the path climbs high above the river. Ahead, the Lairig Ghru, a U-shaped breach cutting a swathe through

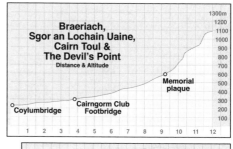

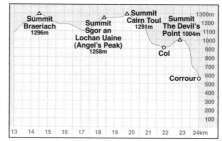

the Cairngorm massif, begins to make itself known. Continue towards this gaping pass, across the heather moor, until you reach a small, narrow gully that holds the stream and the path. The Sinclair Hut, which used to conveniently sit at this spot, was demolished over a decade ago but there is a handy patch of grass by the stream that could make a good campsite for anyone who wants to use this as a base. The site of the hut is marked by a **memorial plaque**.

The path crosses the stream a little further on and begins a short sharp climb out of the gully (Map 24b). At the top leave the main path and instead take the path on the right that doubles back slightly and begins the climb up the heathery flanks of the western side of the Lairig Ghru. This well-trodden path leads onto a small **col** in a cleft just below some steep slopes. Follow the path up this steep shoulder and continue along the broad ridge. Steep slopes drop down into the Lairig Ghru on the eastern side and the high northern corries of Braeriach come into view to the south.

On the approach to the top of Sron na Lairige (an outlying top of the Braeriach massif) you can choose to follow the path to the top or take the other path that skirts below the summit on the eastern side. Both eventually drop a short way to a prominent grassy col. The path climbs about 70m to gain the back of the narrower east ridge of Braeriach. Bear west to follow the line of sheer cliffs above Coire Bhrocain. Continue to follow the line of the cliffs, now in a WSW direction to quickly reach the summit cairn perched on the edge of the corrie.

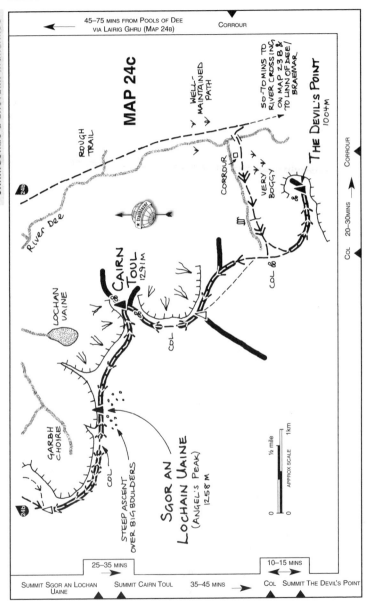

MAP 24c

45–75 MINS FROM POOLS OF DEE
VIA LAIRIG GHRU (MAP 24B)

CORROUR

ROUGH TRAIL

WELL-MAINTAINED PATH

50–70 MINS TO RIVER CROSSING ON MAP 23B & TO LINN OF DEE/ BRAEMAR

THE DEVIL'S POINT 100+M

CORROUR

River Dee

24B

CORROUR

VERY BOGGY

COL 20–30MINS

CAIRN TOUL 1291M

COL &

COL

LOCHAN UAINE

COL

GARBH CHOIRE

COL

STEEP ASCENT OVER BIG BOULDERS

SGOR AN LOCHAIN UAINE (ANGEL'S PEAK) 1258M

24B

★ trailblazer

½ mile   1km
APPROX SCALE
0   0

25–35 MINS

SUMMIT SGOR AN LOCHAN
UAINE

SUMMIT CAIRN TOUL

35–45 MINS

10–15 MINS

COL SUMMIT THE DEVIL'S POINT

The summit of **Braeriach** looks out across the widest part of the Lairig Ghru to the 700m slopes of Britain's second highest peak, Ben Macdui. From the summit head SW over the flat rocks of the plateau. Take care not to stray too far south here. To do so would lead down the slopes into Garbh Choire. Instead aim for the **Falls of Dee**, a spectacular cascade rolling off the lip of the plateau into Garbh Choire. Just over half a mile (about 1km) SW of these falls are the Wells of Dee, the source of the River Dee. They are only a short detour away and in the height of summer make a great bivvy spot in good weather.

From the Falls of Dee, aim SSW along the edge of the cliffs for about 300m. Continue in a SSW direction across the plateau. Don't be tempted to stick unerringly to the edge of the cliffs; you will find yourself walking onto the steep rocky spur that juts out into the corrie. Once past this spur you reach the edge of the cliffs again. Continue round to the SE (Map 24c) and begin the descent to a low point of 1130m and then climb over large boulders to the peak of **Sgor an Lochain Uaine**, known as Angel's Peak in English although the actual translation from the Gaelic is Peak of the Green Lochan. The lochan lies in the deep corrie below the mountain.

Head SE to descend to a **col** and then climb east to the summit of **Cairn Toul**. The views up the length of the Lairig Ghru and back across Garbh Choire to Braeriach are magnificent.

The first significant descent of the day begins here. Descend SSW to a **col** above Coire an t-Saighdeir and briefly climb to an outlying top before continuing the descent over drawn-out grassy slopes, boggy in places, to a broad saddle.

The bothy at Corrour is tantalisingly close at the foot of the Coire Odhar path but having come so far it would be a shame to miss out on the **Devil's Point**. By Cairngorms standards this is, at 1004m, a small hill but it is one of immense stature. Having been carved out and polished by ice on three sides, it is one of nature's little works of art. A path climbs SE and then E to reach the summit from where there are fine views over the meandering River Dee and back along the Lairig Ghru.

Retrace your steps to the col and follow the steep, well-trodden path to **Corrour Bothy**. This historic little hoowf has been sheltering hill folk for well over a hundred years. As bothies go it is very small and very basic and is under increasing pressure from overuse and misuse by walkers who are unfamiliar with the bothy code (see box p11). If you take shelter, be it for an hour or a night, be sure to leave it tidy.

The bothy can make a good overnight stop for those who have lugged all their kit over the hill but if you have come with a lightweight pack you will need to start the long walk back through the Lairig Ghru (for the continuation onto the Linn of Dee and Braemar see pp298-300). Begin by crossing the rather squelchy peat bog outside the bothy and cross the Dee by way of a **footbridge**. Climb up to the main path, which is well maintained at its lower reaches, and follow this north through the Lairig Ghru.

This glacial trough breaches the Cairngorm plateau dividing the Cairngorm side from the Braeriach side, providing a natural through route from one side of the massif to the other. Indeed the long trek from Aviemore to Braemar via the Lairig Ghru is a deservedly popular one. The high point of the pass is at 820m, just north of the Pools of Dee (Map 24b). From here it is a long steady descent back to the path junction where the morning ascent began. Retrace your steps through the Rothiemurchus Forest for the return to Coylumbridge (Map 24a).

Alternative routes

Rather than return through the Lairig Ghru from Corrour Bothy a great expedition can be made by continuing on to the road at Linn of Dee via Derry Lodge (see p152). This, however, involves carrying all your gear which makes the traverse far more demanding. It would also involve an overnight stop, either at Corrour Bothy or, if the weather is good, and you have the right gear and experience, a bivvy on the plateau.

CAIRN GORM (1245m/4080ft)   [MAP 25]

Overview

The mountain that lends its name to the entire range of mountains is one of the easiest of Cairngorm peaks to climb, not least because developers took it upon themselves to build a railway to within touching distance of the summit. Despite the railway and the ski tows decorating Coire Cas it is still possible to feel the essence of the mountain by walking up the Fiacaill Ridge. The walk is neither technically difficult nor long but do not be lulled into a false sense of security. The plateau is a featureless place and it is still easy to get lost if you let your attention slip.

CAIRN GORM (Blue Hill or Cairn)
Technical grade ▲
Navigation grade ▲▲▲
Terrain grade ▲▲
Strenuousness ▲
Return time 2-2½hrs
Return distance 4miles/6km
Total ascent 1970ft/600m
OS maps Landranger 36, Explorer 403
Gateways Glenmore (see p174) Aviemore (see p173)

Route

The (Stagecoach) bus from Aviemore climbs to 650m at the Cairngorm ski centre **car park**. Take the track between the ski centre buildings and under the railway and continue up the track which runs parallel to the railway. Again pass under the railway just below the **Shieling station**. Keep to the track as it traverses the slopes and then begins to zigzag upwards. Just past the sharp left-hand bend look out for a smaller path climbing away from the track. Follow this path as it climbs gradually up the western side of Coire Cas. It soon comes onto the back of the **Fiacaill Ridge**, a rocky nose that separates Coire Cas from neighbouring Coire an t-Sneachda, a popular spot for winter climbing.

The ridge is rocky but easy and culminates at a top marked by a **cairn**. This is the edge of the Cairngorm plateau, where you'll find snow buntings and ptarmigan and hopelessly lost hill walkers. To avoid joining them take a bearing, which will probably be essential in poor visibility, directly east. After crossing a brief dip the ground suddenly steepens but not for too long. As it begins to shallow the summit weather station and a big cairn marking the **true summit** come into view.

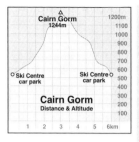

The descent is made particularly easy as a line of very closely laid cairns, and then guiding posts, lead north from the summit to the **Ptarmigan Restaurant**, which is also the final terminal for the mountain railway. Move round to the right of the restaurant and pass under the first ski tow. Keep to the left of the fence (do not rely on this fence as it is part of the ski run and its position may change) and begin to descend the broad mountainside. After five to ten minutes the fence disappears to the north while a faint trail continues to the NW, marked in places by small cairns. After passing the end of another fence, head west to find the path that drops through steep slopes of heather back to the ski centre buildings and car park.

Alternative routes
In clear weather the walk can be lengthened by continuing SW from the summit of Cairn Gorm to follow the edge of the plateau, above the cliffs of Coire an t-Sneachda and Coire an Lochain, taking in the summit of Cairn Lochan. The crowds thin out away from Cairn Gorm and the views over the northern corries are worth the extra effort. From Cairn Lochan's summit bear WSW for about 500m before turning to the NW down the slope to gain a path that leads back to the ski centre car park.

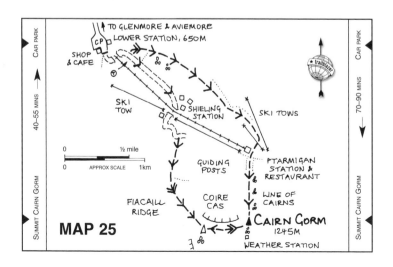

MEALL A' BHUACHAILLE (*'Myowl-a Voo-keler'*, 810m/2655ft)
[MAP 26a; MAP 26b, p168]

Overview

These low hills, forming the north side of Glen More, are completely over-shadowed by the looming mass of the Cairngorms to the south. Nevertheless, they shouldn't be ignored as they offer an easy and thoroughly exhilarating walk along a three-mile ridge. Not only that but they are also the perfect place from which to take in the grandeur of the Cairngorms' northern corries as well as the Abernethy Forest stretching across the low ground to the north.

> **MEALL A'
> BHUACHAILLE
> (Hill of the
> Shepherd)**
>
> **Technical grade**
> ▲
> **Navigation grade**
> ▲▲
> **Terrain grade**
> ▲
> **Strenuousness**
> ▲▲
> **Return time**
> 3½-5hrs
> **Return distance**
> 10miles/16km
> **Total ascent**
> 2300ft/700m
> **OS maps**
> Landranger 36,
> Explorer 403
> **Gateways**
> Glenmore (see p174)
> Aviemore (see p173)

Route

At Glenmore take the single-track road to **Glenmore Lodge** (see p175; the National Outdoor Training Centre). At the road end, a track continues through the beautiful Ryvoan Pass, an old glacial meltwater channel with steep sides and now dominated by Caledonian pine forest. Pass the milky green Lochan Uaine (which appropriately translates as green lake) and take the left-hand track at the following junction.

This leads onto the open heath and to **Ryvoan** bothy. A path leaves the track here and climbs steep slopes of heather to the west. The relentless climb is eased somewhat by the good path and before long the gradient eases as the heather peters out. Continue to a cairn and then head WSW to the summit cairn of **Meall a' Bhuachaille**. After a sandwich stop to admire the northern corries of the Cairngorms continue west down a broad ridge to a col. (There is an escape path back to Glenmore just before reaching the col).

At the col a path climbs quite directly to the summit of **Creagan Gorm** and from there follow the ridge that dips and rolls, but does not lose much altitude, to a subsidiary top. After this the final stretch of the ridge swings to the north for the final summit of **Craiggowrie** (Map 26b).

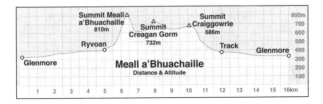

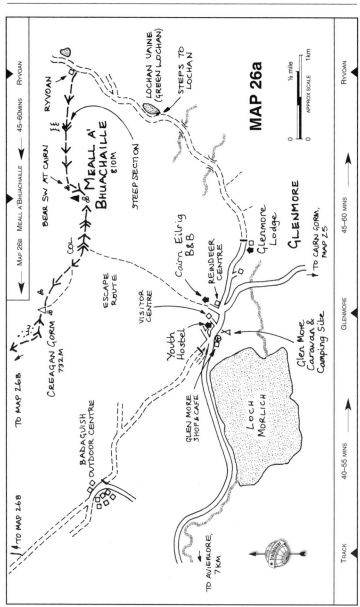

MAP 26a

Text visible within map:

TO RYVOAN

← MAP 26B   Meall a'Bhuachaille 45–60MINS RYVOAN →

RYVOAN

LOCHAN UAINE (GREEN LOCHAN)

STEPS TO LOCHAN

BEAR SW AT CAIRN

MEALL A' BHUACHAILLE 810M

STEEP SECTION

COL

ESCAPE ROUTE

CREAGAN GORM 732M

TO MAP 26B

TO MAP 26B

BADAGUISH OUTDOOR CENTRE

VISITOR CENTRE

Cairn Eilrig B&B

REINDEER CENTRE

Glenmore Lodge

GLENMORE

TO CAIRN GORM, MAP 25

YOUTH HOSTEL

GLEN MORE SHOP & CAFE

Glen More Caravan & Camping Site

LOCH MORLICH

TO AVIEMORE, 7 KM

APPROX SCALE

0 _____ ½ mile

0 _____ 1km

TRACK 40–55 MINS GLENMORE 45–60 MINS RYVOAN →

trailblazer

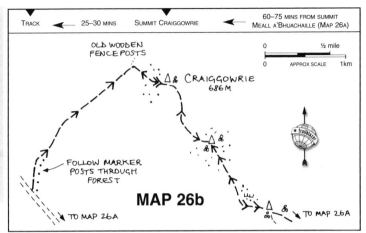

TRACK ← 25–30 MINS   SUMMIT CRAIGGOWRIE ← 60–75 MINS FROM SUMMIT MEALL A'BHUACHAILLE (MAP 26A)

OLD WOODEN FENCE POSTS

△ & CRAIGGOWRIE 686M

FOLLOW MARKER POSTS THROUGH FOREST

MAP 26b

TO MAP 26A

TO MAP 26A

0   ½ mile
0   APPROX SCALE   1km

Descend NW from this summit to a line of old fence posts where a boggy path leads SW to the forest below. Follow the way-marker posts a short distance through the pine trees to a wide forest track. Turn left here towards the Badaguish Outdoor Centre (Map 26a).

Notice the difference between this commercial area of forestry and the native pine forest from the Ryvoan Pass at the start of the walk. Here, the forest is a monoculture of tightly packed non-native spruce and of limited benefit to other species. The biodiversity in the native forest is far greater and, let's be honest, the native forest looks a lot prettier. At **Badaguish** take the **track** that crosses through the complex. At the far end turn left at the junction and follow this track back to Glenmore, keeping to the right-hand track.

Alternative routes
To cut the walk short take the path that drops back to Glenmore, from just east of the col between Creagan Gorm and Meall a' Bhuachaille.

❑ **Other hills in the area**
● **Bynack More (1090m/3575ft)** A long walk from Glenmore, through Strath Nethy, leads to the most northerly of the Cairngorm mountains, whose summit ridge is decorated with granite tors known as the Barns of Bynack.
● **Beinn a' Bhuird ('Ben a _Voorsht_', 1197m/3925ft)** This enormous hill hides some beautiful cliffs and corries on its eastern flanks that are best appreciated from the broad plateau above. Start at Invercauld Bridge just east of Braemar.
● **Sgor Gaoith ('Skor _Gu-ye_', 1118m/3670ft)** In the western Cairngorms, Sgor Gaoith lies between the forests of Glen Feshie and the deep trench of Glen Einich. The summit forms but a small part of an extensive plateau that eventually leads all the way to Braeriach. The best approach is from Glen Feshie.

❏ **Rainy days**

● **Cairngorm Mountain Railway** (☎ 01479-861261, 🖳 www.cairngormmountain .com) This highly controversial £15 million development, that went ahead despite vociferous opposition from those who recognise the value of keeping wild land wild for the benefit of all, carries passengers from the ski centre development at Coire Cas to a restaurant high up on Cairn Gorm. Here you can get fed whilst admiring the 'postcard' view safe in the knowledge that you are protected from the elements and therefore from any sense of actually being up a mountain at all. The return journey costs £9.25 or you can walk up for free.

● **Rothiemurchus Forest** This large expanse of Caledonian pine forest, north of the main Cairngorm massif, is beautiful even in the rain. It is criss-crossed by well-maintained paths and is a great place to spot wildlife such as roe deer, red squirrels and, if you are really lucky, capercaillie. Good places to start a walk are at Coylumbridge, Loch an Eilean or Glenmore. There is an information centre with a ranger service at Coylumbridge (☎ 01479-812345, 🖳 www.rothiemurchus.net).

● **Abernethy Forest and Loch Garten Osprey Centre** (☎ 01479-831476, 🖳 www .rspb.org/reserves) The Abernethy Forest reserve, near Boat of Garten, is managed by the RSPB and includes the famous osprey hide where you can view these magnificent birds nesting in the summer months. See also p57.

● **Cairngorm Reindeer Centre** (☎ 01479-861228, 🖳 www.reindeer-company .demon.co.uk, centre open 10am-5pm daily, visits to herd all year at 11am, also at 2.30pm May-Sep) The reindeer in the Cairngorms National Park were introduced from Scandinavia. Reindeer can be seen in the paddocks at the centre at Glenmore year-round or there are guided walks to see the semi-wild herd out on the hill.

● **Cairngorm Sled-dog Centre** (☎ 07767-270526, 🖳 www.sled-dogs.co.uk) For a chance to visit the huskies in the kennels or even go on a sled-dog trip along a forest trail, head to the sled-dog centre on the Rothiemurchus estate. Booking essential.

● **Pitlochry Hydro-electric Power Station** (☎ 01882-473152, Apr-Sep, Mon-Fri 10.30am-5.30pm, exhibition entry £2.50) The hydro-electric dam at Loch Faskally, near Pitlochry, has a visitor centre and exhibition explaining how Scotland's network of rivers and lochs and the energy they contain help to keep the lights on. There is also a fish ladder where you can watch the salmon leaping.

● **Distilleries** For tours and the chance to sample some malts try: **Blair Atholl**, Pitlochry (☎ 01796-482003); **Edradour**, Pitlochry (☎ 01796-472095, 🖳 www.ed radour.co.uk) **Royal Lochnagar**, at Crathie, near Ballater (☎ 01339-742700); **Cragganmore** at Ballindalloch (☎ 01340-872555), or **Cardow** at Knockando (☎ 01340-872555).

CAIRNGORMS & EASTERN HIGHLANDS – TOWNS & VILLAGES

PITLOCHRY   [see map p170]

The small bustling town of Pitlochry sits above the north bank of the River Tummel with Ben Vrackie as a backdrop. This is a popular tourist centre, decorated with tartan and shortbread shops, and in summer the population balloons as walkers, coach parties and passing A9 motorists stop off here. Despite a wide range of accommodation, it is a wise move to book well in advance.

Services

Trains and **buses** (see pp32-6) pass through Pitlochry on their way north to Aviemore and Inverness, and south to Perth and Edinburgh. The **TIC** (☎ 01796-472215) is at 22 Atholl Rd; the staff are knowledgeable and can help find a bed for the night during the busy summer season. There is a **launderette** on West Moulin Rd, along with the **Co-op supermarket**. Atholl Rd is Pitlochry's main drag and is where you will find the **post office**. There are a couple of **banks** with cash machines and a number of **outdoor equipment shops**: Escape Route Outdoor, Munros, Pine Valley and The Wilderness Factory.

For a **taxi** (useful for getting to the start of the Ben Vrackie or Schiehallion walks) call ☎ 01796-470123 or 01796-473931.

Where to stay

A good place to start looking for a bed is on East Moulin Rd where *Almond Lee Guest House* (☎ 01796-474048, 🖳 www.almond lee.com, 3D/1T), a modern bungalow, has B&B from £27/pp. Next door, *Birchwood Hotel* (☎ 01796-472477, 🖳 www.birch woodhotel.co.uk) with its beautiful wood-panelled hallway, has 13 rooms from £36/pp.

If these are full, look along Lower Oakfield Rd where almost every house is a B&B. The first you will see is *Poplars* (☎ 01796-472129, 🖳 www.poplars-pitlochry

.com, 3D/2T/1F) offering B&B for £32.50/pp, followed by *Derrybeg* (☎ 01796-472070, 🖳 www.derrybeg.com, 2S/6D/2T/1F) from £25 to £35/pp.

Both *Ardvane Guest House* (☎ 01796-472683) and *Craigroyston House* (☎ 01796-472053, 🖳 www.craigroyston.co.uk, 4D/2T/2F) offer B&B from £31/pp and *Carra Beag Guest House* (☎ 01796-472835, 🖳 www.carrabeag.co.uk, 2S/2D/3T/1F), a traditional home with a log fire and wooden beams, does B&B from £23 to £29/pp. A similar rate can be found on Toberargan Rd at *The Well House* (☎ 01796-472239, 🖳 www.wellhouseandar rochar.co.uk, 4D/1T/1F). *Pitlochry Youth Hostel* (☎ 01796-472308; 63 beds, Feb-Oct, £14-17/pp) lies just round the corner.

There is more accommodation on Atholl Rd which acts as the high street. At the eastern end is *Acarsaid Hotel* (☎ 01796-472389, 🖹 01796-473952, 🖳 www.acarsaidhotel.com, 29 rooms) with beds from £38, *Buttonboss Lodge* (☎ 01796-472065, 🖳 www.buttonbosslodge.co.uk,

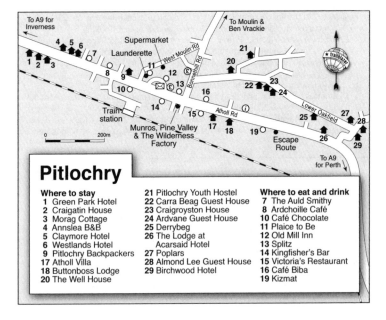

Pitlochry

Where to stay
1 Green Park Hotel
2 Craigatin House
3 Morag Cottage
4 Annslea B&B
5 Claymore Hotel
6 Westlands Hotel
9 Pitlochry Backpackers
17 Atholl Villa
18 Buttonboss Lodge
20 The Well House

21 Pitlochry Youth Hostel
22 Carra Beag Guest House
23 Craigroyston House
24 Ardvane Guest House
25 Derrybeg
26 The Lodge at
    Acarsaid Hotel
27 Poplars
28 Almond Lee Guest House
29 Birchwood Hotel

Where to eat and drink
7 The Auld Smithy
8 Ardchoille Café
10 Café Chocolate
11 Plaice to Be
12 Old Mill Inn
13 Splitz
14 Kingfisher's Bar
15 Victoria's Restaurant
16 Café Biba
19 Kizmat

CAIRNGORMS & EASTERN HIGHLANDS

1S/4D/2T/2F) from £22.50/pp and *Atholl Villa* (☎ 01796-473820, 🖳 www.athollvilla.co.uk, 3D/2T/4F), a beautiful old Victorian house with B&B from £25/pp.

In the centre of the village *Pitlochry Backpackers Hotel* (☎ 01796-470044, 🖳 www.pitlochrybackpackershotel.com) has dorm beds for £13-15/pp, twin rooms from £17.50/pp and breakfast for a bargain £1.90. They also have internet access 80p/half hour.

The other hot spot for beds is at the western end of the street where you will find *Westlands Hotel* (☎ 01796-472266, 🖳 www.westlandshotel.co.uk) with 15 rather plush rooms priced at £44/pp. Of a comparable standard and price (£35-55/pp) is *Claymore Hotel* (☎ 01796-472888, 🖳 www.claymorehotel.com, 2S/3D/3T/2F en suite) while *Annslea B&B* (☎ 01796-472430, 🖳 www.pitlochryguesthouse.com) is cheaper at £22-28/pp.

Continuing on the same road is *Morag Cottage* (☎ 01796-472973, 🖳 www.moragcottage.co.uk, 1D/1T/1F) which has rooms from £23/pp, *Craigatin House* (☎ 01796-472478, 🖳 www.craigatinhouse.co.uk, 13 rooms) with contemporary décor and huge beds for £37.50-50/pp and then there is the impressive *Green Park Hotel* (☎ 01796-473248, 🖳 www.thegreenpark.co.uk), an enormous place with around 51 rooms, and gardens stretching down to the shore of Loch Faskally. Beds here start at £68/pp.

One mile north of Pitlochry, in **Moulin** village, *Moulin Hotel* (see Map 20, p144; ☎ 01796-472196, 🖳 www.moulinhotel.co.uk, 15 rooms) is a wonderfully historic coaching inn with rooms from £35/pp, representing excellent value for the high standard of accommodation.

Where to eat and drink

Most of the eateries are on Atholl Rd, including *Café Biba* (☎ 01796-473294), one of the best places for better-than-average burgers (£7.25) as well as healthier options such as Greek salad (£8.95). *Café Chocolaté* (☎ 01796-470318) where you can tuck into an all-day breakfast for £6.95 or sit on the sofa and indulge in one of their many cakes, *Victoria's Restaurant* (☎ 01796-472670, 🖳 www.victorias-pitlochry.co.uk), serving everything from baked potatoes (£5.85) to salmon (£10.95), and *The Auld Smithy* (☎ 01796-472356), with their pan-fried haggis in onion gravy, are also excellent choices.

Pubs that serve food include *Kingfisher's Bar* (☎ 01796-472027) which can be a bit noisy with a TV screen in almost every corner, a pool table and loud music. A better choice is the *Old Mill Inn* (☎ 01796-474020, 🖳 www.old-mill-inn.co.uk), behind the post office (look out for the old waterwheel). The extensive menu includes bacon and brie ciabatta (£5.25) and grilled sea bass (£11.95).

Indian food can be found at *Kizmat* (☎ 01796-474400) and quick bites are available from *Ardchoille Café* (☎ 01796-472170) where the **fish and chips** are excellent, *Plaice to Be* for more fish and chips and *Splitz* (☎ 01796-472050) which specialises in baked potatoes (from £1.90) and fruit smoothies to take away.

Finally, try not to miss out on the *Moulin Hotel* (see Where to stay). This authentically traditional pub sets the standard with its cosy, bustling bar, scrumptious traditional food, and lack of piped music. If that wasn't enough they also have their own micro-brewery across the road.

CLOVA

There are few facilities in this long glen but there is accommodation. *Glen Clova Hotel* (☎ 01575-550350, 🖳 www.clova.com, 5D/5T), a 150-year-old drovers' inn, has very clean and comfortable en suite rooms, and the odd four-poster bed, with prices from £45/pp. In the summer there is often live music and quite a buzz about the place as walkers stumble off the surrounding hills to recount their exploits over a pint of real ale. There are cheaper beds in their adjacent *Steading Bunkhouse* (contact details as for Glen Clova Hotel) with a similarly high standard of cleanliness and room for 32 smelly walkers. Linen is provided and there are kitchen facilities and a drying room. Beds are £11/pp (£19 with breakfast).

The hotel is also the best place for **food** with an excellent restaurant (Sun-Thu noon-8pm, Fri & Sat noon-9pm) offering local curiosities such as chicken and haggis fillet and Clova venison casserole.

The closest hostel is 14 miles south of Clova in **Glen Prosen**: *Prosen Hostel*

(☎ 01575-540238, 🖥 www.prosenhostel.co.uk, 18 beds) opened in 2007 and charges £18/pp.

There are two **postbuses** (see pp32-6) per day Monday to Friday (only one on Saturday) from Kirriemuir to Glen Clova. The morning departure runs to the end of the glen while the afternoon bus only goes as far as Clova.

BRAEMAR

In winter Braemar acts as a kind of après-ski centre to the Glen Shee ski resort. In summer it is no less busy with the attractions of Royal Deeside and the Cairngorms within easy reach. The heart and soul of the village is along Invercauld Rd.

There is a **post office** and **shop**, as well as a **TIC** (☎ 01339-741600) in The Mews. The **cash machine** is by the TIC and not, more logically, at the bank. **Braemar Mountain Sports** is ideal for any last-minute hill gear you may have forgotten.

To get from Braemar to Linn of Dee (for access to the southern Cairngorms) call ☎ 01339-741456 for a **taxi**.

For a cheap sleeping option try *Rucksacks Braemar* (☎ 01339-741517, from £7 to £15/pp), or *Braemar Youth Hostel* (☎ 01339-741659, 50 beds, £13.50-18/pp), a former shooting lodge at 21 Glenshee Rd. If these are full try the tiny *Inverey Youth Hostel* (see map 23a, p154; ☎ 01339-741017, 14 beds, mid May-early Sept, £12.50-13.50/pp) five miles down Mar Rd, near **Linn of Dee**. There is **camping** at *Invercauld Caravan Site* (☎ 01339-741373) near Braemar Youth Hostel on Glenshee Rd.

Back on Glenshee Rd there is B&B for £25-32/pp at *Cranford Guest House* (☎ 01339-741675, 🖥 www.cranfordbraemar.com, 15 Glenshee Rd, 3D/3T) and *Schiehallion House* (☎ 01339-741679, 🖥 www.schiehallionhouse.com, 1S/3D/3T/2F), a large detached home with log fires.

For a tasty snack try the apple pie for £3.25 at *Gordon's Tearoom* (☎ 01339-741247, 🖥 www.gordonsbraemar.com) or the toasties for £3 at *The Old Bakery Coffee House* (☎ 01339-741415). They

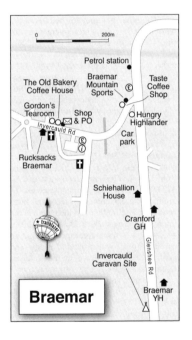

Braemar

also do all-day breakfasts for £5.50 and their menu promises that most of their dishes are '90% home-made'! Alternatively there are fish and chips at the *Hungry Highlander* (☎ 01339-741556) by the main road junction and various healthy snacks such as butternut squash and ginger soup for £3.20 and more filling meals such as lemon salmon for £9.70 at *Taste Coffee Shop* (☎ 01339-741425, 🖥 www.tastebraemar.co.uk) by Braemar Mountain Sports.

AVIEMORE

Aviemore, tucked between the noisy A9 and the River Spey, is the home of Scottish skiing and the infamous hub for tourism in Cairngorms National Park. Having suffered some thoughtless and rushed development during the 1960s it was derided as an eyesore. In recent years, however, this busy outdoor centre has enjoyed a little facelift, although it could still do with a few more nips and tucks here and there.

Services

Everything you might need is stretched out along the main street, Grampian Rd. The **TIC** (☎ 01479-810930) is at the southern end of town and there are plenty of **shops** including a **supermarket** with a **cash machine**, a couple of **banks** also with cash machines and a **post office**. There is also a good choice of **outdoor shops** including Mountain Spirit, Nevisport, Blacks and

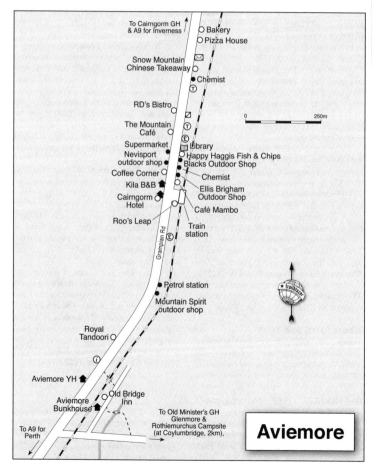

To Cairngorm GH & A9 for Inverness

Bakery
Pizza House
Snow Mountain Chinese Takeaway
Chemist

RD's Bistro
The Mountain Café
Supermarket
Nevisport outdoor shop
Coffee Corner
Kila B&B
Cairngorm Hotel
Roo's Leap

Library
Happy Haggis Fish & Chips
Blacks Outdoor Shop
Chemist
Ellis Brigham Outdoor Shop
Café Mambo
Train station

Grampian Rd

Petrol station
Mountain Spirit outdoor shop

Royal Tandoori

Aviemore YH
Aviemore Bunkhouse
Old Bridge Inn

To A9 for Perth

To Old Minister's GH
Glenmore & Rothiemurchus Campsite (at Coylumbridge, 2km),

Aviemore

0   250m

Ellis Brigham, all well stocked with maps, stove fuel and the usual array of expensive Gore-Tex clothing, tents and sleeping bags. In addition to the **chemist** there are **public shower** facilities at the toilet block opposite RD's Bistro. **Buses** and **trains** (see pp32-6) serve all stops to Inverness and Edinburgh and there is a frequent local bus to Glenmore and Cairn Gorm that departs outside the station.

Where to stay
The nearest campsite is *Rothiemurchus Caravan and Camping Site* (see Map 24a, p159; ☎ 01479-812800, 🖳 www.rothie murchus.net, £7/pp) two miles down the Cairn Gorm road (the B970) at **Coylumbridge**. The cheapest beds are at *Aviemore Youth Hostel* (☎ 01479-810345, 94 beds, £13.75-17/pp), south of the station, and at *Aviemore Bunkhouse* (☎ 01479-811181, 🖳 www.aviemore-bunk house.com, £15/pp) right next to the Old Bridge Inn by the river.

The most central places to stay are *Kila B&B* (☎ 01479-810573) and the more opulent *Cairngorm Hotel* (☎ 01479-810233, 🖳 www.cairngorm.com, 8S/12D/7T/4F) conveniently positioned opposite the train station with beds from £44/pp.

Outside the village, to the north, is *Cairngorm Guest House* (☎ 01479-810630, 🖳 www.cairngormguesthouse.com, 7D/3T/2F) charging £25-40/pp, while heading east on the Cairn Gorm road is *Old Minister's Guest House* (☎ 01479-812181, 🖳 www.theoldministershouse.co.uk, 2D/2T) set amongst the trees of Rothiemurchus estate, with B&B from £42 to £45/pp.

Where to eat and drink
Visitors are spoilt for choice in Aviemore with a range of excellent restaurants and pubs. A good place to start is *Old Bridge Inn* (☎ 01479-811137, 🖳 www.oldbridgeinn

.co.uk), near the river, which has a cosy bar and restaurant with a well-stoked fireplace. The menu includes venison steak (£12.95) and courgettes and risotto (£12). They also have **internet** access (£1 for 30 mins).

All the other choices are along Grampian Rd, the best of which is *The Mountain Café* (☎ 01479-812473, 🖳 www .mountaincafe-aviemore.co.uk) where one can sit by the fireplace whilst reading books and magazines on walking and climbing. The food here is innovative and very, very tasty but most importantly comes in huge portions. The all-day breakfast is £8 and the soup and falafel wrap just £6.75.

Trendy *Café Mambo* (☎ 01479-811670, 🖳 www.cafemamboaviemore .com) turns into a **nightclub** in the evening but during the day it is a relaxed and informal place serving baguettes and huge mugs of hot chocolate. *RD's Bistro* does haggis wraps and burgers while *Roo's Leap* (☎ 01479-811161) by the station is, supposedly, an Australian-themed restaurant, although most of the dishes on the menu appear to be Tex-Mex, with prices from £7.45. Across the road, *Cairngorm Hotel* (see Where to stay) has plenty of Scottish dishes with venison for £13.75 and fish pie for £10.25. They also have regular live folk music.

For quick bites to eat there is a **bakery** at the northern end of the village which is handy for lunchbox bits and pieces, and the *Coffee Corner* (☎ 01479-810564), a small café with toasties from £3.25.

Those who like a taste of Asia should try the *Royal Tandoori Restaurant* (☎ 01479-811199) at the southern end of town for curries around £8, or at the other end of the village, *Snow Mountain Chinese Takeaway* (☎ 01479-810705). Finally there are pizzas for £6 at the *Pizza House* (☎ 01479-810799) and chips at *Happy Haggis Fish and Chip Shop* (☎ 01479-810430).

GLENMORE   [SEE MAP 26a, p167]
Away from the relative metropolis of Aviemore is a collection of buildings by Loch Morlich deep in the beautiful Forest Park of Glenmore. **Glenmore Forest Park Visitor Centre** (☎ 01479-861220, daily

9am-5pm) has a gift shop and **café** and exhibition about the pine forest. There is a small **shop** by the main road which also incorporates a **café** where you can fill up on bacon, egg and chips for £4.95.

There is limited accommodation around Loch Morlich but everyone is catered for. Campers should pitch at *Glen More Caravan and Camping Site* (☎ 01479-861271). On the other side of the road is the capacious *Cairngorm Lodge Youth Hostel* (☎ 0870-004 1137, 76 beds, Jan-Oct, £14-17). The best B&B is *Cairn Eilrig* (☎ 01479-861223, 🖳 www.bedand breakfast-aviemore-glenmore.com, 1T/1F) where you can keep an eye on the mountain weather whilst tucking into breakfast in the conservatory. B&B is £22/pp. Glenmore is the home of **Glenmore Lodge National Outdoor Training Centre** (☎ 01479-861256, 🖳 www.glenmorelodge.org.uk) where you can brush up on your mountain skills and safety awareness. They organise regular summer and winter skills courses covering everything from hillwalking to climbing as well as other outdoor activities. The excellent **bar** is the place for real ale and steaks. They also have **B&B** for £24-£30/pp which includes use of the gym, pool and climbing wall.

Sunart to Knoydart

The further north and west you go in the Highlands the more dramatic the mountains become. It all starts here on the west coast. The combination of

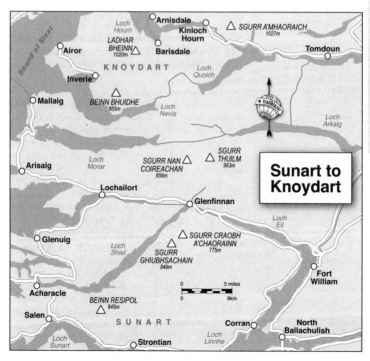

jagged peaks, the brooding sea, the distant dark islands and the big, big sky make this a simply beguiling area to explore. The magical light that catches the hillsides and the sea lochs more than makes up for the weather, which changes fast and often for the worst.

BEINN RESIPOL (*'Bayn Ress-ee-pol'*, 845m/2770ft)   [MAP 27]

Overview
Standing alone between the sea loch of Loch Sunart and the freshwater of Loch Shiel, this is the most prominent hill in the area and for very little effort gives uncluttered views of the west coast, including the Ardnamurchan peninsula, the most westerly point on the British mainland.

BEINN RESIPOL
(Homestead Mountain)

Technical grade
▲▲
Navigation grade
▲▲
Terrain grade
▲▲▲
Strenuousness
▲▲
Return time
4-4³/₄hrs
Return distance
7miles/11km
Total ascent
2770ft/845m
OS maps
Landranger 40,
Explorer 390
Gateways
Strontian (see p197)
Salen (see p198)
Acharacle (see p198)

Route
A track leads through the Resipole campsite (three miles east of Salen) and follows the east bank of the river as far as a modern **barn**. Bear right here to gain the path that climbs through the pastureland ahead. The path continues through a large swathe of **oak woodland** that is typical of the Sunart area.

After just over half a mile (1km) cross the stream to the left and continue over sometimes boggy ground to the open hillside ahead. The path runs roughly parallel to the river on the left-hand side, climbing steadily with the cone of the mountain ahead.

Continue up steeper ground to a small **lochan** to the south of the summit. The going gets a little tougher here. Aim NNE up these steep slopes. A careful eye can pick out the best route that avoids all the rocky outcrops. After a couple of false summits the **true summit** soon comes into view, marked by a big cairn.

The views from this isolated peak are among the finest along this stretch of the west coast, encompassing the Ardnamurchan peninsula and the islands of Skye, Rum, Eigg and Canna. To the east is the unmistakable bulk of Ben Nevis.

The return to Resipole campsite is by the route of ascent. Alternatively, drop off the north side of the summit and carefully descend rough steep ground to the stream below. Follow this west to join the ascent path.

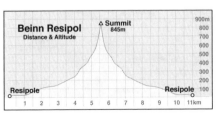

Beinn Resipol
Distance & Altitude

△ Summit
845m

Resipole   Resipole

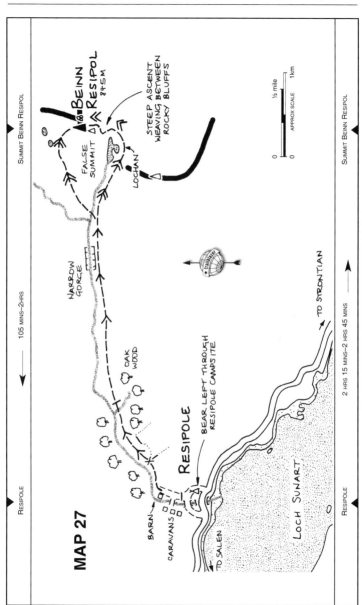

MAP 27

SUMMIT BEINN RESIPOL

BEINN RESIPOL 845M

STEEP ASCENT WEAVING BETWEEN ROCKY BLUFFS

FALSE SUMMIT

LOCHAN

105 MINS–2HRS

NARROW GORGE

OAK WOOD

RESIPOLE

BEAR LEFT THROUGH RESIPOLE CAMPSITE

BARN

CARAVANS

TO SALEN

LOCH SUNART

TO STRONTIAN

2 HRS 15 MINS–2 HRS 45 MINS

½ mile   1km

APPROX SCALE

0   0

RESIPOLE

SUMMIT BEINN RESIPOL

SUNART TO KNOYDART

Alternative routes

An even quieter path approaches the mountain from the NE by Loch Doilet, which is accessible from the single-track road to Polloch.

SGURR GHIUBHSACHAIN (*'Skor Yusaken'*, 849m/2785ft)
SGORR CRAOBH A' CHAORAINN (*'Skor Crerv-a-Herran'*, 775m/ 2545ft)
[MAP 28a; MAP 28b, p180]

Overview

Sgurr Ghiubhsachain is often overlooked, which is a shame because it is a beautiful peak with a fine north ridge snaking up from the shore of Loch Shiel; itself one of the most attractive lochs in the Highlands. The best view of the mountain is from Glenfinnan at the head of the loch. The neighbouring hill of Sgorr Craobh a' Chaorainn is ideally positioned for inclusion in a circular walk from Callop Forest car park. Appearances are somewhat deceptive with these two lonely hills. The ridges of Sgurr Ghiubhsachain can be confusing even in clear weather. There are few, if any, paths and many rocky bluffs along the ridges make navigation a little challenging, even in clear weather.

SGURR GHIUBHSACHAIN (Peak of the Firs)
SGORR CRAOBH A' CHAORAINN (Rowan Tree Peak)
Technical grade ▲▲▲
Navigation grade ▲▲▲▲
Terrain grade ▲▲▲▲
Strenuousness ▲▲▲
Return time 4¹/₂-6¹/₂hrs
Return distance 10¹/₂miles/17km
Total ascent 3379ft/1050m
OS maps Landranger 40, Explorer 391
Gateways Glenfinnan (see p198)

(side margin: SUNART TO KNOYDART *)*

Route

It is about 20 minutes from Glenfinnan Visitor Centre, along the road to Callop Forest. Head NW from **Callop Forest car park** along the forest track which soon bends round to the SW to hug the eastern shore of Loch Shiel. After about one hour the track comes to a bridge next to **Guesachan**, a private house. Just past the bridge turn left onto the lower slopes of the mountain (Map 28b) and follow the faint deer tracks that skirt the foot of the north ridge. Rather than tackle the ridge directly, continue to contour round to its eastern side to avoid the numerous cliffs. A steep grassy slope soon comes into view providing access to the spine of the north ridge. There are a series of rocky bluffs and **buttresses** on this ridge that can either be tackled head on by competent scramblers, or avoided by keeping to the right-hand side of the ridge where steep grassy slopes give access to the col at 600m.

From the **col** the upper section of the mountain comes into view, an impressive pyramidal peak of slanting cliffs and scree. Choose your line of ascent carefully to avoid the cliffs. The best route is to contour to the left to gain the lower of two **stone chutes**. Ascend by way of this chute and bear round to the right and climb very steep grassy slopes to gain the summit ridge. The summit of **Sgurr Ghiubhsachain**

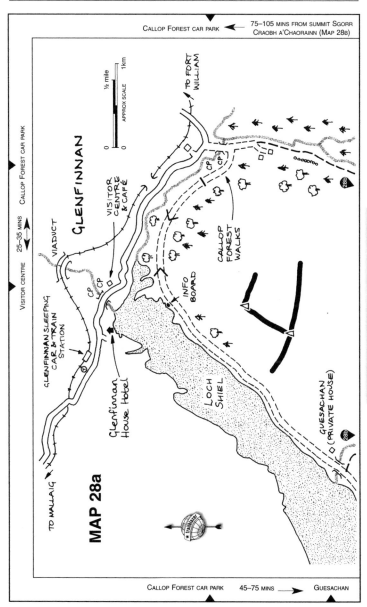

CALLOP FOREST car park ← 75–105 MINS FROM SUMMIT SGORR CRAOBH A'CHAORAINN (MAP 28B)

TO FORT WILLIAM

GLENFINNAN

VISITOR CENTRE & CAFÉ

½ mile   1km

APPROX SCALE

0   0

VIADUCT

CP

CP

CALLOP FOREST WALKS

INFO BOARD

GLENFINNAN SLEEPING CAR & TRAIN STATION

CP   CP

Glenfinnan House Hotel

LOCH SHIEL

GUESACHAN (PRIVATE HOUSE)

28B

TO MALLAIG

MAP 28a

SUNART TO KNOYDART

CALLOP FOREST CAR PARK ▲

CALLOP FOREST CAR PARK ◀ 25–35 MINS ▶ VISITOR CENTRE ◀

CALLOP FOREST CAR PARK ◀ 45–75 MINS → GUESACHAN ▲

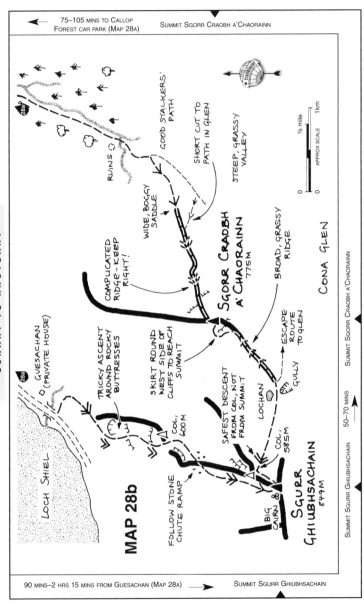

SUNART TO KNOYDART

75–105 MINS TO CALLOP FOREST CAR PARK (MAP 28A)

SUMMIT SGORR CRAOBH A'CHAORAINN

GOOD STALKERS' PATH

SHORT CUT TO PATH IN GLEN

STEEP, GRASSY VALLEY

RUINS

WIDE, BOGGY SADDLE

SGORR CRAOBH A'CHAORAINN 775M

BROAD, GRASSY RIDGE

CONA GLEN

COMPLICATED RIDGE – KEEP RIGHT!

GUESACHAN (PRIVATE HOUSE)

TRICKY ASCENT AROUND ROCKY BUTTRESSES

SKIRT ROUND WEST SIDE OF CLIFFS TO REACH SUMMIT

ESCAPE ROUTE TO GLEN

GULLY

LOCH SHIEL

COL, 600M

SAFEST DESCENT FROM COL, NOT FROM SUMMIT

LOCHAN

COL, 585M

MAP 28b

FOLLOW STONE CHUTE RAMP

BIG CAIRN

SGURR GHIUBHSACHAIN 849M

APPROX SCALE

SUMMIT SGURR GHIUBHSACHAIN

SUMMIT SGORR CRAOBH A'CHAORAINN

50–70 MINS

90 MINS–2 HRS 15 MINS FROM GUESACHAN (MAP 28A)

SUMMIT SGURR GHIUBHSACHAIN

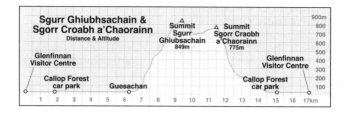

is five minutes along this ridge to the SW. From the summit there are views over the lower end of Loch Shiel and out to the islands of Rum and Skye. To the east is the perfectly U-shaped Cona Glen, a text-book example of a glaciated valley, stretching for ten miles to the shores of Loch Linnhe.

The saddle to the east is best reached by returning back along the summit ridge in a NE direction and descending grassy slopes towards the SE. Cross the broad boggy **saddle** to the east and ascend the easy grassy ridge that leads to the summit of **Sgorr Craobh a' Chaorainn**. The summit of this hill is a seemingly impenetrable ten-metre wall. It is possible to climb this short cliff but it is also easily avoided by moving round to the north side of the summit and climbing shallower slopes to the cairn on the top.

The descent back to Callop Forest car park is by way of the NE ridge. Five to ten minutes after leaving the summit the ridge falls away abruptly. Move round to the right to find a useful grassy gully that leads the way down to a wide boggy ridge. The small peak ahead can be avoided by contouring the southern edge of the ridge. Continue down steep slopes to join the stalkers' path in the glen where there are remnants of Caledonian Pine Forest. It is less than an hour from here back to Callop Forest car park.

Alternative routes

From the saddle between the two peaks there is a descent route back to Guesachan via Coire Ghiubhsachain for a return along the forest track used for the approach. Another route of descent is to follow the undulating north ridge of Sgorr Craobh a' Chaorainn and descend the steep slopes back to Guesachan.

One final alternative is to drop off early towards the SE from the SW ridge of Sgorr Craobh a' Chaorainn to join the path that leads down the glen back to Callop Forest car-park.

SUNART TO KNOYDART

❏ **Important note – walking times**

All times in this book refer only to the time spent walking. You will need to add 20-30% to allow for rests, photography, checking the map, drinking water etc.

THE CORRYHULLY HORSESHOE
SGURR NAN COIREACHAN
('*Skoor nan Corr-a-chen*', 956m/3135ft)
SGURR THUILM ('*Skoor Hool-em*', 963m/3160ft)
[MAP 29a; MAP 29b, p184]

Overview
If ever two mountains were designed for mountain walkers it is the pair of munros sitting at the head of Corryhully north of Glenfinnan. A near perfect horseshoe ridge makes for an ideal outing into the wild and rugged depths of Morar. However, the undulating terrain is characterised by rocky bluffs and knolls making navigation a little confusing at times.

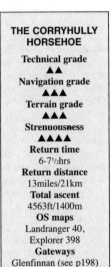

THE CORRYHULLY HORSESHOE

Technical grade
▲▲
Navigation grade
▲▲▲
Terrain grade
▲▲▲
Strenuousness
▲▲▲▲
Return time
6-7½hrs
Return distance
13miles/21km
Total ascent
4563ft/1400m
OS maps
Landranger 40,
Explorer 398
Gateways
Glenfinnan (see p198)

Route
The car park on the west bank of the River Finnan, next to the main road through **Glenfinnan**, marks the start of the approach to these two mountains. Follow the **private driveway** north below the impressive arches of the Glenfinnan viaduct; over 100 years old and star of several *Harry Potter* films. It is about one hour to a bridge that marks a fork in the track. Take the right-hand fork past **Corryhully bothy** and continue northwards for 15 minutes to a small cairn on the left-hand side of the track. The cairn marks the point where the ascent path begins. Follow the path on a gentle gradient as it climbs to some **zigzags**, which ascend sharply on to the back of a wide ridge.

The path continues up the spine of the ridge (Map 29b), negotiating a number of rocky bluffs as it does so. The ridge levels out briefly as it approaches the final steep slopes to the summit and then skirts round to the left of these slopes before zigzagging steeply up the side of the mountain to reach an outlying peak at **850m**.

Continue northwards from this peak along a confusing ridge of rocky shelves and knolls. The summit of **Sgurr nan Coireachan** is straight ahead and the path soon begins to climb the steep slopes up to the cairn on the top. There is one slightly awkward rocky step on this final stretch that necessitates a quick, easy scramble. The views to the NW of Loch Morar, the peaks of Knoydart and the Isle of Rum are sensational.

From the summit follow the ridge down in an ENE direction and keep to the path as it heads eastwards along the broad, rolling two-mile ridge. Despite the confusing nature of the terrain, navigation is aided by the presence of a well-worn path along with a line of rusty fence posts. Just over halfway along the ridge there is a brief climb to the central top of **Beinn Garbh** ('*Bayn Garrav*')

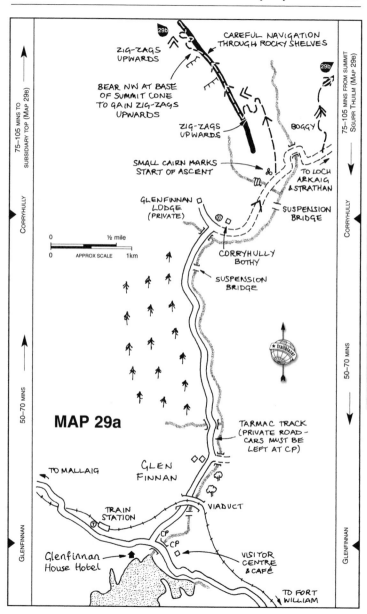

ZIG-ZAGS
UPWARDS

CAREFUL NAVIGATION
THROUGH ROCKY SHELVES

BEAR NW AT BASE
OF SUMMIT CONE
TO GAIN ZIG-ZAGS
UPWARDS

ZIG-ZAGS
UPWARDS

BOGGY

SMALL CAIRN MARKS
START OF ASCENT

TO LOCH
ARKAIG
& STRATHAN

GLENFINNAN
LODGE
(PRIVATE)

SUSPENSION
BRIDGE

CORRYHULLY
BOTHY

SUSPENSION
BRIDGE

0   ½ mile
0   1km
APPROX SCALE

MAP 29a

TARMAC TRACK
(PRIVATE ROAD -
CARS MUST BE
LEFT AT CP)

TO MALLAIG

GLEN
FINNAN

TRAIN
STATION

VIADUCT

CP

CP

Glenfinnan
House Hotel

VISITOR
CENTRE
& CAFÉ

TO FORT
WILLIAM

75-105 MINS TO
SUBSIDIARY TOP (MAP 29b)

CORRYHULLY

50-70 MINS

GLENFINNAN

75-105 MINS FROM SUMMIT
SGURR THUILM (MAP 29b)

CORRYHULLY

50-70 MINS

GLENFINNAN

SUNART TO KNOYDART

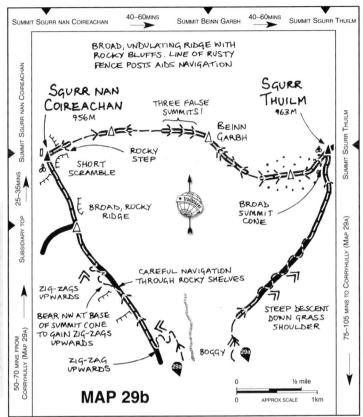

SUNART TO KNOYDART

MAP 29b

before a descent to a col. Climb the steep grassy slopes ahead to a small grassy plateau. Continue eastwards to the end of this flat ground and begin the climb NE up grassy slopes to the summit of **Sgurr Thuilm**. Loch Arkaig can be seen stretched out to the east while the mountain immediately to the south is Streap, a fine corbett with a knife-edged summit ridge.

Descend from Sgurr Thuilm in a south direction over easy slopes. The ridge soon turns to face SW. Follow the path which winds down the steep spine of this ridge leading swiftly back to the glen below at a point just east of a river junction (Map 29a). Follow the track as it swings round to the west over a **bridge** and then south back to Corryhully bothy and the driveway back to Glenfinnan.

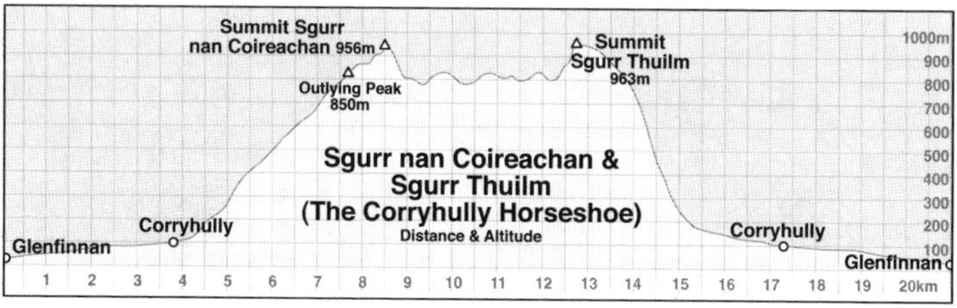
Summit Sgurr nan Coireachan 956m
Outlying Peak 850m
Summit Sgurr Thuilm 963m
Sgurr nan Coireachan & Sgurr Thuilm (The Corryhully Horseshoe)
Distance & Altitude
Glenfinnan
Corryhully
Corryhully
Glenfinnan
1000m
900
800
700
600
500
400
300
200
100
1 2 3 4 5 6 7 8 9 10 11 12 13 14 15 16 17 18 19 20km

Alternative routes

Either mountain can be climbed on its own but the return from either would be by the same route of ascent. The only other way of 'doing' both peaks in one expedition is to tackle them from Glen Pean to the north which can be reached from the road-head at the end of Loch Arkaig. The normal and preferred route, however, is the one described on p182, starting at Glenfinnan.

BEINN BHUIDHE (*'Bayn Voo-ya*, 855m/2805ft) [MAP 30a, p186; MAP 30b, p187]

Overview

There are a number of hills worth taking your boots up on Knoydart but this one is often overlooked, discriminated against because of a lack of height or good looks. However, appearances are deceptive and once on the long gnarly ridge the rewards soon come. The profile of the mountain is far better appreciated from its spine while it easily offers the best views of Loch Nevis as well as vistas to the islands of Skye, Eigg, and even the Outer Hebrides. There are a couple of surprisingly steep sections where hands may come in useful. The first is on the initial climb onto the main ridge and the other at the eastern end of the ridge, otherwise there are few problems.

Route

Beginning at **Inverie pier** walk east along the shore-side road. After 10-15 minutes there is a junction by a white house. Bear left here and then left again at the sign for Kinlochhourn. Climb the track by the long mossy wall and pass through the white gate at the hairpin. Continue along this track towards **Lord Brocket's Monument**, a memorial to a former land-lord who in 1930 began evicting local crofters to make way for his sporting and shooting interests. His insensitive attitude to land ownership was high-

BEINN BHUIDHE (Yellow Mountain)

Technical grade
▲▲▲
Navigation grade
▲▲▲
Terrain grade
▲▲▲
Strenuousness
▲▲
Return time
5-7½hrs
(6-8½hrs including Meall Bhasiter)
Return distance
11miles/18km
(14miles/22km including Meall Bhasiter)
Total ascent
3199ft/975m
(3691ft/1125m including Meall Bhasiter)
OS maps
Landranger 33 or 40, Explorer 398
Gateways
Mallaig (see p198)
Inverie (see p200)

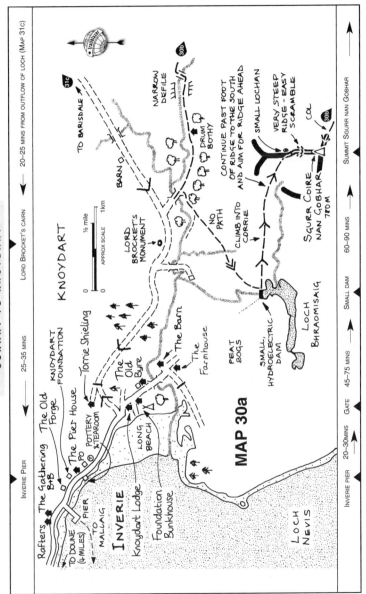

SUNART TO KNOYDART

INVERIE PIER — 20–30MINS — GATE — 45–75 MINS — SMALL DAM — 60–90 MINS — SUMMIT SQURR NAN GOBHAR

20–25 MINS FROM OUTFLOW OF LOCH (MAP 31c)

TO BARISDALE

TO DOUNE (4 MILES)

TO MALLAIG

LOCH NEVIS

KNOYDART

INVERIE

Rafters
The Gathering BnB
The Old Forge
The Pier House
PO
Pottery & Tearoom
Knoydart Lodge
Foundation Bunkhouse
Long Beach

KNOYDART FOUNDATION
Torrie Shieling
The Old Byre
The Barn
The Farmhouse
PEAT BOGS

LORD BROCKET'S MONUMENT

BARN

DRUM BOTHY

NARROW DEFILE

SMALL LOCHAN

VERY STEEP RIDGE - EASY SCRAMBLE

COL

SGURR COIRE NAN GOBHAR 770M

SMALL HYDROELECTRIC DAM

LOCH BHRAOMISAIG

CONTINUE PAST FOOT OF RIDGE TO THE SOUTH AND AIM FOR RIDGE AHEAD

NO PATH

CLIMB INTO CORRIE

APPROX SCALE
0   ½ mile
0   1km

MAP 30a

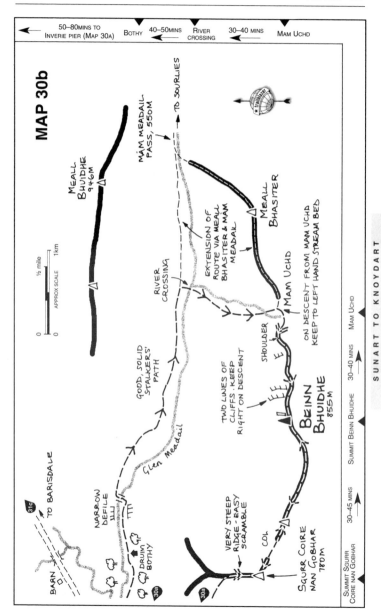

MAP 30b

MEALL BHUIDHE 946M

MÀM MEADAIL PASS, 550M

TO SOURLIES

½ mile   1km
APPROX SCALE
0   0

EXTENSION OF ROUTE VIA MEALL BHASITER & MÀM MEADAL

MEALL BHASITER

RIVER CROSSING

MAM UCHD

ON DESCENT FROM MAM UCHD KEEP TO LEFT HAND STREAM BED

GOOD, SOLID STALKERS' PATH

Glen Meadal

SHOULDER

TWO LINES OF CLIFFS. KEEP RIGHT ON DESCENT

BEINN BHUIDHE 855M

TO BARISDALE

31c

NARROW DEFILE

BARN

DRUIM BOTHY

30c

VERY STEEP RIDGE - EASY SCRAMBLE

COL

SGURR COIRE NAN GOBHAR 780M

30b

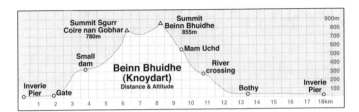

Beinn Bhuidhe (Knoydart) Distance & Altitude

lighted by the so-called Seven Men of Knoydart who, in 1948, defied him by claiming a section of land on which they continued crofting. The cross at the top of the monument hints at Lord Brocket's stance as a nazi-sympathiser.

Just beyond the monument take a right for the bridge over Inverie River. On the other side of the bridge turn right and begin to climb the slopes in a SW direction. The hill is steep here; the best route is to aim for the burn ahead and follow its west bank. As the gradient eases head SW towards Loch Bhraomisaig at 330m. At the outflow of the loch there is a **small dam**, part of the hydro-electric installations, the energy from which powers the whole of Inverie village laid out along the shore of Inverie Bay below.

Head east from the outflow towards Coire nan Gobhar. You are aiming for the northern ridge of Sgurr Coire nan Gobhar which forms the shallow backwall of this corrie. Do not be tempted to climb the smaller spur that juts into the corrie. The ridge in question is higher up at 670m and is obvious once you reach it. There is a small lochan on this knobbly ridge from where it is a short climb over rocky bluffs and grassy ledges up the north ridge to the top of **Sgurr Coire nan Gobhar**. The wide but attractive ridge of Beinn Bhuidhe stretches out towards the depths of Knoydart and by now the views of the islands beyond the mouth of Loch Nevis should come into view.

Follow the ridge to the east, dropping down to a small **col** (Map 30b), before ascending gentle slopes over an outlying top to the summit of **Beinn Bhuidhe**.

The descent along the east ridge begins in a less than demanding fashion until it drops off quite suddenly in a series of low cliffs. The first two are easy enough to avoid by keeping to the right-hand side of both. The third and final cliff requires more care with a faint path picking its way down the right-hand side of the precipice. As soon as you can take your eyes off the ground train them ahead to the beautiful head of Loch Nevis, a wild and remote spot dominated by the pyramidal peak of Sgurr na Ciche and its smaller neighbour Ben Aden. Continue down the left side of some very steep grassy slopes to the saddle of **Mam Uchd**.

Keep to the left as you descend north from here to avoid the steep, rocky ground further to the right. Eventually the gradient eases as you reach the floor of Glen Meadail. The **river** is usually quite easy to cross, unless it is in spate, in which case you will need to follow the trackless southern bank of the river. On the other side, however, is a good **stalkers' path** following the north bank, eventually recrossing the river at the bridge at the mouth of the glen. Continue along the path, through the narrow entrance to the glen and past **Druim bothy** (see p200) set in open birch woodland.

The path leads back to the wooden bridge across the Inverie River (Map 30a) from where it is a question of retracing your steps back to Inverie.

Alternative routes

It is possible to extend the walk and take in the entire ridge that forms the northern side of Loch Nevis by continuing up the ridge from the Mam Uchd saddle to the top of Meall Bhasiter at 710m (2329ft). Descend over a knolly ridge in a north-westerly direction to reach the Mam Meadail col and join the aforementioned stalkers' path back to Inverie.

LADHAR BHEINN ('*Lar-ven*', 1020m/3345ft)
[MAP 31a, p190; MAP 31b, p191; MAP 31c, p192]

Overview

There can be little argument that Ladhar Bheinn is among Scotland's top ten mountains. Standing proudly over the quiet waters of Loch Hourn on the Knoydart peninsula, this distinctive mountain with the deeply enclosed Coire Dhorrcail, has an aura of grandeur and impenetrability. Getting there is an expedition in itself, which only serves to accentuate the sense of wildness. Some scrambling is involved on the traverse described here.

Route

The quickest way to get to Barisdale for the start of the ascent of Ladhar Bheinn is by the Arnisdale ferry (☎ 01599-522247) based in Arnisdale on the north side of Loch Hourn. The boat is a tiny wee thing which can take about eight folk at a push. It only runs on demand so needs to be booked in advance. The traditional route to Barisdale is on foot from Kinlochhourn. There is a long-term car park at Kinlochhourn where one can leave a car for a small charge. The walk starts dramatically as the path squeezes its way along the southern shore of Loch Hourn below steep mountain walls.

It is hard to lose the path at any point from here to Barisdale since it is protected by the narrow stretch of seawater on one side and the impenetrable mountain wall on the other. The going is easy at first although high rucksacks might get tangled up in the rhododendron bushes. These soon peter out and the path continues along the beautiful loch shore to Skiary.

LADHAR BHEINN (Claw or Hoof Mountain)
Technical grade ▲▲▲
Navigation grade ▲▲
Terrain grade ▲▲▲
Strenuousness ▲▲▲
Return time 4-5½hrs from Barisdale (2½-3hrs Kinlochhourn to Barisdale)
Return distance 8miles/13km from Barisdale (6miles/10km Kinlochhourn to Barisdale)
Total ascent 4365ft/1330m from Barisdale (1110ft/340m Kinlochhourn to Barisdale)
OS maps Landranger 33, Explorer 413
Gateways Tomdoun (see p201) Kinlochhourn (p201) Barisdale (see p201) Inverie (see p200)

SUNART TO KNOYDART

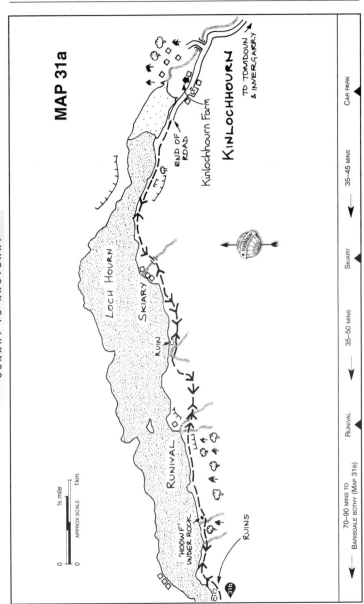

MAP 31a

LOCH HOURN

KINLOCHHOURN

TO TOMDOUN & INVERGARRY

Kinlochhourn Farm

END OF ROAD

SKIARY

RUIN

RUNIVAL

'HOOWF' UNDER ROCK

RUINS

31b

½ mile
APPROX SCALE
0 ————— 1km

| CAR PARK | 35–45 MINS | SKIARY | 35–50 MINS | RUNIVAL | 70–90 MINS TO BARISDALE BOTHY (MAP 31B) |

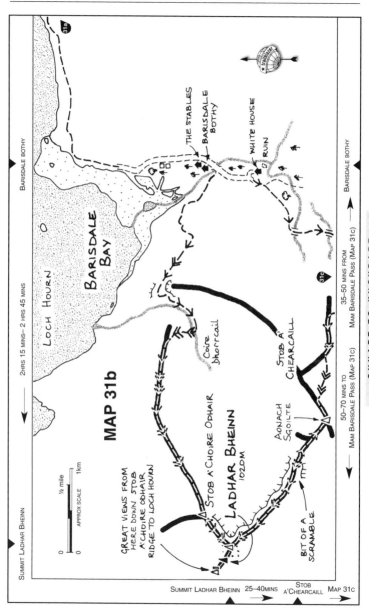

MAP 31b

SUMMIT LADHAR BHEINN

2HRS 15 MINS– 2 HRS 45 MINS

BARISDALE BOTHY

LOCH HOURN

BARISDALE BAY

THE STABLES

BARISDALE BOTHY

WHITE HOUSE
RUIN

BARISDALE BOTHY

35–50 MINS FROM
MAM BARISDALE PASS (MAP 31c)

50–70 MINS TO
MAM BARISDALE PASS (MAP 31c)

SUNART TO KNOYDART

Coire Dhorrcaill

Stob a'
CHEARCAILL

Stob a'Choire Odhair

LADHAR BHEINN
1020M

AONACH
SGOILTE

GREAT VIEWS FROM
HERE DOWN STOB
A'CHOIRE ODHAIR
RIDGE TO LOCH HOURN

BIT OF A
SCRAMBLE

½ mile   1km
APPROX SCALE
0   0

SUMMIT LADHAR BHEINN 25–40MINS

STOB
A'CHEARCAILL

MAP 31c

SUNART TO KNOYDART

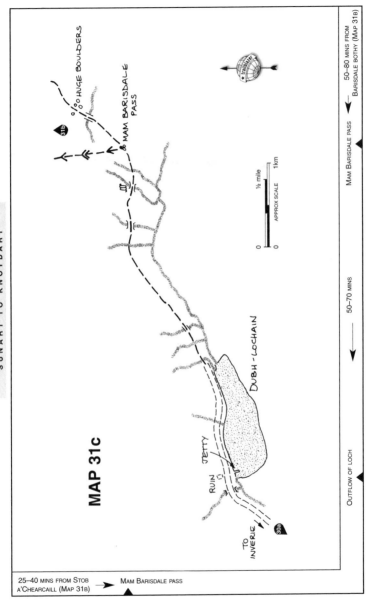

MAP 31c

HUGE BOULDERS

31b

MAM BARISDALE PASS

DUBH-LOCHAIN

RUIN

JETTY

TO INVERIE

30a

APPROX SCALE

0 ½ mile
0 1km

50–80 MINS FROM
BARISDALE BOTHY (MAP 31B)

MAM BARISDALE PASS

50–70 MINS

OUTFLOW OF LOCH

25–40 MINS FROM STOB
A'CHEARCAILL (MAP 31B) ► MAM BARISDALE PASS

The first big climb of the walk starts soon after, climbing 100m over a high brow before dropping back down to sea level on the other side. After crossing a

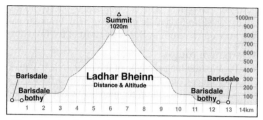

couple of streams the path, rather teasingly, rises again to an even higher point before dropping steadily through a shallow heathery gully, dotted with ancient Scots pine trees, to the private house at **Runival**. This is a magnificent spot with a huge rocky buttress set behind a flat, green alluvial fan on the loch shore.

From Runival continue along a path that clings to a wooded cliff plunging into deep cold waters. A little further on the trees thin out and the path continues on an even keel for a while before a final climb past some ruins onto the last high point of the day. Descend from here, through a shallow gully to a broad track on the shore of Barisdale Bay (Map 31b). Continue south to Barisdale. From **Barisdale bothy** continue SW along the four-wheel-drive track. After crossing the bridge follow the stalkers' path on the right which leads across the flat alluvial plain next to Barisdale Bay. At the edge of this plain the path climbs suddenly and works its way around the lower mountainside into the hidden Coire Dhorrcail, a stunning corrie that only reveals its true nature to those who venture into it.

Leave the path just past the mouth of the corrie and cross the stream below before climbing up increasingly steep slopes of grass and heather to gain the **Stob a' Choire Odhair** ridge above.

In places the ridge is quite narrow on its journey to the summit ridge. Once you reach the eastern end of the summit ridge head west. The ridge drops ever so slightly before climbing again to the summit of **Ladhar Bheinn**. It is worth taking the short detour to the lower top to the NW (marked by a concrete trig point – recently shattered by a bolt of lightning) where there is a much-photographed view over Stob a' Choire Odhair (*'Stop a Horra Ower'*) and the narrow upper reaches of Loch Hourn beyond. To the north is the wider channel of the loch as it approaches the Sound of Sleat and on the far side are the unmistakable curtains of scree on Beinn Sgritheall. Looking south, the view is dominated by the other Knoydart munros of Luinne Bheinn and Meall Buidhe with the strikingly pointed peak of Sgurr na Ciche beyond.

To continue the traverse leave the summit by the SE ridge which drops quite sharply at first before levelling out at a low top. Once past this, the ridge becomes a little more complicated with some fairly easy scrambling involved. Descend steeply again to a col and then climb easier slopes to the summit of Aonach Sgoilte.

A fairly wide ridge runs NE towards the shapely top of **Stob a' Chearcaill** (*'Stop a Hearkeel'*). Before reaching this peak strike off right and begin to descend. The ground here is exceptionally steep and it's a long 450-metre drop SE to the **Mam Barisdale pass** (Map 31c). From the pass follow the path to the left for a quick return to Barisdale or right for Inverie.

Alternative routes
For Inverie, the long traverse of the three-mile (5km), knobbly Aonach Sgoilte ridge to Sgurr Coire Choinneachan makes a far more spectacular approach to the village than the path in the glen below but it's a rollercoaster ridge which is deceptively long.

SGURR A' MHAORAICH ('_Skor a Ver-eech_', 1027m/3370ft)
[MAP 32]

Overview
An overlooked hill deserving of more attention, Sgurr a' Mhaoraich is remote yet easily accessible. Its twisting eastern ridge leads to a high summit that provides one of the most beguiling views of what is probably the most beautiful of sea lochs, Loch Hourn. Apart from a potentially confusing descent from the summit, and a punishingly steep descent from Am Bathaich, this is an easy day that can even be fitted into an afternoon if you are feeling up for it, with time to spare for a pint in Tomdoun Hotel to boot.

**SGURR A'
MHAORAICH**
(Shellfish Peak)

Technical grade
▲▲
Navigation grade
▲▲▲
Terrain grade
▲▲▲
Strenuousness
▲▲
Return time
3¹/₂-5hrs
Return distance
8miles/13km
Total ascent
3576ft/1090m
OS maps
Landranger 33,
Explorer 414
Gateways
Tomdoun (see p201)

Route
The walk begins at a layby on the single-track road to Kinlochhourn, just over half a mile (1km) SW of the bridge over Loch Quoich's northern arm. A deer-stalking information sign by the roadside indicates the start of the path which steadily ascends a long, broad ridge. The ridge shallows briefly at about 650m before climbing in **zigzags** to the top of Sgurr Coire nan-Eiricheallach. Steep slopes drop away dramatically into the glen on the north side while the ridge drops away to the west. Follow this ridge which narrows on occasion and crosses over a well-preserved **old stone wall**. After passing the low point of the ridge some dramatic cliffs come into view and appear to bar further progress. The path, however, skirts below this intrusion on the south side of the ridge and climbs past some massive **boulders** to rejoin the crest of the ridge above the cliffs. Continue climbing westwards along a path that skirts below another line of cliffs, this time on the north side of the ridge. The path rises up to the short summit ridge and swings round to the NW to reach the **summit cairn**.

When the cloud is down the descent from the summit to the **col** before Am Bathaich can be problematic. The shallowest part of the ridge imperceptibly

SUNART TO KNOYDART

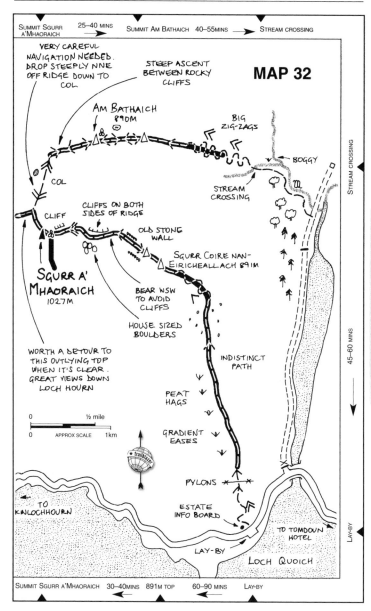

VERY CAREFUL NAVIGATION NEEDED. DROP STEEPLY NNE OFF RIDGE DOWN TO COL

STEEP ASCENT BETWEEN ROCKY CLIFFS

MAP 32

AM BATHAICH 890M

BIG ZIG-ZAGS

BOGGY

COL

STREAM CROSSING

STREAM CROSSING

CLIFF

CLIFFS ON BOTH SIDES OF RIDGE

OLD STONE WALL

SGURR A' MHAORAICH 1027M

SGURR COIRE NAN- EIRICHEALLACH 891M

BEAR WSW TO AVOID CLIFFS

HOUSE SIZED BOULDERS

WORTH A DETOUR TO THIS OUTLYING TOP WHEN IT'S CLEAR. GREAT VIEWS DOWN LOCH HOURN

INDISTINCT PATH

PEAT HAGS

GRADIENT EASES

0   ½ mile
0   APPROX SCALE   1km

trailbtezer

PYLONS

TO KINLOCHHOURN

ESTATE INFO BOARD

TO TOMDOUN HOTEL

LAY-BY

LAY-BY

LOCH QUOICH

SUNART TO KNOYDART

45–60 MINS

LAY-BY

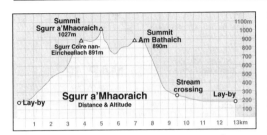

Summit
Sgurr a'Mhaoraich △
1027m
△
Sgurr Coire nan-
Eiricheallach 891m

Summit
△ Am Bathaich
890m

Stream
crossing

Sgurr a'Mhaoraich
Distance & Altitude

o Lay-by
o Lay-by

1100m
1000
900
800
700
600
500
400
300
200
100

1 2 3 4 5 6 7 8 9 10 11 12 13km

swings westwards to a subsidiary top whereas the actual route to the col drops off the side over steep slopes. From the summit head NNW for about 300m before beginning the steep descent over uneven ground in a NNE direction to reach the col at 780m. If, however, the conditions are clear, the side trip to the subsidiary top is worth taking for the magnificent views down the length of Loch Hourn, the narrowest and most deeply cut loch on the western seaboard.

From the col climb very steep slopes to gain the ridge that leads east to the summit of **Am Bathaich** (*'Am Baheech'*). Continue along this undulating ridge from where there are great views down Glen Loyne, surely one of the most perfect examples of a U-shaped valley in the Highlands.

The descent begins in earnest with a knee-jerking stagger down the grassy slopes. A stalkers' path soon appears. Follow the **zigzagging path** down to the floor of the glen and cross the burn. A path on the right bank leads through scattered birch and beech trees and past a beautiful waterfall to reach a **broad track** by a bridge over the River Quoich. Head south along this track to reach the Kinlochhourn road and follow this for five minutes back to the start.

Alternative routes

To shorten the walk, descend from the summit by the south ridge and drop into Coire nan Eiricheallach to gain a stalkers' path for a fast return to the road. It is then 1 1/4 miles (2km) back along the road to the start.

❏ **Other hills in the area**
● **Garbh Bheinn** (*'Gar-vayn'*, **885m/2905ft**) Garbh Bheinn, the hill that stands out across Loch Linnhe when heading north up the A82, is a great place for escaping the crowds of nearby Glen Coe and Glen Nevis. It lies on the north side of the A861 halfway between the Corran ferry and Strontian.
● **Rois Bheinn** (*'Rosh-ven'*, **882m/2895ft**) Accessible from Lochailort on the West Highland railway, Rois Bheinn is an easy climb: the views (of Knoydart and the islands of Skye, Rum and Eigg) start early as it stands uninterrupted on the western seaboard.
● **Sgurr na Ciche** (*'Skor na Kee'*, **1040m (3410ft)**) If you ask a child to draw a mountain you may well end up with a picture of Sgurr na Ciche. This pyramid of a hill competes with nearby Ladhar Bheinn in terms of magnificence and remoteness. It is accessible by chartered boat from Mallaig or Inverie, or a long day's walk from the road end at Loch Arkaig.

SUNART & KNOYDART – TOWNS & VILLAGES

STRONTIAN [see map p198]

The small village of Strontian, famous for lending its name to the element strontium which was first discovered in the nearby lead mines, sits almost at the head of the long tapering Loch Sunart. It makes an excellent base for exploring the area with Beinn Resipol just a few miles down the road.

The **shop** is well stocked and there is a **cash machine** on the wall outside (which charges £1.75 per transaction!). Next door is the **TIC** (☎ 01967-402131) with information on accommodation and things to see and do in the area.

There is a smaller **shop** on the road leading south which incorporates the **post office** and also has a **cash machine** (which does not charge you for withdrawals, unlike the aforementioned one).

Where to stay

There is limited accommodation but *The Strontian Hotel* (☎ 01967-402029, 🖥 www .thestrontianhotel.co.uk, 3D/3T en suite), overlooking the head of the loch, has B&B for £40/pp. The hotel is also the best place for an evening drink.

Glenview Caravan Park and Campsite (☎ 01967-402123) is a small site among the trees behind the village, with pitches from £4/pp. If this is full try *Resipole Campsite* (see Map 27; ☎ 01967-431235, 🖥 www.resipole.co.uk) seven miles west towards Salen, where they have their own licensed **bar**. It is ideally positioned at the start of the Beinn Resipol walk, with pitches for £11-15.50 (for up to six people).

Whilst in the vicinity it is worth mentioning two excellent pubs further along the

---

❏ **Rainy days**

● **Whale watching** Killer whales and minke whales often visit the Sound of Sleat and the waters around the Small Isles. Contact **Sea Knoydart** (☎ 01687-460046, 🖥 www.seaknoydart.co.uk) for trips to the islands on their rigid inflatable boat. Mark, the guide, is an expert in marine wildlife and has a keen eye for finding whales and other cetaceans. Even when they are not there the speedy boat ride is an exhilarating experience.

● **Beaches** It doesn't have to be hot and sunny to go to the beach. The silver sands of Morar and Camusdarach (three miles south of Mallaig) look just as good on a wet and wild day.

● **Ardnamurchan Natural History Centre** This remarkable centre (☎ 01972-500209, 🖥 www.ardnamurchannaturalhistorycentre.co.uk), located at Glenmore, nine miles west of Salen, was the inspiration of Michael MacGregor, a highly accomplished local wildlife and landscape photographer with a real passion for the native beasts of the west coast. It incorporates a café and the 'Living Building', a turf-roofed interactive barn where you can come face to face with frogs and newts in the glass-sided pond and learn about the diversity of life in those wet bogs that you squelch through in the hills. You can even see if any wild pine martens have holed themselves up in the purpose-built den and watch live footage of the local golden eagles (Apr-Oct, Mon-Sat 10.30am-5.30pm; Sun noon-5.30pm). Admission is £5.

● **Ardnamurchan Point and lighthouse** Unfortunately there is no bus to Ardnamurchan Point lighthouse. If you have a car it is a twisty 25 miles along the single-track road from Salen to this most westerly point of the British mainland. There is a small café and gift shop at the road end but it is really the rugged coastline, pitted with small sandy beaches, that you will have come to see.

Glenview
Campsite

★ trailhead

To Resipole
Campsite (7 miles),
Salen Hotel (10 miles)
&Loch Shiel Hotel
(13 miles)

A861

Shop
CP ℹ

Loch Sunart

0   250m

Strontian
Hotel

To
Corran

Shop

Strontian

road to Lochailort. The first in **Salen** is *Salen Hotel* (☎ 01967-431661, 🖥 www .salenhotel.co.uk, 3D), ten miles west of Strontian, which has been tastefully refurbished yet still retains some old Highland character. They serve some great home-cooked food: deep-fried haddock (£8.95) and pork loin chops with blue cheese (£9.50) and they also have beds from £30/pp.

The other, three miles further north from Salen at **Acharacle**, is *Loch Shiel Hotel* (☎ 01967-431224, 🖥 www.loch shielhotel.com, 6D/2T/1F en suite), a traditional former shooting lodge with a welcoming and relaxed atmosphere. It's a wonderful place to have a long lunch on a rainy afternoon. The menu covers everything from venison to burger and chips and B&B costs from £32.50/pp.

GLENFINNAN   [SEE MAP 28a, p179]

Trains (see pp32-6) from Fort William stop regularly at Glenfinnan, a place that has more claims to fame than a village of such diminutive stature really deserves. To begin with there are the historical associations with Bonnie Prince Charlie who led the Jacobite uprisings in 1745 (see p49). The striking monument to Charlie is down by the loch shore and there is a **visitor centre** and **café** with informative displays on the local history.

Glenfinnan's second claim to fame is the quite spell-binding views down Loch Shiel which find their way onto calendars and postcards all over Scotland. Finally there is the curving viaduct behind the village which is over 100 years old.

More importantly for hillwalkers, Glenfinnan is the gateway to the Corryhully

Horsehoe and Sgurr Ghiubhsachain walks. Unfortunately, there is little accommodation here but Fort William (see p114), where there is a greater choice, is only a short train ride away.

In Glenfinnan it is one extreme or the other with dorm beds for £12 at *Glenfinnan Sleeping Car* (☎ 01397-722295) at the station, or a huge bed for £57.50/pp or above at the 250-year-old *Glenfinnan House Hotel* (☎ 01397-722235, 🖥 www.glenfinnanhouse.com, 3D/2F). The whole building oozes history and class and if the rooms are a bit too expensive console yourself with a wee dram in the bar or maybe indulge in the venison sausages.

MALLAIG

Mallaig, a small west-coast fishing town hugging a tiny harbour at the end of the West Highland Railway line, commands enviable views across the Sound of Sleat to Skye and the Small Isles.

One of the best viewpoints of these islands is actually two miles south of

Mallaig at the immaculate shell-sand beaches of Morar and Camusdarach, where much of the film *Local Hero* was shot.

Services

Trains run daily to and from Fort William with some of these connecting with the

Skye **ferry**. Calmac operates a ferry service to Rum. See pp32-6 for details of these services.

To reach Knoydart climb aboard the *MV Western Isles* (office hours ☎ 01687-462320, 🖳 www.knoydart-ferry.co.uk) which departs Mallaig Harbour for Inverie at 10.15am and 2.15pm on Mon, Wed and Fri (also Tue and Thu, May-Sept).

Next to the harbour Way Out West is a great **outdoor shop** which can supply any last-minute bits of hill kit you've forgotten; they also sell maps of the area. There are also two **banks** with **cash machines**, a **newsagent**, two **shops** including a sizeable Co-op, a **pharmacy** and a **post office**. For a **taxi** call ☎ 01687-462232 or 01687-462370.

Where to stay
In the centre of the village, with its raised patio overlooking the bustle of the harbour is *Sheena's Backpackers' Lodge* (☎ 01687-462764, 🖳 www.mallaigbackpackers.co.uk) which has 12 dorm beds in two rooms at £13.50/pp. Opposite the Co-op is the *Marine Hotel* (☎ 01687-462217, 3S/5D/9T/2F) which offers B&B from £25/pp. *The Moorings* (☎ 01687-462225) is a friendly guest house overlooking the harbour with B&B from £23/pp. Both *Seaview Guest House* (☎ 01687-462059, 🖳 www.seaviewguesthousemallaig.com, 1D/1T/2F) and *The Anchorage* (☎ 01687-462454, 🖳 www.anchoragemallaig.co.uk, 3D) offer B&B for £25/pp. Finally, up the hill is the *Chlachain Inn* (☎ 01687-460289, 🖳 www.westscotlandinn.co.uk, 3D/1T) with B&B from £30 to £37.50/pp.

Where to eat and drink
Being a fishing village, Mallaig is a good place to enjoy fresh seafood. Try the *Fishmarket Restaurant* (☎ 01687-462299), appropriately positioned next to the harbour and the place for locally caught seafood and fish dishes.

The cheapest fish is at the *Fisherman's Mission* (☎ 01687-462086) or one of the two **fish and chip shops**; one is at the back of the Cornerstone Restaurant

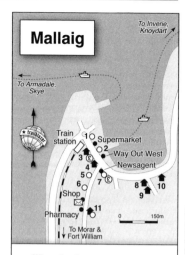

Mallaig

To Inverie, Knoydart
To Armadale, Skye
Train station
Supermarket
Way Out West Newsagent
Shop
Pharmacy
To Morar & Fort William
0   150m

Where to stay
3 Marine Hotel
4 Sheena's Backpackers' Lodge
8 Seaview GH
9 The Anchorage B&B
10 The Moorings
11 Chlachain Inn

Where to eat and drink
1 Fisherman's Mission
2 Fishmarket Restaurant
5 Fish & Chips
6 Mallaig Spice
7 Cornerstone Restaurant
11 Chlachain Inn

(see below) and the other is hidden in an alley-way by *Mallaig Spice* (01687-462393), Mallaig's very own Indian restaurant with the usual array of curries. The chicken balti is £6.95.

Finally, *Cornerstone Restaurant* (☎ 01687-462306, 🖳 www.seafoodrestaurantmallaig.com) specialises in seafood but also does pork chops and steaks while the contemporary *Chlachain Inn* (see Where to stay) with its rather optimistic outside decking and more realistic open fire has a variety of pub food including local mussels (£7.95) and pizza (from £5.50).

SUNART TO KNOYDART

INVERIE   [SEE MAP 30a, p186]
The occasional sailor has been known to turn up in Inverie and ask when the next bus leaves for Fort William, only to discover that there is none. The reason: Inverie, on the southern shore of Knoydart, is unconnected to the rest of the mainland road network, giving the peninsula a kind of island mentality.

This is a magical place with an overwhelming sense of community spirit among the one hundred or so permanent residents; it is a warmth which extends to the many curious visitors who cross the water during the summer.

The only access is on foot from Kinlochhourn (two days, see pp300-1) or Glenfinnan (three days), or by passenger ferry; the *Western Isles* **ferry** (☎ 01687-462320, 🖳 www.knoydart-ferry.co.uk) departs Inverie for Mallaig at 11am and 3pm, Mon, Wed and Fri, also Tue and Thu May-Sept; see p199 for times from Mallaig to Inverie.

Services
Services in Inverie are limited to the **post office** and small **shop** stocking essentials such as midge repellent and spam. Dial-up **internet** access is available in The Old Forge pub.

Where to stay, eat and drink
For such a small community there is a wealth of accommodation options (all of which should be booked in advance) including a **campsite** on the broad stretch of grass by Long Beach. Facilities include a standpipe and compost toilet and there are plans to install a solar shower. A pitch is £4/tent (£6 for a 3-man tent or larger).

There is also the *Foundation Bunkhouse* (☎ 01687-462242, www.knoydart-foundation.com) with beds for £14/pp, *Torrie Shieling* (☎ 01687-462669) with 12 beds costing from £25/pp and the *Old Byre Bunkhouse* (☎ 01687-460099, 🖳 www .theoldbyre-knoydart.com), a beautifully converted cow-shed with beds for £25/pp.

There four bed-and-breakfasts in Inverie: *Rafters* (☎ 01687-462622, 🖳 www

.knoydartbedbreakfast.co.uk, 1D/1T/1F) opened in 2009 and charges £40-45/pp. The double is en suite but the twin and family room (one double and one single) share a bathroom but the proprietors usually only rent out one of these rooms at a time. Each room at *The Gathering* (☎ 01687-460051, 🖳 www.thegatheringknoydart.co.uk; £35-45/pp) can sleep up to four people and it is a very smart and friendly place with great views and possibly the biggest, tastiest breakfasts in the Highlands while the very welcoming *Knoydart Lodge* (☎ 01687-460129, 🖳 www.knoydartlodge .co.uk) has a huge dining area, grand piano and four en suite rooms (£40/pp).

In the heart of the village is *The Pier House* (☎ 01687-462347, 🖳 www.thepier houseknoydart.co.uk, 1D/2T/1F) which does a full-board package for £60/pp. It is also one of two excellent places for an evening meal with a menu that changes daily. The chef is a dab hand at everything from seafood to curry (prices are around £10-15).

The other place for dinner is 'mainland Britain's remotest pub': *The Old Forge* (☎ 01687-462267, 🖳 www.theold forge.co.uk), the beating heart of the village where one can tuck into langoustines or lobster, washed down with a good Highland ale. On a good night The Old Forge puts a night on the tiles in London to shame with live folk music and lively clientele keeping the windows rattling into the early hours.

For breakfast and lunch the delightful *Knoydart Pottery and Tearoom* (☎ 01687-460191) is a wise choice. Soup of the day is £3.50 and there are baked potatoes with various fillings for £4.95, all served in a cosy room with sofas, stove and a sea view.

In the neighbouring estate of **Kilchoan**, about half a mile east up the glen, there is a wide choice of self-catering accommodation for groups who want to stay more than just one night. These range from the remote *Druim Bothy* (£7/pp) at the mouth of Gleann Meadail to the *Barn* (from £15/pp)

and the *Farmhouse* (£200/pp per week for up to eight people). To book any of these contact Kilchoan estate on ☎ 01687-462133/462724, 🖳 www.kilchoan-knoydart.com.

If you are planning to stay in Knoydart for any length of time a great place is

Doune (☎ 01687-462667, 🖳 www.douneknoydart.co.uk), four miles west of Inverie on the tip of the peninsula. It's inaccessible by road but the owners will ferry you to and from Mallaig. It's a great base for exploring Knoydart and you can also arrange boat trips to Skye and the Small Isles.

TOMDOUN   [OFF MAP 31a, p190]

The best place, in fact the only place, for an after-walk drink and a bite to eat is by the log fire at the beautiful *Tomdoun Hotel* (☎ 01809-511218, 🖳 www.tomdoun.com, 1S/4D/3T/2F), seven miles down the Kinlochhourn road.

The interior of this historic sporting lodge is decorated with deep red carpets, dead fish in glass cases, stags' antlers on the walls, and whippets racing round the table

legs. As one would expect the food is local produce and tastes fantastic. The venison casserole is £9.95. A room costs from £45/pp. Those who decide to stay can look forward to breakfast in the resplendent dining room.

Sadly the postbus service between Tomdoun and Kinlochhourn, which was discontinued some years ago, looks unlikely to be reinstated.

KINLOCHHOURN
[SEE MAP 31a, p190]

Kinlochhourn is the tiny hamlet at the end of the 22-mile dead-end road from Invergarry and is the start of the hike into Barisdale and Inverie in Knoydart. There are no services here but *Kinlochhourn Farm* (☎ 01809-511253, 🖳 www.kinlochhourn

.com, Apr-Oct) does offer **bed and breakfast** (£26/pp) and a **self-catering flat** sleeping up to five (£50 per night). They also run a **tearoom**. They have no set opening hours so it's best to call in advance.

BARISDALE   [SEE MAP 31b, p191]

For walkers, Barisdale is almost a Scottish Shangri-la. This beautiful wild bay of white sand below sheer mountain walls is a hard nine-mile walk from the road end at Kinlochhourn.

You can also get to Barisdale by boat by booking the **Arnisdale ferry** (☎ 01599-522247, 🖳 www.arnisdaleferry.co.uk), a tiny passenger boat based in Arnisdale across Loch Hourn.

Despite its isolation those who run the estate have made sure that walkers have plenty of places to stay. You can **camp** (£1/pp) by the **bothy** (£3/pp) which has

electricity but no heating. You will need a sleeping bag and a stove. If tents and bothies are not your thing book a bed at *The Stable* next door, a self-catering flat with space for five people (£40-85 per night for the whole flat) or *The White House* which is the lonely building further up the glen. Rental is for groups of up to 12 with prices ranging from £70 to £140 depending on the number in the party.

For further information on all these options contact the estate (☎ 01764-684946, 🖳 www.barisdale.com).

Midtown

Tuirnaig

Fionn Loch

Dundonnell

AN TEALLACH
1062m

RUADH STAC MOR
918m

Poolewe

A'MHAIGDEAN
967m

Gairloch

Kerrysdale

Loch a'Bhraoin

Talladale

Loch Maree

Loch Fannich

BEINN AN EOIN
855m

Kinlochewe

Achnasheen

Upper Loch Torridon

BEINN ALLIGIN
986m

BEINN EIGHE
1010m

Torridon

Shieldaig

BEINN DAMH
902m

Lair

0 5 miles
0 8km

Kishorn

Strathcarron

Loch Kishorn

Loch Carron

Lochcarron

Loch Monar

Stromeferry

Loch Long

Loch Mullardoch

Kyle of Lochalsh

Auchtertyre

CARN EIGE
1183m

MAM SODHAIL
1181m

SGURR NA LAPAICH
1036m

Kylerhea

Tomich

Glenelg

Shiel Bridge

BEINN SGRITHEALL
974m

THE SADDLE
1010m

SGURR NA SGINE
946m

Cluanie Inn

Arnisdale

Glen Shiel to Torridon & Fisherfield

Glen Shiel to Torridon & Fisherfield

This stretch of the west coast around Torridon contains some of the most lauded peaks in Scotland, and rightly so. These delicately terraced sandstone mountains stand detached from each other giving each perfectly sculpted mountain a distinct character and beauty. Add to this the remoteness, the seascapes, the lochs and the native forests and you have an area that will enchant the hardest of souls and will draw you back time and again. The only problem is deciding which is the most magnificent mountain: Beinn Eighe? Liathach? An Teallach?

BEINN SGRITHEALL ('*Bayn Skree-ul*, 974m/3195ft)   [MAP 33, p205]

Overview
There are few mountains in the Highlands that can offer such outstanding views across the Western seaboard as Beinn Sgritheall which rears up from the north shore of Loch Hourn in an unrelenting slope patterned with grey scree.

The ascent of 960m in two miles (3km) is punishing but the views get better with every step. The only tricky part of the walk is the extremely steep descent off the mountain's east ridge but this can be avoided by returning via the ascent route.

Route
It can be a little awkward finding the ascent path, which leaves the road at GR816119. A **small cairn** on the roadside marks the spot. The first 350m of ascent are quite steep passing through some beautifully lush oak woodland with branches draped in moss.

At the top of the woodland there is a fence with a **stile** that leads onto open moorland. From here it is a short climb to a small lochan on the back of a broad ridge.

Once at the **lochan** turn right and follow the rollercoaster ridge as it climbs eastwards over a number of short sharp steep sections interrupted by flat grassy stretches.

A faint path leads towards the final steep pull to the summit. Follow this path up the crest of the ridge, which in places is rocky. You may sometimes need your hands to help pull yourself ever upwards but the going is relatively easy.

BEINN SGRITHEALL (Scree Mountain)
Technical grade
▲▲
Navigation grade
▲▲
Terrain grade
▲▲▲
Strenuousness
▲▲
Return time
3½-5hrs
Return distance
6miles/10km
Total ascent
3346ft/1020m
OS maps
Landranger 33, Explorer 413
Gateways
Glenelg (see p231) Shiel Bridge (see p231)

The relentless ascent finishes at the **summit cairn** where there is also a shattered trig point. Be sure to spend plenty of time at the summit if the conditions are good. The views across to Rum, Eigg, the Cuillin of Skye and even the Outer Hebrides, must surely rank among some of the best seascapes in Europe. Inland you can often see as far as Ben Nevis and the Glen Coe peaks while the Torridon Top Three of Beinn Alligin, Liathach and Beinn Eighe stand out to the north.

For those who don't like very steep descents it is best to return by way of the ascent route, otherwise continue in an ESE direction to a narrow grassy ridge interrupted by a small rocky step. This attractive ridge drops down to a **col** and a path continues eastwards to a stony top.

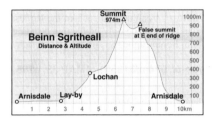

Just east of the cairn at the top, the mountain falls away in a sheer slope of 300m that may cause a few butterflies in unprepared stomachs. Nevertheless, there is a useful path that avoids the scree slope and picks its way instead down a small gully. Just above a short cliff the path swings to the right and continues to descend to the Bealach Arnasdail.

Aim for the steep slopes on the other side of this col and follow the path by the stream that tumbles down towards Arnisdale. The going is steep and in parts a little boggy but the descent is rapid. Just before reaching the village of **Arnisdale** a sign points to the right indicating the way to the road. Cross the **stream** and climb briefly over a heathery shoulder to reach the roadside at the western end of the village. It is two miles (3km), along the lane back to the start point.

Alternative routes

There is a longer approach from the north, starting at the road-heads in either Gleann Beag or Glen More. The ascent is via the fine north ridge of Beinn Sgritheall.

Fit walkers can extend the walk by continuing over the corbetts of Beinn-na-h-Eaglaise and Beinn nan Caorach to the east of Beinn Sgritheall. The descent from the latter peak is possible by heading directly south over scree slopes to join the path to Corran at the end of the Arnisdale road.

❏ **Important note – walking times**
All times in this book refer only to the time spent walking. You will need to add 20-30% to allow for rests, photography, checking the map, drinking water etc.

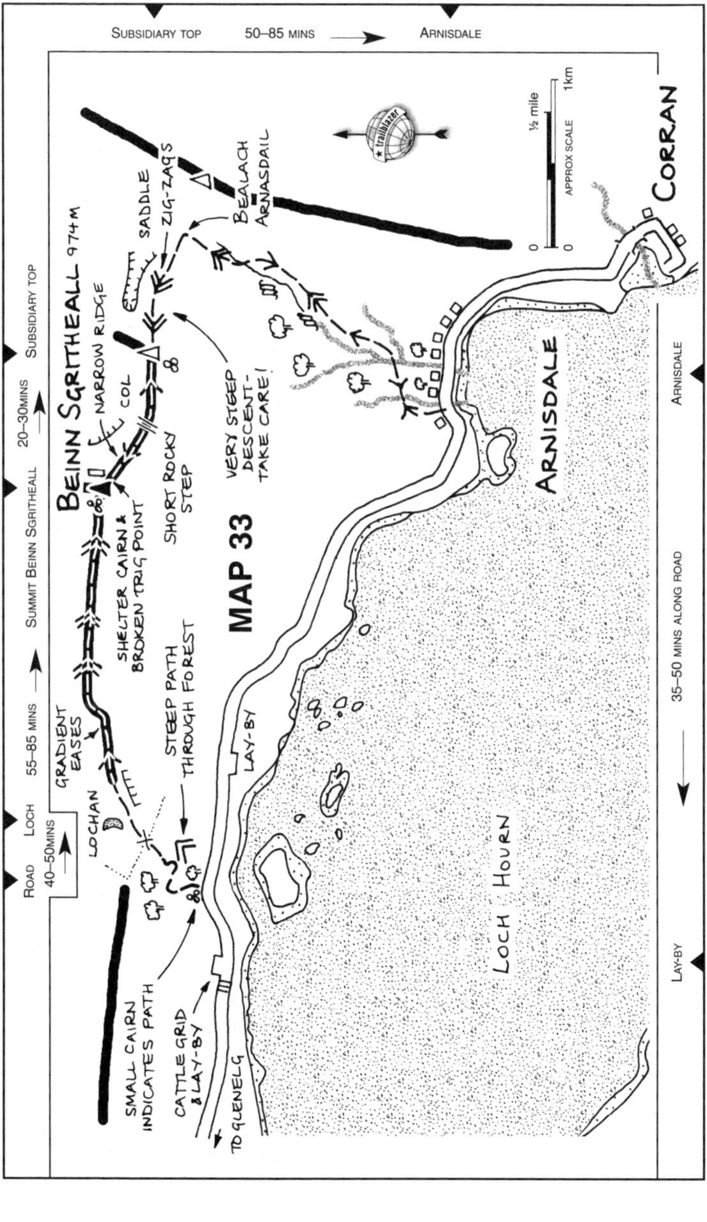
MAP 33
SUBSIDIARY TOP
50–85 MINS
ARNISDALE
ROAD
40–50MINS
LOCH
55–85 MINS
SUMMIT BEINN SGRITHEALL
20–30MINS
SUBSIDIARY TOP
LAY-BY
35–50 MINS ALONG ROAD
ARNISDALE
BEINN SGRITHEALL 974M
NARROW RIDGE
COL
SADDLE
ZIG-ZAGS
BEALACH ARNASDAIL
SHELTER CAIRN & BROKEN TRIG POINT
SHORT ROCKY STEP
VERY STEEP DESCENT- TAKE CARE!
GRADIENT EASES
LOCHAN
STEEP PATH THROUGH FOREST
SMALL CAIRN INDICATES PATH
CATTLE GRID & LAY-BY
TO GLENELG
LAY-BY
LOCH HOURN
ARNISDALE
CORRAN
APPROX SCALE
½ mile
1km
0
trailblazer

THE SADDLE (1010m/3315ft) [MAP 34]
SGURR NA SGINE ('*Skor na Skeen-er*', 946m/3105ft)

Overview

Narrow ridges, deep corries and views over countless high peaks make this one of the great mountain days in the Highlands. The highlight is undoubtedly the Forcan Ridge, a steep, rocky crest leading spectacularly to the summit. Although not technically difficult there are one or two hairy sections. Those who have little scrambling experience should take the alternative route described.

Route

Begin the ascent by leaving the A87 road just south of the farm buildings at Achnangart (GR968143) and about 50m south of a parking **lay-by**. A well-maintained path climbs in a series of switchbacks up the lower flanks of the glen before turning sharply to climb steadily across the face of the hillside in a NW direction. This soon leads to a col on the ridge between Biod an Fhitich and Meallan Odhar. From the col the first great views of The Saddle open up ahead with the jagged Forcan Ridge dominating the skyline.

The path swings round to the south to climb the western edge of Meallan Odhar and then aims SW to the foot of the Forcan Ridge. Here the **path splits** and it's decision time. Continue straight ahead, following an old collapsed stone wall, to gain the upper slopes of The Saddle and a final steep climb to the summit, or take the right-hand path for the challenge of the Forcan Ridge.

The obstacles for the latter start immediately with a slanting slab of rock. There is a good pattern of narrow ledges on this outcrop making progress easier than expected. After this first hurdle the ridge climbs unrelentingly in a series of rocky towers and steps making hands almost as vital as feet in the quest for the summit. Near the top of the ridge is a short yet formidable **pillar of rock** that can either be tackled directly (for those with climbing experience) or by skirting below the northern side of the tower and scrambling up an easier route. This leads quickly to the summit of the **Forcan Ridge**.

The reward is the view ahead of the ridge slicing towards the summit of the mountain. The narrowest section of all is little more than a shattered edge of rock dipping steeply on one side and dropping vertically on the other. A path below this short stretch avoids all the difficulties. The final awkward step is a notch in the ridge. There is a difficult down-climb into this cleft but again there

THE SADDLE

SGURR NA SGINE
(Knife Peak)

Technical grade
▲▲▲▲

Navigation grade
▲▲▲

Terrain grade
▲▲▲▲

Strenuousness
▲▲▲▲

Return time
4-6 hrs

Return distance
8miles/12km

Total ascent
4593ft/1400m

OS maps
Landranger 33,
Explorer 413

Gateways
Glen Shiel and Shiel
Bridge (see p231)

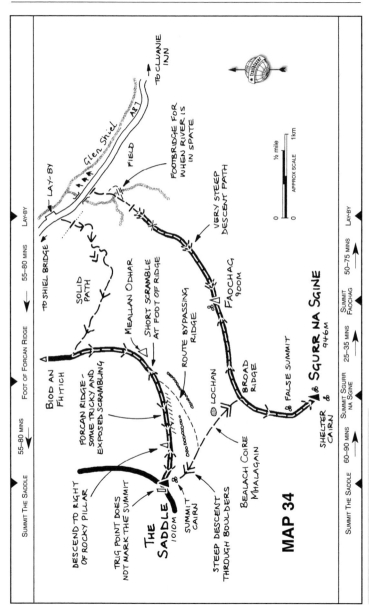

SUMMIT THE SADDLE — 55–80 MINS — FOOT OF FORCAN RIDGE — 55–80 MINS — LAY-BY

TO CLUANIE INN

AB1

Glen Shiel

LAY-BY

TO SHIEL BRIDGE

FOOTBRIDGE FOR WHEN RIVER IS IN SPATE

FIELD

VERY STEEP DESCENT PATH

SOLID PATH

MEALLAN ODHAR

SHORT SCRAMBLE AT FOOT OF RIDGE

ROUTE BYPASSING RIDGE

FAOCHAG 900M

BIOD AN FHITICH

FORCAN RIDGE – SOME TRICKY AND EXPOSED SCRAMBLING

DESCEND TO RIGHT OF ROCKY PILLAR

TRIG POINT DOES NOT MARK THE SUMMIT

THE SADDLE 1010M

SUMMIT CAIRN

STEEP DESCENT THROUGH BOULDERS

BEALACH COIRE MHALAGAIN

LOCHAN

BROAD RIDGE

FALSE SUMMIT

SGURR NA SGINE 946M

SHELTER CAIRN

MAP 34

½ mile   1km
0   APPROX SCALE

SUMMIT THE SADDLE — 60–90 MINS — SUMMIT SGURR NA SGINE — 25–35 MINS — SUMMIT FAOCHAG — 50–75 MINS — LAY-BY

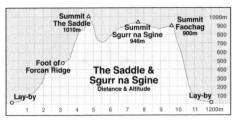

are easier alternatives. Two steep chutes lead down, either side of the precipice, to reach the floor of the gap and the path climbs back out to continue along the ridge. Avoid the rocky buttresses on the final climb to the summit by keeping to the steep grassy slopes to the right. From the **summit** of The Saddle the full intricacy of the mountain is clear and by continuing on to the trig point a few minutes SW there are somewhat vertiginous views down into the gaping depths of Coire Uaine.

From the summit descend by the steep ground to the SE or descend the way you came for about 50m and locate one of the steep grassy gullies that drop down onto a boulder field. Cross an old stone wall and continue ESE over occasionally boggy terrain to the saddle known as the Bealach Coire Mhalagain, where there is a small **lochan**. Climb the steep slopes on the far side of this saddle. The path is indistinct but it is only a short pull to gain the ridge. If there is time it is worth heading south along this easy ridge to the summit of **Sgurr na Sgine**. A path follows a line of old rusty fence posts before climbing steep stony ground to reach a false summit. Drop briefly before climbing once again to the true summit from where there are views south over the head of Loch Hourn, possibly the most beautiful sea loch in Scotland, and the remote tops of Knoydart.

Retrace your steps along the ridge and continue to the far end over easy grassy turf to the summit of **Faochag**. This is the smallest of the three peaks but is no less interesting. It towers over Glen Shiel and with deep corries on either side the effect is one of elation in every way.

The descent is less appetising and is not kind on the knees. Nevertheless there is a good path that drops down the NE ridge all the way back to the glen. Near the foot of the mountain cross through a pair of gates, over the river (which can be forded but the bridge is only a very short detour upstream) and through a field that is often home to inquisitive cattle. The track through the field reaches a gate from where it is a five-minute stroll down the tarmac to the day's starting point.

Alternative routes

Only competent scramblers should attempt the Forcan Ridge. If you are unsure of your ability, follow the bypass route, which begins at the foot of the ridge where the path splits. Follow the left-hand fork by an old fallen stone wall. The path contours the hillside and climbs the steep upper slopes of the mountain where shattered boulders fill the high corrie below the summit.

The route described above can, of course, be shortened by ignoring Sgurr na Sgine and Faochag and descending into Coire Mhalagain from the bealach.

Another good expedition is the long circular route that takes in not just the Forcan Ridge, but many of the Saddle's other fine ridges. Start at the campsite at Shiel Bridge and follow the long A'Mhuing ridge to join the route described above. Continue over the Forcan Ridge and across the summit ridge to Spidean Dhomhuill Breac and Sgurr Leac nan Each. Head along the ridge in a northerly direction to join a stalkers' path that leads back to Shiel Bridge. Although this route does not take in Sgurr na Sgine or Faochag, it is still a lengthy trek involving a lot of ascent. Only for the very fit!

SGURR NA LAPAICH (*'Skor na La-peech'*, 1036m/3400ft), MAM SODHAIL (*'Mam Sowel'*, 1181m/ 3875ft), CARN EIGE (*'Carn Ay-ga'*, 1183m/3880ft)
[MAP 35a, p211; MAP 35b, p210]

Overview
High ridge walking above one of the most unspoilt and longest glens in Scotland. These are the highest peaks north of the Great Glen and are just the beginning of a complex maze of ridges that stretch all the way to Kintail on the western seaboard. Come late in the year to make the most of the beautiful autumnal colours.

Route
The public road ends at a large car park on the south side of the River Affric. Cross back over the road-bridge and follow the estate track along the north shore of the tapered end of Loch Affric. After 15 minutes this brings you to a **keeper's cottage**, set on a beautiful wooded promontory on the loch. Before the cottage take the **stalkers' path** on the right that climbs up through the fringes of the pine forest and then over open moorland. The path turns sharply to the west to contour the hillside, climbing gradually to a hairpin. Follow this round and look for the small cairn that marks the start of a fainter path on the left-hand side.

Follow this north for a few minutes, following a line of **small cairns**, before swinging west again to cross the wide **boggy moorland**. The trail follows the north bank of the Allt na Faing with the precipitous east face of Sgurr na Lapaich looming closer and closer all the time.

Aim for the lower slopes of the SE ridge of the mountain where a burn runs down grassy slopes. This is the easiest approach route. Once on this SE ridge follow the path as it climbs to the summit of **Sgurr na Lapaich**.

SGURR NA LAPAICH (Bog Peak)
MAM SODHAIL (Barns Hill)
CARN EIGE (File Hill or Cairn)
Technical grade ▲▲
Navigation grade ▲▲▲
Terrain grade ▲▲
Strenuousness ▲▲▲▲
Return time 6½-8½ hrs
Return distance 14miles/23km
Total ascent 4710ft/1436m
OS maps Landranger 25, Explorer 414 & 415
Gateways Tomich (see p232)

GLEN SHIEL TO TORRIDON & FISHERFIELD

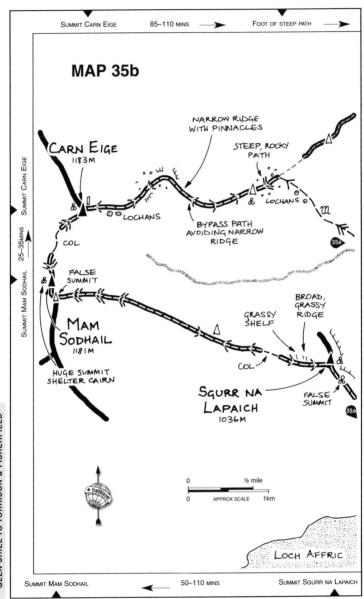

MAP 35b

SUMMIT CARN EIGE — 85–110 MINS ⟶ FOOT OF STEEP PATH ⟶

CARN EIGE
1183M

NARROW RIDGE
WITH PINNACLES

STEEP, ROCKY
PATH

LOCHANS

BYPASS PATH
AVOIDING NARROW
RIDGE

LOCHANS

35a

COL

FALSE
SUMMIT

MAM
SODHAIL
1181M

HUGE SUMMIT
SHELTER CAIRN

GRASSY
SHELF

BROAD,
GRASSY
RIDGE

COL

SGURR NA
LAPAICH
1036M

FALSE
SUMMIT

35a

SUMMIT CARN EIGE

25–35MINS

SUMMIT MAM SODHAIL

trailblazer

0   ½ mile
0   APPROX SCALE   1km

LOCH AFFRIC

SUMMIT MAM SODHAIL ⟵ 50–110 MINS — SUMMIT SGURR NA LAPAICH

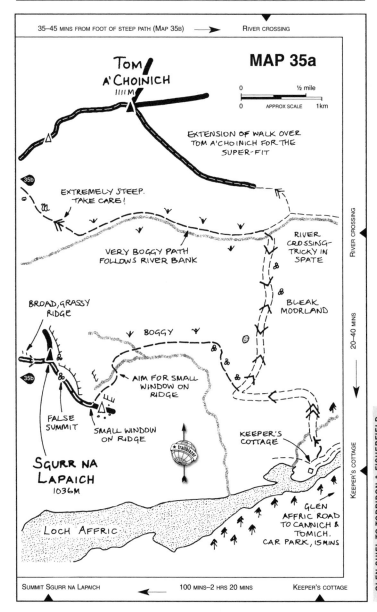

35–45 MINS FROM FOOT OF STEEP PATH (MAP 35B) ⟶ RIVER CROSSING

TOM A'CHOINICH
1111M

MAP 35a

0   ½ mile
0   APPROX SCALE   1km

EXTENSION OF WALK OVER
TOM A'CHOINICH FOR THE
SUPER-FIT

35b

EXTREMELY STEEP.
TAKE CARE!

VERY BOGGY PATH
FOLLOWS RIVER BANK

RIVER
CROSSING -
TRICKY IN
SPATE

RIVER CROSSING

BLEAK
MOORLAND

20–40 MINS

BROAD, GRASSY
RIDGE

BOGGY

35b

AIM FOR SMALL
WINDOW ON
RIDGE

FALSE
SUMMIT

SMALL WINDOW
ON RIDGE

★ trailblazer

KEEPER'S
COTTAGE

KEEPER'S COTTAGE

SGURR NA
LAPAICH
1036M

GLEN
AFFRIC ROAD
TO CANNICH &
TOMICH.
CAR PARK, 15MINS

LOCH AFFRIC

SUMMIT SGURR NA LAPAICH ⟵ 100 MINS–2 HRS 20 MINS   KEEPER'S COTTAGE

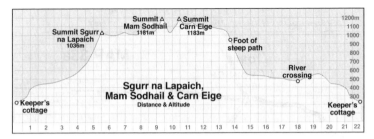

Sgurr na Lapaich, Mam Sodhail & Carn Eige
Distance & Altitude

A **broad ridge** descends gradually from the summit, passing a large rocky shelf that slices along the northern side of the slope. The ridge is long and undulating but the path is easy to follow as it hugs the south side just below the crest. Towards the end of the ridge the path climbs steeply to a **false summit**. The true summit of **Mam Sodhail** is a short distance away, across the flat grassy top in a NNW direction. It is hard to miss the cairn. It is a massive circular affair with a hollow centre offering very welcome shelter from any inclement elements that might be in the air.

Descend north from the summit down to the **col** and begin the ascent of **Carn Eige**'s SW ridge. A trig point marks the **summit** of this almost identical twin peak. Anyone contemplating the ascent of Beinn Fhionnlaidh that lies at the end of a northerly spur will have to descend NW from the summit and return the same way back to Carn Eige. This adds over 500m to the total ascent and 2^1/$_2$ miles (4km) to the total distance for the day, so make sure you have plenty of daylight if you are contemplating it.

For the continuation of the walk, follow the long ridge to the east. For the first 1^1/$_4$ miles (2km) the ridge is unremarkable but this all changes when it swings round to the SE, narrowing sharply with some interesting scrambling for those with a head for heights. These obstacles can be avoided by following the path on the south side of the ridge. The ridge continues its narrow, arête-like theme for some time before broadening just before it reaches an abrupt end with a steep drop to the col below. Carefully follow the **steep path** down to this col.

Head down from the col to a pair of **lochans**. There are two options here. Keep to the west bank of the burn flowing from the lochans for a very steep descent to the glen below or bear east into Coire Mhic Fhearchair to locate a stalkers' path that leads down into Gleann nam Fiadh. A boggy path follows the north bank of the river in the glen. Follow this across the quagmire for 1^1/$_4$ miles (2km) and **cross the river** where a path appears on the other side. The river crossing may be tricky if in spate. Use a trekking pole or a reliable hill-chum for support and face upstream when crossing.

The path on the other side is wide and solid and climbs the shallow slopes to the south across the moorland, soon reaching the point where you left it earlier in the day. Continue down the path back to the keeper's cottage and follow the track back to the car park.

Alternative routes

A look at OS map 25 will show any number of possible routes on these beautiful ridges. If there is time it is worth taking in the peak of Beinn Fhionnlaidh that lies along a ridge to the north of Carn Eige, from where there are spectacular views across remote Loch Mullardoch to the even remoter peaks of An Riabhachan and Sgurr na Lapaich (not the same as the one on this route). Munro-baggers with extra reserves of energy might like to continue the traverse from Carn Eige to include the munros of Tom a' Choinich and Toll Creagach. This makes for a very long day and although the views are good these final two peaks are less interesting than those that have gone before.

BEINN DAMH (*'Bayn Daf'*, 902m/2960ft)   [MAP 36, p214]

Overview

Beinn Damh is probably the least famous of the Torridon peaks yet it is certainly worthy of attention. Defined ridges lead to the summit that looks out across Loch Torridon and the awesome bulks of Beinn Alligin and Liathach. A relatively easy ascent makes this a perfect introduction to the beautiful terraced sandstone slopes of Torridon, before tackling one of the more challenging beasts across the glen.

Route

From the The Torridon Hotel head west along the main road for about 100m. The Beinn Damh path leaves the **road** about 20m on from the bridge over the Allt Coire Roill, climbing up through some rhododendron bushes and into a lovely pine forest. The path climbs high above the west bank of the tumbling river until, after about 200m of ascent, the forest begins to thin and the pine trees become more stunted. Look out for the **big waterfall** at this point. Unlike many waterfalls marked on maps this one really is worth seeing: a torrent falling some 30m into the deep mossy gorge below.

A couple of minutes on from the waterfall the **path divides**. Take the right-hand fork and follow the stalkers' path across the heather and up the steep slopes into the corrie above. The trail continues to climb straight ahead up the side of the corrie to gain the NW ridge of the mountain where there are a couple of small **cairns**. Head SE up the broad ridge keeping the corrie wall below to your left. The terrain soon becomes rockier on the approach to the first false summit above the backwall of the corrie. This marks the beginning of the summit ridge, characterised by shattered rock. The ridge drops briefly before passing over a second false summit, dropping again and finally swinging round in an east direction to rise to

**BEINN DAMH
(Stag Mountain)**

Technical grade
▲▲
Navigation grade
▲▲
Terrain grade
▲▲
Strenuousness
▲▲
Return time
2¹/₂-3¹/₂hrs
Return distance
7miles/11km
Total ascent
3215ft/980m
OS maps
Landranger 24,
Explorer 428
Gateways
Torridon (see p232)

GLEN SHIEL TO TORRIDON & FISHERFIELD

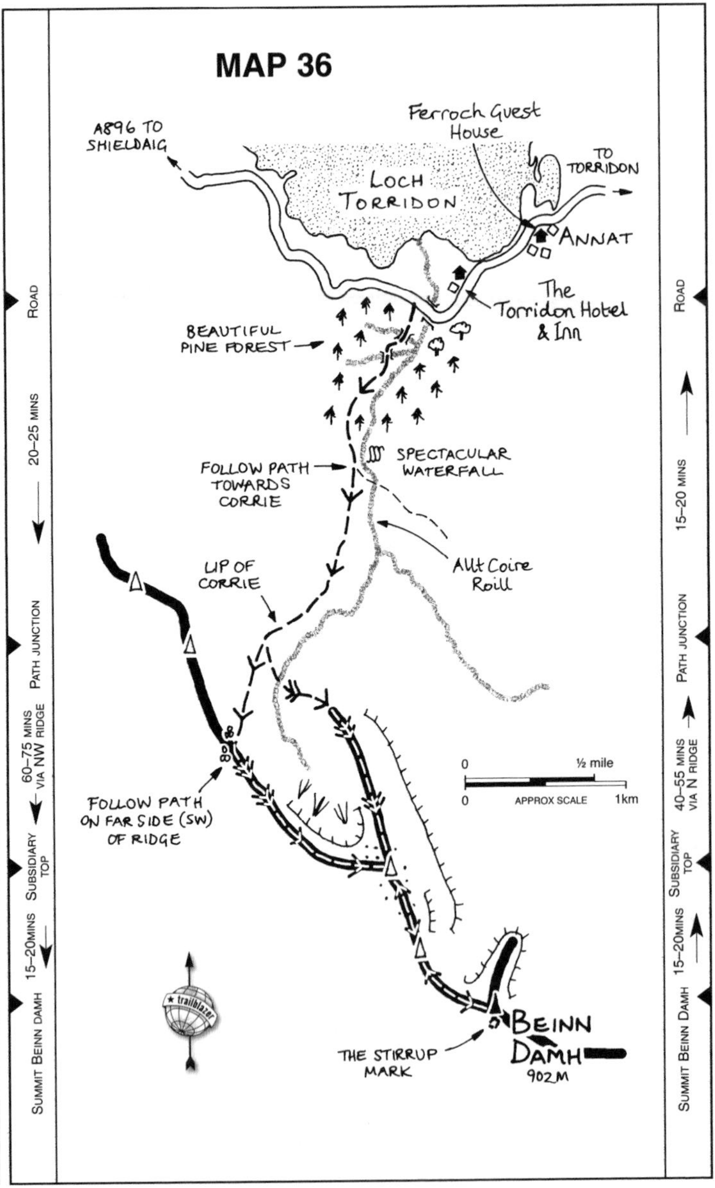

MAP 36

A896 TO SHIELDAIG

Ferroch Guest House

TO TORRIDON

LOCH TORRIDON

ANNAT

The Torridon Hotel & Inn

BEAUTIFUL PINE FOREST

SPECTACULAR WATERFALL

FOLLOW PATH TOWARDS CORRIE

Allt Coire Roill

LIP OF CORRIE

FOLLOW PATH ON FAR SIDE (SW) OF RIDGE

0   ½ mile

0   APPROX SCALE   1km

BEINN DAMH 902M

THE STIRRUP MARK

GLEN SHIEL TO TORRIDON & FISHERFIELD

SUMMIT BEINN DAMH ←15-20MINS→ SUBSIDIARY TOP ←60-75 MINS VIA NW RIDGE→ PATH JUNCTION ←20-25 MINS→ ROAD

ROAD ←15-20 MINS→ PATH JUNCTION ←40-55 MINS VIA N RIDGE→ SUBSIDIARY TOP ←15-20MINS→ SUMMIT BEINN DAMH

the **summit**. Just south of the summit there is a rocky pattern in the ground known as the **Stirrup Mark**. Despite its perfect symmetry this is an entirely natural feature.

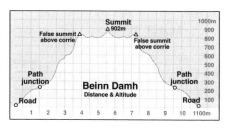

Beinn Damh — Distance & Altitude

The views from Beinn Damh are sensational with Beinn Alligin across the sheltered waters of Upper Loch Torridon and the Isle of Skye to the west. Looking east, towering over the glacial trough of Glen Torridon, are the smooth sheer sides of Liathach and the quartzite scree of Beinn Eighe in the distance.

To vary the return a little, head back along the summit ridge to the first false summit above the backwall of the corrie and follow the north ridge down over some rocky knolls and ribs to reach the lip of the corrie. Cross the **stream** above the gully that drops over the lip of the corrie and rejoin the path from earlier in the day for the descent back across the moor and down through the forest.

Alternative routes

An alternative descent, or ascent, is possible via the very steep SE ridge which involves some very careful route planning and a little scrambling.

BEINN ALLIGIN (*'Bayn Al-ik-in'*)
TOM NA GRUAGAICH (*'Tom na Gruagich'* 922m/3025ft)
SGURR MHOR (*'Skoor Mor'*, 986m/3235ft) [MAP 37, p216]

Overview

One of the big Torridon mountains, standing above the shores of Loch Torridon with terraced sandstone slopes leading up to the two main summits. The east ridge involves a spell of scrambling over the exposed Horns of Alligin.

Route

Start at the **car park** by the roadside on the Torridon to Diabaig road. Cross the rising moorland and head straight for the wide corrie ahead, **Coir' nan Laogh** (*'Cor nan Looerg'*).

Once in the corrie, keep to the right-hand side of the stream and follow its true left bank. The ground steepens towards the back of the corrie. After much effort the gradient eases near the top and soon arrives at the summit of **Tom na Gruagach**, the lower of

BEINN ALLIGIN (Jewelled Mountain)

Technical grade
▲▲▲▲

Navigation grade
▲▲

Terrain grade
▲▲▲▲

Strenuousness
▲▲

Return time
3-4½ hrs

Return distance
6miles/10km

Total ascent
3800ft/1150m

OS maps
Landranger 24, Explorer 433

Gateways
Torridon (see p232)

GLEN SHIEL TO TORRIDON & FISHERFIELD

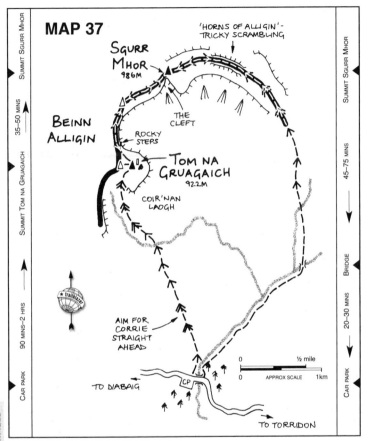

MAP 37

'HORNS OF ALLIGIN'-
TRICKY SCRAMBLING

SGURR
MHOR
986M

BEINN
ALLIGIN

THE
CLEFT

ROCKY
STEPS

TOM NA
GRUAGAICH
922M

COIR'NAN
LAOGH

★ trailblazer

AIM FOR
CORRIE
STRAIGHT
AHEAD

TO DIABAIG

CP

TO TORRIDON

0   ½ mile

0   APPROX SCALE   1km

Left margin (top to bottom):

SUMMIT SGURR MHOR ▶ | 35–50 MINS ▲ | SUMMIT TOM NA GRUAGAICH ▲ | 90 MINS–2 HRS ▲ | CAR PARK ▶

Right margin (top to bottom):

SUMMIT SGURR MHOR | 45–75 MINS ▼ | BRIDGE | 20–30 MINS ▼ | CAR PARK ◀

Far left vertical text:

GLEN SHIEL TO TORRIDON & FISHERFIELD

the mountain's two munros. Descend by the north ridge and follow this down to the col. There are a couple of large steps on the way down but they pose little difficulty.

After passing over a small top on the ridge continue to the next col and then begin the steep ascent NE to the main summit, that of Sgurr Mhor. On the way up look out for the great **cleft** in the ridge on the right-hand side. Below in the corrie one can see the huge fan of old debris that fell away from this natural gully. It is a dramatic spot and makes a great photograph, especially if a friend agrees to pose on the edge of the cliff.

At the summit of **Sgurr Mhor** there are views across to the Hebrides. Looking east is one of the most impressive views anywhere in Torridon, the eye being drawn over the Horns of Alligin and the successive summits of the Torridon giants: Liathach and Beinn Eighe.

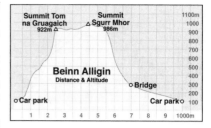

The next section of the walk is the most challenging. Those who are not confident of their scrambling ability should return the way they came.

To continue, descend NE at first, and then east to a narrow col. The way continues up and over the so-called **Horns of Alligin**, a trio of little tops at the end of a narrow ridge. In places the scrambling becomes easy climbing and is exposed.

Once past these obstacles follow the broader slopes, at first SE and then S, down to the moorland floor below. Join the path when it appears and follow this over a **bridge** and back to the road.

Alternative routes
To avoid the Horns of Alligin, retrace your steps from Sgurr Mhor.

BEINN EIGHE ('*Bayn-Ey*')   [MAP 38, p218]
SPIDEAN COIRE NAN CLACH ('*Spee-jyan Cora nan Clach*', 993m/3260ft)
RUADH-STAC MOR ('*Roo-er Stak Mor*', 1010m/3235ft)

Overview
Although not the highest of the Torridon giants, Beinn Eighe is the grandest and most complex. The characteristic sheets of quartzite scree on its southern slopes contrast greatly with the wide rocky corries on the north side. The most intimidating of these is Coire Mhic Fhearchair and its Triple Buttress. Most of the walk poses little difficulty but it does involve one very steep and slippery descent and a long walk out.

Route
On the Kinlochewe to Torridon road, park in the small **car park** by a stand of pine trees at GR 977578. A stalkers' path climbs north towards the imposing wall of the mountain. Hidden within these slopes is a small, east-facing **corrie**. The path swings round into this high corrie and climbs steep slopes of grass and moss to gain the ridge above.

Follow this ridge north to a **false summit**. The true summit of **Spidean Coire nan Clach** is a five-minute detour further NE. The fun starts here. Head west along the main spine of the mountain with quite

BEINN EIGHE
(File Mountain)

Technical grade
▲▲▲
Navigation grade
▲▲▲
Terrain grade
▲▲▲
Strenuousness
▲▲▲▲
Return time
5-6 hrs
Return distance
10miles/16.5km
Total ascent
3870ft/1180m
OS maps
Landranger 19 and 25,
Explorer 433
Gateways
Kinlochewe (see p233)
Torridon (see p232)

GLEN SHIEL TO TORRIDON & FISHERFIELD

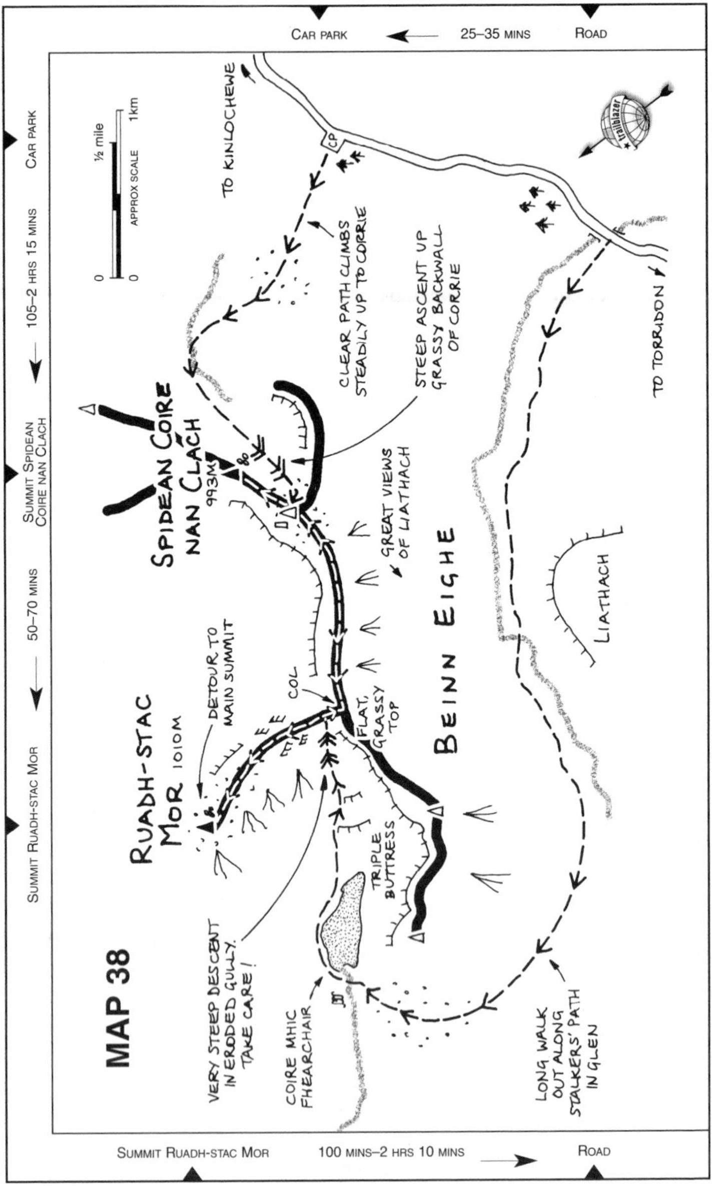

MAP 38

CAR PARK ← 25–35 MINS ROAD

TO KINLOCHEWE

CP

CLEAR PATH CLIMBS STEADILY UP TO CORRIE

STEEP ASCENT UP GRASSY BACKWALL OF CORRIE

TO TORRIDON

SPIDEAN COIRE NAN CLACH 993M

GREAT VIEWS OF LIATHACH

LIATHACH

BEINN EIGHE

RUADH-STAC MOR 1010M

DETOUR TO MAIN SUMMIT

COL

FLAT, GRASSY TOP

TRIPLE BUTTRESS

VERY STEEP DESCENT IN ERODED GULLY. TAKE CARE!

COIRE MHIC FHEARCHAIR

LONG WALK OUT ALONG STALKERS' PATH IN GLEN

½ mile
1km
APPROX SCALE
0   0

SUMMIT RUADH-STAC MOR 100 MINS–2 HRS 10 MINS → ROAD

CAR PARK

105–2 HRS 15 MINS

SUMMIT SPIDEAN COIRE NAN CLACH

50–70 MINS

SUMMIT RUADH-STAC MOR

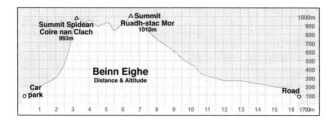

remarkable views to the west of Liathach and Beinn Alligin with the sea beyond. The ridge is not difficult although there are some sections of big uneven boulders that need a little more attention. On the left-hand side the scree spills away to the glen below while on the right are black cliffs dropping into the northern corries.

The path climbs increasingly mossy ground to a flat top. Ignore the main ridge which continues west and instead head north down a narrowing ridge to a small col. The descent begins here but first there is the main summit to reach.

Continue north from the col up big slabs of rock and boulders to a broadening summit ridge. The summit of **Ruadh-stac Mor**, not to be confused with the mountain of the same name in Fisherfield, is marked by a cairn. It is like a satellite of the massif and is the best place to admire the sheer scale of this complicated mountain.

From the summit return south to the col and descend by the sheer, eroded gully to the west. This is quite a difficult descent and extra care is needed on what is very loose rock and scree. At the foot of this slope head NW through **Coire Mhic Fhearchair**. There are a number of short cliffs on the approach to the lochan so pay attention to route planning. It is best to keep to the right-hand side of the corrie to avoid the worst of these rocky shelves.

At the **lochan** there is a path on its eastern shore that leads round to, and crosses, the outflow of the lochan where there is a waterfall and wild views north across the barren Flowerdale Forest to the isolated inselbergs (island peaks) of Baosbheinn and Beinn an Eoin. If you haven't looked over your shoulder yet, this is your last chance to admire the Triple Buttress, the 300-metre cliffs that form the back wall of Coire Mhic Fhearchair.

The long walk out really starts here. Follow the path as it descends from the lip of the corrie and swings around the foot of the Sail Mhor buttress to the west. The trail, a stalkers' path, follows the floor of the glen, slipping between Beinn Eighe and Liathach to arrive back at the **road**, from where it is about half an hour back to the start point.

Alternative routes

Beinn Eighe is a complicated mountain with a myriad of ridges. There are any number of ways of climbing the mountain. From Kinlochewe the eastern ridges can be explored, including the Black Carls which throw up some interesting scrambling.

BEINN AN EOIN *('Ben an E-yan'*, 855m/2805ft)

[MAPS 39a & 39b]

Overview

Lying some distance from the road, this hill involves a long but enjoyable walk in. The mountain itself is a typical inselberg, standing isolated from any other mountain. As such the views are far-reaching taking in the rest of the sandstone peaks of Torridon and the Fisherfield Forest to the north. There are no major difficulties.

BEINN AN EOIN
(Bird Mountain)

Technical grade
▲▲

Navigation grade
▲▲

Terrain grade
▲▲

Strenuousness
▲▲▲

Return time
4–5½hrs

Return distance
12½miles/20km

Total ascent
2950ft/900m

OS maps
Landranger 19,
Explorer 433

Gateways
Kinlochewe (see p233)
Gairloch (see p234)
Poolewe (see p233)

Route

On the Kinlochewe to Gairloch road, about four miles west of Talladale, is a small **car park** next to a green shed. A sign marks the start of a forest trail through the Bad na Sgalag native pinewoods. The woods have been fenced off to prevent grazing by deer and sheep which should help the regeneration of the native Scots pine trees that have been planted here. Follow the path through the forest and then continue south as it crosses the **rocky moorland**. After about half an hour the trail passes alongside and above a river before climbing further towards the mountains ahead, with Baosbheinn to the right and Beinn an Eoin to the left. The almost symmetrical mountains are separated by a loch. Before the path reaches this loch, turn left (leaving the **main path**, Map 39b)) and head across the trackless slopes of heather to the northern end of Beinn an Eoin.

Climb the steepening slopes and pass around the northern foot of the mountain to reach a **hidden corrie** on its NE side. Climb SW up onto the spine of the mountain, taking care to choose the right route to avoid the rocky bluffs and cliffs. Continue SSE along the broad back of the mountain. After an hour or so, a short steep section leads to the summit ridge and the **summit** itself, marked by a **cairn**. The return is by the same route.

GLEN SHIEL TO TORRIDON & FISHERFIELD

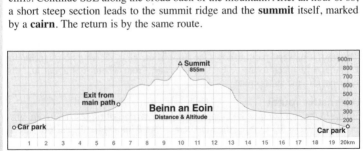

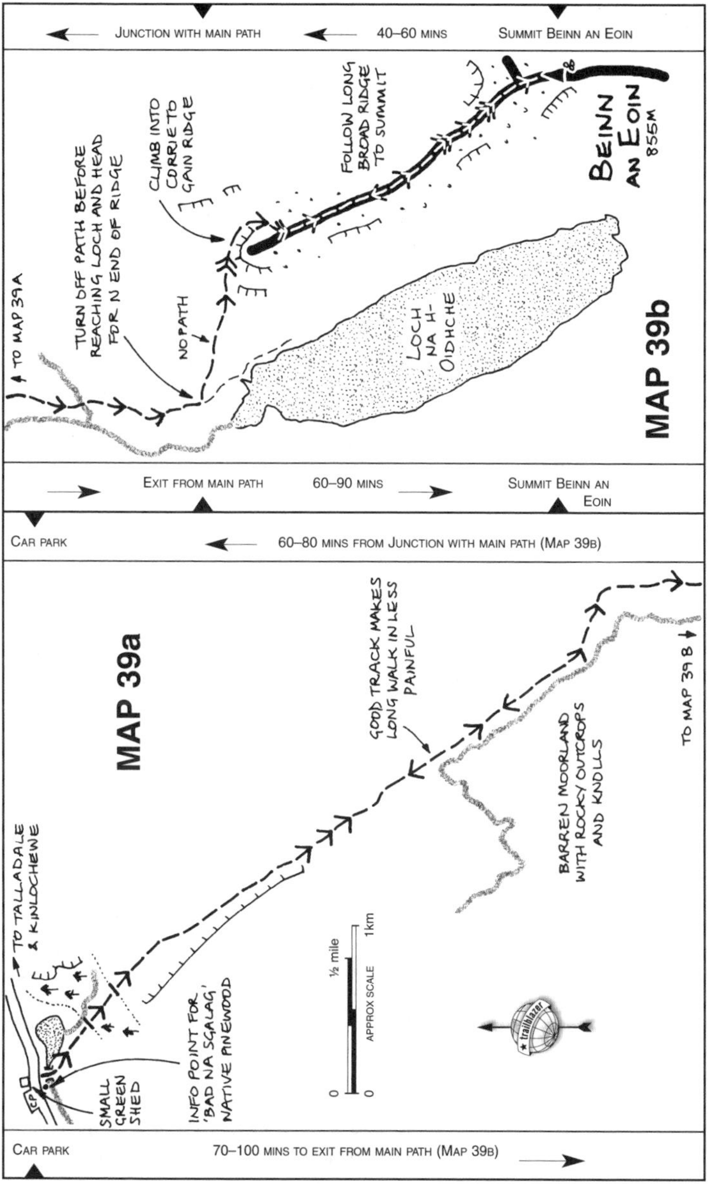

MAP 39b

JUNCTION WITH MAIN PATH ← ← 40–60 MINS ← SUMMIT BEINN AN EOIN

TURN OFF PATH BEFORE REACHING LOCH AND HEAD FOR N END OF RIDGE

CLIMB INTO CORRIE TO GAIN RIDGE

FOLLOW LONG BROAD RIDGE TO SUMMIT

NO PATH

BEINN AN EOIN 855M

LOCH NA H-OIDHCHE

TO MAP 39A

EXIT FROM MAIN PATH → 60–90 MINS → SUMMIT BEINN AN EOIN

CAR PARK ← 60–80 MINS FROM JUNCTION WITH MAIN PATH (MAP 39B)

MAP 39a

GOOD TRACK MAKES LONG WALK IN LESS PAINFUL

TO MAP 39 B

BARREN MOORLAND WITH ROCKY OUTCROPS AND KNOLLS

TO TALLADALE & KINLOCHEWE

INFO POINT FOR 'BAD NA SGALAG' NATIVE PINEWOOD

SMALL GREEN SHED

½ mile   1km

APPROX SCALE

CAR PARK   70–100 MINS TO EXIT FROM MAIN PATH (MAP 39B) →

GLEN SHIEL TO TORRIDON & FISHERFIELD

Alternative routes

The walk can be extended, quite considerably, by walking back over the neighbouring peak of Baosbheinn. To do so, descend the very steep western slopes of the mountain and cross the moor to the south of the loch. Climb west onto the end of the ridge for the start of the traverse of Baosbheinn. At the northern end of the ridge, descend east to rejoin the path back to the road.

A' MHAIGDEAN ('A _Vayen_', 967m/3175ft)
RUADH STAC MOR ('_Roo-er Stak-Mor_', 918m/3010ft)
[MAP 40a; MAP 40b, p224; MAP 40c, p225]

Overview

Famed as being the two most remote munros in Scotland these twin peaks provide the best vantage point across the wilds of the Fisherfield Forest with the deep Dubh Loch and Fionn Loch dominating the view. The very fit can tackle the whole walk in a day with an early start but the Poolewe to Carnmore section is a day's walk in itself so it is better to camp here or stay in the barn that is left open for walkers and climbers.

A' MHAIGDEAN (The Maiden)
RUADH STAC MOR (Big Red Peak)
Technical grade ▲▲▲
Navigation grade ▲▲▲
Terrain grade ▲▲▲
Strenuousness ▲▲▲▲▲
Return time Poolewe to Carnmore and back 5½-8¾hrs Carnmore to A' Mhaigdean and Ruadh Stac Mor and back 4½-6¼hrs
Return distance 26miles/42km
Total ascent 4430ft/1350m
OS maps Landranger 19, Explorer 433, 434 & 435
Gateways Poolewe (see p233) Gairloch (see p234)

Route

At **Poolewe** cars can be left at the small car park by the bridge (Map 40a). The actual path starts by the last white building at the northern end of the village, just before Inverewe Gardens. Follow the path through a couple of **gates** and a brief patch of woodland and then on through a forest of **gorse bushes**. The path soon emerges into open country where the first views of the Fisherfield mountains come clearly into view. Follow the stalkers' path along the north shore of Loch Kernsary. At the far end of this small loch the path crosses a bridge and then a **stile** and drops through a field to another rickety bridge over a stream. Climb past the dog kennels to reach a wide track by the estate buildings of **Kernsary**.

Continue east along this track to a fork. Take the right-hand branch through a **gate** and follow it through the forestry plantation, eventually reaching a **stile** on the edge of the trees. On the other side pick up a good, solid path that rises onto the high **open moorland**. The views get more and more enthralling with every step. To the right are the cliffs and gullies of Beinn Airigh Charr, a relatively low mountain but a spectacular one all the same.

Just past a small **lochan** (Map 40b) there is an enormous **rockfall** that must have made quite a

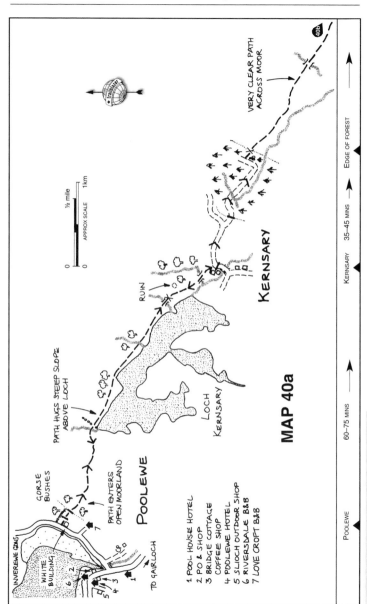

½ mile
APPROX SCALE
1km

MAP 40a

VERY CLEAR PATH
ACROSS MOOR

KERNSARY

RUIN

PATH HUGS STEEP SLOPE
ABOVE LOCH

LOCH
KERNSARY

POOLEWE

GORSE
BUSHES

PATH ENTERS
OPEN MOORLAND

INVEREWE GDNS

WHITE
BUILDING

TO GAIRLOCH

1 POOL HOUSE HOTEL
2 PO & SHOP
3 BRIDGE COTTAGE
   COFFEE SHOP
4 POOLEWE HOTEL
5 SLIOCH OUTDOOR SHOP
6 RIVERSDALE B&B
7 LOVE CROFT B&B

POOLEWE   60–75 MINS   KERNSARY   35–45 MINS   EDGE OF FOREST

GLEN SHIEL TO TORRIDON & FISHERFIELD

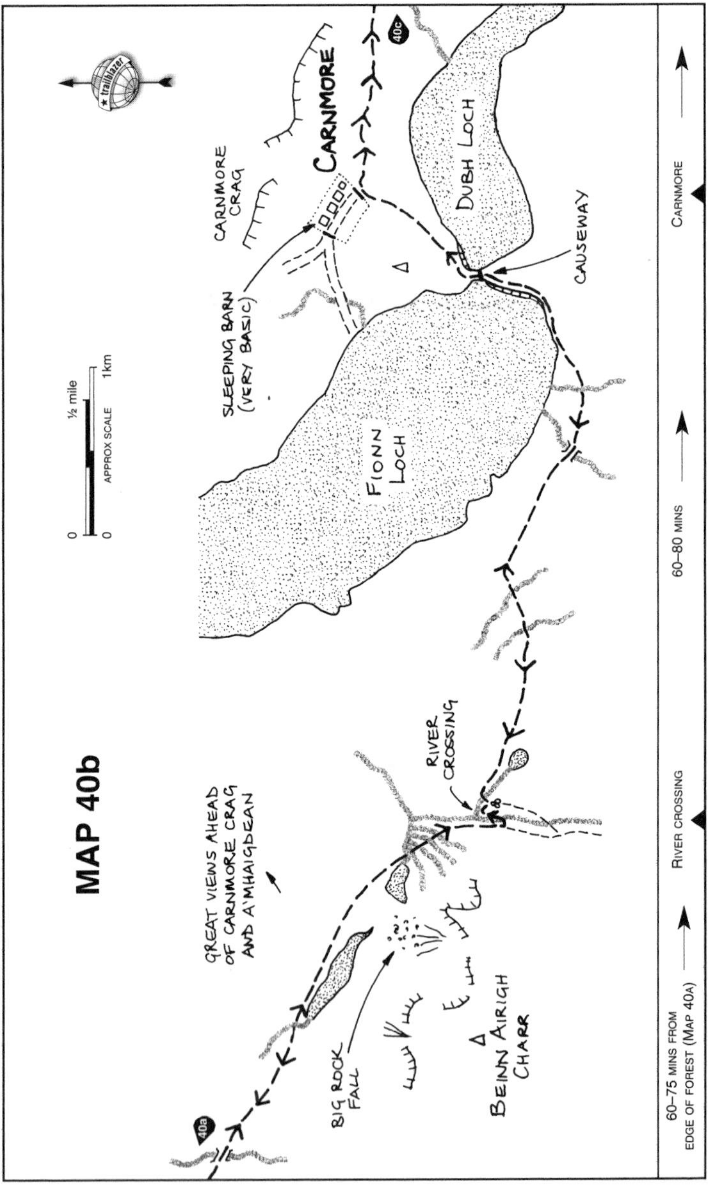

MAP 40b

GLEN SHIEL TO TORRIDON & FISHERFIELD

CARNMORE

CARNMORE CRAG

SLEEPING BARN (VERY BASIC)

DUBH LOCH

CAUSEWAY

FIONN LOCH

GREAT VIEWS AHEAD OF CARNMORE CRAG AND A'MHAIGHDEAN

RIVER CROSSING

BIG ROCK FALL

BEINN AIRIGH CHARR

½ mile   1km
APPROX SCALE
0   0

40a

40c

60–75 MINS FROM EDGE OF FOREST (MAP 40a) → RIVER CROSSING → 60–80 MINS → CARNMORE

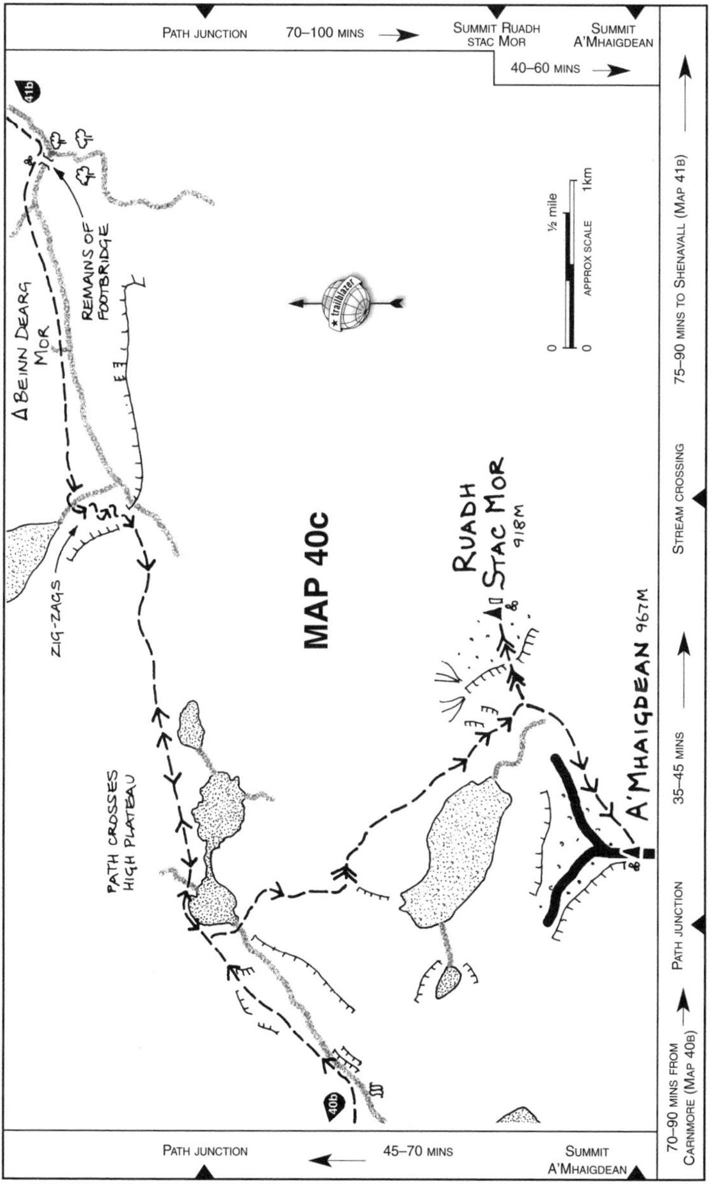
PATH JUNCTION
70–100 MINS
SUMMIT RUADH STAC MOR
SUMMIT A'MHAIGDEAN
40–60 MINS
75–90 MINS TO SHENAVALL (MAP 41B)
STREAM CROSSING
35–45 MINS
PATH JUNCTION
70–90 MINS FROM CARNMORE (MAP 40B)
PATH JUNCTION
45–70 MINS
SUMMIT A'MHAIGDEAN
MAP 40C
41b
40b
BEINN DEARG MOR
REMAINS OF FOOTBRIDGE
ZIG-ZAGS
PATH CROSSES HIGH PLATEAU
RUADH STAC MOR 918M
A'MHAIGDEAN 967M
trailblazer
0
½ mile
0
1km
APPROX SCALE

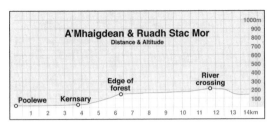

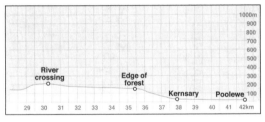

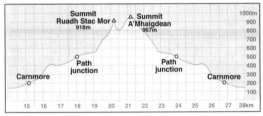

noise when it came crashing down the mountainside. A little further on the path swings round into a breach in the mountains. Ignore the main path as it climbs into this narrow defile and follow, instead, the path that drops down to the river. **Cross the river**, which is not too deep unless it has been raining a lot, and climb the short steep slope on the other side to rejoin the main path which twists and turns across the moorland eventually dropping down to the shore of **Fionn Loch**. All around there are enormous crags and faces of splintered rock. The path keeps to the shore of the loch, crossing a couple of thin stretches of sand before reaching the causeway that separates Fionn Loch from Dubh Loch.

Cross over and follow the path round the knoll to the estate buildings at **Carnmore**.

The small stone barn at the foot of the field is kept open especially to give shelter to walkers and climbers who come to dance around on Carnmore Crag. Remember to adhere to the usual bothy etiquette (see box p11) when staying here. The only other alternative is to camp.

From Carnmore follow a clear path that climbs steadily up the flank of the hill. After a climb of some 200m the path swings round into a small hanging valley (Map 40c). Continue NE above a small gorge to the high ground beyond. At the head of this high valley the path climbs sharply in a couple of switchbacks to reach some lonely **lochans**. A trail leaves this main path just before the first loch, crosses the stream flowing from the lochans, and climbs into the high, rocky corrie where there is another lochan. The path passes below slopes of scree and above the waters of the loch.

The ground gets a little steeper as it approaches the **col**, from which both summits can be tackled. For **Ruadh Stac Mor** (not to be confused with the mountain of the same name in Torridon) pick your way up the very steep and rocky slopes to gain the summit. Return to the col for the easier ascent of **A' Mhaigdean's** NE summit slopes. Return to the col again for the descent.

Alternative routes
An alternative descent from A'Mhaigdean is via the NW ridge. At the foot of this ridge cross the outflow of the lochan to return to the path.

AN TEALLACH (*'An Challoch'*)   [MAP 41a, p228; MAP 41b, p229]
BIDEAN A' GHLAS THUILL (*'Beeyen a Glas Hool'*, 1062m/3484ft)
SGURR FIONA (*'Skor Fee-o-ner'*, 1060m/3478ft)

Overview
Many people, quite rightly, regard An Teallach as mainland Scotland's centre-fold mountain, and also one of the most difficult. The very name sends shivers of awe and fear down the spine. The ascent of the two munros is not too taxing but the traverse of the Corrag Bhuidhe ridge requires some rock-climbing skills and a serious head for heights.

Route
The path for An Teallach leaves the **road** at a lay-by two miles south of Dundonnell Hotel. Follow this path through a brief stretch of woodland and up the north bank of the stream that tumbles down from the mountain ahead. There are two satellite peaks of An Teallach straight ahead. Follow the path to the foot of the left-hand (and most southerly one) and begin the hard pull up the slope.

This leads directly onto the east ridge of **Bidean a' Ghlas Thuill** (Map 41b), the first munro and one of the best places on the mountain from which to admire the centrepiece of the whole massif – the cliffs above Loch Toll an Lochain.

From Bidean a' Ghlas Thuill drop SW down to the col before ascending again up the ridge rising to the summit of the second munro, **Sgurr Fiona**. Take time to enjoy the vista to the south across the very remote Fisherfield Forest. The mountain on the opposite side of Strath na Sealga is Beinn Dearg Mor. With its sharp profile and defined arêtes and peaks it looks much like a diminutive relative of An Teallach. All attention now needs to be placed on the ridge to the south, the summit of which is Corrag Bhuidhe. This is the crux of the whole day. Anyone who is not comfortable with very exposed scrambling on what is a mightily challenging

AN TEALLACH (The Forge)
Technical grade
▲▲▲▲▲
Navigation grade
▲▲▲
Terrain grade
▲▲▲▲▲
Strenuousness
▲▲▲▲
Return time
5-7hrs
Return distance
9miles/14km
Total ascent
4450ft/1350m
OS maps
Landranger 19,
Explorer 435
Gateways
Dundonnell (see p234)
Ullapool (see p249)

GLEN SHIEL TO TORRIDON & FISHERFIELD

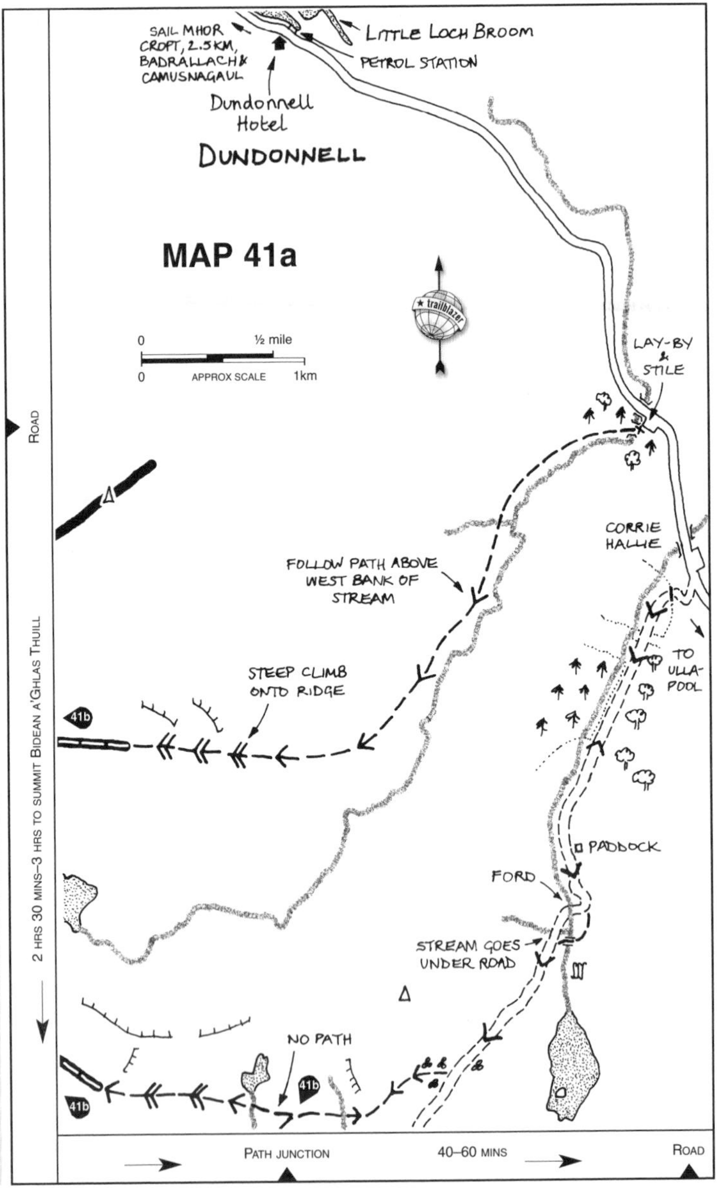

SAIL MHOR
CROFT, 2.5 KM,
BADRALLACH &
CAMUSNAGAUL

LITTLE LOCH BROOM

PETROL STATION

Dundonnell
Hotel

DUNDONNELL

MAP 41a

★ Trailblazer

0 ½ mile
0 APPROX SCALE 1km

LAY-BY
&
STILE

CORRIE
HALLIE

FOLLOW PATH ABOVE
WEST BANK OF
STREAM

TO
ULLA-
POOL

STEEP CLIMB
ONTO RIDGE

41b

PADDOCK

FORD

STREAM GOES
UNDER ROAD

NO PATH

41b

41b

GLEN SHIEL TO TORRIDON & FISHERFIELD

2 HRS 30 MINS–3 HRS TO SUMMIT BIDEAN A'GHLAS THUILL

ROAD

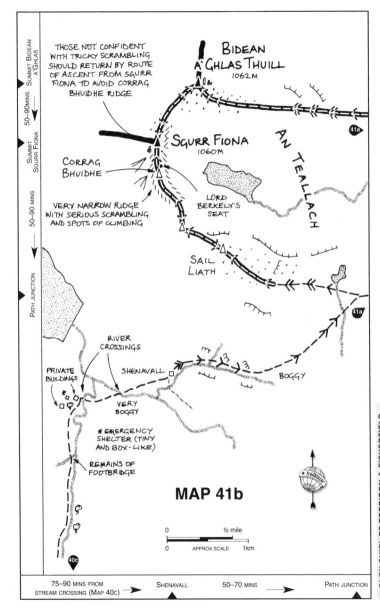

THOSE NOT CONFIDENT WITH TRICKY SCRAMBLING SHOULD RETURN BY ROUTE OF ASCENT FROM SGURR FIONA TO AVOID CORRAG BHUIDHE RIDGE

BIDEAN A'GHLAS THUILL 1062M

SGURR FIONA 1060M

AN TEALLACH

41a

CORRAG BHUIDHE

LORD BERKELY'S SEAT

VERY NARROW RIDGE WITH SERIOUS SCRAMBLING AND SPOTS OF CLIMBING

SAIL LIATH

41a

PATH JUNCTION

RIVER CROSSINGS

PRIVATE BUILDINGS

SHENAVALL

BOGGY

VERY BOGGY

* EMERGENCY SHELTER (TINY AND BOX-LIKE)

REMAINS OF FOOTBRIDGE

MAP 41b

0   ½ mile
0   APPROX SCALE   1km

★ trailblazer

40c

Summit Bidean A'Ghlas — 50–90mins — Summit Sgurr Fiona — 50–90 MINS — Path Junction

75–90 MINS FROM STREAM CROSSING (MAP 40c) → SHENAVALL 50–70 MINS → PATH JUNCTION

GLEN SHIEL TO TORRIDON & FISHERFIELD

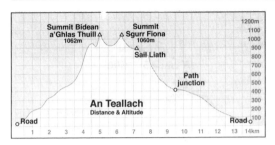

Summit Bidean a'Ghlas Thuill △ 1062m

Summit △ Sgurr Fiona 1060m

△ Sail Liath

Path junction ○

An Teallach
Distance & Altitude

○ Road

Road ○

1200m
1100
1000
900
800
700
600
500
400
300
200
100

1 2 3 4 5 6 7 8 9 10 11 12 13 14km

ridge should either retrace their steps from here or negotiate the bypass trail on the west side of the ridge.

To continue, descend via the south ridge of Sgurr Fiona and ascend to the summit of **Lord Berkely's Seat**, a tapering tower of rock that seems to overhang the corrie below. There are more towers to negotiate further along the Corrag Bhuidhe ridge which is where the scrambling comes in. Once past these, the ridge drops sharply and then rises again before finally coming to the end, at the summit of **Sail Liath**, the most southerly of the mountains tops.

With the hard work done, descend SE over, at first, gentle slopes, and then more inclined lower slopes. Avoid the short cliffs and exposed rock by passing them to the north or south and join the stalkers' path just below the **lochan**. Follow this path E to a track and then NNE when on the track, which leads down to the road at Corrie Hallie, about half a mile south of the start point.

Alternative routes
Another stalkers' path winds up the steadily rising northern slopes of the mountain, starting near Dundonnell Hotel. This is an easier, longer approach to the two munros but misses many of the good views of the mountain.

❏ **Rainy days**
● **Eilean Donan Castle** The most photographed castle in the Highlands with its backdrop of cold loch and mountain is open to the public daily from April to October (10am-6pm, £4.95, ☎ 01599-555202, 🖳 www.eileandonancastle.com). A castle has stood on the small island just off the shore of Loch Duich since the 13th century, although the present-day building is less than 100 years old. As well as appearing on thousands of postcards and calendars, it has been used for location shots in the films *Highlander*, *Loch Ness* and the James Bond film *The World is Not Enough*.
● **Falls of Glomach** Waterfalls always look better on a rainy day, especially this one, the highest free-falling waterfall in Britain with a drop of 113m. From Morvich it is a ten-mile return trip to the falls. Follow the path over the bleak Bealach na Sroine.
● **Low-level walks by Loch Torridon** The shores of Loch Torridon are just as fascinating as the mountains. One of the best walks is a two-mile return trip from the village of Shieldaig to a small hillock at the end of the peninsula. Head north from the primary school on a good path leading along this rocky slither of land, for a grandstand view across the waters of Lochs Torridon and Shieldaig.
   There is another great coast walk, of about three miles, from Alligin to Diabaig on the north side of the loch.

❏ **Other hills in the area**

● **Five Sisters of Kintail – Sgurr Fhuaran** (*'Skor Oor-un'*, **1067m/3500ft**) The Five Sisters of Kintail loom over Glen Shiel and Loch Duich. Access to and from the ridge is sheer but once up there the sense of elevation and freedom is utterly exhilarating. Apart from the knee-jarring ascent and descent the walk is relatively easy, but strenuous.

● **Liathach** (*'Lee-a-huch'*, **1055m/3460ft**) One of the Torridon giants and certainly the toughest. A punishing ascent leads to a frightening yet scintillating ridge of pinnacles strung between two high peaks. Like all Torridon mountains the views of the surrounding terraced slopes and corries are humbling in the extreme.

● **Slioch** (*'Slee-och'*, **981m/3220ft**) This rampart of a mountain could have been transplanted from the Canadian Rockies. Simply put, Slioch is what makes the view down Loch Maree one of the most talked about in Scotland. The walk to the summit from Kinlochewe is very long but not technically difficult.

GLEN SHIEL TO TORRIDON & FISHERFIELD – TOWNS & VILLAGES

GLENELG   [OFF MAP 33]

Glenelg is reached by way of the Ratagan pass, a single track road that climbs 350m from Loch Duich before plunging down to the village overlooking Skye. Nearby is Sandaig where Gavin Maxwell wrote his best-selling *Ring of Bright Water*.

Glenelg is a region of great historical interest with the old Hanovarian barracks, built during the 18th-century Jacobite uprisings, lying in ruins just outside the village. A mile or so up the glen are the famous brochs of Dun Telve and Dun Troddan, 2000-year-old stone towers believed to be Pictish defensive dwellings.

The village has a small **shop** and the quite brilliant *Glenelg Inn* (☎ 01599-522273, 🖳 www.glenelg-inn.com), a no-nonsense pub that does not pander to modern ideas of tourism. There is a great bar, cosy, dark, low-slung beams, dogs on ropes, fiddles, bodhrans and old wooden fish crates for chairs. The rooms are beautifully

decorated and stylish and cost from £30/pp for B&B. The scrumptious bar food is more affordable and covers everything from local haddock to chicken fajitas. There is also a handy **cash machine** in the porch that will charge you £1.50 for the thrill of withdrawing your own money.

Skyeways (☎ 01599-555477, 🖳 www .skyeways.couk) operates the 378a **bus** from Kyle of Lochalsh to Glenelg via Shiel Bridge Mon-Fri 1/day. They also operate a dial-a-bus service (378) to Corran car park via Arnisdale; this must be prebooked and operates on demand.

A small car **ferry** (see p33 for details) crosses to Kylerhea from Glenelg. The ferry service had been threatened with closure following the end of the tolls on the Skye bridge but thankfully the local community successfully campaigned for funding to operate the service as a community initiative.

GLEN SHIEL & SHIEL BRIDGE
      [OFF MAP 34]

Considering the number of munros either side of **Glen Shiel** it is surprising that the area has not been exploited commercially. This, of course, is a good thing and we

can forgive *Cluanie Inn* (☎ 01320-340238, 🖳 www.cluanieinn.com) for being the only interruption on the otherwise empty road at the high end of the glen. This white-washed inn has been offering shelter to travellers for over one hundred years, although it is unlikely that the inside of the place was as plush back then as it is today. There is good food on offer with paninis from £4.50 and haggis, neeps and tatties also for £4.50, and good ale too. The accommodation comprises 10 very posh rooms, some with Jacuzzis, from £49.50/ pp, or cheaper clubhouse accommodation for £35/pp, which is only marginally less luxurious than the hotel rooms. There is also the offer of Land-Rover lifts up and down the glen for £8.

At the foot of the glen is **Shiel Bridge**, a small hamlet comprising a **shop** and **café** with cheap and tasty bacon rolls and **internet** access (£1 per hour). There is also a **campsite** (☎ 01599-511221) with 50 pitches (£4 each) and, a little further down the shore of Loch Duich, *Ratagan Youth Hostel* (☎ 01599-511243, 40 beds, Mar-Oct, £12.50-14/pp). Along the A87 towards Morvich is *Kintail Lodge Hotel* (☎ 01599-

511275, 🖳 www.kintaillodgehotel.co.uk) with 12 en suite rooms costing £42-57/pp. Dormitory beds in their *Wee Bunkhouse* and twin rooms in the *Trekkers' Lodge* cost from £13.50/pp. Their bar menu includes traditional dishes such as haggis and cock-a-leekie pie.

A few paces away is the *Jac-o-bite Café* for lighter snacks and meals, and almost next door *Glomach House* (☎ 01599-511222, 🖳 www.glomach.co.uk, 2D/1T) has B&B for £35/pp and free views up Loch Duich.

Continue along the minor road up Strath Croe for the NTS *Kintail Outdoor Centre* (☎ 0131-243 9331, 🖳 www.nts .org.uk, 20 beds) where there is bunkhouse accommodation for £15/pp.

For a taxi up or down the glen call **Glenshiel Taxis** on ☎ 01599-511384. Alternatively the Glasgow to Skye Citylink **bus** runs six/seven times a day in each direction: see pp32-6.

TOMICH   [OFF MAP 35a]

The pretty cottages of Tomich have earned the village heritage status. In the centre of the village is *Tomich Hotel* (☎ 01456-415399, 🖳 www.tomichhotel.co.uk, 5D/ 3T), an old Victorian hunting lodge which has put up the likes of George V and Winston Churchill. It's a very friendly place with a well-stoked stove and cuddly toy labradors on shelves. The Golden Retriever was first bred here in the 1860s.

The food is excellent with salmon and venison on the menu. B&B is from £46.50/pp.

Opposite the hotel is a **post office** (only open Mon, Tue & Thu 11am-noon).

Tomich and the upper reaches of Glen Affric are hard to get to without a car but Ross's Minibuses (see p35) operate a **bus** from Inverness/Dingwall via Beauly railway station to the car park in Glen Affric.

TORRIDON

The village of Torridon, on the shore of the sea loch of the same name, lies in the shadow of Liathach's sheer slopes, scarred by an enormous old landslide.

The small **shop** stocks most essential foodstuffs, with fresh fruit and vegetables. Along the same stretch of road is *Torridon Youth Hostel* (☎ 01445-791284, 60 beds, Mar-Oct, from £12.50 to £15) and a free **campsite** which even has a toilet block with free hot showers!

Torridon Countryside Centre (☎ 01445-791368, 🖳 www.nts.org.uk, daily 10am-5pm end Mar-Oct, £3) is the place to learn about the local wildlife, particularly

the deer, in the deer museum. There is also a wildlife hide where one can watch red deer at close quarters.

Contact Stagecoach (see p35) to see if they still run the one **bus** a day (Mon-Sat) that Rapsons operated between Torridon and Achnasheen (for the **train** station). In the opposite direction a **post bus** (☎ 08457-740740, 🖳 www.postbus.royalmail.com) runs to Shieldaig and Strathcarron (for the train station). There are no buses on Sundays.

About a mile south of Torridon, at **Annat** (see map 36, p214), is *The Torridon Hotel* (☎ 01445-791242, 🖳 www.lochtor

ridonhotel.com) whose 19 en suite rooms cater for those with money to burn. The cheapest rooms, all of which have duck down duvets, are £82.50/pp which includes dinner and breakfast.

Next door, and part of the same establishment, is the ***Torridon Inn*** (☎ 01445-791242, 🖳 www.thetorridon.com/inn) which has 12 en suite rooms, some sleeping up to six people, from £40/pp. The bar and restaurant have tiled floors, log fires and maps on the wall. The meals range from fish and chips to scallops and king prawns. The nearest B&B to the pub is ***Ferroch Guest House*** (see map 36, p214; ☎ 01445-791451, 🖳 www.ferroch.co.uk), a pine-clad modern home with B&B from £35 per person.

KINLOCHEWE

Kinlochewe sits at the junction of the Torridon, Gairloch and Achnasheen roads. It is a tiny place with a small **store** (Mon, Wed, Fri 9am-5.30pm; Thu, Sat, Sun 9am-1pm) that also incorporates the **post office**, **Moru Outdoor Shop** (☎ 01445-760252) – the place for stove fuel and other camping bits and pieces – and the ***Teapot Café*** where you can sit in with a burger (£4.95) or fried breakfast (£6.95). There is another café, the ***Tipsy Laird***, at the petrol station. Bacon rolls here are £2.60. Other than that the main attraction is ***Kinlochewe Hotel*** (☎ 01445-760253, 🖳 www.kinlochewehotel .co.uk, 1S/4D/4T) which does B&B for £40/pp. They also have a constantly changing bar menu with main courses for around £7-11. Next door is their **bunkhouse** with very basic accommodation on sleeping platforms (bring your own sleeping bag), and a kitchen. There is space for 12 people (£10/pp). For B&B try ***Hillhaven*** (☎ 01445-760204, 🖳 www.kinlochewe.info,

POOLEWE   [SEE MAP 40a, p223]
There is a **shop** and **post office** in the village and, opposite the **swimming pool**, the excellent **Slioch Outdoor Shop** (☎ 01445-781412, 🖳 www.slioch.co.uk) where they make their own outdoor garments. The cheapest beds are from £15 at ***Riversdale B&B*** (☎ 01445-781227, 1D/1F) while ***Poolewe Hotel*** (☎ 01445-781241, 🖳 www .poolewehotel.co.uk, 2S/1D/2T) also

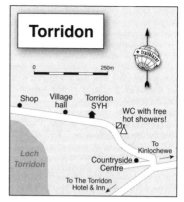

2D/1T en suite) where beds are £30/pp.

Scotbus's No 708 (Jun-Sep 3/day) **bus** goes from Achnasheen to Inverewe via here, Gairloch and Poolewe. Contact Stagecoach about any other bus services to/from here. See p35 for details.

offers B&B from £47/pp. In amongst the crofts on the edge of the village is the cosy yet contemporary ***Love Croft*** (☎ 01445-731048, 🖳 www.lovecroft.co.uk, 2D/1F) which offers B&B from £26/pp.

As an antidote to bothy living, ***Pool House Hotel*** (☎ 01445-781272, 🖳 www .poolhousehotel.com, 50 en suite rooms) is sheer extravagance. With its themed bedrooms, billiard room and antiques all over the place, this is an exclusive retreat for special occasions and large wallets.

Prices start at £150/pp for dinner, bed and breakfast rising to an astonishing £410/pp for the 'flagship suite'. And if you plan on spending that much why not pull out a few extra notes for their romantic packages: the 'Isle of Ewe (I Love You)' package includes truffles and champagne and costs an extra £100 while the 'Ever So Slightly Naughty Weekend Kit' is well worth an extra £90 just for the edible body dust and ostrich feather. I'd pay for that even if I was in a single room.

The *Bridge Cottage Coffee Shop* is the place for a filling snack before hitting the mountain trails.

Scotbus's No 708 (Jun-Sep 3/day) **bus** calls here en route between Achnasheen and Inverewe; see p35 for details. Contact Stagecoach and Westerbus for details of **bus services** (see p35) in the area. There are no usually no buses on Sundays.

GAIRLOCH

The main reason Gairloch gets a mention in this book is *The Old Inn* (☎ 01445-712006, 🖳 www.theoldinn.net, 1S/6D/4T/3F), one of the best pubs in the Highlands. It's steeped in history, tastefully refurbished to expose its original 300-year-old stone walls and has a constantly changing array of real ales (including their own Blind Piper of Gairloch ale), friendly staff, live folk music at weekends, huge portions of tasty food (including burgers, sandwiches and salads) and plush accommodation from £27.50 to £44.50/pp.

If you want to stay in the area the most spectacular spot is at *Rua Reidh Lighthouse* (☎ 01445-771263, 🖳 www .ruareidh.co.uk, 4T or D/4F/1 bunk room with 3 beds). The old keeper's dwelling has been converted into cosy self-catering accommodation with both hostel beds (£10/pp) and private rooms (£16/pp). It's a spectacular spot on a windswept rocky headland with views across The Minch to Skye and Lewis. The only drawback is that you will need your own wheels to get there; Rua Reidh is ten miles north of Gairloch at the end of a dead-end road.

In Gairloch itself there are a few **B&Bs**, **cafés**, a **chemist**, a **bank** with **cash machine**, and a **campsite** (☎ 01445-712373, 🖳 www.gairlochcaravanpark.com, £6/pp) but for those about to set foot on the Fisherfield trek, Poolewe is a more convenient place to stay.

Scotbus's No 708 (Jun-Sep 3/day) **bus** calls here en route between Achnasheen (for the train station) and Inverewe; see p35 for details.

DUNDONNELL [SEE MAP 41a, p228]

There is not much to Dundonnell, at the head of Little Loch Broom. There are a few crofts, an SMC mountaineers' hut, the Dundonnell mountain rescue team, and a herd of feral goats. This is a quiet and deserted region but there are places to lay your head after a hard day on An Teallach.

In the adjoining crofting hamlet of **Camusnagaul** is *Badrallach* (☎ 01854-633281, 🖳 www.badrallach.com) which has everything from a **bothy** (£5/pp) to a **campsite** (£3/pp) to a **caravan** (sleeps 2, £40/night).

At *4 Camusnagaul* (☎ 01854-633237, 🖺 01854-833382, 🖳 www.camusnagaul .com, 1D/1T/2F) there are beds from £24/pp.

Sail Mhor Croft (☎ 01854-633224, 🖳 www.sailmhor.co.uk) has further bunkhouse-style beds for £12/pp or £16/pp with breakfast thrown in.

Dundonnell Hotel (☎ 01854-633204, 🖳 www.dundonnellhotel.com) is the only place to find an evening meal (Mar-Oct only), with both sea bass and beef on the menu, unless you are prepared to drive round to Ullapool. They have nearly thirty smart rooms from £40 to £55/pp. There is little else in the area, except for a tiny **shop** at the **petrol station** opposite the hotel.

Contact Stagecoach and Westerbus for details of **bus services** (see p35) in the area. There are no usually no buses on Sundays.

GLEN SHIEL TO TORRIDON & FISHERFIELD

The Far North

The north-west corner of the Highlands from Torridon to Loch Eriboll on the north coast is wild land characterised by a bed of gneiss decorated with Torridonian sandstone peaks. These very individual mountains, detached from

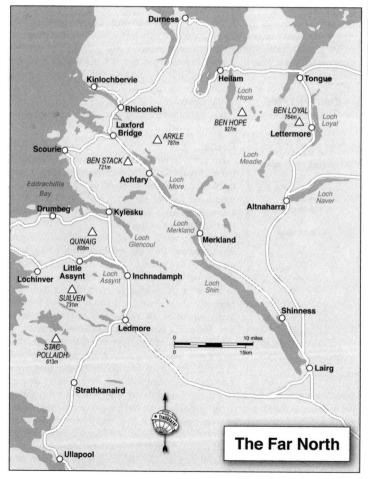

their neighbours by large swathes of bog, rock and heather, are not particularly high but they are distinct in appearance and quite stunning to look at from any angle. The view from the top of any of them takes in an undulating and barren landscape patterned with lochans, pools and rivers. It may be a long way from anywhere but that is another part of the appeal. This is relatively unspoilt land and is certainly Scotland's most raw and savage landscape. If it fails to capture your spirit you should stick to the city.

STAC POLLAIDH (*'Stak Pol-ee'*, 613m/2010ft)   [MAP 42]

Overview
This is the smallest of the Assynt peaks but, as with many of its neighbours, size means nothing in Assynt. With its splintered crown of sandstone pillars and pinnacles, this distinctive little hill demands attention, and gets it. The southern slopes were, once, heavily scarred from the passage of thousands of boots but some good work by the Footpath Trust has repaired much of the damage. As a result, access to the crest of the mountain could not be simpler. Reaching the actual summit, however, does involve a reasonably awkward scramble.

Route
A **car park** on the single track road to Achiltibuie is the start point for the Stac Pollaidh footpath. Climb up through the native birch woods and take the right-hand fork at the path junction. The path is almost impossible to lose as it climbs up and around the eastern flank of the hill.

On the north side of the mountain the path divides again. Take the left-hand fork which leads quickly up to the crest of the hill. A quick detour to the left leads to a good viewpoint but the summit is to the west. A number of trails thread their way along the ridge, weaving between, up and over the many pinnacles, chimneys and towers that make Stac Pollaidh a hill of such great character.

One of the easiest approaches to the summit is on the path that hugs the south side of the ridge, just below the pinnacles. Just before the summit there is a notch in the ridge with precipitous drops on each side. The summit is tantalisingly close but the only way to tackle this gap is by negotiating the buttress on the far side of this gap. There are three ways of tackling it: there is a tricky chimney down and to the right, there is an exposed and difficult climb straight ahead, or a scramble to the left. The latter is by far the easiest option. After negotiating this obstacle it is a short stroll along a flat ridge to the summit with views north to Suilven and beyond. To the south-east is Beinn Mor Coigach and its distinctive Fiddler ridge.

STAC POLLAIDH
(Steep Hill of the Peat Bog)

Technical grade
▲▲▲
Navigation grade
▲
Terrain grade
▲▲▲
Strenuousness
▲

Return time
1¹/₂-2¹/₂hrs
Return distance
2¹/₂miles/4km
Total ascent
1900ft/580m
OS maps
Landranger 15,
Explorer 439
Gateways
Ullapool (see p249)
Lochinver (see p252)

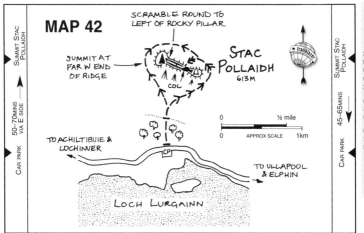

Descend back to the path junction on the north side of the hill and follow the path bearing west to complete a circumnavigation of the hill.

Alternative routes
It is best to stick to the path to avoid a recurrence of the terrible erosion that scarred the hill for so long.

SUILVEN ('*Sool-ven*')   [MAP 43a, p238; MAP 43b, p239]
CAISTEAL LIATH ('*Cas-ul Lee-u*', 731m/2400ft)

Overview
Suilven is Scotland's sugar-loaf mountain; like a punched fist through a cold floor of rock and water. Many walkers are so beguiled by this inselberg, spared by the giant ice sheets of long ago, that it often comes first on their list of favourite peaks. It is certainly the most individual and most recognisable of Scotland's many mountains and manages to attract all the plaudits despite its very modest height. Reaching the top is easier than it looks but it does involve a long walk in.

Route
Cars can be driven as far as the lay-by just before **Glencanisp Lodge**, about a mile east of Lochinver. For those without a car it's a 15- to 20-minute walk. Follow the track past the lodge and continue on it through a small field of gorse. A path continues beyond this field and follows the north bank of the river over open ground for about an hour, with the mighty pillar of Suilven's main peak, Caisteal Liath ('*Cashowl Leea*'), ahead. Just before the hut at **Suileag** (Map 43b) the **path splits**. Follow the right-hand fork for another half

THE FAR NORTH

**SUILVEN
(The Pillar)**

Technical grade
▲▲

Navigation grade
▲▲

Terrain grade
▲▲

Strenuousness
▲▲▲

Return time
6-8hrs

Return distance
13½miles/22km

Total ascent
2620ft/800m

OS maps
Landranger 15,
Explorer 442

Gateways
Lochinver (see p252)

an hour. Soon after crossing a **bridge** a less obvious path deviates from the main riverside path before a second bridge. Follow this very boggy trail up and over the rough ground ahead. The path rises in a series of rolling shelves and passes by small lochans on each side.

Shortly beyond this the sheer side of the mountain is reached. The path continues straight ahead, up the very steep slope. The climb is a tough slog but is not difficult and is soon over. Once on the spine of the mountain the views across the surrounding bedrock of Lewisian gneiss can be fully appreciated. All of the Assynt peaks come into view with spiky Stac Pollaidh to the south across the lochans and knolls, Quinaig and Canisp to the north and, in the east, the only two munros in the area: Ben More Assynt and Conival.

The summit is not far from the saddle. Follow the rising ridge to the west, past a rather unexpected stone wall that straddles the back of the hill, to the flat grassy summit of Caisteal Liath. A short excursion along the ridge to the east top of the mountain is strongly recommended but be warned that the final climb is for competent rock-climbers only. Non-climbers can still venture a little way along the ridge, which is narrow and quite spectacular in

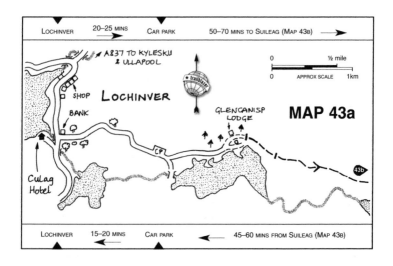

LOCHINVER 20–25 MINS ──▶ CAR PARK 50–70 MINS TO SUILEAG (MAP 43B) ──▶

A837 TO KYLESKU & ULLAPOOL

★ trailsign

SHOP LOCHINVER

BANK

GLENCANISP LODGE

MAP 43a

0   ½ mile
0   APPROX SCALE   1km

CP

CULAG HOTEL

43b

LOCHINVER 15–20 MINS ◀── CAR PARK ◀── 45–60 MINS FROM SUILEAG (MAP 43B)

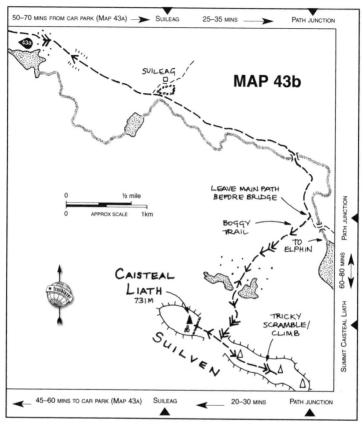

SUILEAG

MAP 43b

0   ½ mile
0   APPROX SCALE   1km

trailblazer

LEAVE MAIN PATH BEFORE BRIDGE

BOGGY TRAIL

TO ELPHIN

CAISTEAL LIATH 731M

PATH JUNCTION

60–80 MINS

SUMMIT CAISTEAL LIATH

TRICKY SCRAMBLE/CLIMB

SUILVEN

45–60 MINS TO CAR PARK (MAP 43A) ← SUILEAG ← 20–30 MINS ← PATH JUNCTION

places. The return is along the same route or, alternatively via the southern approach path which comes out a few miles south of Lochinver at Inverkirkaig.

Alternative routes

The southern approach to Suilven from Inverkirkaig is about the same length as the route described opposite.

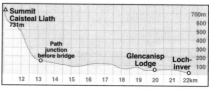
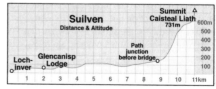

THE FAR NORTH

QUINAIG ('*Koo-nyak*') [MAP 44]
SAIL GHARBH ('*Say-ul Garv*', 808m/2650ft)
SAIL GORM ('*Say-ul Gorm*', 776m/2545ft)
SPIDEAN COINICH ('*Spit-yan Con-ich*', 764m/2505ft)

Overview

The most northerly of the Assynt hills maintains the character of the region; an isolated mountain subtly carved into shape by massive ice sheets. The dramatic cliffs on the west side give an air of impenetrability but from the road on the east side a path leads easily to the sweeping ridges that link the shapely tops. Quinaig estate is now owned and managed by the John Muir Trust (see p45) whose ethic is to preserve wild land in the Highlands.

Route

Follow the path from the **car park** on the A894, two miles north of the Skiag road junction. The trail climbs the shallow slopes into the wide-mouthed corrie ahead and skirts the north shore of the **lochan**. At the backwall of the corrie, the ground gets progressively steeper but at no point is the terrain particularly awkward. A relatively short ascent leads to a flat-bottomed grassy **col**.

The main summit of Quinaig lies out on a satellite spur of the mountain. To get there climb north up a short, steep section to a broad knoll at a junction of ridges. Head east along an easy ridge which drops very little before rising gradually to the trig point that marks the summit of **Sail Gharbh**, the highest point of this complex mountain.

The walk can be cut short by retracing your steps to the saddle and returning to the road via the ascent route. However, rather than end the walk prematurely return to the knoll at the ridge junction and walk north along an undulating ridge which eventually rises steadily to the summit of the northern peak, **Sail Gorm**. The views from here take in the small islands and skerries of Eddrachillis Bay.

QUINAIG (The Pail)
Technical grade ▲▲
Navigation grade ▲▲
Terrain grade ▲▲
Strenuousness ▲▲
Return time 3½-5hrs
Return distance 8miles/13km
Total ascent 3280ft/1000m
OS maps Landranger 15, Explorer 442
Gateways Lochinver (see p252) Kylesku (see p253)

Return to the saddle and ascend south up a grassy ridge which leads over an exposed top before continuing up a ridge of grey boulders to the top of **Spidean Coinich**. To the south

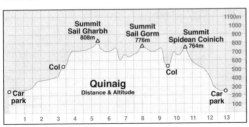

Quinaig
Distance & Altitude

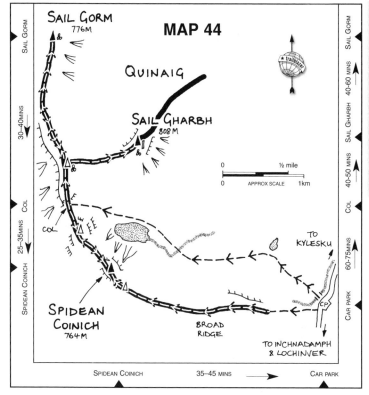

there are inspiring views across Loch Assynt. Beyond this dogleg of water are the chiselled peaks of Canisp and Suilven breaking from the flat bedrock below.

The very wide slope of Spidean Coinich's SE ridge gently lowers happy walkers back to the road.

Alternative routes

Quinaig essentially consists of three ridges, distinguished by three peaks so the walk can be shortened by omitting one or two of the summits, although most walkers will want to visit Sail Gharbh which represents the true summit of the whole massif.

❏ **Important note – walking times**
All times in this book refer only to the time spent walking. You will need to add 20-30% to allow for rests, photography, checking the map, drinking water etc.

BEN STACK (721m/2365ft)   [MAP 45]

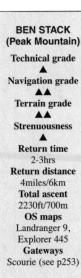

**BEN STACK
(Peak Mountain)**

Technical grade
▲

Navigation grade
▲▲

Terrain grade
▲▲

Strenuousness
▲

Return time
2-3hrs

Return distance
4miles/6km

Total ascent
2230ft/700m

OS maps
Landranger 9,
Explorer 445

Gateways
Scourie (see p253)

Overview

Of all the isolated peaks in this region Ben Stack is probably the loneliest, well-detached from its kin. Consequently the summit, which is a short and easy climb from the road, is an excellent vantage point for the view north to Foinaven and Arkle.

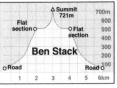

Route

A few metres south of the turn-off for Lone there is the beginning of a four-wheel-drive track. Follow this towards the obvious rocky rib that runs up the wide slopes of the ridge ahead. The track dies almost as soon as it starts, becoming little more than a wet trail over very squelchy peat bog. Aim for the rocky rib and follow it up the hillside, keeping to the left at all times. Near the top of this rib, at about 500m, the **ground flattens** out. Continue in a NW direction to

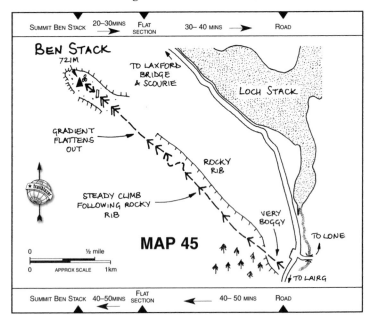

the foot of the summit cone. The ground once again gets steeper and leads up rocky slopes to the twin summit of the mountain.

The descent is via the same route as the ascent.

Alternative routes

Another path climbs up the mountain's NW ridge from the stalkers' path that begins at the northern end of Loch Stack. This route is much steeper and a little more exerting.

ARKLE (787m/2580ft)   [MAP 46, p244]

Overview

A distinctive hill whose sheets of grey scree over terraced ledges can only really be bettered by its neighbour, Foinaven. However, Arkle is the more accessible of the two hills although reaching the summit is still a significant little expedition.

Route

Turn east off the **A838 road** at the southern end of Loch Stack onto a track over a bridge. Follow the track past some private buildings to **Lone**. Once past Lone the track peters out to become a stalkers' path. Follow it as it passes through a small copse and then zigzags up a steep slope to the left of a stream. After a climb of about 100m the path emerges onto wide open slopes of scattered boulders and flat bedrock.

Look out for a small cairn on the left-hand side of the path and from here follow a faint trail NW up the long flat back of the mountain keeping the sheer cliffs and scree to the left. It is a long ascent of about a mile and a half in distance but it is not particularly steep, eventually topping out at the lower of Arkle's two peaks; a flat top that offers the first views of the gaping eastern corrie of the mountain to the north.

The main summit is along the spectacular arête that can be seen across the corrie. Descend from the southern top in a WNW direction to a rocky col. From here it is a short sharp climb up a broad, rocky slope to gain the crest of the ridge as it swings round to the north over a knoll. It is another half a mile along an, at times, very **narrow ridge** of rocky slabs and

**ARKLE
(The Level-Topped Mountain)**

Technical grade
▲▲▲
Navigation grade
▲▲
Terrain grade
▲▲▲
Strenuousness
▲▲▲
Return time
4¹/₂-6hrs
Return distance
8¹/₂miles/14km
Total ascent
2740ft/830m
OS maps
Landranger 9, Explorer 445
Gateways
Scourie (see p253)

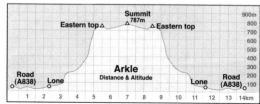

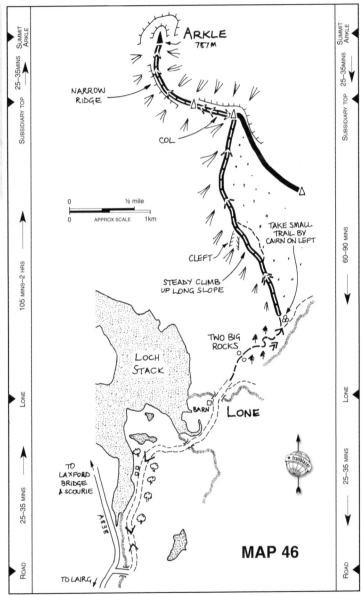

ARKLE
787M

NARROW
RIDGE

COL

TAKE SMALL
TRAIL BY
CAIRN ON LEFT

CLEFT

STEADY CLIMB
UP LONG SLOPE

TWO BIG
ROCKS

LOCH
STACK

BARN

LONE

TO
LAXFORD
BRIDGE
& SCOURIE

A838

TO LAIRG

0   ½ mile
0   APPROX SCALE   1km

MAP 46

trailblazer

Left side margin (top to bottom):
SUMMIT ARKLE
25-35MINS
SUBSIDIARY TOP
105 MINS-2 HRS
LONE
25-35 MINS
ROAD

Right side margin (top to bottom):
SUMMIT ARKLE
25-35MINS
SUBSIDIARY TOP
60-90 MINS
LONE
25-35 MINS
ROAD

steps to the main summit of the mountain, from where there are views across the wide strath to the grey rock of Foinaven.

Retrace your steps for the return to the start.

Alternative routes
Arkle is so well defended by cliffs and loose scree that it throws up very little chance to vary the walk. The route described offers the only sensible approach to the summit.

THE FAR NORTH

BEN HOPE (927m/3040ft)   [MAP 47, p246]
Overview
Ben Hope is the most northerly of all 284 munros in Scotland. It is a long way from any other munro and as such stands proudly alone. The long southerly slopes of the mountain provide the easiest access to a rugged summit overlooking the wild north coast. There is no public transport so anyone planning to walk here would definitely need a car.

Route
The start of the walk is a few metres south of a barn on the minor road running through Strath More (GR462477). Follow a rough old path up the south bank of the stream. The path is fairly steep at first as it climbs up and into a broad gully falling away from a wide shelf on the mountainside. Cross the **stream** and continue straight up the steep muddy path through the heather. The path swings briefly south before continuing east and north to reach the top of the steep section at about 400m.

At this point there is a **wide grassy bowl** straight ahead while to the north the slopes of Ben Hope rise steadily to the summit in the far distance. A faint path zigzags up the steep lower flank of this wide ridge but soon the gradient eases and the last half a mile is a relatively easy walk.

The only difficulty on this approach is the risk of getting lost in poor visibility. This is a very broad ridge with a sudden and precipitous cliff for company on the left, so careful map and compass work may be needed in mist. In clear weather the view from the summit is sensational, taking in Ben Loyal to the east and Foinaven to the south-west and, of course, the cold sea to the north.

BEN HOPE
(Bay Mountain)

Technical grade
▲
Navigation grade
▲▲
Terrain grade
▲▲
Strenuousness
▲
Return time
3-3¹/₂hrs
Return distance
4miles/6km
Total ascent
3020ft/920m
OS maps
Landranger 9, Explorer 447
Gateways
Durness (see p253)
Tongue (see p254)

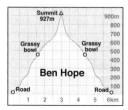

Ben Hope

Alternative routes

You can also start from the farm at Alltnacaillich where a path joins the lower end of the long southern slope of the mountain. This cuts out the steep start of the walk described on p245 but is longer.

BEN LOYAL (764m/2505ft)   [MAP 48]

Overview

Easily the most recognisable mountain in the far north, Ben Loyal is worth the long journey. Its steep sides sweep majestically from the heather moors to a ridge that dips and rolls in beautiful symmetry. The main summit is easy to reach despite the imposing look of the mountain from the nearby Kyle of Tongue. There is a postbus (see p35) to Tongue but in general terms you would need a car to be able to reach the start of this walk.

Route

From Tongue follow the minor road as far as the turn-off for Ribigill Farm. Cars can be parked in the space provided just before the gate and cattle grid. Now on foot, follow the lane south turning left at the first junction and left again at the

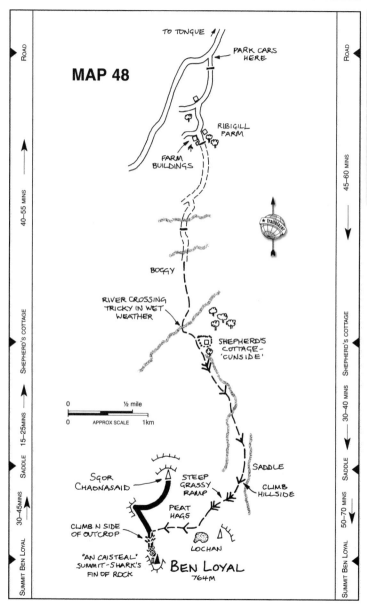

THE FAR NORTH

MAP 48

TO TONGUE

PARK CARS HERE

RIBIGILL FARM

FARM BUILDINGS

BOGGY

RIVER CROSSING TRICKY IN WET WEATHER

SHEPHERD'S COTTAGE - 'CUNSIDE'

0   ½ mile
0   APPROX SCALE   1km

SGOR CHAONASAID

STEEP GRASSY RAMP

SADDLE

CLIMB HILLSIDE

PEAT HAGS

CLIMB N SIDE OF OUTCROP

LOCHAN

"AN CAISTEAL" SUMMIT - SHARK'S FIN OF ROCK

BEN LOYAL 764M

ROAD — 40-55 MINS — SHEPHERD'S COTTAGE — 15-25MINS — SADDLE — 30-45MINS — SUMMIT BEN LOYAL

ROAD — 45-60 MINS — SHEPHERD'S COTTAGE — 30-40 MINS — SADDLE — 50-70 MINS — SUMMIT BEN LOYAL

**BEN LOYAL
(Elm Tree
Mountain)**

Technical grade
▲

Navigation grade
▲▲

Terrain grade
▲▲

Strenuousness
▲

Return time
3½-5hrs
Return distance
8miles/13km
Total ascent
2460ft/750m
OS maps
Landranger 10,
Explorer 447
Gateways
Tongue (see p254)

farm buildings of Ribigill. The road becomes a track after passing through a gate at the farmyard. Ignore the path that breaks away to the right and continue across the rough grazing land, through another gate and across a couple of rivers.

The climb proper begins just after the second crossing and the old **shepherds' cottage** at Cunside. A clear path negotiates the peaty slopes ahead and leads to a very wide **saddle**. To the right is the outlying top of Ben Loyal: Sgor Chaonasaid. It is possible to climb the very steep slopes to the summit of this peak but an easier approach is to continue past and climb onto the saddle ahead. Before the cliffs on the right head straight up the steep slopes of grass and deep heather where a small stream runs out of a shallow bowl.

It is only a short climb and very soon the slopes give way to an expanse of upland peat moor. Weave your way around the **peat hags** and aim for the ridge ahead. It is a short pull up steep slopes of tussocky grass to the broad back of the mountain and it is then just a short step onto the shark's fin summit of Ben Loyal: **An Caisteal**. Another short pull up steep slopes of tussocky grass leads to the broad back of the mountain and it is then not far to the real summit. The south side of the huge wedge of exposed rock that is the summit is one big cliff. Access to the trig point, which is perched precariously on the edge of this drop, is from the north side

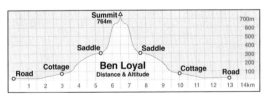

where a little light scrambling is all that is needed. The quickest return is via the ascent route.

Alternative routes

For a longer day continue south from the summit of the mountain and descend west via the southernmost peak, Carn an Tionail. Continue west past the lower top of Sgor Fhionnaich, taking care to avoid the cliffs on this peak's east face. Then head north, again avoiding the cliffs at the lower margins of the mountain, for the return NE through woodland to Cunside and the path back to Ribigill Farm.

❏ Other hills in the area

● **Ben Mor Coigach** (*'Bayn Mor Coyach'*, **743m/2440ft**) A seaside mountain with walls of rock running into the ocean on its south side, and deep corries to the north. The highlight is the Fiddler, a wedge of rock stretching from the boggy moorland to the high plateau above. Access is across rough grassland but most of the walk is free of major obstacles.

● **Ben More Assynt** (**998m/3275ft**) and **Conival** (**987m/3240ft**) The only two munros in the area can be climbed in one long exhausting expedition. The views from the summits take in all the smaller Assynt peaks laid out across a bogland of rock and lochan.

● **Foinaven** (*'Funaven'*, **911m/2990ft**) Foinaven is Arkle's bigger brother, sharing the same characteristics of grey scree and defined arêtes. It involves a lot more leg work lying some way from any road but rewards those who make the effort with some remarkable vistas across barren mountains and moor.

THE FAR NORTH – TOWNS & VILLAGES

ULLAPOOL [see map p250]

Occupying an alluvial fan on the shore of Loch Broom, Ullapool has developed into the largest town on the north-west coast. It is a quiet, friendly place and acts as an excellent base for exploring the area, positioned halfway between Torridon and Fisherfield to the south and Assynt to the north.

Services

The **TIC** (☎ 0845-225 5121) is a good starting point for anyone unfamiliar with the region. On West Argyle St and Argyle St there is a small **supermarket**, a **post office**, two **banks** with **cash machines** and, in the converted church, a small **museum** (☎ 01854-612987, 🖳 www.ullapoolmuse um.co.uk, £3) highlighting local history. For mountain equipment look for **North-West Outdoors** (☎ 01854-613383) on the same street. There is **internet** access at the **bookshop** and also at the **library** where it is free. The **chemist** is on Shore St. There is a large Somerfield **supermarket** on the outskirts of town to the north.

Ferries (operated by Caledonian MacBrayne) to Stornoway on the Isle of Lewis depart at least twice daily. **Citylink buses** from Inverness terminate at Ullapool and connect with the ferries. There is at least one bus a day, Monday to Saturday. See pp32-6 for more details.

For **taxis** and **local buses** to Inverness and Gairloch contact Ewen's of Ullapool (☎ 01854-612966, 🖳 www.ewensofulla pool.co.uk).

Where to stay

There are two cheap hostels: *Ullapool Youth Hostel* (☎ 01854-612254, 50 beds, Mar-Oct, £12.50-15.75/pp), on Shore St, and the independent *Scotpackers Hostel* (☎ 01854-613126, 🖳 www.scotpackers-hos tels.co.uk, £15) on the corner of West Lane.

A good place to look for a bed is on West Terrace where *The Old Surgery Guest House* (☎ 01854-612520, 🖳 www.oldsur gery.co.uk, 1D/1T/1F en suite) does B&B from £20 to £30/pp. Further up the road there are beds for around £20/pp at *Loggie Bank B&B* (☎ 01854-612042) and at *Dalshian Guest House* (☎ 01854-612413).

At the east end of Castle Terrace is *Riverside Hotel* (☎ 01854-612239, 🖳 www .riversideullapool.com, 4S/4D/4T/2F) with B&B from £27/pp.

A convenient place to base oneself is along the seafront. Try *Waterside House* (☎ 01854-612140, 3D en suite) which does B&B from £25/pp. At the opposite end of this street is the *Ferry Boat Inn* (☎ 01854-612366, 🖳 www .ferryboat-inn.com) whose beds are so

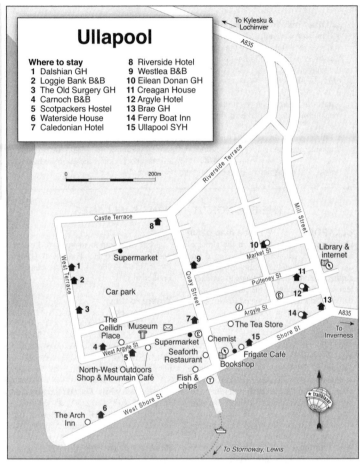

Ullapool

Where to stay
1 Dalshian GH
2 Loggie Bank B&B
3 The Old Surgery GH
4 Carnoch B&B
5 Scotpackers Hostel
6 Waterside House
7 Caledonian Hotel
8 Riverside Hotel
9 Westlea B&B
10 Eilean Donan GH
11 Creagan House
12 Argyle Hotel
13 Brae GH
14 Ferry Boat Inn
15 Ullapool SYH

0   200m

To Kylesku &
Lochinver

A835

Riverside Terrace

Mill Street

Castle Terrace

Supermarket

West Terrace

Car park

Market St

Library &
internet

Pulteney St

Quay Street

The
Ceilidh   Museum
Place

Argyle St

The Tea Store

A835

To
Inverness

West Argyle St

Supermarket

Chemist

Shore St

Seaforth
Restaurant

Frigate Café

North-West Outdoors
Shop & Mountain Café

Bookshop

Fish &
chips

The Arch
Inn

West Shore St

trailblazer

To Stornoway, Lewis

comfortable you won't want to go up the hill the next morning. Prices start at £35/pp. Next door is ***Brae Guest House*** (☎ 01854-612421) with B&B from £20/pp.

In the centre of the village B&B costs £25/pp at the traditional ***Carnoch B&B*** (☎ 01854-612749, 🖳 www.carnoch.com, 2D) and £50/pp at the extensive ***Caledonian Hotel*** (☎ 01854-612306, 🖳 www.oxford hotelsandinns.com, 9S/18D45T/1F). Both ***Argyle Hotel*** (☎ 01854-612422, 🖳 www .theargyllullapool.com, 2D/2T/2F) and ***Creagan House*** (☎ 01854-612397, 🖳 www .ullapool.co.uk/creaganhouse, 5D) charge around £30-40 for B&B.

Finally, ***Westlea B&B*** (☎ 01854-612594, 🖳 www.westlea-ullapool.co.uk, 1S/3D/1T) and ***Eilean Donan Guest***

House (☎ 01854-612524, 💻 www.eilean donan.fsbusiness.co.uk, 1S/2D/2T), are tucked away in a quiet part of the town on Market St; both charge around £30/pp.

Where to eat and drink

The Ceilidh Place (☎ 01854-612103, 💻 www.ceilidhplace.com) is possibly the best place for a meal in Ullapool. The menu is imaginative and varied with stalker's pie for £8.50 and locally smoked hake for £16.50. Also here is an excellent **bookshop** selling tomes on all things Scottish.

The Mountain Café (☎ 01854-613769) above the North-West Outdoors shop is another good place to while away a rainy hour or two. Their baked potatoes are £3.95 and their all-day breakfast is £5.95. You can also get breakfast for £4.70 at the tiny *Tea Store* (☎ 01854-612995).

The *Frigate Café* (☎ 01854-612969, 💻 www.ullapoolcatering.co.uk) on Shore St is a relaxing and spacious place with a wonderful array of dishes including venison pie for £9.95. They also do take-away food, including baked potatoes from £4.75.

There are several **fish and chips** places near the harbour.

Many of the pubs do good bar food: the best place to combine a meal with a pint is the *Ferry Boat Inn* (see p249). They do smoked haddock for £12.50 and soup of the day for £3.50. The *Arch Inn* (☎ 01854-612454, 💻 www.thearchinn.co.uk) and *Argyle Hotel* (see opposite) also do pub grub with the latter offering scampi and chips for £7.95.

Some specialist restaurants to try include *Seaforth Restaurant* (☎ 01854-612122, 💻 www.theseaforth.com) which acts as a contemporary restaurant during the day, serving duck, langoustines and good old fish and chips, but at night it becomes a lively bar with a fairly young crowd. The Seaforth has forged a reputation for live music, having attracted some fairly big bands in the past such as Shed Seven, Ash and The Mull Historical Society. Check their website for listings.

Over at the *Eilean Donan Guest House* (see opposite) things are less raucous. They specialise in sumptuous meals such as salmon and butterbean mash.

❏ **Rainy days**

● **Beach walks at Clach Toll, Achmelvich and Sandwood Bay** The beaches of Clach Toll and Achmelvich, just north of Lochinver, are easily accessible from the road and give a taste of the wild seascapes that characterise this area. But it is Sandwood Bay, lying six miles south of the Cape Wrath sea cliffs, that attracts all the attention. It is a four-mile walk from Oldshoremore, near Kinlochbervie, to this two-mile strand, with its dunes, loch and the sea stack of Am Buchaille. The wilder the weather the more beautiful this place seems but don't go alone! Sandwood Bay is reputedly haunted.

● **Eas a' Chual Aluinn waterfall** The highest waterfall in Britain, just short of 200m, is remarkably undeveloped, largely thanks to its isolation. To get there one needs to walk along the stalkers' path heading east from the hairpins on the A894 about three miles south of Kylesku. Unfortunately, the falls can be little more than a significant dribble in dry weather so pray for rain.

● **Smoo Cave** Smoo Cave (see map p253) is a sea cave at the end of a geo. It is right by the roadside at the village of Smoo but you need to climb down into the cove below to appreciate it. Inside, a short walkway leads into the depths of the cavern where the thundering roar of an underground waterfall shakes the walls. The top of the waterfall can be seen disappearing into the ground on the other side of the road. Well worth the short walk.

LOCHINVER

Lochinver lies on the harbour of the same name with the sugar-loaf mountain of Suilven dominating the view behind.

A **bus** from Inverness stops here on its way to Durness (May-Sept, Mon-Sat, once daily, daily July-Aug): contact Tim Dearman Coaches (☎ 01349-883585, 💻 www.timdearmancoaches.co.uk). Contact Stagecoach (see p35) for details of services they operate in this area. For a **taxi** call ☎ 01571-844607.

The **TIC** (☎ 01571-844330) is opposite the village hall. There is also a **newsagent** and **shop** and a **post office** on the main street, and a **bank** at the southern end. The **health centre** (☎ 01571-844226) is also on the main street. Assynt Adventures is an extremely small **outdoor shop** with limited mountain and camping supplies.

A bed for the night can be found for £30/pp at *Polcraig Guest House* (☎ 01571-844429, 3D/3T) behind the village hall.

Achmelvich Beach Youth Hostel (☎ 01571-844480, 35 beds, mid Mar-Sep, £13-15/pp) is two miles from the village in a stunning position by Achmelvich beach. There is also the independent *Inchnadamph Hostel* (☎ 01571-822218, 💻 www.inch-lodge.co.uk; 50 beds; dorm beds £15/pp, private rooms £30/pp, all including a self-service breakfast), ten miles east of Lochinver.

Back in the village, *Culag Hotel* (☎ 01571-844270, 📠 01571-844483) has B&B from £25/pp.

There are some excellent local dishes such as haggis stuffed chicken (£10.50) at *Caberfeidh Restaurant* (☎ 01571-844321). Next door is the *Riverside Bistro* (☎ 01571-844356) specialising in pies: the wild boar and apricot pie is £5.45.

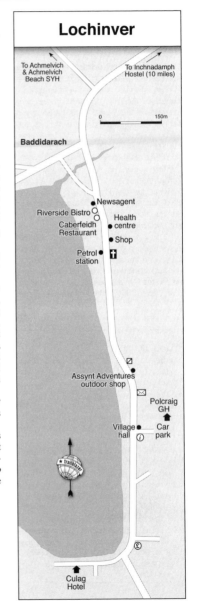

Lochinver

To Achmelvich & Achmelvich Beach SYH

To Inchnadamph Hostel (10 miles)

0   150m

Baddidarach

Newsagent
Riverside Bistro
Health centre
Caberfeidh Restaurant
Shop
Petrol station

Assynt Adventures outdoor shop

Polcraig GH

Village hall   Car park

Culag Hotel

KYLESKU   [OFF MAP 44]

The hamlet of Kylesku looks down to the rough-hewn mountains above the twin sea lochs of Glencoul and Glendhu.

This is a savage landscape but *Kylesku Hotel* (☎ 01971-502231, 🖳 www.kylesku hotel.co.uk, 5D/2T/1S) acts as an island of comfort, offering classy B&B for £47/pp. Their excellent restaurant uses local ingredients such as salmon, and venison from the hill. A three-course meal costs £28.50 or they do cheaper bar meals from £7.95.

About a mile south is slightly cheaper B&B (from £42/pp) at *Newton Lodge* (☎ 01971-502070, 🖳 www.newtonlodge.co .uk, 3D/4T) which has a wonderful panoramic conservatory overlooking Loch Glencoul.

Contact Stagecoach (see p35) for details of services they operate in this area.

SCOURIE   [OFF MAPS 45 & 46]

Scourie is one of the only villages of any significance on the long desolate road from Ullapool to Durness. The scattering of crofts and houses almost seem to have been squeezed out of the rumbling rocks all around.

It is a useful base for anyone wishing to tackle the likes of Ben Stack or Arkle. There is a small **shop** on the main street but it is *Scourie Hotel* (☎ 01971-502396, 🖳 www.scourie-hotel.co.uk, 20 rooms) that

dominates the area. They have rooms looking towards Ben Stack and Arkle. B&B is from £45/pp. Cheaper beds (£25) can be found at *Greenhill B&B* (☎ 01971-502351) and at *Scourie Guest House* (☎ 01971-502001, 🖳 www.scourieguesthouse.btin ternet.co.uk) where B&B is £30/pp.

Contact Stagecoach (see p35) for details of services they operate in this area.

DURNESS

If you look north from Durness the next piece of land is Russia beyond the North Pole. Durness is a far-flung village clinging to the rugged north coast of Scotland. To the east and west are cold, empty beaches, windy headlands and some of the highest cliffs in Britain.

Despite the harsh environs this is a friendly place where the locals seem to have retained a rather pleasant Scandinavian lilt to their accents. For walkers on Ben Hope it is the nearest settlement of any significance. There is a **post office** in a big **shop** which sells enough to keep one fed and smiling, a

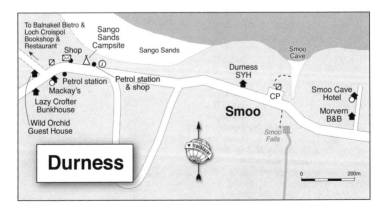

smaller shop in the **petrol station**, and a **TIC** (☎ 0845-225 5121) with displays on local wildlife and history.

There is a good spread of accommodation with the *Lazy Crofter Bunkhouse* (☎ 01971-511202, 🖳 www.durnesshostel .com, £14/pp) catering for budget travellers. There is a **campsite** (☎ 01971-511222) on the shore above Sango Sands with pitches for around £5/pp while more comfort can be gleaned from *Mackay's* (☎ 01971-511202, 🖳 www.visitmackays.com, Easter-Oct, 1S/1D/3T/1F), the big white building on the corner. The simple yet beautiful rooms cost from £25/pp with breakfast. In the restaurant, wild boar and arctic char are just some of the delicacies that may appear on the ever-changing menu. Most main courses are good value at around £10-15.

The *Wild Orchid Guest House* (☎ 01971-511280, 🖳 www.wildorchidguest house.co.uk, 1D/1T) is a modern bungalow

TONGUE

Overlooking the Kyle of Tongue, this is the nearest village to Ben Loyal and claims to be home to Britain's most northerly palm tree.

There is not much here but there is a very small **shop** and **post office**. There is a **post bus** (see p35) once a day (except Sunday) in each direction between Tongue and Lairg (for the train station).

Ben Loyal Hotel (☎ 01847-611216, 🖳 www.benloyal.co.uk, 2S/5D/3T/1F) charges from £35/pp. They also do sumptuous meals, much of it locally sourced. The Mediterranean vegetable crêpe is £11 and a 'tower' of haggis with neeps and tatties is £11.50. *Tongue Hotel* (☎ 01847-611206, 🖳 www.tonguehotel.co.uk, 12D/4T/2F) is a former Victorian sporting lodge, once owned by the Duke of Sutherland. B&B is from £50/pp. They also boast a fine restaurant; try the breasts of wood pigeon for £16.50. *Tigh-nan-Ubhal Guest House* (☎ 01847-611281, 🖳 www.spanglefish.com /tigh-nan-ubhal, 2T/2F) has B&B for £30/pp while *Rhian Guest House* (☎ 01847-611257, 🖳 www.rhiancottage.co.uk, 2D/2T/1F) on the lane to Ben Loyal has a pleasantly rustic feel. B&B is from £28/pp.

close to the centre of the village; B&B here is from £25/pp.

In neighbouring **Smoo** there is *Durness Youth Hostel* (☎ 01971-511264, 38 beds, mid Mar-mid Sep, £12.50-13.50/pp), and B&B from just £25/pp at *Smoo Cave Hotel* (☎ 01971-511227, 🖳 www.smoocavehotel .co.uk, 1D/1T/1F). They also do cheap but filling bar meals. On the same stretch of road *Morvern B&B* (☎ 01971-511252, 1D/1T/1F) has beds for £28/pp.

Finally, about half a mile west of Durness is **Balnakeil Craft Village**, home to a number of artists and crafts people who, in 1964, converted this 1950s military encampment into a craft village. Here you will find the *Balnakeil Bistro* (☎ 01971-511232), and the *Loch Croispol Bookshop and Restaurant* (01971-511777) which does vegetarian haggis among other things.

Contact Stagecoach (see p35) for details of services they operate in this area.

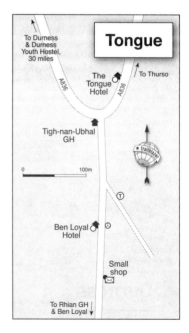

The Islands

The west coast of Scotland is patterned with hundreds of islands and skerries. Apart from the Argyll islands such as Arran most of these lie in two archipelagos: the Inner Hebrides and the Outer Hebrides, or Western Isles. Many of these islands are uninhabited or at best support tiny crofting and fishing communities. All of them are geologically part of the Highlands and, with their rocky hills and heather moorland, have a similar feel. And then there are the empty white beaches and high coastal cliffs, home to a diverse array of seabirds. This combination of sea and hills makes walking on the islands the closest one can get to a wilderness experience in Scotland.

ARRAN – GOATFELL (874m/2865ft)   [MAP 49, p257]

Overview

The highest peak on Arran, although beautiful, is not the most eye-catching. It is, however, the best viewpoint from which to admire the fearsome ridges and peaks that make up the rest of Arran's no-nonsense mountain terrain.

The ascent is easy, with good views over Brodick Bay and across the water to Ayrshire but the best vistas are not until those final few steps to the summit when the mountains to the west open out before you. Simply spectacular stuff.

Route

The starting point is by the **Arran brewery**, a 10-minute bus ride, or 20 to 30 minutes' walk, from Brodick Ferry Terminal. Resist the temptation to spend all day in the brewery and follow a wide track up through deciduous woodland. A private road crosses the track; stay on the latter which continues through coniferous woodland.

Go straight ahead at the next junction but leave the **track** when it curves to the right and join a path. The **path** is very well-maintained by the National Trust for Scotland and as such is very hard to lose!

The trees soon get left behind and the path climbs to a **gate**. From here the trail is a little rougher but the gradient is gentle on the feet. Follow the path as it winds up to the flat ridge on the skyline. To the left are the summit slopes of Goatfell, while to the east are great views across to the mainland. On clear days Ben Lomond and the Arrochar Alps are visible to the north.

GOATFELL
Technical grade
▲
Navigation grade
▲
Terrain grade
▲▲
Strenuousness
▲
Return time
3-4hrs from brewery, 4-5 hrs from ferry terminal
Return distance
7miles/11km from brewery, 10miles/16km from ferry terminal
Total ascent
2854ft/870m
OS maps
Landranger 69, Explorer 361
Gateways
Brodick (see p283)

Once on the skyline ridge the path swings westwards to begin the ascent of a steep ridge leading directly to the summit. This is rocky in places and occasionally you may need to call on your hands for help but generally the ascent is quick and easy. Near the top the gradient gets particularly steep but there is an easier route that bears SW briefly to gain the summit ridge.

The **summit** is characterised by rocky outcrops and is marked by an indicator dial pointing out all the hills that can be seen on a clear day. The pointed peak to the NW is Cir Mhor, a remarkable mountain and the location of some famous climbing routes. Directly across Glen Rosa are the A'Chir and Beinn a' Chliabhain ridges, both narrow in the extreme, particularly the former.

Further north is the second highest peak on Arran, Caisteal Abhail. It is hard to draw your eyes away from these incredible mountains but take a look too at Brodick Bay with the mighty hulk of Holy Isle rising up behind. Imaginative eyes might see it as a mini Rio de Janeiro and Sugar Loaf mountain. Just stick a statue of Christ on the top of Holy Isle and the picture would be complete. This is unlikely ever to happen however, since Holy Isle is owned by Tibetan Buddhist monks.

The quickest descent is by the same route of ascent but ambitious hillwalkers should think seriously about the alternative route described below.

Alternative routes

Goatfell is the highest of a string of stunning peaks. However, most of the neighbouring ridges and peaks offer more exhilarating and challenging walks. Fit, experienced hillwalkers should definitely consider tackling the long horseshoe traverse of the main chain of mountains.

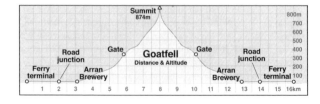

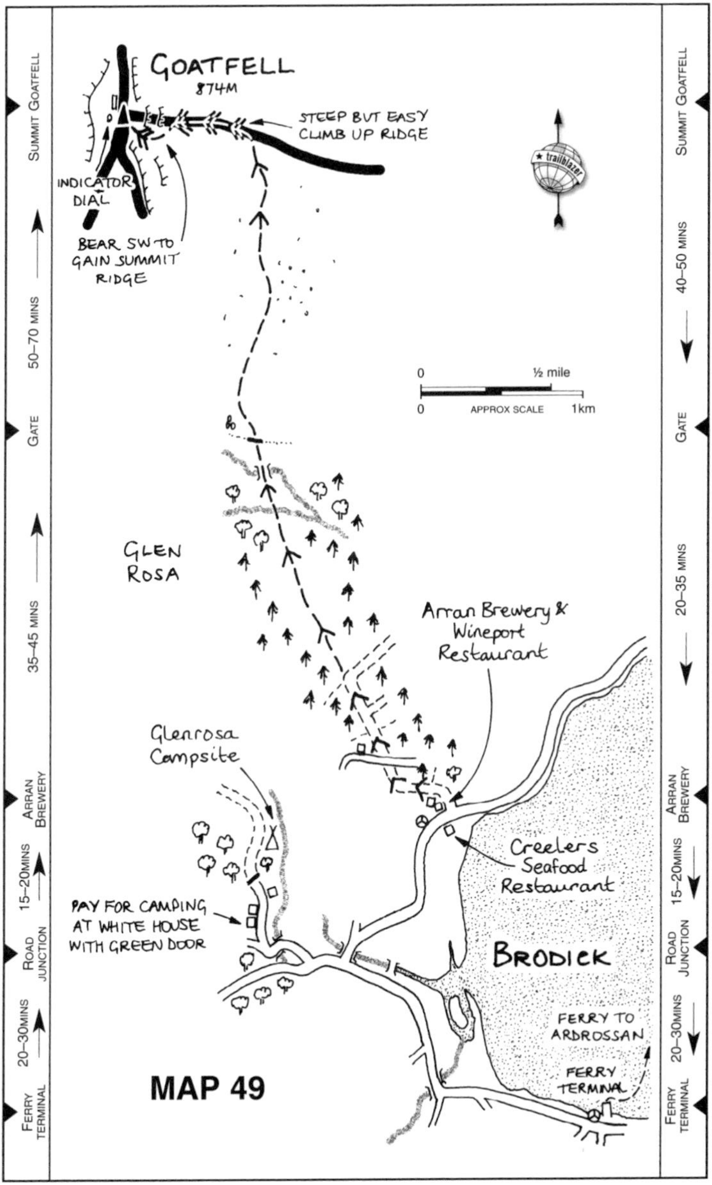

GOATFELL
874M

STEEP BUT EASY
CLIMB UP RIDGE

INDICATOR
DIAL

BEAR SW TO
GAIN SUMMIT
RIDGE

GLEN
ROSA

Arran Brewery &
Wineport
Restaurant

Glenrosa
Campsite

PAY FOR CAMPING
AT WHITE HOUSE
WITH GREEN DOOR

Creelers
Seafood
Restaurant

BRODICK

FERRY TO
ARDROSSAN

FERRY
TERMINAL

MAP 49

0   ½ mile
0   1km
APPROX SCALE

SUMMIT GOATFELL — 50-70 MINS — GATE — 35-45 MINS — ARRAN BREWERY — 15-20MINS — ROAD JUNCTION — 20-30MINS — FERRY TERMINAL

SUMMIT GOATFELL — 40-50 MINS — GATE — 20-35 MINS — ARRAN BREWERY — 15-20MINS — ROAD JUNCTION — 20-30MINS — FERRY TERMINAL

THE ISLANDS

Start in Glen Rosa and follow the path up the banks of the Allt Garbh for an easy walk to the summit of Beinn Nuis, the first peak on the horseshoe. From here head north along the ridge to Beinn Tarsuinn (to cut the day short, head back south along the narrow ridge of Beinn a' Chliabhain).

North from Beinn Tarsuinn the going gets decidedly interesting with the traverse of the A'Chir ridge, a very narrow crest involving some tricky scrambling. A bypass path cuts out most of these difficulties on the west side. Drop down to a col and then begin the very steep ascent of Cir Mhor, arguably the most fantastic peak on the island – a sharp cone of jagged rock – and continue down steep slopes to the next col.

Finally ascend SE to North Goatfell from where it is a few strides along the ridge to the main summit. Descend by the route described in the main route description above. The whole traverse should take between seven and eight hours.

MULL – BEINN TALAIDH ('*Bayn Tal-ee*', 762m/2500ft)　　　[MAP 50a & b]

Overview

While Ben More to the west, with its exposed ridges, is the hill of choice among munro-baggers, Beinn Talaidh, a hill of sweeping curves and a volcanic past, makes a fine alternative. The hill sits in the centre of the island making this a great vantage point from which to admire the rest of the island including Ben More itself. It is easy to reach, easy to climb and quieter than its more famous neighbour to the west.

Route

If coming by public transport from the ferry at Craignure, take the Tobermory bus (see p286) and ask to be dropped at Glen Forsa. A farm track heads south down the glen, through pastures grazed by disturbingly inquisitive Highland

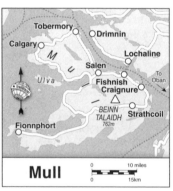

cattle. Follow the track for about an hour, ignoring the left-hand branch that follows a more circuitous route by the river, to some old buildings in a field on the right. Again, ignore the left-hand track that crosses the river and continue straight ahead. The track bends to the right and climbs to a ford. In heavy rain this can be quite an obstacle. Just past the ford the track splits by an **old propeller** set in concrete as a memorial to the airman who died when his plane, from which the propeller came, crashed in bad weather towards the end of World War II.

Take the right-hand track up the hill and continue as far as **Tomsleibhe** bothy. At the bothy, leave the track and climb the boggy ground to the SE. The small hillocks and humps across the lower hillside, which make the walking

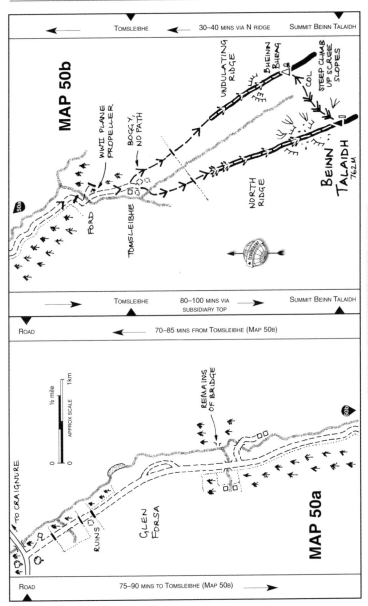

MAP 50b

TOMSLEIBHE ← 30–40 MINS VIA N RIDGE ← SUMMIT BEINN TALAIDH

UNDULATING RIDGE

BHEINN BHEAG

COL

STEEP CLIMB UP SCREE SLOPES

WWII PLANE PROPELLER

BOGGY, NO PATH

FORD

TOMSLEIBHE

NORTH RIDGE

BEINN TALAIDH 762M

Trailblazer

SUMMIT BEINN TALAIDH

TOMSLEIBHE → 80–100 MINS VIA → SUBSIDIARY TOP

ROAD ← 70–85 MINS FROM TOMSLEIBHE (MAP 50B)

½ mile   1km
APPROX SCALE
0   0

TO CRAIGNURE

RUINS

GLEN FORSA

REMAINS OF BRIDGE

MAP 50a

ROAD   75–90 MINS TO TOMSLEIBHE (MAP 50B) →

THE ISLANDS

BEINN TALAIDH
(Happiness
Mountain)

Technical grade
▲

Navigation grade
▲

Terrain grade
▲

Strenuousness
▲▲

Return time
4-5½hrs

Return distance
11½miles/18km

Total ascent
2560ft/780m

OS maps
Landranger 49,
Explorer 375

Gateways
Craignure (see p286)
Oban (see p284; on
mainland)

here so awkward, are called drumlins, a glacial feature that can be seen in many Highland glens. Scattered all over these drumlins are large boulders that were carried along by glaciers until the ice melted and the boulders came to rest wherever they were. Glaciologists know them as erratics. Everyone else knows them as rocks.

A faint trail leads up to a **gate** in the fence above and from here it is open hillside all the way. Follow the broad, shallow ridge to the top of **Bheinn Bheag** from where it is a short drop SW to the col below Beinn Talaidh's summit. It is about a 250m climb up steep scree slopes to the summit of **Beinn Talaidh**. Looking north is the Ardnamurchan peninsula, the most westerly point of mainland Britain, and beyond that the small isles of Canna, Eigg and Rum with Skye behind. Mull's highest mountain, and only munro, towers to the west.

Bear at first N and then NNW for the descent down the mountain's long and, in places, steep **N ridge**. Look for the gate in the fence at the foot of the mountain and continue along a track to a stream and, soon afterwards, the bothy at Tomsleibhe. From here, it is a case of retracing one's steps along the Glen Forsa track.

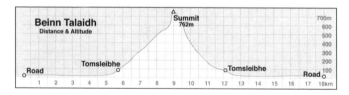

Beinn Talaidh
Distance & Altitude

△ Summit
762m

Tomsleibhe

○ Road ○ Tomsleibhe ○ Tomsleibhe Road ○

700m
600
500
400
300
200
100

1 2 3 4 5 6 7 8 9 10 11 12 13 14 15 16 17 18km

Alternative routes

There is a shorter sharper ascent route from the south starting at GR642328 on the A849 road (take the Fionnphort bus from Craignure). Climb the steep hillside onto the shoulder of Maol nam Fiadh and from there follow the ridge to the summit of the mountain.

RUM – AINSHVAL (*'Ayn-sha-val'*, 781m/2560ft) & ASKIVAL (812m/2665ft)
[MAP 51a, p262; MAP 51b, p263]

Overview

The Rum Cuillins are, almost literally, overshadowed by the Cuillins of Skye which is a shame because they are similar in name only and should not really

Western Isles, Skye & Rum

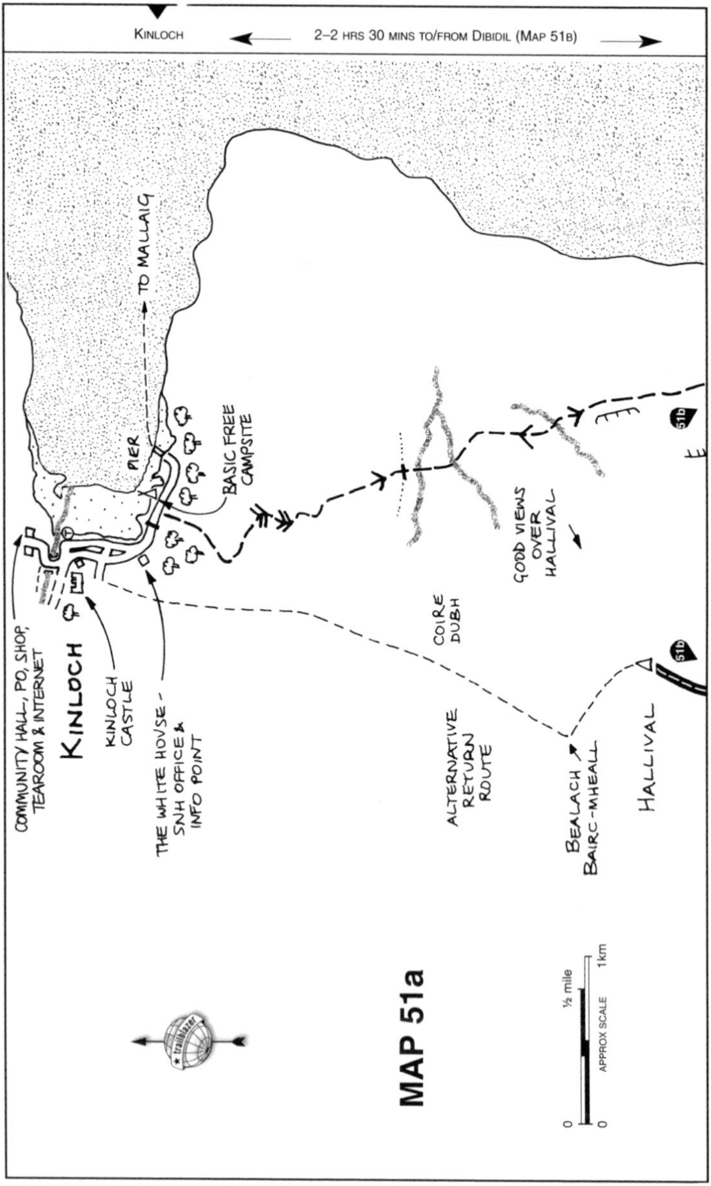
Kinloch
2–2 hrs 30 mins to/from Dibidil (Map 51b)
MAP 51a
TO MALLAIG
PIER
BASIC FREE CAMPSITE
COMMUNITY HALL, PO, SHOP, TEAROOM & INTERNET
KINLOCH
KINLOCH CASTLE
THE WHITE HOUSE - SNH OFFICE & INFO POINT
ALTERNATIVE RETURN ROUTE
COIRE DUBH
GOOD VIEWS OVER HALLIVAL
BEALACH BAIRC-MHEALL
HALLIVAL
51b
51b
APPROX SCALE
0
½ mile
0
1km
trailblazer

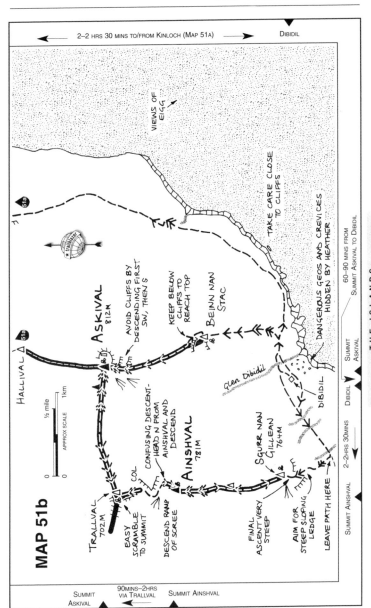

MAP 51b

DIBIDIL

2–2 HRS 30 MINS TO/FROM KINLOCH (MAP 51A)

VIEWS OF EIGG

TAKE CARE CLOSE TO CLIFFS

DANGEROUS GEOS AND CREVICES, HIDDEN BY HEATHER

60–90 MINS FROM SUMMIT ASKIVAL TO DIBIDIL

HALLIVAL △ 51a

ASKIVAL 812M

AVOID CLIFFS BY DESCENDING FIRST SW, THEN S

KEEP BELOW CLIFFS TO REACH TOP

BEINN NAN STAC

Glen Dibidil

DIBIDIL

SUMMIT ASKIVAL

THE ISLANDS

TRALLVAL 702M

EASY SCRAMBLE TO SUMMIT

COL

DESCEND RAMP OF SCREE

CONFUSING DESCENT- HEAD N FROM AINSHVAL AND DESCEND

AINSHVAL 781M

SGURR NAN GILLEAN 764M

FINAL ASCENT VERY STEEP

AIM FOR STEEP SLOPING LEDGE

LEAVE PATH HERE

2–2HRS 30MINS

DIBIDIL

½ mile
APPROX SCALE   1km
0   0

SUMMIT ASKIVAL ▲ ← 90MINS–2HRS VIA TRALLVAL → ▲ SUMMIT AINSHVAL

SUMMIT AINSHVAL

AINSHVAL (Hill of the Strongholds)

ASKIVAL (Hill of the Ash Trees)

Technical grade
▲▲▲

Navigation grade
▲▲

Terrain grade
▲▲▲

Strenuousness
▲▲▲▲

Return time
Kinloch to Dibidil
2-2½hrs; from
Dibidil 6½-8½hrs

Return distance
Kinloch to Dibidil
5miles/8km; from
Dibidil 8miles/13km

Total ascent
Kinloch to Dibidil
985ft/300m; from
Dibidil
5150ft/1570m

OS maps
Landranger 39,
Explorer 397

Gateways
Kinloch (see p287)

be compared. The Rum Cuillins are grassier, far more compact and less crowded than the Skye Cuillins. Occupying such a small island as Rum means the seascapes are some of the best on the west coast. There are a couple of scrambles on the circumnavigation of this horseshoe of peaks but the traverse is infinitely easier than any expedition to the Black Cuillin of Skye.

Route

Start by following the path from Kinloch to Dibidil, a wonderful walk in its own right, climbing above the high sea cliffs of the island's south-east coast. There are all sorts of birds to look out for including huge gannets that plunge into the sea in their search for fish. Keep an eye out too for porpoises and minke whales in the waters between Rum and Eigg.

There is a bothy at **Dibidil** which makes a good overnight stay for breaking the walk into manageable chunks. There are a number of geos and crevasses hidden underneath the heather below the bothy so tread very carefully if exploring this area. A path continues behind the bothy to the foot of Sgurr nan Gillean. At the highest point on this path, leave it and strike NW to gain the southern spur of the mountain. In places the ground is very steep, especially near the top where a small gravelly ledge provides the easiest access to the summit.

Sgurr nan Gillean is the most southerly of the peaks in the horseshoe and has some of the best views, across the sea to the Isle of Eigg. From the summit bear NW along an easy ridge over a minor top, followed by a steep drop to a col. From the col climb back up steep ground to the summit of Ainshval. Some careful navigation is needed here. The instinct is to continue along the ridge but this only leads to dangerous cliffs.

The actual descent is to the north down a ramp of loose rock and grass, keeping the aforementioned cliffs above and to the left. At the foot of the cliffs

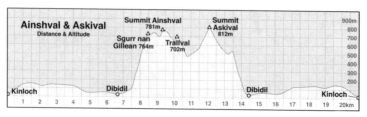

Ainshval & Askival
Distance & Altitude

Summit Ainshval 781m
Summit Askival 812m
Sgurr nan Gillean 764m
Trallval 702m

Kinloch   Dibidil   Dibidil   Kinloch

1 2 3 4 5 6 7 8 9 10 11 12 13 14 15 16 17 18 19 20km

900m 800 700 600 500 400 300 200

a ramp of **scree** leads west to avoid a small buttress. Do not follow the scree too far down. As soon as you reach the foot of the buttress bear north again to reach the **col**.

It is a short but very steep ascent from here to the summit of Trallval. The approach path leaves the col on its eastern extreme. In places hands will help negotiate the rocky shelves with the path doing much of the route finding for you. The tiny rocky summit of **Trallval** is the lowest of the day's peaks but has the most character.

Descend east to a wide grassy saddle at a lowly 450m. It is almost 400m of ascent from here to the summit of **Askival**, Rum's highest peak, but a good path makes the going quite straightforward. Look out for the burrows on the way up which are home to manx shearwaters, seabirds that spend all day at sea only to return at night amid a cacophony of noise.

At the summit take care to avoid the cliffs immediately south when descending. Move slightly SW from the summit before picking your way down rough slopes of boulders and scree to gain the easier grassy slopes further south. Follow this broad ridge as it rises gently to the imposing wall of rock ahead. This is the minor top of **Beinn nan Stac**, the final peak of the day. Ascend via the ledge on its eastern side which avoids all the sheer cliffs. The top is quite a good spot from which to admire the rest of the chain of peaks arcing around Glen Dibidil.

Continue south from this top and descend steep slopes of heather to join the Dibidil path. The bothy is back across the stream or it is 2-2 1/2 hours back to Kinloch.

Alternative routes

If an overnight stop at Dibidil is not an option the return to Kinloch is best made from the summit of Askival via the outlying peak of Hallival. From there descend via its NW ridge to the Bealach Bairc-mheall and drop down to the village through Coire Dubh.

Be aware that the traverse of Hallival involves some fairly awkward scrambling while the north ridge of Askival hides the Askival pinnacle which is the domain of rock-climbers. It can be avoided by keeping to the east side of the ridge.

SKYE – BLA BHEINN (*'Bla-vayn'*, 928m/3045ft)   [MAP 52, p266]

Overview

Bla Bheinn is the only peak in the Black Cuillin that is not part of the main ridge. This air of independence coupled with its forbidding appearance makes Bla Bheinn a mountain of great character. The summit can be reached by a short but fairly relentless climb from the shore of Loch Slapin.

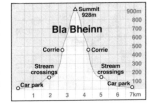

**BLA BHEINN
(Blue Mountain)**

Technical grade
▲▲▲
Navigation grade
▲▲
Terrain grade
▲▲▲
Strenuousness
▲▲
Return time
3-4hrs
Return distance
4½miles/7km
Total ascent
3020ft/920m
OS maps
Landranger 32,
Explorer 411
Gateways
Torrin (see p288),
Broadford (see p287)

THE ISLANDS

Route

There is a car park on the western shore of Loch Slapin, just over a mile from Torrin. Take the path on the north side of the river, through a **gate**, and follow the well-maintained path towards the menacing cliffs of the mountain. After passing through another gate the path continues above a small gorge to the upper reaches of the corrie, below a stunning backdrop of cliffs that appear to have been thrust from the bowels of the Earth.

After crossing the main **stream**, cross the tributary that runs into it and bear SW up a **wide gully** keeping to the north side of the stream in the bouldery gorge below. At the top of this gully is an open corrie of boulders and bedrock, almost enclosed on all sides by steep mountain walls.

The easiest route of ascent is to locate a faint path picking its way between the small cliffs and rocky terraces on the north side of the **corrie**. A short ramp of scree leads up between two buttresses and emerges on a long **steep rocky** ridge. Ascend this east ridge of the mountain with more precipices dropping away without warning on its north side.

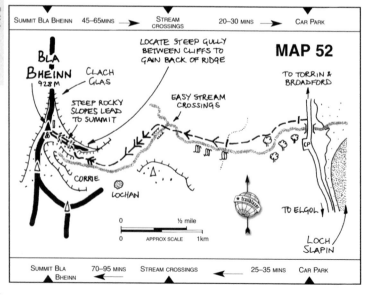

Eventually the ridge reaches a climax near the top where some light scrambling over rocky outcrops leads to the **flat-topped summit**.

This is a great place from which to appreciate the main Cuillin ridge with both the Inaccessible Pinnacle, roughly halfway along the ridge, and the pinnacle ridge of Sgurr nan Gillean, at the northern extreme, clearly visible. The contrast between the savage-toothed Black Cuillins and the altogether smoother, curvier Red Cuillin hills to the north could not be greater.

Alternative routes

A longer approach from the remote bay at Camasunary takes in the mountain's long south ridge while climbers will enjoy the obstacles thrown up by the neighbouring peak of Clach Glas along the very difficult north ridge of the mountain.

SKYE – SGURR NAN GILLEAN   (*'Skor nan Gee-yen'*, 964m/3165ft)   [MAP 53, p268]

Overview

Sgurr nan Gillean, at the eastern end of Skye's famed Cuillin ridge, is the most recognisable of Skye's mountains, forming an almighty backdrop to Sligachan Hotel. This is not an easy climb but it is one of the more accessible of the Cuillin peaks. Those with no scrambling experience may find the exposed final pitch a little intimidating but even if the summit eludes you the SE ridge is still a magnificent viewpoint.

Route

Head down the A863 road from Sligachan Hotel for about two minutes until you reach a path on the left (just past the mountain rescue building). Follow this path through the heather to a bridge and continue on the far side of the stream.

The path continues past a **lochan**, over another bridge, with the imposing pinnacle ridge of Sgurr nan Gillean looming ever closer. The path climbs gradually to a high point marked by a cairn just to the north of the pinnacle ridge. At the **cairn** continue straight on, ignoring the path off to the right, and follow it down into the corrie. Cross the stream in the corrie floor and begin the climb up the steep backwall.

SGURR NAN GILLEAN
(Peak of the Young Men)

Technical grade
▲▲▲▲▲
Navigation grade
▲▲
Terrain grade
▲▲▲▲▲
Strenuousness
▲▲
Return time
3-4¹/₂hrs
Return distance
7miles/11km
Total ascent
3180ft/970m
OS maps
Landranger 32,
Explorer 411
Gateways
Sligachan (see p288)
Portree (see p289)

THE ISLANDS

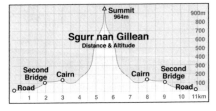

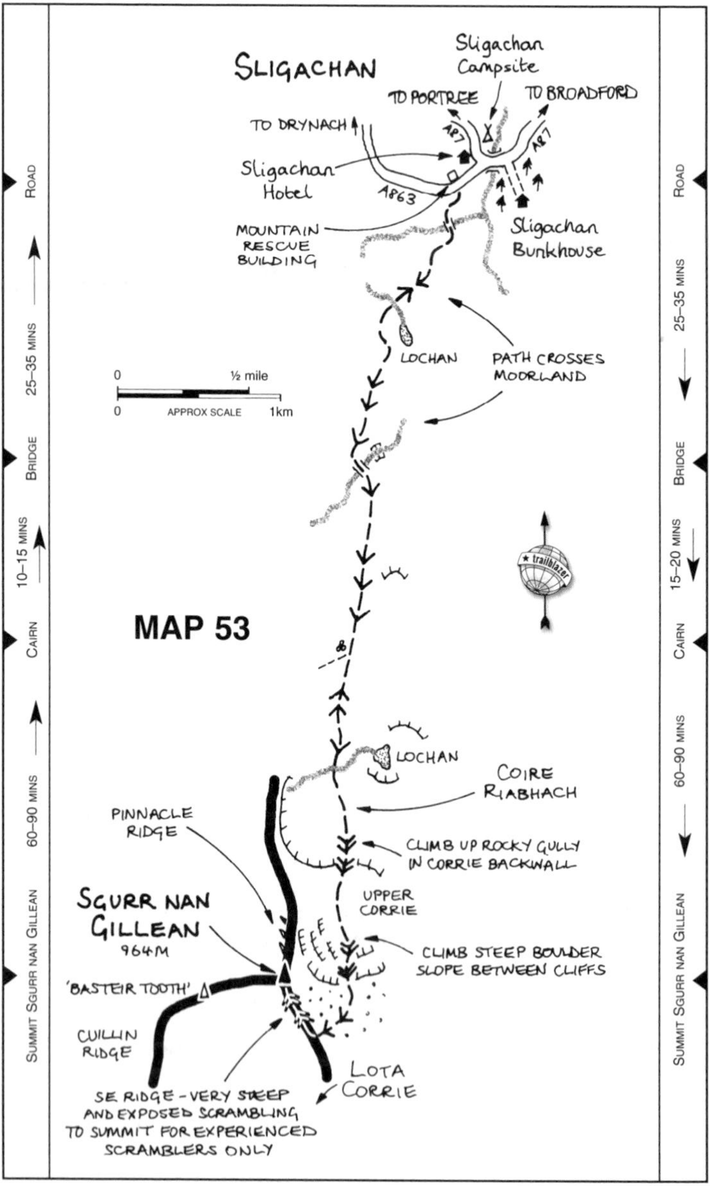

SLIGACHAN

Sligachan Campsite

TO PORTREE

TO BROADFORD

TO DRYNACH

A87

A87

Sligachan Hotel

A863

MOUNTAIN RESCUE BUILDING

Sligachan Bunkhouse

LOCHAN

PATH CROSSES MOORLAND

0 ½ mile

0 APPROX SCALE 1km

★ trailblazer

MAP 53

LOCHAN

COIRE RIABHACH

PINNACLE RIDGE

CLIMB UP ROCKY GULLY IN CORRIE BACKWALL

UPPER CORRIE

SGURR NAN GILLEAN
964M

'BASTEIR TOOTH'

CLIMB STEEP BOULDER SLOPE BETWEEN CLIFFS

CUILLIN RIDGE

LOTA CORRIE

SE RIDGE - VERY STEEP AND EXPOSED SCRAMBLING TO SUMMIT FOR EXPERIENCED SCRAMBLERS ONLY

THE ISLANDS

ROAD

25-35 MINS

BRIDGE

10-15 MINS

CAIRN

60-90 MINS

SUMMIT SGURR NAN GILLEAN

ROAD

25-35 MINS

BRIDGE

15-20 MINS

CAIRN

60-90 MINS

SUMMIT SGURR NAN GILLEAN

A **rocky gully** avoids all the cliffs and leads into a higher upper corrie. Continue upwards and aim for the steep slope of boulders in the far corner of this corrie where the black walls of the pinnacle ridge drop down menacingly to the floor.

Again the path up this **steep boulder slope** avoids the precipices on each side. This path leads onto a third and final ramp of rocks that leads easily onto the spine of the SE ridge. The views really are breathtaking, with the rest of the Cuillin ridge arcing away across Lota Corrie. A keen eye can pick out the famous Inaccessible Pinnacle (the most difficult munro) while closer to hand is the even more menacing Basteir Tooth, a prow of rock to the west of Sgurr nan Gillean, interrupting the flow of the ridge. Looking south-east, the ridge you are on curls away beautifully to the peak of Sgurr na h-Uamha. Enjoy the views now because the next stretch requires careful attention to the ground at one's feet.

Follow the obvious ridge as it tapers NW to the tiny pointed **summit** of the mountain. The scrambling starts in earnest but it is the final, exceedingly steep and narrow 50m, that is the most difficult and most exposed. Return from the summit via the same route.

Alternative routes
The pinnacle ridge of Sgurr nan Gillean is even more technical and requires a certain amount of climbing experience. The route described is by far the least difficult.

SKYE – GLAMAIG (775m/2545ft)
[MAP 54, p270]

Overview
In 1889, Harkabir Thakpa, a Gurkha soldier, ran from Sligachan Hotel to Glamaig's summit in 37 minutes. This monumental feat becomes all the more remarkable when you realise just how awkward it is to walk up the steep fans of scree that make this mountain so immediately recognisable. Glamaig is part of the Red Cuillins, more rounded and benign than their illustrious Black Cuillin cousins across the Sligacan Glen.

The ascent of Glamaig really is quite tough considering how short a walk it is; the ascent is sheer and relentless and made all the more difficult by the uninterrupted and unstable scree.

Route
The start is by a roadside gate about a mile north of **Sligachan**. Once through the **gate** a faint trail heads directly for the foot of Glamaig's uniform grey slopes. The gradient gets progressively more severe and it is not long before the wet grass and moss at the foot of

GLAMAIG (The Greedy Woman)

Technical grade
▲▲
Navigation grade
▲▲
Terrain grade
▲▲▲▲
Strenuousness
▲▲
Return time
from Sligachan 3½-4½hrs
Return distance
from Sligachan
5miles/8km
Total ascent
from Sligachan
2490ft/760m
OS maps
Landranger 32,
Explorer 411
Gateways
Sligachan (see p288)
Portree (see p289)

THE ISLANDS

the mountain gives way to the loose **scree** for which Glamaig is famous. The going can be quite treacherous in places and progress quite slow. Try and stick to the faint trail that often seems to disappear. After much huffing and puffing and slipping and sliding, the shoulder of the ridge comes into view and a very

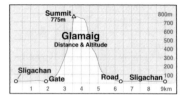

welcome stretch of flat ground gives some respite. Follow the obvious ridge and pick up the path as it climbs again to the summit. Now is the time to relax and enjoy the views of the Black Cuillins and Bla Bheinn.

Continue along the main ridge and descend to the col and then descend into the wide corrie below and to the left. Take care on the descent as it gets quite steep and in places there is some very slippery moss. At the narrow mouth of the corrie there is a cliff so be sure to choose the correct route to avoid it. Bear right and pick your way down more steep and slippery ground towards the road

THE ISLANDS

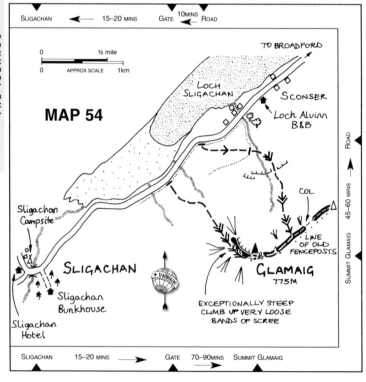

below. Cut across the sheep grazings, through a gate and back to the road from where it is five minutes back to the start point.

Alternative routes
The northern top of Glamaig is only a short diversion away from the saddle and has great views of the rest of the Red Cuillins.

SKYE – THE STORR (719m/2360ft)   [MAP 55, p272]

Overview

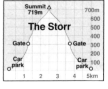

Skye does not get more other-worldly than on the Trotternish peninsula, where there's the Quiraing and the Old Man of Storr: pinnacles of bare rock slipping imperceptibly from the hills to the sea. The latter is the more famous of the two and deservedly so, with a number of other pinnacles and towers adding to the almost Narnian atmosphere.

The walk to the summit of the Storr (not the pinnacle, but the hill behind it) is short and quite easy with only two points that require a little scrambling. The biggest danger is from falling rocks near the pinnacles.

Route
A few miles north of Portree on the Staffin road, just past Loch Leathan is a small forestry plantation on the left and a **car park**. A very well-made path snakes up through the trees to a **gate** just below the pinnacles.

The sign on the gate warning of falling rocks is not exaggerating. The cliffs above the pinnacles seem to have become more and more unstable in recent years and rockfalls occur with shocking frequency. Keep to the lower path below the pinnacles. The path above is regularly showered in skull-cracking debris.

The **Old Man of Storr** and the other rocky protrusions around this area have all, over the years, slipped away from the cliff face. Indeed, all of these uneven lower slopes are part of a huge slump that has gradually shifted towards the sea. After passing the Old Man of Storr, the path climbs further up the grassy slopes towards the northern end of the cliff. At the **stile** turn round for a wonderful view back over the pinnacles. The path bears round to the left after the stile and after negotiating a small rocky shelf climbs into a wide, shallow corrie. Aim for the back of the small **gap in the cliff** at the top of the corrie's backwall for access to the summit.

From the **summit** there is an interesting perspective looking down on the pinnacles while fur-

THE ISLANDS

THE STORR
Technical grade
▲▲
Navigation grade
▲▲
Terrain grade
▲▲
Strenuousness
▲
Return time
2-2¹/₂hrs
Return distance
3miles/5km
Total ascent
1900ft/580m
OS maps
Landranger 23,
Explorer 408
Gateways
Portree (see p289)
Sligachan (see p288)
Uig (see p290)

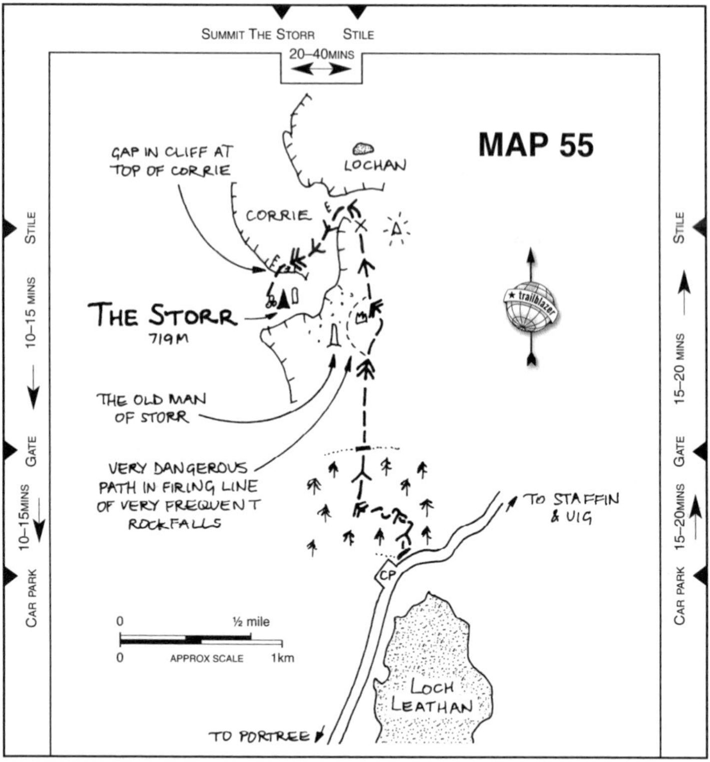

SUMMIT THE STORR   STILE

20–40MINS

GAP IN CLIFF AT
TOP OF CORRIE

LOCHAN

MAP 55

CORRIE

THE STORR
719M

THE OLD MAN
OF STORR

VERY DANGEROUS
PATH IN FIRING LINE
OF VERY FREQUENT
ROCKFALLS

TO STAFFIN
& UIG

CP

0   ½ mile
0   APPROX SCALE   1km

LOCH
LEATHAN

TO PORTREE

STILE
10–15 MINS
GATE
10–15MINS
CAR PARK

STILE
15–20 MINS
GATE
15–20MINS
CAR PARK

THE ISLANDS

ther afield there are views of the Cuillins and, on the mainland, the Torridon
mountains. Return by descending the same way.

Alternative routes

There are no real alternatives to this walk, although a much longer excursion (a
full day or more) can be enjoyed by following the Trotternish ridge north for an
epic journey along the spine of the peninsula, culminating in the other great feature of the area, the Quiraing.

❏ **Other hills in the area**
● **Sgurr Alasdair** (*'Skor Al-is-der'*, **992m/3255ft**) Large parts of the Cuillin ridge
are out of reach of those with no climbing experience. Sgurr Alasdair, the highest
mountain on Skye, is certainly not easy but experienced hillwalkers and scramblers
will find access to the top via the famous Great Stone Chute, a 300m scree slope on
the east side of Coire Lagan, by Glen Brittle.

SOUTH UIST – BEINN MHOR (620m/2035ft), BEN CORODALE (527m/1730ft) & HECLA (606m/1990ft)
[MAP 56a, p274; MAP 56b, p275]

Overview
From Beinn Mhor's narrow summit ridge to the castellated peak of Ben Corodale and the scree slopes of Hecla, these three hills exude individuality and provide a strenuous but thoroughly rewarding expedition across the skyline of South Uist's wild east coast with views across the machair and the Little Minch to Skye.

Route
Leave the A865 road about a mile south of Tobha Mor and a few metres south of a road bridge over the River Rog. A track leads the way past some crofters' houses and soon arrives at a **gate**. Continue along this track which gradually peters out as it crosses boggy peat moorland. At this point bear SE towards a small lochan. Pass this lochan on its north side and turn east towards the slopes of Beinn Mhor's NW ridge. The gradient is reasonably gentle but there is no clear path and the heather can slow progress somewhat.

Once on the back of this broad ridge, known as **Maola Breac**, head SSE aiming for the obvious continuation of the ridge which steepens and narrows as it rises to the northern end of the main spine of the mountain at 550m. Remember this point as you will need to return to it for the descent towards Ben Corodale. But first you need to reach the summit of Beinn Mhor just over half a mile (1km) SSE

BEINN MHOR (Big Mountain)
BEN CORODALE (Corodale Mountain)
HECLA (Hooded Peak)
Technical grade ▲▲
Navigation grade ▲▲▲
Terrain grade ▲▲▲
Strenuousness ▲▲▲
Return time 5¼-7hrs
Return distance 11miles/18km
Total ascent 3740ft/1140m
OS maps Landranger 22, Explorer 453
Gateways Tobha Mor (Howmore) (see p292)

THE ISLANDS

along the summit ridge, a surprisingly narrow affair interrupted by a series of 'teeth'. These are easy to negotiate being molar in appearance rather than canine. A path skirts just below them to avoid them altogether.

As you approach the summit take time to admire the fearsome cliffs of Beinn Mhor's north face, scarred by two steep gullies. At the **summit** there is a shelter cairn and a trig point and good views over Loch Aineort and south to Barra and the Isle of Eriskay where the ship *SS Politician* ran aground in 1941,

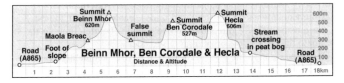

Beinn Mhor, Ben Corodale & Hecla – Distance & Altitude

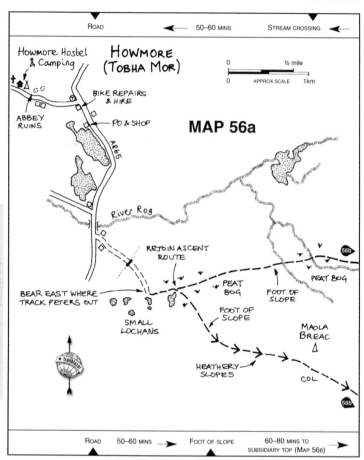

spilling hundreds of bottles of whisky that were gleefully scooped up by the locals. The story has been immortalised in the film *Whisky Galore!*

Retrace your steps along the ridge to the northern end at 550m and bear east down the ridge to the col. The ridge needs careful attention as there are a number of rocky shelves and steps particularly near the bottom. From the col the slopes immediately ahead are steep and impenetrable. To reach the ridge, contour the hillside in a SE direction for five minutes before climbing the steep slopes onto the back of the broad grassy shoulder.

Climb the ridge to the NW and then bear N over undulating ground to the summit of **Ben Corodale**. The west and north sides of the summit are protected by sheer cliffs. These are particularly pronounced on the north side so care should be taken in mist on approach to the top.

The descent from Ben Corodale is safest by retracing your steps to avoid the short cliffs on the west side of the summit. However, there are two short easy gullies that cut through this obstacle to reach a long grassy slope that stretches to the north. Follow this natural ramp down towards some small **lochans** and peat bogs. Continue NNE over rough ground that dips and rolls to the foot of Hecla. Climb the slopes ahead, keeping to the left of the large rocky slabs to gain the broad back of **Hecla**. Climb steadily east over grassy slopes and a band of shattered rock to reach the summit of the mountain. Before descending take time to take in the view over Loch Coradail and the rocky eastern coastline of South Uist. To the north-west is Loch Druidibeg, a large expanse of water and a national nature reserve, home to greylag geese, red-throated divers and corncrakes.

The most direct route back to the road is to return to the saddle between Hecla and Ben Corodale and descend directly west across the heather moor.

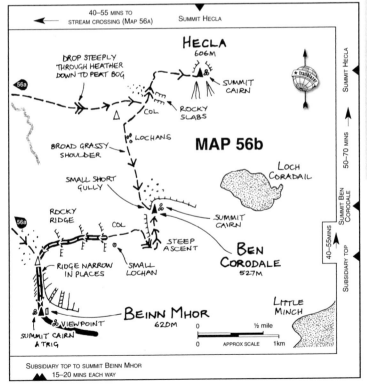

Aim for the foot of the ridge ahead and cross the raised **peat bog** in the glen. When in spate the river might cause wet feet but is not particularly dangerous. Continue across the peat bog which can be squelchy after rain and continue west past the foot of Beinn Mhor's north ridge and back to the track that leads to the road where the walk began.

Alternative routes
There are escape routes back to the road from the col between Beinn Mhor and Ben Corodale and also from the col between Ben Corodale and Hecla.

HARRIS – CEAPABHAL (*'Keep-a-val'*, 365m/1195ft)   [MAP 57]

Overview
A low hill of unique character. But for a half-mile wide isthmus this heathery hill would be an island. Its modest height and easy approach make for a great short walk offering sweeping views of the beaches along the east side of Harris and the scattering of islands in the Sound of Harris.

Route
Walk through An Taobh Tuath village and pass through the gate at the road end. A jeep track continues across flat grazing land. Listen out for corncrakes in the iris beds to the right. At the next **gate** the track splits and becomes indistinct. Take the right-hand trail and aim for the old **sheep pens** at the foot of the hill where a gate leads onto the steep hillside.

There is no obvious path up the slopes of heather, apart from a few random sheep trails. The best route of ascent is to climb the slopes to the left of the large stream gully that cuts an obvious line diagonally across the hillside. In places the heather is shin deep and quite annoying to brush through.

After about three-quarters of an hour of ascent the gradient eases. Just past a small rocky outcrop the trig point comes into view. This is not the true summit, which is a few boggy paces further on at a **large cairn**.

The views all around are sensational, encompassing white sand beaches, the hills of North Harris and the rocky coastline below. To the north-east is the barren Isle of Taransay (made famous as the location of the BBC *Castaway* reality series in 2000), while to the south is the island-studded Sound of Harris and the Isles of North Uist and Berneray, a favourite haunt of Prince Charles. On the clearest of

CEAPABHAL	
Technical grade	▲
Navigation grade	▲
Terrain grade	▲▲
Strenuousness	▲
Return time	2-2½hrs
Return distance	5miles/8km
Total ascent	1214ft/370m
OS maps	Landranger 18, Explorer 455
Gateways	An Taobh Tuath (Northton; see p292) An t-Ob (Leverburgh; see p292)

Ceapabhal profile: Road junction – Sheep pens – Summit 365m – Sheep pens – Road junction

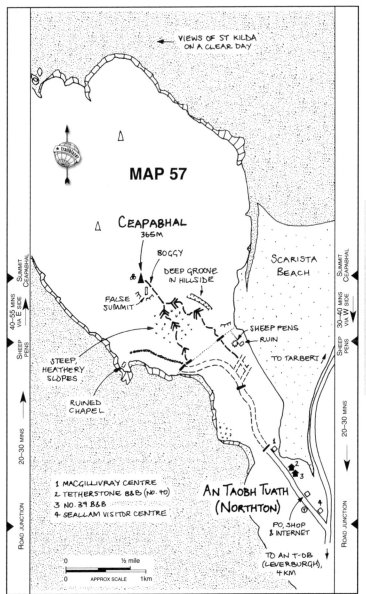

VIEWS OF ST KILDA ON A CLEAR DAY

MAP 57

CEAPABHAL
365M

BOGGY

DEEP GROOVE IN HILLSIDE

SCARISTA BEACH

FALSE SUMMIT

SUMMIT CEAPABHAL

SHEEP PENS
RUIN

TO TARBERT

STEEP, HEATHERY SLOPES

RUINED CHAPEL

40-55 MINS VIA E SIDE   SUMMIT CEAPABHAL

30-40 MINS VIA W SIDE   SUMMIT CEAPABHAL

SHEEP PENS

SHEEP PENS

20-30 MINS

20-30 MINS

ROAD JUNCTION

ROAD JUNCTION

THE ISLANDS

1 MACGILLIVRAY CENTRE
2 TETHERSTONE B&B (NO. 40)
3 NO. 39 B&B
4 SEALLAM VISITOR CENTRE

AN TAOBH TUATH (NORTHTON)

PO, SHOP & INTERNET

TO AN T-OB (LEVERBURGH), 4 KM

0   ½ mile
0   APPROX SCALE   1km

clear days St Kilda can be seen some fifty miles to the west, although from this distance it is impossible to appreciate the stunning cliff scenery, home to gannets, puffins and guillemots. Rather than return by the same route it is better to follow the steep south-facing shoulder of the hill (a faint path is intermittently visible).

There are three small sandy beaches strung out in a row below with a ruined chapel next to the one that lies furthest west. Aim instead for the **middle beach**. On approaching this beach a wall blocks the way but a small gate in the corner of the field gives access to a track that passes the beach and heads inland through grassy dunes back to the gate for the return along the track to An Taobh Tuath.

CLISHAM

Technical grade
▲▲
Navigation grade
▲▲
Terrain grade
▲▲▲
Strenuousness
▲▲▲
Return time
4-5hrs –
Bunavoneader to
Ardhasaig ½hr
(2km), Ardhasaig to
Tarbert 1hr (4km),
Bunavoneader
road/main road junction to start of walk
¾hr (3km);
Ardhasaig to start of
walk 1hr (4km)
Return distance
5miles/8km (extra
6km each way of
road walking from
Bunavoneader to
Tarbert)
Total ascent
2690ft/820m
OS maps
Landranger 14,
Explorer 456
Gateways
Ardhasaig (see p294)
Tarbert (see p293)

Alternative routes

The walk can be extended by following the ridge from the summit to a top marked by a cairn. Heathery slopes lead northwards down to some spectacular rocky coastline with natural arches and blowholes. Follow the eastern coastline back to the start point over trackless terrain.

HARRIS – CLISHAM (799m/2620ft)
[MAP 58]

Overview

The highest mountain in the Western Isles provides a thoroughly exhilarating day out. The summit is easily reached and there is quite a narrow and enjoyable ridge linking it with the neighbouring peak of Mulla-fo-dheas (743m/2440ft). There is some rough terrain to negotiate but nothing technically difficult. Buses stop in Ardhasaig but not in Bunavoneader.

Route

The ascent begins on the main **road**, opposite a small lochan (GR157052), where a short steep slope leads onto a wide open moorland. Continue across this trackless high ground to the foot of Clisham's SE ridge which rises sharply for 300m. After negotiating this steep climb over bands of boulders, the summit ridge leads quickly to the main **summit** which is marked by a trig point enclosed by an immaculate wall of rocks.

From the summit head NNW down the rocky ridge and then descend west to reach the col on the ridge leading to Mulla-fo-dheas. Just past the **col** the ridge narrows markedly and rises sharply for a time

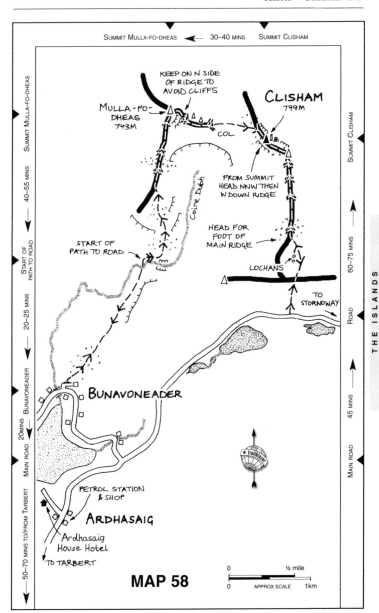

SUMMIT MULLA-FO-DHEAS ← 30–40 MINS SUMMIT CLISHAM

KEEP ON N SIDE OF RIDGE TO AVOID CLIFFS

MULLA-FO-DHEAS 743M

CLISHAM 799M

COL

FROM SUMMIT HEAD NNW THEN W DOWN RIDGE

Coire Dubh

HEAD FOR FOOT OF MAIN RIDGE

START OF PATH TO ROAD

LOCHANS

TO STORNOWAY

SUMMIT MULLA-FO-DHEAS

40–55 MINS

START OF PATH TO ROAD

20–25 MINS

BUNAVONEADER

MAIN ROAD 20MINS

50–70 MINS TO/FROM TARBERT

SUMMIT CLISHAM

60–75 MINS

ROAD

45 MINS

MAIN ROAD

THE ISLANDS

BUNAVONEADER

PETROL STATION & SHOP

ARDHASAIG

Ardhasaig House Hotel

TO TARBERT

trailblazer

MAP 58

0   ½ mile
0   APPROX SCALE   1km

Wind farms
The recent expansion of wind farms has created quite a stir, even within environmental groups. The arguments both for and against wind farms are strong.
Those in favour cite the need to embrace renewable and sustainable energy
sources if we are to tackle the issue of greenhouse gas emissions and climate change
while those against express concern for local ecosystems – specifically raised bogs
and golden eagle habitat – as well as the huge visual impact the turbines have on the
landscape.

Renewable energy companies have lodged hundreds of applications for wind
farm developments across the Highlands. The most high profile of these are the ones
earmarked for some of our most beautiful places, notably Skye and Lewis. Local
action groups have campaigned against the proposals; the Lewis Wind Farm propos-
al was rejected by the authorities in 2008 but the one at Edinbane on Skye looks likely to go ahead.

The key to this issue is surely a little common sense; yes to renewable energy but
no to indiscriminate development. Some sensible decisions need to be made to ensure
that we can use the energy in the wind whilst preserving our natural heritage.

before passing over a couple of knolls and dropping back down to another col.
The intimidating east ridge of Mulla-fo-dheas is marked by some fairly severe
cliffs. Avoid these by skirting round to the north side of the ridge and following
a faint trail that climbs the steep grassy slopes towards the top. Scramble up the
rocky outcrops to reach the spine of the ridge and soon after the summit of
Mulla-fo-dheas (*'Mulla-fo-Yes'*).

There are great views south along the length of the Western Isles and in
clear weather the incredible sea cliffs of the St Kilda islands, the remotest in
Britain, can be seen over fifty miles to the west.

Descend via the south ridge of the mountain which drops awkwardly over
a band of huge boulders before the gradient eases. Another steep drop leads onto
the lower reaches of the ridge. Bear SSE to avoid the cliffs at its foot and drop
down slippery slopes by the stream to join the **path** in the main glen.

From here it is less than half an hour down the glen to the village of
Bunavoneader where there used to be a whaling station. The old chimney stack
is still visible.

It is another 20 minutes along this road to the junction with the **main road**.
Turn left to head back to the start point (45 mins) or right for Tarbert (1¼hrs).

Alternative routes

There is another starting point about a mile further east from the one described but it starts at a lower elevation and crosses much boggier ground on its way to the SE ridge of the mountain.

LEWIS – SUAINEABHAL (*'Soon-a-val'*, 429m/1405ft) [MAP 59, p282]

Overview

The combination of no paths and no people gives a real sense of isolation to this small rocky hill in the wild and lonely Uig District of Lewis.

Route

The start point is by the cutting in the road at GR108311. Look out for the bridge across the burn on the west side of the road. Cross this bridge and weave across boggy peat moor to the lowest point on the skyline ahead. At this saddle descend to the northern end of Loch a' Phealair Mor.

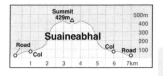

There are two choices here: the more confusing terrain of rocky outcrops and slabs to the right, or the grassy but boggy ramp to the left. The latter is the easier of the two. At the top of the **grassy ramp** bear north to join the former route at an unusual alleyway, caused by a small fault, cutting north–south across the ridge.

Continue up rocky ground to a **false summit** and head west, dropping briefly into a narrow depression and then up to the **huge summit cairn** that is somewhat disproportionate to the size of the hill it decorates.

There are views of Uig Sands to the west, the largest such expanse of shell sand on Lewis, while the rest of the Uig hills lie stretched out on the far side of Loch Suaineabhal below. The dramatic islands of St Kilda can be seen on a clear day way out west. Descend by the route of ascent.

Alternative routes

Another route to the summit comes in from the west at the end of the minor road at the north end of Loch Suaineabhal (no public transport). Cross the small dam over the river and head east towards the impressive west face of the hill. To avoid these sheer slopes bear NE to gain the northern side of the hill and climb the less severe ground in a southerly direction to the summit.

SUAINEABHAL

Technical grade
▲▲
Navigation grade
▲▲
Terrain grade
▲▲
Strenuousness
▲
Return time
2-2½ hrs
Return distance
4miles/7km
Total ascent
1444ft/440m
OS maps
Landranger 13,
Explorer 458
Gateways
Timsgearraidh (see p294)

THE ISLANDS

THE ISLANDS

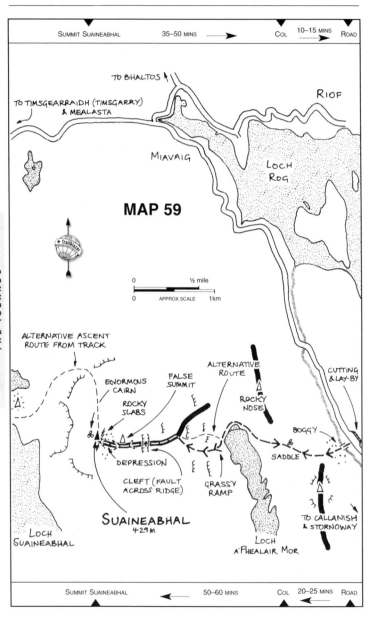

SUMMIT SUAINEABHAL 35–50 MINS → COL 10–15 MINS ROAD

TO BHALTOS

TO TIMSGEARRAIDH (TIMSGARRY)
& MEALASTA

RIOF

MIAVAIG

LOCH
ROG

MAP 59

0 ½ mile
0 APPROX SCALE 1km

ALTERNATIVE ASCENT
ROUTE FROM TRACK

ENORMOUS
CAIRN

FALSE
SUMMIT

ALTERNATIVE
ROUTE

ROCKY
NOSE

CUTTING
& LAY-BY

ROCKY
SLABS

BOGGY

SADDLE

DEPRESSION

CLEFT (FAULT
ACROSS RIDGE)

GRASSY
RAMP

SUAINEABHAL
429M

TO CALLANISH
& STORNOWAY

LOCH
SUAINEABHAL

LOCH
A'PHEALAIR MOR

SUMMIT SUAINEABHAL ← 50–60 MINS COL 20–25 MINS ROAD

THE ISLANDS – TOWNS & VILLAGES

ARRAN
Brodick

The tourist board call the Isle of Arran 'Scotland in a nutshell'; a fairly accurate description considering that it includes rocky coasts, fertile pastures, heather moorland and high jagged mountains. Brodick, the main town on Arran, is strung out along one main road hugging the shore of the bay.

Services The **TIC** (☎ 01770-303776, 🖥 www.visitarran.net), right by the **ferry terminal** (where there are **left-luggage** facilities), is well stocked with information on where to eat and sleep.

There are six **ferries** (Mon-Sat) to and from Ardrossan on the mainland (four on Sunday) and regular trains between Ardrossan and Glasgow. The main **bus station** is directly opposite the TIC. **Buses** circumnavigate the island regularly, passing the start of the Goatfell path, throughout the day. See pp32-6 for transport details.

There are two Co-op **supermarkets** in the village, one (Mon-Sat 8am-10pm, Sun 9am-7pm) near the ferry terminal (with **internet access**) and the other (Mon-Wed 8am-6pm, Thu-Sat 8am-8pm, Sun 11am-5pm) about five minutes' walk along the

seafront at the west end of the village . This is also where you will find the **post office** (☎ 01770-302245, Mon-Fri 9am-5.30pm, Sat 9am-12.45pm), **library** and the **chemist** (☎ 01770-302250), while the **health centre** (☎ 01770-302175) is about halfway along the main street. There are also two **banks** with cash machines.

Where to stay Brodick offers plenty of places to stay but these get booked up quickly in the summer.

Campers should head for *Glenrosa Campsite* (see Map 49, p257; ☎ 01770-302380, 🖥 www.glenrosa.com), a simple but beautiful site about one hour's walk west then north from the ferry terminal, in the mouth of Glen Rosa (enquire at the white house near the end of the lane). The grassy plain is right by the river: a great place to chill out, but watch for flooding in wet weather!

For more sturdy accommodation just look in the village. Starting from the TIC head west along the shore. *Dunvegan House* (☎ 01770-302811, 2D/6T/1F) does B&B for £36/pp and *The Invercloy* (☎ 01770-302225, 🖥 www.theinvercloyarran

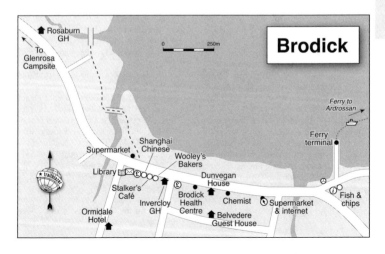

.com, 9D/1T) charges from £29/pp for B&B. On Alma Rd you will find the **Belvedere Guest House** (☎ 01770-302397, 🖳 www.visionunlimited.co.uk/belvedere, 1S/3D/1T) which has very smart and spacious rooms beneath its ivy-clad exterior. B&B is £28-53/pp.

On Knowe Rd **Ormidale Hotel** (☎ 01770-302293, 🖳 www.ormidale-hotel .co.uk, 2S/2D/3T/1F) has beds from £38/pp and, finally, **Rosaburn Lodge Guest House** (☎ 01770-302383, 🖳 www.rosaburnlodge .co.uk, 2D/1T) at the western edge of the village is a smart choice; a beautiful old house, with a lovely garden and hens in a pen. B&B is £27-35/pp.

Where to eat and drink For cheap, tasty meals try the cosy, no-nonsense *Stalker's*

OBAN (FOR MULL)
Oban is not actually on Mull, but is the main ferry port to the island and to many of the other Hebridean islands. As such, it has developed into a significant Highland town and not an unattractive one, tucked around a sheltered natural harbour with McCaig's Tower, a Colosseum-like folly, dominating a backdrop of wooded hillsides.

Services
The **TIC** (☎ 01631-563122) is in an old church on Argyll Sq. There is no cash machine in Craignure on Mull so it is best to fill your pockets here; there are **banks** with **cash machines** along George St. This is where you will also find the **chemist**.

There is a **post office** on Corran Esplanade and the two biggest **supermarkets** are off Soroba Rd to the south of the town centre.

Citylink **buses** to Oban come from Glasgow (seven a day), Perth (two a day) and Fort William (four a day, not Sunday). There are also regular **trains** from Glasgow Queen St. **Ferries** to Craignure on Mull run daily. See pp32-6 for public transport map and details.

Oban **taxis** can be reached on ☎ 01631-564666.

Café (☎ 01770-302579), for burger and chips and jacket potatoes. Next to this is *Wooley's Bakers* (☎ 01770-302280) for even cheaper snacks and lunches. There is also a **fish and chip shop** next to the TIC and the **Shanghai Chinese Takeaway** (☎ 01770-303777) at the west end of the street.

Finally, there are two excellent restaurants outside Brodick, perfectly situated at the foot of **Goat Fell** (see Map 49, p257). First is the **Wineport Restaurant** (☎ 01770-302977) a smart choice for well-presented tasty dishes from a varied menu, while on the opposite side of the road is *Creelers Seafood Restaurant* (☎ 01770-302810) where you can enjoy three courses for £25. As well as seafood (baked scallops, king scallops) they also serve Sika venison and veggie dishes.

Where to stay
There are two hostels: *Oban Youth Hostel* (☎ 01631-562025, Jan-Oct, 96 beds) on Corran Esplanade charging £13-16.25/pp and *Oban Backpackers* (☎ 01631-562107, 🖳 www.obanbackpackers.com) on Breadalbane St charging £13.50/pp.

The best street for B&Bs is Dunollie Rd: try *Torlundy B&B* (☎ 01631-562961) or *Alderlea B&B* (☎ 01631-562937, 🖳 www .alderlea.co.uk), both charging from £15/pp, and on the opposite side of the road, *Hamilton House* (☎ 01631-562384) and *Dana Villa* (☎ 01631-564063, 🖳 www .danavilla.co.uk), where beds are from £20 to £30/pp.

Continuing down the street towards the centre are *Arbour Guest House* (☎ 01631-564394, 🖳 arbourhouseoban@aol .com, 2S/2D/2T/1F) which has B&B from £20 to £25/pp, and *St Anne's Guest House* (☎ 01631-562743, 🖳 www.victorianvillas oban.com, 1S/2D/3F) with beds for £18-£29/pp. *Glengorm Guest House* (☎ 01631-564386, 🖳 www.glengorm-oban.co.uk, 1S/1D/1T/6F) does B&B from £20 to £35/pp.

If these are full, aim for the harbour and look for the flashing neon sign above *Columba Hotel* (☎ 01631-562183, 🖳 www

.mckeverhotels.co.uk). This swish, contemporary hotel is not cheap with prices for B&B starting at £79.50/pp.

Where to eat and drink

A good street to search for culinary pleasures is George St. Here you will find Indian food at the *Taj Mahal* (☎ 01631-566400) and *Saifoor* (☎ 01631-567467; chicken dopiaza £5.40) restaurants. The nearby *Coast Restaurant* (☎ 01631-569900, 🖳 www .coastoban.co.uk) is another classy, arty affair serving Scottish lamb for £16.95.

Snacks and coffees are on offer at the *Pancake Place* (☎ 01631-562593) along with pizzas for £5.95, while *Nevis Bakery* (☎ 01631-562262) on Stevenson St is the place to rustle up some lunch. There are also two **fish and chip shops** (*Oban* and *Norie*) on George St.

For pub grub head for the *Oban Inn* (☎ 01631-562484), a tiny little stone-floored pub with ships' wheels on the wall. A couple of pipe-smoking white-bearded old timers in wellies would really complete the picture. The haddock is £4.95.

Continue along the north pier for the twin restaurants *Piazza* (☎ 01631-563628) and *EE.USK* (☎ 01631-565666, 🖳 www .eeusk.com), both offering pricey meals in a

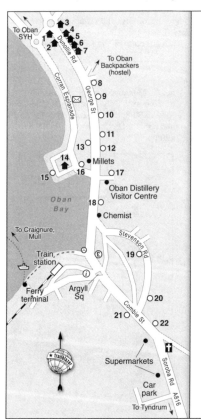

Oban

Where to stay
1 Torlundy B&B
2 Alderlea B&B
3 Hamilton House
4 Dana Villa
5 Arbour Guest House
6 St Anne's Guest House
7 Glengorm Guest House
14 Columba Hotel

Where to eat
8 Taj Mahal Indian Restaurant
9 Saifoor Indian Restaurant
10 Oban Fish & Chip Shop
11 Coast Restaurant
12 Norie's Fish & Chips
13 The Pancake Place
15 Piazza Restaurant & EE.USK Restaurant
16 The Oban Inn
17 China Restaurant
18 Cuan Mor
19 Nevis Bakery
20 Light of India Restaurant
21 Bossards Patisserie
22 Hong Kong Chinese

THE ISLANDS

0   200m

minimalist environment of straight lines and floor-to-ceiling glass, for that intimate feel. The former does pizza and pasta from £7.95 while the latter is the place for seafood, with langoustines for £17.95. Incidentally, the EE.USK's name is the pronunciation of 'fish' in Gaelic.

There is Chinese food at *China Restaurant* (☎ 01631-565317) opposite Oban Distillery Visitor Centre (see box below) and also at the *Hong Kong Chinese Takeaway* (☎ 01631-563415) on Combie St. On Stevenson St, *Light of India*

Restaurant (☎ 01631-563728) is a good spot for a curry.

Also in the vicinity, on Combie St, is *Bossards Patisserie* (☎ 01631-564641) which does quiche, cake and coffee among other delights.

Finally there is *Cuan Mor* (☎ 01631-565078) on the waterfront, a restaurant that effortlessly blends contemporary with traditional. The menu has something for everyone with veggies, meat-eaters and seafood aficionados all catered for. Try the pan-fried sea bass for £10.95.

❏ **Rainy days**
● **Oban Distillery Tour** To find out how one of Scotland's finest single malt whiskies is made head to the Oban distillery (Easter-Oct 9.30am-5pm, until 7.30pm Mon-Fri, Jul-Aug, ☎ 01631-572004, 🖳 www.malts.com) on Stafford St, Oban.

THE ISLANDS

MULL
Craignure
Services The ferry (see p33) from Oban drops passengers off here. The main **bus stop** is by the pier and is the place to catch a lift along the southern road to Fionnphort and Iona, or the northern road to Tobermory (for Beinn Talaidh). Contact Bowmans Coaches (☎ 01631-566809, 🖳 www.bowmanstours.co.uk) for timetables.

The **TIC** (☎ 01680-812377, 🖳 craignure@visitscotland.com) is opposite the pier. Turn right from the pier for the local **supermarket**, which has all the food you might need for a day on the hill, and the **post office**.

Where to stay and eat A little further on from the post office there is cheap food at *MacGregor's Roadhouse* (☎ 01680-812471). The most extravagant beds are at the *Isle of Mull Hotel* (☎ 01680-812351, 🖳 www.crerahotels.com, 86D/T). Most of the rooms in this modern functional hotel have sea views; beds cost from £60/pp.

Turn left from the pier for *Craignure Inn* (☎ 01680-812305, 🖳 www.craignure-inn.co.uk), an old 18th-century drovers' inn which appears in Robert Louis Stevenson's

novel, *Kidnapped*, under the moniker 'Inn of Torosay'. They have cheap, filling bar food (5.30-8pm) with fish cakes for £8.50 and pork for £9.95. They also do B&B from £20/pp.

Continue along the road for *Aon a' Dha* (☎ 01680-812318, 2D/1T) which has the cheapest beds in the village at £20/pp. About 500m south of the village at Druim Mhor is *Dee-Emm B&B* (☎ 01680-812440, 🖳 www.dee-emm.co.uk, 1D), a homely place run by ornithologists who can advise you of the best places to see Mull's wildlife which includes sea eagles and otters. B&B here is £25-28/pp.

Turn left at the southern end of Craignure Bay for *Pennygate Lodge* (☎ 01680-812333, 🖳 www.pennygatelodge .com, 4D/3T) which does B&B from £28 to £40/pp. Almost next door is the *Shieling Holidays Camping and Caravan Site* (☎ 01680-812496, 🖳 www.shielingholidays .co.uk) in a beautiful spot overlooking Craignure Bay with views up the length of Loch Linnhe. **Camping** pitches are £15.50 for a tent and two campers. They also have **hostel** beds for £11.50/pp.

RUM
Kinloch   [see Map 51a, p262]
Rum is a national nature reserve (NNR), owned and managed by Scottish Natural Heritage (SNH). And it is wildlife that Rum is most famous for, be it the sea eagles that were reintroduced in the 1970s, the red deer, that are subject to the longest-running deer study in the world, or the noisy manx shearwaters that nest on the high mountain tops.

There are **ferries** from Mallaig on Mon, Wed, Fri and Sat (☎ 0800-066 5000, 🖳 www.calmac.co.uk); see pp32-6 for public transport map and details. Failing this, the *MV Sheerwater* (☎ 01687-450224, 🖳 www.arisaig.co.uk) sails here from Arisaig on Tuesday and Thursday, and in summer also on Saturday.

The new community hall incorporates the **post office** and a small **shop** selling essential groceries and knick-knacks. Also in the hall there is a **tearoom** (☎ 01687-460328, daily 10am-7.30pm) selling soup for £3 as well as cakes and hot drinks. You can access the **internet** here for £1 per 20 minutes.

Information about the island, its role as a NNR and access rights is available from the **SNH office** (Mon-Fri 9am-12.30pm) at The White House. If it isn't open you can get essential information and leave a route card on the display boards outside. There are plans to build a new visitor centre so this may have changed by the time you read this.

There is a basic free **campsite** (with standpipe and toilet) between the village and the pier. For cheap beds head to **Kinloch Castle** (☎ 01687-462037) which houses the **hostel** (dorm beds and twin rooms with four poster beds £14/pp). The castle also has a self-catering kitchen (£5/pp), laundry (£2.50) and hot showers (£1/pp). The extravagant Victorian sandstone castle was once home to Sir George Bullogh who used the building to entertain his many deer-stalking guests. The daily tours of the castle (which begin just after the ferry arrives) are well worth the £6 entry fee.

On the southern side of the island at Dibidil (see Map 51b, p263) there is a very cosy **MBA bothy** conveniently positioned at the foot of the mountains. To check the availability of these options contact the SNH office on ☎ 01687-462026.

SKYE
Broadford [see map p288]
Broadford is well kitted-out with a **TIC** (☎ 0845-225 5121), a **bank** with a cash machine, a **post office** and a large **supermarket** also with a cash machine. At the **petrol station** there is a **launderette** and internet access. *Broadford Youth Hostel* (☎ 01471-822442, 59 beds, Mar-Oct, £13.50-16/pp), on the west side of Broadford Bay, is the cheapest place to stay. There is also a range of B&Bs closer to the centre of the village. Starting at the

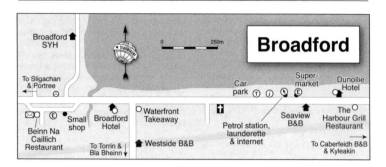

east end is **Caberfeidh B&B** (☎ 01471-822664, 🖳 www.caberfeidhskye.co.uk, 1S/2D en suite), a modern bungalow charging £25-30/pp, while opposite the Co-op supermarket **Seaview B&B** (☎ 01471-820308, 🖳 www.accommodation-isle-of-skye.co.uk, 1S/2D/2T/1F) has beds from £20/pp. A short distance down the road to Elgol is another modern bungalow B&B: **Westside** (☎ 01471-820243, 🖳 www.isleof skye.net/westside, 1S/1D/1T), charging from £22.

Broadford has two main hotels: The first, imaginatively named, **Broadford Hotel** (☎ 01471-822204, 🖳 www.broad fordhotel.co.uk) is by the bridge at the west end of the village and does B&B from a pricey £64/pp, while the large **Dunollie Hotel** (☎ 01471-822253, 🖳 www.oxford hotelsandinns.com, 19S/18D/48T) is at the other end of the village near the Co-op. B&B here is also quite expensive at £54/pp.

Hungry tummies are well catered for in Broadford. A great place for tasty sandwiches and hot drinks is the **Waterfront Takeaway** by the junction with the road for Elgol. For a more substantial meal try either of the two hotels (see above) or the **Beinn na Caillich Restaurant** (☎ 01471-822616), a small bistro-style café which also does takeaways. Finally, there is the **Harbour Grill Restaurant** (☎ 01471-822687, 🖳 www.harbourbroadford.co.uk) for steaks and lighter snacks.

Torrin   [off Map 52, p266]
The crofting community of Torrin is seven

miles south of Broadford and just a few miles from the start of the Bla Bheinn path but it has limited amenities. There is a B&B for £22/pp in the old croft at **Slapin View** (☎ 01471-822672, 1F).

Sligachan   [see Map 53, p268]
Sligachan Hotel (☎ 01478-650204, 🖳 www .sligachan.co.uk, 21 rooms), or 'The Slig' to regulars, and those who can't face the pronunciation, is a traditional resting spot for travellers and a popular base for walkers and climbers.

This historic drovers' inn lies in a spectacular spot with the pinnacled ridge of Sgurr nan Gillean and the Bhasteir Tooth on the Cuillin ridge forming an almighty backdrop. Hillwalkers and climbers have long used the hotel as a base for excursions into these most revered of mountains and this has not been lost on the family who run the place.

They have set up a **bunkhouse** just across the old bridge with space for 20 folk, let on a weekly basis, at a rate of £12/pp. The hotel rooms are more of a luxury with prices from £45/pp for B&B. Food is available in the hotel (venison sausages for £7.50) and they even operate their own in-house micro-brewery, the results of which can be found at the bar.

Conveniently placed, across the road at the head of the loch is **Sligachan Caravan and Campsite** (☎ 01478-650204) where pitches cost £5 per camper.

The nearest B&B to Sligachan is two miles away near **Sconser** at **Loch Aluinn** (see Map 54. p270; ☎ 01478-650288, ⌨ www.isleofskye.net/loch-aluinn, 1D/1T en suite, £30/pp). Anyone considering a hike up Glamaig will find it conveniently positioned at the foot of the hill.

Portree

On the east coast of Skye is Portree, the capital of the island. The name Portree is a corruption of the Gaelic 'Port an Righ' which, roughly translated, means King's Harbour. It is certainly a spot fit for royalty; a lively and pretty little town set on a natural harbour enclosed by dramatic green cliffs.

For anyone planning on spending any time on Skye, Portree is an ideal base, lying half-way between the Cuillin hills and the Trotternish peninsula.

Services The **TIC** (☎ 0845-225 5121) is well stocked with maps and books about the island and they can help book accommodation. Being the largest town on the island Portree has all the services one might need: there is a **post office**, plenty of **shops**, a **supermarket** and two or three **banks** with **cash machines**. Island Outdoors (daily 9am-6pm), five minutes out of town on the A87, is an **outdoor equipment shop**.

Getting to the town is easy with three Citylink **buses** (see pp32-6) a day to and from Fort William and Glasgow. For access to some of the remoter spots on the island call **A1 taxis** on ☎ 01478-611112 or **Don's taxis** on ☎ 01478-613100.

Where to stay *Portree Independent Hostel* (☎ 01478-613737, ⌨ www.hostel

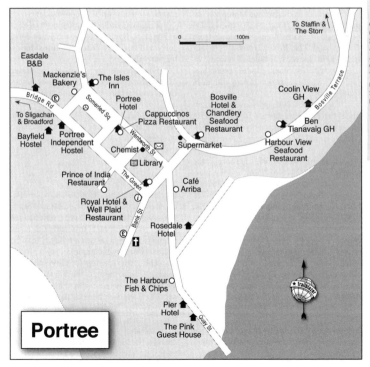

skye.co.uk, £12-13.50/pp) has over 60 beds and is the unmistakable yellow building just off the square. Behind it, down the steps, is the very functional **Bayfield Hostel** (☎ 01478-612231, 🖳 www.skyehostel .co.uk, 24 beds) with beds from £13/pp.

On Bosville Terrace, overlooking the harbour, almost every house seems to be a B&B. Two to consider are **Coolin View Guest House** (☎ 01478-611280, 🖳 www .coolinview.co.uk, 3S/2D/2T/1F) and **Ben Tianavaig Guest House** (☎ 01478-612152, 🖳 www.ben-tianavaig.co.uk), both offering B&B for around £35/pp.

For a little luxury one could do worse than the opulent **Bosville Hotel** (☎ 01478-612846, 🖳 www.bosvillehotel.co.uk, 1S/11D/5T/2F) where B&B costs from £64/pp. **Rosedale Hotel** (☎ 01478-613131, 🖳 www.rosedalehotelskye.co.uk, 19 rooms) charges around £40/pp.

The most exclusive hotels in town are probably **Portree Hotel** (☎ 01478-612511) on the square, with 24 en suite rooms from £45/pp, and **The Royal Hotel** (☎ 01478-612525, 🖳 www.royal-hotel-skye.com, 21 rooms); with its fitness centre, sauna and room service is a bit of a luxury with rates from £57/pp.

The cheapest beds on Somerled Square are at the **The Isles Inn** (☎ 01478-612129, 🖳 www.accommodationskye.co.uk, 4D/3T/1F), a traditional old pub. B&B here is £22.50-45/pp.

Down on the colourful harbour is the **Pier Hotel** (☎ 01478-612094, 🖳 www.pier-hotel.co.uk) where B&B is £30/pp and the nearby **Pink Guest House** (☎ 01478-612263, 🖳 www.pink-guest-house.co.uk, 5D/1T/4F) which has B&B from £30 to £35/pp. Finally, **Easdale B&B** (☎ 01478-613244, 2D/1T), just off the square, is a friendly place with beds for £28/pp.

Where to eat and drink The laid-back and colourful **Café Arriba** (☎ 01478-611830, 🖳 www.cafearriba.co.uk) is a great place for a leisurely bite to eat, and is deservedly popular with locals on their lunch breaks. The menu changes daily but the food is always top notch with the likes of chorizo and tomato pasta for £5.45.

Many of the hotels (see Where to stay) have good restaurants open to non-residents: **Well Plaid Restaurant** in Royal Hotel is a modern, functional bistro with a varied menu including MacNab's steak pie for £8.50, while **Cappuccinos Pizza Restaurant** in Portree Hotel serves pizza for £5.95.

Chandlery Seafood Restaurant is part of Bosville Hotel and matches the rooms for style and expense, but the dishes are quite special and include roast guinea fowl and Portree langoustines.

There is more local seafood next door at the **Harbour View Seafood Restaurant** (☎ 01478-612069, 🖳 www.harbourview skye.co.uk), where the Skye king scallops are worth every penny of the £16 asking price.

Ben Tianavaig Guest House (see Where to stay) doubles up as a vegetarian restaurant that is open to non-residents.

Prince of India Restaurant (☎ 01478-612681) on Bayfield Rd is the place for a curry and there is a **fish and chip shop** by the harbour.

For something a little healthier **Mackenzie's Bakery** on the square offers cakes and savouries either to eat in or take away.

The Isles Inn (see Where to stay) is one of the better pubs in the town centre with an open fire, good beer and regular live music. They also do good pub grub with haddock for £7.95.

Uig

For exploring the Trotternish peninsula, home to the Quiraing and Old Man of Storr, Uig is a good base. It is also the terminal for **ferries** to Tarbert on Harris and with boats running just once or twice a day it may be necessary to stay the night.

The main bus stop for Citylink **buses** heading south through the island to Fort William and Glasgow is by the ferry terminal. There are two buses a day in summer but only one in winter. See also public transport map and table, pp32-6.

The **shop**, **post office** and a **bakery** are all tucked into one building about a mile east of the pier by the Ferry Inn.

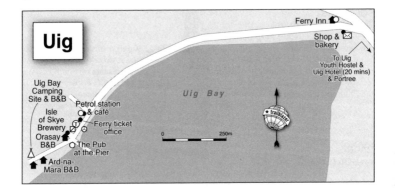

Where to stay, eat and drink This is a popular holiday spot so do book in advance. *Uig Bay Camping and Caravan Park* (☎ 01470-542714, 🖥 www.uig-camping-skye.co.uk) is just five minutes from the pier. Pitches are £5/pp and they also do **B&B** (2D/1T) from £18 to £25/pp.

Uig Youth Hostel (☎ 01470-542746; 62 beds, mid Mar-Oct, £13-15.25/pp) is a 20-minute walk up the hill to the south (if coming by bus ask the driver to drop you at the hostel, not in the village).

Most of the B&Bs are located close to the pier, the most convenient of which are *Orasay* (☎ 01470-542316, 🖥 www.holiday-skye.co.uk, 1S/1D/1T) by the brewery, with B&B from £22.50/pp and *Ard-na-Mara* (☎ 01470-542281, 🖥 www.bandbisleofskye.co.uk, 2D/1F) with similar prices.

About a mile east of the pier is the *Ferry Inn* (☎ 01478-611216, 🖥 www.ferryinn.co.uk) where rates begin at £37/pp.

Even further out of the village, with enviable views over the bay towards the Western Isles, is *Uig Hotel* (☎ 01470-542205, 🖥 www.uighotel.com), a substantial establishment with 18 luxurious rooms from £40/pp.

Good food is limited in Uig. There is a cheap and cheerful **café** at the **petrol station** while the *Pub at the Pier* (☎ 01470-542212) offers meals of debatable quality in a building that would win a blot-on-the-landscape competition in Hackney, let alone Skye. The best place by far is up the hill at the *Ferry Inn* (see column opposite) where you can indulge in Scottish steak and salmon whilst sampling some Skye ales from the Cuillin Brewery at Sligachan. Curiously, they do not appear to stock any ales from Uig's very own brewery, the **Isle of Skye Brewery** (see map of Uig).

THE ISLANDS

❏ **Rainy days**
● **Kilt Rock waterfall** The sea cliffs on the east coast of the Trotternish peninsula of Skye are decorated with dancing trails of water spilling over the edges. The best of these waterfalls is the one at Kilt Rock, two miles south of Staffin. It involves a walk of about five metres from the car park so don't plan on pencilling in a whole day to see it.

SOUTH UIST
Tobha Mor (Howmore)
[see Map 56a, p274]

The most convenient base for a day on the South Uist hills is the Gatliff Trust *Howmore Hostel* (no phone), a traditional Hebridean blackhouse with simple bunks for £8/pp and a few spaces for **camping**, at £5/pp, in the field next door. There is a small **shop** and **post office** (Mon 9.30am-12.30pm, Tue-Fri 10am-12.30pm, Sat

10.30am-12.30pm) down the road past the bicycle hire and repair shop. Ferries from Oban serve Lochboisdale on South Uist on Tue, Thu, Sat and Sun (🖳 www.calmac.co .uk). There are buses three times a day (Mon-Sat); contact Hebridean Transport (☎ 01859-705050). Buses run the length of the Western Isles. See also pp32-6

HARRIS
An t-Ob (Leverburgh)
[off Map 57, p277]

An t-Ob, on the south coast of Harris, is the arrival and departure point for the Caledonian MacBrayne (see p35) **ferry** from Berneray. It is not a particularly attractive village but the surrounding countryside makes up for that and it makes a good base for walkers intent on climbing Ceapabhal.

The **Cauldron** is a small **shop** and **post office** (Mon, Tue, Thu, Fri 9am-5pm, Sat 9am-12.30pm) near the road junction for the ferry terminal. They have a **cash machine** inside. A little further along there is a craft and exhibition centre incorporating a **café** and **grocery shop** (☎ 01859-520370, Mon-Sat 10am-4pm).

The cheapest beds are at the purpose-built *Am Bothan Bunkhouse* (☎ 01859-520251, 🖳 www.ambothan.com, 18 beds) with cabins, wigwams and bunks from £15/pp. For a little more comfort try any of the numerous B&Bs, the most central of which is *Caberfeidh House* (☎ 01859-520276, 2D/1F) with beds from £20/pp.

Heading out on the road to An Taobh Tuath is the very quaint *Sorrel Cottage* (☎ 01859-520319, 🖳 www.accommodation isleofharris.co.uk, 2T/1F) with its blooming

garden and B&B from £32.50/pp (bike hire available for £10). If this is full, there are a few more B&Bs along this road, including *Eggs*, although this is probably a reference to their hens' offerings, rather than the name of the house.

There are regular **buses** on the route from An t-Ob to Tarbert and Stornoway (Mon-Sat). Contact Hebridean Transport (☎ 01859-705050).

An Taobh Tuath (Northton)
[see Map 57, p277]

About a mile out of An t-Ob, below the hill Ceapabhal, is the small hamlet of An Taobh Tuath, boasting **Seallam Visitor Centre** (Mon-Sat 10am-5pm, 🖳 www.seallam .com), specialising in local genealogy and incorporating an exhibition on local history and nature (£2.50). **Internet access** is available for £1 per 20 mins. At the end of the lane is the **MacGillivray Centre** (free) celebrating the work of the late naturalist William MacGillivray who studied the local wildlife on his father's farm.

The **post office** and small **shop** is at No 34 (Mon 9am-noon, Tue & Wed 10am-noon, Thu 10am-1pm, Fri 10am-noon). There are comfortable beds at *Tetherstone B&B* at No 40 and more of the same at the **B&B** next door at No 39.

❑ Beaches

On the west-facing coasts of the Western Isles are some of the biggest, most unspoilt, and beautiful beaches in Europe. There are no beach huts or ice-cream vendors; just sand, marram grass and the evocative whistling of sandpipers. Beaches of note include those on South Uist and Berneray but the finest are on Harris, at Scarista and Luskentyre, and on Lewis, at Uig Sands (not to be mistaken with Uig on Skye).

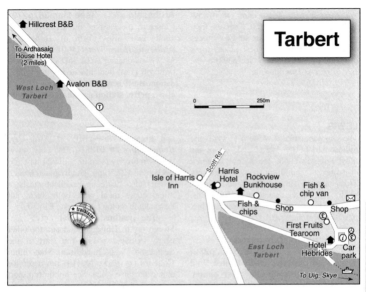

Tarbert

Tarbert
The isthmus that gives Tarbert its name (Tairbeart means isthmus in Gaelic) separates the moonscape of South Harris from the hills of North Harris. In fact this neck of land is so narrow that the two are almost separate islands.

Tarbert, although not big, is the main village on Harris. It is a friendly place and is a good base from which to approach the Harris hills.

Ferries run Mon-Sat between Uig on Skye and here. Hebridean Transport (☎ 01859-705050) runs regular **bus** services (Mon-Sat) between Stornoway on Lewis and Leverburgh on Harris, all of which pass through Tarbert and the start of the Clisham and Ceapabhal walks. See public transport map and table on pp32-6.

The **TIC** (☎ 01859-502011, Apr-mid Oct, Mon-Sat 9am-5pm) is in the car park near the ferry terminal and the helpful staff can sort out your accommodation worries.

Tarbert has two **shops** that should cover most people's gastronomic demands, a **bank** and a **cash machine** (located by the TIC, not the bank). Head east along Main St for the **post office**.

The first place offering accommodation that one sees when departing the ferry is **Hotel Hebrides** (☎ 01859-502364, 🖳 www.macleodmotel.com, 8S/8D/3T/2F) which has been transformed from a run-down motel into a posh hotel; B&B is £55/pp. Continue up the hill onto the main street for **Rockview Bunkhouse** (☎ 01859-502081) which has dormitory-style rooms with beds for £10/pp.

At the other end of the price scale is the very friendly **Harris Hotel** (☎ 01859-502154, 🖳 www.harrishotel.com, 2S/10D/10T/2F), built in 1865, where B&B is from £45 to £70/pp. The food in their restaurant is excellent and varied, with beef and ale casserole for £8.50 and fajitas for £7.50.

For something between the two there are some good B&Bs on the Stornoway road with **Avalon B&B** (☎ 01859-502334, 🖳 www.avalonguesthouse.org, 2D/1T) offering beds for £32/pp. **Hillcrest B&B** (☎ 01859-502119, 1D/1T/1F) is the simplest and cheapest option with beds for £25/pp.

First Fruits Tea Room (☎ 01859-502439), opposite the TIC, serves light meals and snacks, and there are two sources of **fish and chips**. The best places for a drink are in *Harris Hotel* (see p293) or the *Isle of Harris Inn* opposite.

LEWIS

The Uig peninsula of western Lewis is the hilliest part of the island and one of the most remote. There are a few scattered crofting communities, namely Timsgearraidh, Bhaltos, Riof and Miavaig, to the east of the spectacular Uig Sands, arguably the most beautiful beach (see box p292) in Scotland.

Timsgearraidh (Timsgarry)
[off Map 59, p282]

Accommodation is extremely limited. Wild **camping** is probably the best option. However, *Baile na Cille* (☎ 01851-672242, 6D/2T) offers B&B from £29/pp,

Ardhasaig   [see Map 58, p279]

Closer to the start of the Clisham walk, about two miles north of Tarbert, is *Ardhasaig House Hotel* (☎ 01859-502066, 🖳 www.ardhasaig.co.uk, 6D en suite), an old croft converted into luxury accommodation. B&B here is from £55/pp. There's also a **petrol station** and **shop**.

and high on the cliffs at Aird Uig, *Bonaventure* (☎ 01851-672474, 🖳 www .bonaventurelewis.co.uk, 2D/2T/1F) do B&B from £27.50/pp. The Irish and French owners also rustle up excellent meals: a three-course meal with both duck and Lewis lamb on the menu costs £30.50.

The **postbus** (Mon-Sat only) from Stornoway to Timsgearraidh and the other nearby villages passes the start of the Suaineabhal walk. In addition, **Maclennan Coaches** (☎ 01851-702114) run a service along the same route. See public transport map and table, pp32-6, for details.

❑ **Rainy days**
● **Callanish (Calanais) standing stones and Garenin** On the west coast of Lewis are the mysterious standing stones of Callanish. They may not be as famous as Stonehenge but this henge is a lot older, dating back to around 1800BC. There are actually four stone circles in the immediate area but the one by the visitor centre is the most complete.

Nearby in the traditional blackhouse village of Garenin one of the old crofters' homes operates as a **Youth Hostel** (no phone, £8/pp, **camping** £5/pp). MacLennan Coaches (☎ 01851-702114) run buses to Callanish and Garenin from Stornoway.

The Big Treks

The treks described below are multi-day expeditions in the hills. The maps for these walks and some parts of the route descriptions are in the main part of the book.

THE GREAT TRAVERSE – CORROUR TO GLEN NEVIS (VIA THE GREY CORRIES, THE AONACHS, CARN MOR DEARG & BEN NEVIS)

[MAP 19a, p134; MAP 19b, p135; MAP 19c, p137; MAP 13b, p108; MAP 13a, p107]

THE GREAT TRAVERSE
Corrour to Glen Nevis (via the Grey Corries, the Aonachs, Carn Mor Dearg & Ben Nevis)
Technical grade ▲▲▲▲
Navigation grade ▲▲▲
Terrain grade ▲▲▲▲
Strenuousness ▲▲▲▲▲
Time 2-3 days
Distance 23miles/37km
Total ascent 9514ft/2900m
OS maps Landranger 41, Explorer 392 & 385
Gateways Corrour (see p141) Glen Nevis (see p113) Fort William (see p114)

Overview

Simply put, this great traverse is one of the finest long-distance ridge walks to be found anywhere in the British Isles. It begins with an easy day of low-level walking from Corrour train station past Loch Treig to the lonely Lairig Leacach glen.

The following day is spent high on the Grey Corries ridge, rarely dropping below 900m and offering outstanding views ahead to the final day's objectives: Aonach Beag, Aonach Mor, Carn Mor Dearg and Britain's highest peak Ben Nevis. Together these hills form some of the most alpine-like scenery in Scotland and the final ascent of 'The Ben' by way of the sweeping knife-edged Carn Mor Dearg arête makes a fitting end to a demanding expedition.

The very fit and experienced hillwalker can complete the route described in three days. The unusually fit may even attempt it in two while the unfit should stay on the train at Corrour. There is no accommodation along the way and an overnight bivvy or camp is necessary. Consequently the traverse is made even more demanding by the need to carry a full pack with cooking equipment, sleeping bag and tent or bivvy bag. Also, bear in mind that being at high altitude for three days means bad weather can be expected on at least one, if not every, day. This is not for the faint-hearted.

Route

The route from Corrour train station to **Lairig Leacach** (2-3hrs) is described on p133. This is the point of ascent for the two munros on the east side of the Lairig

Leacach: Stob Coire Easain and Stob a' Choire Mheadhoin which are described as a separate day walk on p133 and p136. This is where the real business of the trek begins with the ascent of the first peak of the Grey Corries: Stob Ban, a satellite peak of some character, sitting away from the main Grey Corries ridge. From the river next to the Lairig Leacach hut (Map 19c, p137) follow the path which climbs heathery slopes in a southerly direction. After just 20 paces or so a smaller trail branches off to the right to climb the steep slopes of the hill above. Continue up this path. The gradient eases after about 20 minutes and the path contours around the broad lower slopes of Stob Ban's east ridge to gain a saddle just below 800m. The conical summit of the mountain lies ahead and a clear path winds its way directly up the east side to reach the small rocky summit of **Stob Ban**. From the top there is a taste of the views to come with the Mamores to the SW and the Glen Coe hills to the south, most notably the brooding bulk of Buachaille Etive Mor looking out across Rannoch Moor.

The descent route from the cairn on top of Stob Ban is not immediately obvious but can be located by taking a bearing of 285° from the cairn and walking for about 20 paces. A very steep eroded trail drops down scree slopes to a broad and undulating col at 800m. From the small **lochan** at the northern end of the saddle begin the 380m ascent to the summit of the second munro, **Stob Choire Claurigh**, by way of its southern ridge. The gradient eases briefly near the top before the route continues in a north-westerly direction over a steep boulder field to the large summit cairn.

The view from here is quite simply magnificent with the rest of the ridge stretched out before you. The distant peaks of the Aonachs and Ben Nevis can be seen beyond the end of the Grey Corries ridge. It can be a view that leaves you both breathless and bemused in equal measure as you take in the full scale of the walk that lies ahead. The good news is that now you have reached the ridge proper there is less in the way of descent and re-ascent until you reach the massive bulk of Aonach Beag and that's some way off yet.

From Stob Choire Clauright descend the SW ridge to gain the main ridge. As you walk along this **narrow edge** it becomes clear how the Grey Corries got their name as sweeping slopes of grey scree fan down from each side of the ridge. The ridge passes over a small top with a wee **cairn** before dropping briefly to a col at 1040m and continuing along another narrow stretch of ridge with sheer cliffs on the SW side and a steep grassy drop on the other. Head on along the ridge as it broadens somewhat, past beautiful slopes of red scree (that contrasts with the grey scree everywhere else) to another top and a cairn.

The ridge swings to the west, passes over another top and then reaches another short, narrow stretch. This leads down to a section of the ridge somewhat interrupted by the tail ends of a series of high cliffs that make up the north side of the mountain. There is a short but easy scramble to gain the top of them. From here it is a straightforward walk to the summit of the second munro, **Stob Coire an Laoigh**, where there is a shelter cairn. This is a good vantage point for admiring the view back to the first peaks of the day: Stob Ban and Stob Choire Clauright. An easy ridge leads in a NW direction from here to the top of **Stob**

Coire Easain via a small col. There now comes a descent of 140m to a wide saddle. Some concentration is needed here as there is some awkward rocky terrain culminating in a short section of rocky ribs where there is a choice of descent. The direct approach involves scrambling straight down on the main line of the ridge while an alternative sneaks down the west side over large loose boulders. There is a useful escape route from the saddle heading SE into the glen below, from where it is a long trudge to Glen Nevis. Also at the saddle there is a shelter cairn and a number of possible camping spots ($3^1/_2$hrs to 5hrs 40mins from Lairig Leacach).

Unless time is limited it is best to continue over Sgurr Choinnich Mor and Sgurr Choinnich Beag to leave less to do for the next day. The shapely peak of **Sgurr Choinnich Mor** has a well-trodden path leading up its NE ridge. There are a couple of false summits to endure before the path finally continues along the grassy summit ridge to the small cairn at the top. The great eastern walls of Aonach Beag and Aonach Mor loom ahead. Snow lies in their gullies well into summer.

Continue down the grassy SW ridge to a col at 900m where a bypass path skirts around the north side of the small peak of **Sgurr Choinnich Beag** (Map 13b, p108). If you want to do the whole ridge you will have to climb the 60m to the top of this peak before descending steep grassy slopes to the **saddle** at 735m below Aonach Beag (1-1$^1/_2$hrs from the saddle on the NE side of Sgurr Choinnich Mor). This is good spot for a camp before the final day on the Aonachs and Ben Nevis but if legs, weather and time permit it is possible to continue on over the Aonachs to the col below Carn Mor Dearg. Bear in mind, however, that it is a long pull up onto Aonach Beag from here and it may be better to save it for the morning.

It is a daunting prospect looking up at the ascent onto Aonach Beag's SE ridge, trying to work out the best route to take. The sheer walls of the eastern side of the mountain wrap right round towards the satellite peak of Sgurr a' Bhuic. As you face this seemingly impenetrable wall look for the band of rocky strata sweeping diagonally across the face of the mountain and then look for the band of scree further left. There is in fact a faint trail leading up between the spine of this rocky face and the scree but it is very steep and exposed.

An easier route can be found by heading west towards a steep grassy gully. Climb steeply halfway up the gully to a point just below a buttress on the left. The top of the gully holds snow through much of the year, even in summer, and finding a way over the cornice at the top can be almost impossible. For this reason it is better to contour around below the buttress and pick a way up slopes of grass and small rocky shelves to gain the col to the north of Sgurr a' Bhuic. Once on this wide ridge the going is easy. Ascend steadily along the line of the ridge, which swings around to the west to a small col.

From here it is a 140m ascent up the featureless southern sweep of the summit slopes. In poor visibility be sure to take careful compass readings since the 500m cliffs on the eastern side are just a short step away. The broad summit of **Aonach Beag**, the highest of the two Aonachs, offers unrivalled views of Ben

Nevis and the Carn Mor Dearg arête, but before tackling them descend the NW ridge to the col and follow the path in a north direction to the summit of **Aonach Mor**, the highest point of a 1¼ mile/2km-long plateau. Peering over either side of this flat sub-arctic plateau gives a real impression of how the glaciers of 10,000 years ago have eaten into this mountain massif. To the north, and thankfully out of sight from the summit, are the ski lifts of the Nevis Range ski resort and Ptarmigan mountain restaurant high on the northern slopes of the mountain.

Careful navigation is necessary to find the descent to the col below Carn Mor Dearg. Begin by bearing south. A faint path follows the western edge of the plateau. Do not continue all the way back to the col below Aonach Beag. Instead look out for a **small cairn** near the top of the nose that leads off the western side of the mountain. It is an extremely steep descent so it is important to find the path. There are a couple of misleading eroded sheep trails leading down parallel gullies to the south of the nose which should not be followed as they lead to some dangerously steep ground. The path that picks its way down the nose begins at the small cairn (GR 19137222). After a knee-jerking descent the trail eventually shallows out by a stream to reach the **col** at 835m. There are plenty of good spots for camping on this flat grassy col (2½-3½ hrs from saddle SE of Aonach Beag). It is nearly 400m of ascent onto the summit of **Carn Mor Dearg** by way of its beautifully defined eastern ridge. Gaining the ridge at first sight appears tricky but by following a path from an old stone wall at the col round to the NE side of the ridge brings you to easier slopes, just before some slabs of rock. A steep ascent of 50m brings you onto the spine of the ridge. Follow this rocky line to the summit of Carn Mor Dearg.

For the continuation of this walk, across the Carn Mor Dearg arête to Ben Nevis and Glen Nevis see pp106-9 (2½-3½hrs from the col east of Carn Mor Dearg to Ben Nevis Inn in Glen Nevis).

Alternative routes

The first day from Corrour to Lairig Leacach, which essentially acts as an approach route to the walk proper, can be avoided by driving to Corriechoille (GR 250806) and walking to Lairig Leacach from there. However, it is only two miles (3km) shorter than the Corrour route and less interesting. But if you are coming by car it is the only option as Corrour is in a road-free area.

There are a number of escape routes from the ridge into Glen Nevis (see pp106-9).

CAIRNGORMS – AVIEMORE TO LINN OF DEE   [MAP 24a, p159; MAP 24b, p160; MAP 24c, p162; MAP 23b, p155; MAP 23a, p154]

Overview

The Lairig Ghru is a glacial breach that slices the Cairngorm plateau in two. It is also a very useful walking route linking the northern side of the Cairngorms with the southern side. The two-day trek from Aviemore to Linn of Dee near Braemar can get busy in summer but it is deservedly popular, offering inexperienced hillwalkers the chance to immerse themselves in high mountain scenery.

Starting at Aviemore the walk passes through the beautiful Rothiemurchus Forest before climbing into the Lairig Ghru which holds you in its grasp for a good few hours. The high point is over 800m, an extremely high valley floor by Scottish standards. The southern end of the Lairg Ghru is wider and dominated by the gaping Garbh Choire and the shapely peak of Devil's Point. The walk continues through more native pine forest and finally follows the river down to the Linn of Dee.

Route

Opposite the tourist info centre at the southern end of Aviemore's main street there is a path leading away from the busy road. Follow this path below an underpass and turn right at the road. Just past the Old Bridge Inn, cross the road and continue along the path, and over the River Spey, to join the B970. Continue along this road for 1¼ miles (2km) to the Rothiemurchus Caravan and Camping Park, just before Coylumbridge (Map 24a).

For a description of the first stage of this walk from Coylumbridge to the path junction just past the memorial plaque see pp158-61. At this junction the main Lairig Ghru path is straight ahead (Map 24b; for the more experienced hillwalkers out there, the path leading up the hill to the right is the route to take for the high-level trek over the Braeriach plateau; see p161 and p163). Navigating through the **Lairig Ghru** is relatively straightforward. The path is quite clear but the terrain can be quite rough in places with sections of loose rock and scree. However, the steep walls of the Ghru on each side should keep even the most hapless of navigators channelled in the right direction.

It's a steady climb, with a shallow gradient, to the highest point of the pass which at just over 830m is a deceptively lofty spot. It is actually higher than many mountain summits in other parts of the Highlands and should therefore be treated with respect. The weather here can turn pretty foul and can do so very suddenly. After crossing the pass the path winds to the right of the **pools of Dee**, a couple of tiny lochans caught among the rocks. And then the long, slow descent begins with great views ahead down the glen to the shapely Devil's Point (Map 24c) at the bottom. To the right is the vast **Garbh Choire**, among Scotland's most famous corries. The semi-permanent snow beds in these high gullies are said to be the most likely place for the regeneration of glaciers in Scotland, should the climate take a turn for the colder.

On the opposite side of the Dee, across the footbridge, is the tiny **Corrour bothy** which is usually over-crowded. Camping is a better option if you choose to spend the night here. The path from here climbs briefly as it skirts the lower flanks of **Carn a' Mhaim** and then contours through the heather to the river at

CAIRNGORMS

Aviemore to Linn of Dee

Technical grade
▲▲

Navigation grade
▲▲

Terrain grade
▲▲

Strenuousness
▲▲▲

Time
2 days

Distance
20miles/32km

Total ascent
2067ft/630m

OS maps
Landranger 36 and 43, Explorer 403

Gateways
Aviemore (see p173), Braemar (see p172)

THE BIG TREKS

Luibeg. Cross the river, either by fording it or using the bridge a short way upstream, and continue along a good track through the pine trees and then across the flat grassy floodplain of the Dee to a footbridge which leads to the abandoned **Derry Lodge**. From here follow the track down the glen to a **bridge** over the Linn of Dee. Continue on the opposite side and follow the path through the trees to the car park at Linn of Dee.

Alternative routes

For a far more exerting trek via the Braeriach plateau, taking in the summits of four munros, see pp161-4.

KNOYDART – KINLOCHHOURN TO INVERIE [MAP 31a, p190; MAP 31b, p191; MAP 31c, p192; MAP 30a, p186]

Overview

There is an almost mythical aura surrounding Knoydart for hill-goers. It is an isolated and mountainous peninsula bordered by two sea lochs: Nevis and Hourn. There is no road access to the only village, Inverie, so access is by boat from Mallaig or on foot from the remote hamlet of Kinlochhourn, at the end of a 22-mile dead-end road from Invergarry.

The walk is 15 miles of some of the finest west-coast scenery on offer, starting with a trail along the southern shore of Loch Hourn leading to the remote bothy at Barisdale Bay. The second day heads inland and deep into the heart of Knoydart, crossing a high mountain pass and dropping down to the friendly village of Inverie. For added spice, plan on a spare day for the ascent of Ladhar Bheinn from Barisdale.

KNOYDART

Kinlochhourn to Inverie

Technical grade
▲
Navigation grade
▲▲
Terrain grade
▲▲
Strenuousness
▲▲
Return time
2 days
Return distance
15miles/24km
Total ascent
2790ft/850m
OS maps
Landranger 33, Explorer 413 and 414
Gateways
Tomdoun (see p201), Inverie (see p200) Mallaig (see p198)

Route

See pp189-93 for a description of the route from Kinlochhourn to Barisdale. **Barisdale** is the best place for an overnight stop.

It is a good idea to spend the second day climbing **Ladhar Bheinn** (see p193) and then continue from Barisdale to Inverie on the third day. When moving on to Inverie cross the bridge just south of the bothy and follow this track inland. A path climbs away from the track, just before the white house. Take the right-hand fork where it divides. The path contours the mountainside to enter a corrie above the birch woods.

Ahead is the **Mam Barisdale pass** (Map 31c) at 450m. The path climbs gradually to this high point and then descends steadily along the northern flank of Gleann an Dubh-Lochain to the lochan below. It is quite a long trudge from here along a wide track that hugs the northern shore of the lochan.

Follow this track, ignoring the two tracks that approach from the left, to **Lord Brocket's Monument** (see p185). The final push to Inverie begins here as the track continues through a forestry plantation and rises to a gate on the edge of some woodland. Immediately beyond the gate is a sharp bend in a track. Follow the left-hand side as it drops down to the lane that leads along the shore of Loch Nevis to the village of **Inverie** (see p200) and the all-important tearoom and Old Forge pub. From Inverie it is a 45-minute boat ride across to **Mallaig** (see p198).

Alternative routes

There are two other approaches to Inverie that are longer and more challenging, involving a lot of ascent and descent over a number of remote passes. The first starts from the road end at Loch Arkaig and follows the stalkers' path through Glen Dessary to Sourlies and then continues over Mam Meadail pass to Inverie. The second is even harder, starting at Glenfinnan, passing over the summit of Sgurr nan Coireachan to Glen Pean and then continuing by the head of Loch Morar, over the ridge of Sgurr nam Meirleach to Sourlies and finally over Mam Meadail pass to Inverie. These are both strenuous treks, especially the latter where a good deal of experience in route-finding in remote trackless country is needed.

FISHERFIELD – POOLEWE TO DUNDONNELL
[MAP 40a, p223; MAP 40b, p224; MAP 40c, p225; MAP 41b, p229; MAP 41a, p228]

Overview

Everyone raves about Fisherfield. It is the largest expanse of trackless land in the western Highlands and not only that, is home to some cracking mountains such as An Teallach. To cross this beautiful tract of land takes a minimum of two days but it is better to take three for this is a land to be savoured.

The first day is long but easy. The mountains, deep in the heart of Fisherfield, loom large as the day progresses until the massive crags and cliffs around Carnmore tower above you and the dark waters of the Dubh Loch. The second day involves a high-level traverse below the summits of A' Mhaighdean and Ruadh Stac Mor where there is a tangible sense of being in a very remote and beautiful place.

The final day climbs past one of the greatest, if not the greatest, mountains in Scotland, An Teallach. Most of the trek is on good stalkers' paths but there is one potentially difficult river crossing at Shenavall. Combine this with the isolation and high altitude and it becomes clear that this is quite a challenging, but hugely enjoyable, trek.

FISHERFIELD

Poolewe to Dundonnell

Technical grade
▲▲▲
Navigation grade
▲▲▲
Terrain grade
▲▲▲ (▲▲▲▲▲
when river in spate)
Strenuousness
▲▲▲
Time
2-3 days
Return distance
21 miles/33km
Total ascent
3500ft/1080m
OS maps
Landranger 19,
Explorer 433, 434
and 435
Gateways
Gairloch (see p234)
Poolewe (see p233)
Dundonnell (see p234)

THE BIG TREKS

Route

See pp222-6 for the route description from Poolewe to Carnmore. At Carnmore you will either need to stay in the barn (follow the usual etiquette for bothies) or camp.

The next day, pick up the trail which climbs in a rising traverse along the side of the mountain (Map 40c, p225). There are fine views over Dubh Loch to the cliffs that enclose it and up to the peaks of A' Mhaigdean and Ruadh Stac Mor. The path swings round into a high hanging valley and leads on to a **high plateau** decorated with small lochans. Follow the path east over this high ground and then begin the zigzagging descent into the head of the glen below. The mountain immediately ahead is Beinn Dearg Mor. The path descends steadily to the floor of the glen and then joins another path coming down from the neighbouring glen further east. It is about a mile from here to the private buildings at Larachantivore (Map 41b, p229). If the river is in spate here it may not be possible to cross, in which case there is an **emergency shelter** behind the house for those who do not have a tent. Do not plan on staying here, however. The shelter is about the size of a large box and there are absolutely no facilities or trimmings inside. If the river is not too high cross here and then negotiate the extremely boggy flood plain to the next river. This river is even wider and again may not be passable if in spate. If it is passable, the bothy at **Shenavall** is a short step away once on the far side. When crossing these rivers be sure to approach them in the right way (see river crossings on p307).

Shenavall is the best place for the second camp (or stay in the bothy) before spending the third day on the walk out to the road. Climb the path behind the bothy up the side of a stream gully. This leads on to a high moorland of exposed bedrock and erratic rocks. In places the path can be hard to follow but discreet **cairns** ease the way. Keep to the left of the rocky rib that shadows the stream. Cross the stream and continue to another small stream crossing and a short uphill section. At this point it is worth making a short detour from the path to the high ground above. From here the full extent of An Teallach's northern corrie and fearsome cliffs can be appreciated. The path drops down to a wide stony **track** (Map 41a, p228) that itself drops down into a small glen. Cross the river via the footbridge and continue on the track which leads down to the road at **Corrie Hallie**. It is about two miles up the road to Dundonnell. For information on the village and public transport to and from Poolewe and Gairloch see p234.

Alternative routes

Starting at Kinlochewe (see p233) is an option. Follow the path along the north shore of Loch Maree and continue up Gleann Bianasdail. Follow the north shore of Lochan Fada which leads on to Gleann Tulacha and down to Carnmore. From here the route described above can be picked up.

APPENDIX A: MOUNTAIN SAFETY

'Be prepared' **Robert Baden-Powell** (The motto of the Scout Movement)

These two words – be prepared – say it all. The hills can be dangerous but not if you are aware of the hazards and are willing to prepare for them and learn how to minimise the potential for an incident. Start by wearing the right clothes (see 'What to take' pp24-8) and follow this up by packing the extra clothing you may need to cope with a deterioration in the weather.

The next step is to learn about the mountains. If you are already an experienced hill-walker you probably have an almost instinctive awareness of potential dangers. It is only with experience that you learn how to place your feet to avoid spraining an ankle, which rocks look unstable to step on, which slopes lead to an impassable precipice, which line to take when scrambling up an outcrop and, most crucially, what the weather is about to do.

Know your limits

Some of the walks in this book are very long and demanding. Others are relatively quick and easy, so there should be something for everyone. Know your limits and try not to do too much from the outset. It's always a good idea to build up a bit of stamina and fitness before embarking on a strenuous hillwalk. If you are not sure of your level of fitness try starting out with one of the easier walks in the book so that you have a yardstick to judge the other walks by. Each walk is graded for strenuousness.

The weather

'There is no such thing as bad weather, only bad clothing'. **Norwegian saying**

Along with the terrain, the weather is the most important factor affecting a day on the hill, in terms of enjoyment, aesthetics, comfort, difficulty and, most pertinently, safety. Understanding the weather is so important and yet it is often overlooked. The weather at sea level is often very different to the weather at the top of a mountain and, more often than not, it is usually worse at the latter. However, bad weather does not necessarily mean that plans for a day out have to be shelved.

While walking in very extreme weather is quite foolish, walking in less severe rain, snow and wind can make for the most exhilarating of days, if you are prepared and clad for the elements. To know what weather to expect it is important to know how it works. During the summer, high pressure systems, or anti-cyclones, usually bring settled weather, often with sunshine, but not always. Low pressure systems are bad news for walkers as these tend to bring rain and strong winds.

Weather fronts, that mark the boundary between warm and cold air masses, are usually quite benign when associated with high pressure, often leading to cloud and maybe a little light drizzle. Conversely, with low pressure, they are active affairs that produce prolonged precipitation. There are three types of weather front. Cold fronts, where colder air replaces warmer air, bring intense rainfall that generally lasts for around six to twelve hours. Warm fronts, where warmer air replaces colder air, usually result in less intense rain but it can last for 24 hours or longer. After the passage of a cold front the weather usually turns showery but the visibility improves dramatically; a good time to enjoy wide-ranging views. Finally, occluded fronts mark the point where a cold front catches up with a warm front. They also produce precipitation and last about as long as a cold front.

Understanding clouds
The weather, especially in the mountains, is extremely complex and difficult to forecast but there are some indicators that help us predict what is likely to happen. Reading the clouds is the best way of determining the likelihood of a break-down in the weather. Weather fronts bring about the biggest changes and as they pass over they invariably bring precipitation.

In clear weather look out for high cirrus clouds (sometimes called mares' tails). These wispy clouds are over 10km high and signal the approach of a frontal system. In some cases a large area of high pressure may effectively block the weather front or divert it but more often than not expect the weather to deteriorate within the next 12 to 15 hours. If the sky on the horizon looks milky and grey this is an even surer sign that the weather front is making progress as stratus clouds build up. If the cloud appears to be thicker and begins to lower to cut off the tops of all the mountains precipitation is likely at any time.

After the passage of a front there is often a spell of sunshine and showers. However, in the hills it is very hard to predict where the showers are most likely to occur. You can usually see them coming but how long they last depends on a number of factors, including wind direction and topography. As a general rule the lee side of mountains is drier because of the rain shadow effect, in which most of the rain falls on the side of the mountain exposed to the approaching weather. It is for this reason that the west coast of Scotland, exposed to the prevailing south-west winds, gets much more rainfall annually than the east.

Wind While winds do, in general, increase with altitude this is not always the case. It is not unusual to find the wind blowing at gale force on a col while the summit is relatively calm. It often depends on local currents, the topography of the land and the overhead conditions. Once the **windspeed** starts gusting around 40mph walking becomes quite awkward. On narrow ridges it just becomes plain dangerous. Above 50mph the wind can quite easily throw a walker from his or her feet. Add to this the risk of becoming exhausted by fighting against a strong head wind and the wisest course of action is to descend by the nearest safe route.

Everyone knows that it feels colder when the wind blows. This cooling effect caused by the wind is known as **windchill**. Windchill is an important consideration when checking weather forecasts for it can dramatically affect how cold it feels and can lead to exposure and hypothermia. For example in winds of just 10mph a temperature of +5°C will feel more like -2°C and at speeds of 40mph it will feel more like -10°C. With these figures the case for a good windproof jacket and warm clothes becomes quite evident. *(Cont'd on p305).*

Colour section (following pages)
● **C1 Top**: The Cobbler (see pp65-7) from Loch Lomond. **Bottom**: Ben Alder and the Lancet Edge from Culra.
● **C2** Descending from Ladhar Bheinn (see pp189-94), Knoydart, with Loch Hourn beyond.
● **C3 Left (top)**: Ben Nevis in winter, seen from Glenfinnan to the west. **Left (bottom)**: On Carn Mor Dearg arête (see pp106-10), Ben Nevis. This is one of the most alpine of ridges in the Highlands. **Right (top)**: On the Grey Corries Ridge and Ben Nevis. **Right (bottom)**: On Ben Alder's summit plateau (see pp127-8) with late spring cornices still in place.
● **C4** The Moidart hills at sunrise, seen from near Beinn Resipol by Loch Sunart.
● **C5 Top**: Isles of Eigg and Rum from Beinn Resipol (see pp176-8). **Left (bottom)**: Lancet Edge from Geal Charn (see pp122-6), Central Highlands. **Right (bottom)**: Suilven (see pp237-9), seen from Glencanisp Lodge, near Lochinver.
● **C6 Left (top)**: On the Beinn an Eoin Ridge (see pp220-22), Flowerdale Forest. Hill-walking in winter is a much more serious proposition. **Middle**: Climbing from the col to the lower of Arkle's two tops (see pp243-5). The summit is in the background to the right. **Bottom**: Walking through bog cotton in spring. This bog plant is common throughout the glens of the Highlands. **Right**: An Teallach (see pp227-30) – Corrag Bhuidhe from Sgurr Fiona. This ridge is one of the most technically demanding in Scotland, even more so in winter conditions.
● **C7 Left (top)**: Cooking dinner at a bivvy site on the shores of Loch Shiel, Western Highlands. The tarp isn't essential but does keep the rain off the bivvy bag. **Left (middle)**: Bothy on the Isle of Rum. **Left (bottom)**: Bothy life in Glen Feshie in the Cairngorms. **Right (top)**: Wild camping, Knoydart. **Right (bottom)**: Wild camping on a ridge above Loch Nevis, Knoydart. Beinn Bhuidhe is to the left in the background.
● **C8 (Opposite p305)**: Old Man of Storr (see pp271-2), Trotternish, Isle of Skye.

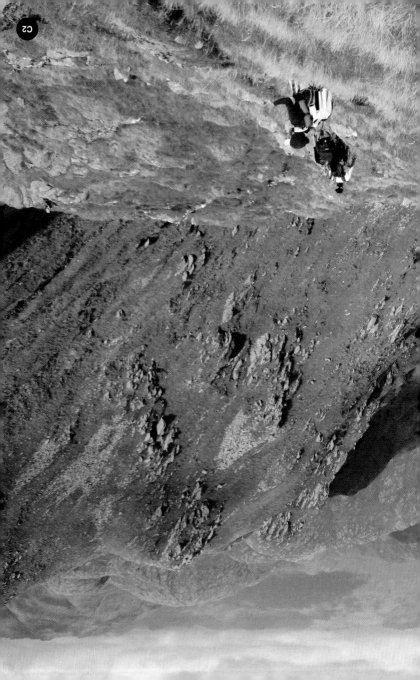

Rain, snow and ice Just as the wind gets stronger with altitude and the temperature decreases so levels of precipitation increase. At 900m there is about twice as much **rainfall** annually as there is at sea level. This is down to the cooling of moist air as it is forced over high ground, leading to condensation and eventually the formation of raindrops that can no longer be suspended in the air. Rainfall is only a problem if the clothing you have is not up to the job of repelling it: a wet hillwalker first becomes an unhappy one and potentially a hypothermic and dead one.

Snowfall occurs as the temperature approaches or drops below freezing point. It is unlikely to be a problem in summer although it can fall at any time of year and is not at all uncommon in spring and autumn. When the ground temperature reaches freezing point, **ice** begins to form and any snow falling begins to settle. In such conditions it is only wise to proceed if you are familiar with winter-walking (see box p20).

Snow that is already on the ground from winter snowfall can and does last on high ground well into May and June with some semi-permanent patches often not melting at all some years, particularly in the Cairngorms. They are most common in northern corries sheltered from the sun. Try to avoid large snow patches if you are not used to walking on them but if they are unavoidable kick steps in (by swinging your toe firmly at the snow to create a firm platform for your foot), if someone has not already done so, and proceed steadily. Cornices (drifts of snow overhanging cliff edges and ridges) also have a long lifespan. Never step on a cornice. They are usually suspended over thin air and are very unstable.

Sun and heat Always apply high-factor suncream (eg Factor 25 or above) to exposed skin when walking in the summer. The sun's rays are surprisingly strong in the mountains and many people are not used to the long exposure to them that comes with a full day on the hill. **Sunburn** even occurs on cloudy days and if there is snow on the ground 99% of the sun's rays are reflected straight back from the surface directly onto vulnerable areas such as bare arms, legs, lips, ears and chins.

As a rule of thumb the **temperature** drops at a rate of 1°C for every 100-150m of altitude. For the Scottish mountains this means a temperature drop of around 6-10°C from sea level to the tops of the higher mountains.

Lightning The frequency of thunderstorms in the Highlands appears to be increasing, perhaps as a result of changing climate patterns. While incidents are still very rare, fatalities do occur.

The best way to avoid a hit is to read the weather and act accordingly. The build up of towering anvil-headed cumulonimbus shower clouds are an obvious sign of a potential thunderstorm. And if you see some distant flashes and hear a rumbling of thunder keep well away from summits and ridges, which receive most direct strikes. Never shelter beneath trees, in caves or below cliffs, all of which act as channels for electrical currents. If a thunderstorm appears to be building the only course of action that should be countenanced is to descend at the next safest opportunity.

Walkers who have been struck by lightning, and survived, report a tingling sensation prior to the strike. Should you start to get that prickling on the nape of your neck get as close to the ground as possible. It is best to kneel with your head between your knees.

Mountain weather While all the above is relevant it is important to remember that local conditions can vary wildly. I have, on more than one occasion, spent a whole day high on a hill in persistent cold drizzle only to find that a friend was basking in warm sunshine on the neighbouring peak. Somehow it never seems to work the other way round. Mountain weather is fickle and often ignores what the forecasters say it should be doing. By all means check the weather forecast the night before but it is often best to wait until the morning and see for yourself which mountains appear to be enjoying the best weather before deciding where to go.

Equipment

Effective pieces of equipment are the ingredients for enjoying a safe day on the hill. The essentials are strong boots, clothing that can cope with the worst the weather can serve up, a comfortable rucksack or day pack, and a water bottle or pouch. There is a huge market for outdoor clothing and boots. So much so that manufacturers have gone to great lengths in researching and developing the best materials for walkers' needs. Unfortunately a lot of outdoor clothing is expensive but don't be tempted to take short-cuts. While it is not necessary to buy the most expensive jacket or boots, it is important to buy the right equipment that will last and will keep you safe in a potentially hostile environment.

The most important consideration when browsing for clothing is to ensure you have all the correct layers: a base layer that wicks moisture away from the body, a mid-layer that traps heat effectively and an outer layer that is waterproof, windproof and breathable (enabling moisture to escape easily). The big no-no is denim jeans which trap moisture, stick to the skin and are very slow to dry out. For more detailed advice on clothing and other equipment see pp24-6.

Hill food and water

Choosing the right type and quantity of food and drinking enough water are both essential for getting the most out of a day. Doing so not only maintains your energy level and keeps morale high but also helps minimise the risk of exhaustion and other ailments such as hypothermia and fatigue which can lead to clumsiness and accidents. The body burns up a lot of calories when walking up mountains so these need replenishing. As a rule, men need between 2500 and 3000 calories per day and women 2000 to 2500 calories, depending on how strenuous the walk is.

Eat a good breakfast: porridge or muesli is a good choice but in a B&B you'll probably be offered a traditional Scottish fry-up. Take plenty of high-energy food for lunch – maybe some peanut butter or tuna sandwiches, bananas, nuts, raisins and chocolate – and for dinner treat yourself to a good meal with lots of carbohydrates, preferably pasta, rice or potato based. If you are staying in a village there can be no better way of rounding off a hill day than treating yourself to a good meal and a pint in the local pub.

Walkers also lose a lot of water through sweating so drink regularly. On average the body will need around two to four litres during the course of a hill day. On particularly warm, sunny days this amount may need doubling. Mountain streams are generally safe to drink from and the majority of walkers happily do so but it is important to use a little common sense when choosing a drinking spot. Choose tributaries rather than main rivers and avoid any water source that is downstream from buildings or farmland. The nearer to the source you are, the less probability there is of there being a sheep carcass upstream.

If you are not happy about drinking directly from streams (there is a very small risk of contracting giardia or finding something smelly and organic in the water after having drunk from it), make sure you fill up your bottle or pouch with tap water at the start of the day or use water purification tablets or a couple of drops of iodine.

Blisters and other foot problems

Blisters occur with excessive friction on vulnerable spots like the heel and the ball of the foot. The chance of a blister developing is even higher with wet feet. Prevention is definitely better than cure when it comes to blisters. Make sure your boots fit well and that there is not too much slippage. Orthotic insoles such as Superfeet are a worthy investment that help stabilise the foot. They also improve overall posture and therefore minimise stress on knees and other joints.

If you feel a blister may be developing, don't ignore it hoping it will go away. Apply a dressing before it gets nasty and becomes too painful to walk on. Blister kits such as

Compeed, Second Skin and Moleskin are excellent at protecting tender spots from further abrasion. If a blister does develop try to avoid popping or tearing it. However, if this hap-pens, apply antiseptic cream to prevent infection and apply a dressing.

Boots must be waterproof. Use a boot wax or spray regularly on leather boots. It is best to 'break in' new boots by wearing them round the house before tramping off into the sticks.

Hypothermia

Hypothermia is the cooling of the core body temperature due to exposure to the elements. It is a potentially lethal condition but is totally avoidable. The wind, cold and rain are all elements that can lead to a case of hypothermia but their potential to cool the body's core (where all the vital organs such as heart, lungs and brain are located) can be minimised by preparing for them.

Make sure the clothing you have insulates well, is breathable, effective in repelling water and windproof. And remember that it is just as important to take layers off to avoid sweating too much (which can lead to cooling of the body) as it is to keep layers on when it is cold. Other factors that can increase the chances of hypothermia include exhaustion and dehydration. Combat these by eating plenty of high-energy food and drinking regularly throughout the day and ensuring you are fit enough for the planned walk. Spending some time training before a trip is very wise.

The early signs of hypothermia to look out for in yourself or a companion include occasional shivering (and complaining of) feeling cold. If nothing is done about this the condition can worsen. A person can be considered hypothermic once the shivering becomes uncontrollable.

Other obvious signs that may or may not be present in an individual with hypothermia include irrational behaviour, slurring of speech, irritability, clumsiness in walking and refusing to accept that anything is wrong. If you are alone it is essential to be aware of the early signs and to act accordingly since it becomes much harder to think straight and be rational once the condition progresses.

Anyone can and must treat an individual if they appear to have hypothermia. Find the nearest shelter or use a bivvy bag and make sure there is some insulation from the ground (a rucksack for example). Replace a patient's wet clothes with dry ones and give him or her food and a hot drink. Stay close to the patient to provide additional shelter and warmth and talk constantly in comforting and encouraging tones. It may take some time for the patient to recover a sense of normality so it is also important to make sure you and anyone else in the group are warm and dry.

When you are sure that it is safe to continue, descend immediately by the quickest and safest route. If it becomes obvious that to continue would be too dangerous you may need to send someone to summon help. The best way of avoiding hypothermia is to not allow it to reach such a stage.

River crossings

Bridges make river crossings quite easy in Scotland and there are a lot of them so having to truly cross a river is quite rare and when it does become unavoidable the rivers or streams in question are often no more than ankle deep. However, in very wet weather what appeared to be a benign babbling brook one day can transform to an almost Himalayan torrent of powerful gushing water. If a stream or river is in spate it may be impossible to cross so be prepared to change plans.

There are a few renowned spots in the Highlands where the crossing of deep, wide rivers is unavoidable, notably on the Fisherfield Trek at the Abhainn Strath na Sealga. The best technique for crossing such a river is to face upstream and cross with the aid of a strong stick or trekking pole which increases stability. Do not cross bare-footed since your boots will help grip on slippery rocks. Move steadily across the river, ensuring that every time you place a foot down you have a firm hold. When there is more than one person cross in

Mountain rescue

The Mountain Rescue Council of Scotland (🖳 www.mrcofs.org) represents all Scotland's mountain rescue, and search and rescue teams. In the Highlands there are mountain rescue teams in Arran, Arrochar, Assynt, Braemar, Cairngorm, Dundonell, Glen Coe, Glenelg, Glenmore Lodge, Grampian (police), Killin, Kintail, Lochaber, Lomond, Oban, Skye, Strathclyde, Tayside, Torridon, RAF Leuchars and RAF Kinloss. In the case of an emergency contact the police on ☎ 999 who will alert the nearest one.

groups of two or three. With two people the partner stands behind the person holding the stick and holds on, moving in time with their partner. Three people can cross in a huddle with arms around each others' backs. Once across, have a break, put on some dry socks and off you go.

Dealing with an accident

- Use first aid to deal with any injuries but do not overstep your own knowledge or ability.
- Work out your position and make a note of the grid reference on the map.
- Try to attract attention by blowing a whistle, or flashing a headtorch if it's dark (six blasts or flashes repeated after a minute is the international distress call).
- In a group, leave at least one person with the casualty while others go for help.
- If there are only two of you, you must decide if it is safe to leave the casualty alone.
- If you decide to go, leave some spare warm clothing and food with the patient and remember to keep a note of the grid reference.
- Call ☎ 999 and ask for the police or mountain rescue (see box above). Tell them the exact location of the casualty and what has occurred.

Bothersome bugs

The main bugs are midges and ticks (see box p26). Other bugs that are less common but worthy of mention include horseflies, or clegs as they are known locally: bee-sized flies that have a knack of landing unnoticed on bare skin and come armed with a hyperdermic-like sting. Finally there are keds or flat flies: intensely ugly, prehistoric-looking insects with a peculiar sideways crawling motion. They are not dangerous but do make you go 'urgh'.

APPENDIX B: GAELIC

The following words are all commonly found in Scottish mountain and place names:

Gaelic	Meaning	Gaelic	Meaning
Abhainn	river	Cruach	stack
Acarsaid	anchorage	Cumain	bucket
Achadh/achaidh	field	Dearg	red
Adhar/adhair	sky	Diallaid	saddle
Aite/àiteachan	place/places	Dorcha	dark
Alba	Scotland	Dorus	door
Albannach/ albannaich	Scot	Drochaid	bridge
Allt/uillt	stream	Druim	back/ridge
Ard/àird	height or promontory	Dubh	black
Bagh/bàigh	bay	Duinne	brown
Baile	town	Each	horse
Bàn	white	Eaglais	church
Bàthach	byre	Earb	roe deer
Beag	small	Eilean	island
Bealach	col/mountain pass	Eòin	bird
Beinn/beinne/bheinn	mountain	Fada	long
Bidean	pinnacle	Fasgadh	shelter
Bó/bà	cow	Feòla	flesh
Bodach/bodaich	old man	Feur	grass
Bruthach	slope	Fiacaill	tooth
Buidhe/Bhuidhe	yellow	Fiadh	deer
Cailleach	old woman	Fitich	raven
Caisteal	castle	Fraoch	heather
Cala	harbour	Fuar	cold
Calman/calmain	dove	Gaidheal	Highlander
Caol	narrows/strait	Gaidhealtach	Highlands
Caora	sheep	Gaoth	wind
Carn	cairn or hill	Geal	white
Cas	steep	Glas	grey
Cath	battle	Gleann	glen/valley
Cathair	chair	Gorm	blue
Ceann	end/at the head of (often anglicised) (to kin)	Innis	meadow
Cearc	hen	Iolair	eagle
Ceum	step	Lach	duck
Ciobair	shepherd	Leathann	broad
Ciste	chest	Liath	grey
Clach/clachan	stone	Linne	pool
Cnap	lump/knob	Loch	lake
Cnoc	hill	Lochan	small lake
Coille	wood/forest	Machair	field
Coire/coireachan	corry/corries (cirque)	Mam	hill or a pass
Craobh	tree	Meall	hill
Creag	rock	Monadh	moor
		Mor/Mhor	big
		Mullach	top
		Neul	cloud
		Nid	nest

Oigh	maiden	*Sròn*	nose
Or	gold	*Stac*	peak
Poca	sack	*Stob*	peak
Ràmh	oar	*Tigh/taigh*	house
Rathad	road	*Tioram*	dry
Ruadh	red	*Toll*	hole
Sail	heel	*Tom*	hillock
Sgor/sgorr/sgurr	peak	*Tràigh*	beach
Sionnach	fox	*Uaine*	green
Slat	rod	*Uamh*	cave
Sneachda	snow	*Uiseag*	lark
Spidean	pinnacle	*Uisge*	water

APPENDIX C: GLOSSARY

Arête – narrow ridge formed by abrasion on each side by glaciers

Bivvy – to sleep outdoors under the stars usually using a waterproof bivvy bag

Blackhouse – a traditional croft

Bothy – simple, unlocked shelter providing refuge in remote areas of the Highlands

Broch – Iron Age stone tower, probably a defensive dwelling

Cairn – man-made pile of stones often used to mark summits and the routes of paths

Col – pass

Coire – bowl-shaped corrie or cirque formed by glacial scouring

Corrie or corry – anglicised spelling of coire

Drumlins – ridges of sediment deposited and shaped by glaciers

Geo – a steep-sided chimney-like inlet on the coast, caused by erosion from wave action

Glen – valley

Gneiss – a metamorphic rock, probably originating from granite, but altered by intense heat and pressure

Howf – a Scots term for a bivvy site, ie: a natural shelter like a cave

Inselberg – an 'island peak' formed when ice sheets scoured away the surrounding rock

Munro – a Scottish peak of 3000 feet (914m) or higher

Munro-bagging – the activity of climbing all 284 munros (see box p9)

Neve – rock hard snow that is impossible to walk on without crampons

Plateau – a flat area of high ground

Pyramidal peak – a sharply pointed summit formed by glacial abrasion on all sides

Ridge – a spine of the mountain that usually leads to or between peaks

Saddle – a wide col or bealach (col/mountain pass)

Scree – slopes of shattered stone and rock, often loose and unstable

Skerry – small rocky island often submerged at high tide

Trig point – pillar owned by Ordnance Survey, once used for mapping the land

U-shaped valley – a valley carved into a U shape by long glaciers

APPENDIX D: MOUNTAIN PHOTOGRAPHY

The art of mountain photography is in the ability to capture, in a two-dimensional image, the essence of these wild places; quite a challenge when one considers that mountains are not just a visual treat but a stimulus to all our senses. The trick then is to use the visual element to convey the sounds, scents and overall mood.

Light is a key consideration in this. The best time to photograph mountains is at dawn and dusk when the sun is low in the sky, casting shadows that capture the true topography of the land. For the same reason, the autumn and spring often throw up some beautifully subtle light.

Digital SLR cameras are steadily taking over from film SLR cameras as the most popular tools for landscape photography. Whichever format you choose there are a few ideas to bear in mind. Take lots of shots. Try different angles, different compositions and use bracketing (trying different exposures for the same subject).

Anyone who takes landscape photography seriously will use a tripod. These are essential for holding the camera steady in low-light conditions when a slow shutter speed is needed. Using a slow shutter speed also helps bring out the natural colours in a photograph.

Composing a picture is down to personal taste. Most photographers agree that the rule of thirds, having a background, middle and foreground, works best. Having something in the foreground, a rock or stream for example, complements the mountains in the background, while natural lines leading to a focal point also work well.

But sticking to rules is the way to stem creativity. There is nothing wrong with filling the frame with sky, if the sky is an interesting one, or shooting into the sun, to capture a dramatic silhouette, while shooting in the rain and cloud can capture that dark, brooding atmosphere.

The key is not to scrimp on film or memory cards. The more photographs one takes the better the chances of catching that one cracking image that ends up in a frame on the mantelpiece.

INDEX

Map references are in bold type.

A' Chailleach 138
A' Mhaighdean **202**, 222,
  225, 226-7
Abernethy Forest 169
access 15, 40-1
accidents 308
accommodation 10-13, 62
Acharacle **175**, 198
Achmelvich 251, 252
Ainshval 260, **261**, **263**,
  264-5
altimeters 27
Alltnafeadh **90**, **92**
Am Bodach 93, **94**
Am Bàtaich **195**, 196
An Stùc 120
Annat **214**, 232-3
An Taobh Tuath (Harris)
  276, **277**, 292
An Teallach **202**, 227, **229**,
  230, 301
An t-Ob (Harris) 292
annual events 22
Aonach Beag **108**, 297
Aonach Eagach ridge (nr
  Bridge of Orchy) **79**, **80**
Aonach Eagach (nr Glen
  Coe) **90**, 93, **94**, 95, 97
Aonach Mòr **108**, 298
Aonach Sgùlaic **191**, 193
Ardgarten 66, **67**
Ardhasaig (Harris) 278,
  279, 294
Ardlui 63, **71**, 86
Ardnamurchan Natural
  History Centre 197
Ardnamurchan Point and
  Lighthouse 197
Arkle **235**, 243, **244**, 245
Armadale **261**
Arnisdale **175**, 201, **202**,
  205
Arran 255-8, **255**, 283-4
Arrochar **63**, **67**, 84-5, **85**
Askival 260, **261**, **263**,
  264-5
Aviemore 22, **142**, 173-4,
  173

Ballachulish **90**, **102**, 113
Ballachulish Horseshoe **90**,
  100-1, **102**, 103
banks 16
Baosbheinn 222
Barisdale **175**, 189, **191**,
  193, 201, 300
beaches 197, 251, 252, 292
beavers 52
bed and breakfasts (B&Bs)
  12, 62
beers 14-15
Beinn a' Bheithir 100-1,
  102, 103
Beinn a' Bhuird 168
Beinn a' Chreachain 77
Beinn a' Ghlo 138
Beinn Achaladair 77
Beinn Alligin **202**, 215-17,
  216
Beinn an Dothaidh **63**,
  74-6, **75**
Beinn an Eòin **202**, 220,
  221, 222
Beinn Bheòil **117**, 127-8,
  128
Beinn Bhuidhe **175**, **185**,
  187, 188-9
Beinn Damh **202**, 213,
  214, 215
Beinn Dorain **63**, 74-6, **75**
Beinn Eighe **202**, 217,
  218, 219
Beinn Fhionnlaidh 213
Beinn Garbh 182, **184**, 184
Beinn Ghlas **117**, 118, **119**,
  120
Beinn Mhor **261**, 273-6,
  275
Beinn nan Caorach 204
Beinn Resipol **175**, 176,
  177
Beinn Sgritheall **202**,
  203-4, **205**
Beinn Talaidh **258**, 258,
  259, 260

Beinn-na-h-Eaglaise 204
Ben Alder **117**, 127-8, **128**
Ben Cordale **261**, 273-6,
  275
Ben Cruachan 81
Ben Hope **235**, 245-6, **246**
Ben Lawers **117**, 118, **119**,
  120
Ben Lèdi **63**, **64**, 65
Ben Lomond **63**, 68, **69**,
  70
Ben Loyal **235**, 246, **247**,
  248
Ben Lui 81
Ben Macdui **142**, 151-3,
  156, 157
Ben Mòr Coigach 249
Ben More **63**, **72**, **73**, 74
Ben More Assynt 249
Ben Nevis **90**, 106, **107**,
  108, 109-10, 298
Ben Nevis distillery 112
Ben Nevis observatory
  107, 109, 110
Ben Stack **235**, 242-3, **242**
Ben Starav 110
Ben Vorlich **63**, **70**, **71**, 72
Ben Vrackie **142**, **143**, 144,
  145
bibliography 29-30
Bidean a' Ghlas Thuill
  227, **229**, 230
Bidean nam Bian **90**, **97**,
  98, **99**, 100
Big Grey Man of Macdui
  157
birds 53-7
bivvy gear 27, 28
bivvying 10-11
Bla Bheinn **261**, 265, **266**,
  267
blisters 306
boots 24
bothies 11-12
bothy code 11
Braemar 22, **142**, 172, **172**
Braeriach **142**, 158, **160**,
  161, 163-4

Bridge of Dee 147, **149**
Bridge of Orchy **63**, **75**, **78**, 89
Broad Cairn 151
Broadford (Skye) **261**, 287-8, **288**
Brodick (Arran) 255, **255**, **257**, 283-4, **283**
Buachaille Etive Mor **90**, 90-1, **92**, 93
bugs 308
Bunavoneader 278, **279**, 280
bunkhouses 12
bus services 35, 36
Bynack More 168

Cairn Bannoch 151
Cairn Gorm **142**, 164-5, **165**
Cairn Lochan 165
Cairn Toul **142**, 158, 161, **162**, 163, 164
Cairngorm Mountain Railway 38, 169
Cairngorm Reindeer Centre 169
Cairngorm Sled-dog Centre 169
Cairngorms National Park 44
Cairngorms region **142**, 142-75, 298-300
cairns 62, 93
Caisteal Leath 237-9, **239**
Caledonian Forest 58, 148, 158
Callander **63**, 81, **82**, 83
Callanish standing stones 294
camping 10
camping gear 28
Camusnagaul 234
Carn a' Choire Bhoidheach **142**, 147-8, **150**, 151
Carn a' Mhaim **142**, 151-3, **155**, 157, 299
Carn an Tionail 248
Carn an t-Sagairt Mor **150**, 151

Carn Dearg (nr Ben Nevis) **107**
Carn Dearg (Central Highlands) **117**, 122, **125**, 126
Carn Eige **202**, 209, **210**, 212-13
Carn Liath 132
Carn Mor Dearg **90**, 106, **107**, **108**, 109-10, 298
Carnmore **224**, 226, 302
Ceapabhal **261**, 276, **277**, 278
Central Highlands region 117-41, **117**
Chancellor, The **94**, 95
Clach Toll 251
Clachaig Gully 95, **96**
climbing definition 116
Clisham **261**, 278, **279**, 280-1
clothes 25-6
Clova 171-2
coach services 34, 35, 36
Cobbler, The **63**, 65-6, **67**
Coire Gabhail 97, **98**, 99, 100
Conival 249
conservation organisations 45
corbetts 9, 204
Corran **175**, 204, **205**
Corrie Hallie **228**, 302
Corriechoille 136, 298
Corrour **90**, 117, **134**, 141, 295
Corrour Bothy 162, **163**, 164, 299
Corryhully Horseshoe 182, **183**, **184**, 185
Coylumbridge **142**, 158, **159**
Craiggowrie 166, **168**
Craignure (Mull) 286-7, **286**
Creag Dhubh **117**, 129-30, **129**
Creag Meagaidh **117**, 130, **131**, 132
Creagan Ghorm 166, **167**
Crianlarich **63**, 87-8, **87**

Cruachan Power Station 84
Culra 122, **125**, 126

Dalwhinnie **117**, 122, **123**, 140, **140**, **142**
daylight hours 21
deer-stalking 23
Derry Cairngorm **142**, 151-33, **156**, 157
Devil's Point **142**, 158, 161, **162**, 163, 164
Dibidil 264, 287
distilleries 14, 112, 138, 169, 286
Driesh **142**, 145, **146**, 147
drinks 14-15
Dundonnell **202**, **228**, 234
Durness **235**, 253-4, **253**

Eas a' Chual Aluinn waterfall 251
Eastern Highlands region 142-75, **142**
economic impact 42-3
Eilean Donan Castle 230
emergencies 307
emergency services 17
emergency signals 27
environmental impact 38-42
equipment 24-8, 306
erosion 39
estates 23

Falls of Dee **160**, 163
Falls of Dochart 138
Falls of Glomach 230
Faochag **207**, 208
Far North region 235-54, **235**
ferry services 33, 36
festivals 22
first-aid kit 27
Fisherfield **202**, 222, 301-2
Five Sisters of Kintail 231
flies 308
flights to Scotland 31
flora and fauna 51-9
flora and fauna guides 30
flowers 58-9
Foinhaven 249

food 13-15, 42-3, 306
foot care 306
Footpath Trust 39
footwear 24-5
Forcan Ridge 206, **207**, 208-9
forests 58
Fort William 22, **90**, 114-16, **115**, **175**

Gaelic 50, 309-10
Gairloch **202**, 234
Garbh Bheinn 196
Garbh Choire **160**, 299
Garenin 294
Geal Charn **117**, 122, **125**, 126
geography 46-7
geology 47-8
Glamaig **261**, 269-71, **270**
Glen Clova 145, **146**, 147
Glen Coe & Glen Nevis region 89-116, **90**
Glen Coe **90**, **94**, 95, **96**, **98**, 111
  see also Glencoe Village
Glen Coe massacre 99, 112
Glen Croe 66, **67**
Glen Doll 145, **146**, 147
Glen Nevis **107**, 113-14
Glen Nevis waterfalls 112
Glen Shiel 208, 231-2
Glen Shiel to Torridon & Fisherfield region **202**, 203-34
Glencoe Village **90**, **96**, 111
Glenelg **202**, 231
Glenfinnan **175**, 178, **179**, 182, **183**, 198
Glenmore **142**, **167**, 174-5
Glenmore Lodge National Outdoor Training Centre **167**, 175
glossary 310
Goatfell **255**, 255-6, **257**, 258
Great Traverse 295-8
Grey Corries ridge 295, 296
guesthouses 12

guidebooks 29
guides 19

Harris **261**, 276-81, 292-4
Hecla **261**, 273-6, **275**
Highland clearances 44, 49, 50
Highland Games 22
hillphones scheme 23
history 48-50
Horns of Alligin **216**, 217
horseflies 308
hostels 12
hotels 12
Howmore (South Uist) **261**, **274**, 292
hypothermia 307

Ice Factor, Kinlochleven 112
inns 13
insurance 17
international distress signal 27
Inverarnan **63**, 86-7
Inverbeg **63**, **69**, 86
Inverie **175**, 185, **186**, 200, 301
Inveroran 77, **78**
Inversnaid 70
Islands region, The 255-94, **255**, **258**, **261**

John Muir Trust 23, 39, 45, 120
  see also Muir, John

Kernsary 222, **223**
Killin **63**, **117**, 138-9, **139**
Kilmahog **82**, 83
Kilt Rock (Skye) 291
Kingshouse **90**, 110
Kinloch (Rum) **261**, **262**, 287
Kinlochewe **202**, 219, 233, **233**
Kinlochhourn **175**, 189, **190**, 201, 300
Kinlochleven **90**, 112
Knoydart **175**, **186**, 300-1
Kyle of Lochalsh **202**

Kylerhea **202**
Kylesku **235**, 253
Ladhar Bheinn **175**, 189, **191**, 193-4, 300
Laggan 140, **117**
Lairig Ghru **160**, 161, 164, 298-9
Lairig Leacach 133, **135**, 136, 295
Lairigmor 106
languages 50
Leverburgh (Harris) **261**, 292
Lewis **261**, 281, **282**, 294
Liathach 231
lichens 59
Linn of Dee **142**, 152, **154**, 157
litter 38-9
Little Hills **71**, 72
Loch Garten Osprey Centre 169
Loch Lomond **69**, **71**
Loch Lomond and the Southern Highlands region 63-89, **63**
Loch Lomond and the Trossachs National Park 44
Loch Long 66, **67**, **71**, 84, **85**
Loch Muick 151
Loch Ossian **134**, 141
Loch Torridon **214**, 230
Lochboisdale **261**
Lochinver **235**, **238**, 252, **252**
Lochnagar **142**, 147-8, **150**, 151
Lost Valley 97, **98**, 99, 100
Luibeg 300

Mad Meg's cairn **131**, 132
Mallaig **175**, 198-9, **199**, 298
Mam Barisdale pass 300
Mam Bhasiter **187**, 189
Mam Meadaill **187**, 189
Mam Sodhail **202**, 209, **210**, 212
Mam Uchd **187**, 188

mammals 51-3
map keys 60
map scales 62
maps 28-9
Mayar **142**, 145, **146**, 147
Meall a' Bhuachaille **142**, 166, **167**, 168
Meall Dearg 9, 93, **94**, 95, 97
Meall Garbh 120
Meall Greigh 120
midges 26
minimum impact walking 37-43
mobile phones 17
money 15
Moulin 143, **144**, 171
mountain-bike trails 138
mountain guides 19
mountain rescue 308
mountain safety 303-8
Muir, John 8, 10, 18
Mull **258**, 258-60, 286-7
Mulla-fo-Dheas **279**, 280
Mullach nan Coirean **90**, 103-4, **105**, 106
munros 9, 39
munro-bagging 9
music 22

Narnain Boulders 66, **67**
national parks 44-5
National Trust for Scotland 23, 45
nature reserves 43, 56
North Uist **261**
Northton (Harris) 276, **277**, 292

Oban 284-6, **285**
Old Man of Storr 271, **272**
ospreys 57, 138, 169
Outdoor Access Code 15, 40-1

photography 311
Pitlochry **117**, **142**, **144**, 169-71, **170**
plants 58-9
Polldubh 103, 104, **105**

Poolewe **202**, 222, **223**, 233-4
Portree (Skye) **261**, 289-90, **289**
post offices 16
Prince's Stone, The **149**, 151
Ptarmigan ridge 68, **69**
public transport 31-5, **32-3**
pubs 13, 16
postbus services 35, 36

Quinaig **235**, 240-1, **241**

rail services 31, 34, 35
rainfall 20, 21
Rannoch Moor 90, **90**, **117**
real ales 14-15
Resipole 176, **177**
Ring of Steall 110
river crossings 307
Rois Bheinn 196
Rothiemurchus Forest 158, **159**, 169, 299
route maps 61-2
Rowardennan **63**, **69**, 86
Roybridge 141, **141**
Ruadh-Stac Mor (Torridon) 217, **218**, 219
Ruadh Stac Mor (Fisherfield) **202**, 222, **225**, 226-7
rucksacks 24
Rum **261**, 260-5, 287

Saddle, The **202**, 206, **207**, 208-9
Sail Garbh 240-1, **241**
Sail Gorm 240-1, **241**
Salen **175**, 198
Sandwood Bay 251
Schiehallion **117**, 120-1, **121**
Sconser **270**, 288-9
Scottish Natural Heritage 23, 43-4, 45
Scottish Outdoor Access Code 15, 40-1
Scourie **235**, 253

Sgor an Lochain Uaine **142**, 158, **162**, 163, 164
Sgor Gaoith 168
Sgor Iutharn **117**, 122, **125**, 126
Sgorr an Iubhair 106
Sgorr Craobh a' Chaorainn **175**, 178, **180**, 181
Sgorr Dhearg 100-1, **102**, 103
Sgorr Dhonuill 100-1, **102**, 103
Sgorr nam Fiannaidh 93, **94**, 95, **96**, 97
Sgurr a' Bhuic **108**
Sgurr a' Mhaim 110
Sgurr a' Mhaoraich **175**, 194, **195**, 196
Sgurr Alasdair 272
Sgurr Choinnich Beag **108**, 297
Sgurr Choinnich Mor **137**, 297
Sgurr Coire Choinneachan 194
Sgurr Coire nan Eiricheallach 194, **195**
Sgurr Coire nan Gobhar **186**, **187**, 188
Sgurr Fhuaran 231
Sgurr Fiona 227, **229**, 230
Sgurr Ghiubhsachain **175**, 178, **180**, 181
Sgurr Mhor **216**, 215-17
Sgurr na Ciche 196
Sgurr na Lapaich **202**, 209, **210**, **211**, 212-13
Sgurr na Sgine **202**, 206, **207**, 208-9
Sgurr nan Coireachan **175**, 182, **184**, 184-5
Sgurr nan Gillean (Rum) **263**, 264
Sgurr nan Gillean (Skye) **261**, 267, **268**, 269
Sgurr Thuilm **175**, 182, **184**, 184-5
shelter cairns 62
Shenavall **229**, 302
Shiel Bridge **202**, 232

Sites of Special Scientific Interest (SSSIs) 43-4
Skye, Isle of 22, 261, 265-72, 287-91
sleeping bags 27-8
Sligachan (Skye) 261, 268, 270, 288-9
Slioch 231
Smoo Cave 251, 253
solo walking 18
South Uist 261, 273-6, 292
Southern Highlands region 63
Spidean Coinich 240-1, 241
Spidean Coire nan Clach 217, 218, 219
Sron a' Choire 131, 132
Stac Pollaidh 235, 236-7, 237
Stank Glen 64
Stob a' Chearcaill 191, 193
Stob a' Choire Mheadhoin 117, 132-3, 135, 136
Stob a' Choire Odhair (Knoydart) 191, 193
Stob a' Choire Odhair (Southern Highlands) 63, 77, 79, 80, 81
Stob Ban (Central Highlands) 137
Stob Ban (Glen Nevis) 90, 103-4, 105, 106, 296
Stob Binnein 63, 72, 73, 74
Stob Choire Claurigh 137, 296
Stob Coire an Laoigh 137, 296
Stob Coire Easain (Central Highlands) 117, 132-3, 134-5, 136, 296-7
Stob Coire Easain (ridge) 137
Stob Coire na Altruim 91, 92
Stob Coire nam Beith 98, 100
Stob Coire nan Lochan 90, 97, 98, 99, 100
Stob Coire Sgreamhach 90, 97, 98, 99, 100

Stob Dearg 90-1, 92, 93
Stob Ghabhar 63, 77, 79, 80, 81
Stob na Broige 90-1, 92, 93
Stob na Doire 91, 92
Stob Poite Coire Ardair 132
Stornoway 261
Storr, The 261, 271-2, 272
Strontian 175, 197-8, 198
Suainebhal 261, 281, 282
Suilven 235, 237-9, 239
Sunart to Knoydart region 175-201, 175
Taladale 202
Tarbert (Harris) 261, 293-4, 293
telephones 17
temperature 20, 21
ticks 26
Timsgarry (Lewis) 261, 294
Timsgearraidh (Lewis) 294
Tobha Mor (South Uist) 261, 274, 292
Toll Creagach 213
Tom a' Choinich 211, 213
Tom na Gruagaich 215-17, 216
Tomdoun 175, 201
Tomich 202, 332
Tomsleibhe 258, 259
Tongue 235, 254, 254
Torridon 202, 232-3, 233
Torrin (Skye) 261, 288
tourist information 31
town map key 60
trail map key 60
train services 31, 34, 35
Treasures of the Earth, Corpach 112
trees 57-8
trekking poles 27
Tulloch 90, 117, 141
Tyndrum 63, 88-9, 88
Uig (Skye) 261, 290-1, 291
Ullapool 235, 249-51, 250

Victoria Bridge 77, 78
walk grades 61
walkers' organisations 30
walking alone 18
walking companies 16-17
walking definition 116
walking magazines 30
walking times 62
water 305-6
water bottles 27
weather 18-21, 303-5
weather forecasts 21
West Highland Way 69, 70, 71, 77, 78
Western Isles 261
whale-watching 197
whistles 27
wild camping 10, 41-2
wilderness 44
wildlife 40, 56
wildlife hides and reserves 56
wind farms 280
Window, The 130, 131
winter hillwalking 20

TRAILBLAZER GUIDES – TITLE LIST

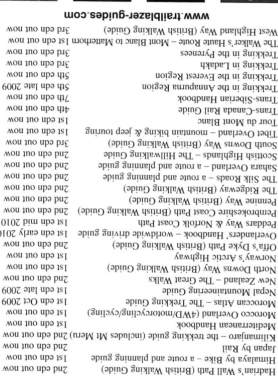

www.trailblazer-guides.com

Adventure Cycle-Touring Handbook	2nd end late 2009
Adventure Motorcycling Handbook	5th edn out now
Australia by Rail	5th edn out now
Azerbaijan	4th edn late 2009
China Rail Handbook	1st edn early 2010
Coast to Coast (British Walking Guide)	3rd edn out now
Cornwall Coast Path (British Walking Guide)	3rd edn out now
Corsica Trekking – GR20	1st edn out now
Cotswold Way (British Walking Guide)	1st edn out now
Dolomites Trekking – AV1 & AV2	2nd edn out now
Inca Trail, Cusco & Machu Picchu	4th edn out now
Indian Rail Handbook	1st edn late 2009
Hadrian's Wall Path (British Walking Guide)	2nd edn out now
Himalaya by Bike – a route and planning guide	1st edn out now
Japan by Rail	2nd edn out now
Kilimanjaro – the trekking guide (includes Mt Meru)	2nd edn out now
Mediterranean Handbook	1st edn out now
Morocco Overland (4WD/motorcycling/cycling)	1st edn out now
Moroccan Atlas – The Trekking Guide	1st edn Oct 2009
Nepal Mountaineering Guide	1st edn late 2009
New Zealand – The Great Walks	2nd edn out now
North Downs Way (British Walking Guide)	1st edn out now
Norway's Arctic Highway	1st edn out now
Offa's Dyke Path (British Walking Guide)	2nd edn out now
Overlanders' Handbook – worldwide driving guide	1st edn early 2010
Peddars Way & Norfolk Coast Path	1st edn mid 2010
Pembrokeshire Coast Path (British Walking Guide)	2nd edn out now
Pennine Way (British Walking Guide)	2nd edn out now
The Ridgeway (British Walking Guide)	2nd edn out now
The Silk Roads – a route and planning guide	1st edn out now
Sahara Overland – a route and planning guide	2nd edn out now
Scottish Highlands – The Hillwalking Guide	2nd edn out now
South Downs Way (British Walking Guide)	3rd edn out now
Tibet Overland – mountain biking & jeep touring	1st edn out now
Tour du Mont Blanc	1st edn out now
Trans-Canada Rail Guide	4th edn out now
Trans-Siberian Handbook	7th edn out now
Trekking in the Annapurna Region	5th edn late 2009
Trekking in the Everest Region	5th edn out now
Trekking in Ladakh	3rd edn out now
Trekking in the Pyrenees	3rd edn out now
The Walker's Haute Route – Mont Blanc to Matterhorn	1st edn out now
West Highland Way (British Walking Guide)	3rd edn out now

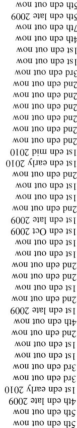

TREKKING GUIDES

Europe
Corsica Trekking – GR20
Dolomites Trekking – AV1 & AV2
Scottish Highlands – The Hillwalking Guide
Tour du Mont Blanc
Trekking in the Pyrenees
Walker's Haute Route: Mt Blanc to Matterhorn

South America
Inca Trail, Cusco & Machu Picchu

Africa
Kilimanjaro
Moroccan Atlas – The Trekking Guide

Australasia
New Zealand – The Great Walks

Asia
Trekking in the Annapurna Region
Trekking in the Everest Region
Trekking in Ladakh

Tour du Mont Blanc Jim Manthorpe
1st edition, 208pp, 60 maps, 30 colour photos
ISBN 978-1-905864-12-6, £11.99

At 4810m (15,781ft), Mont Blanc is the highest mountain in western Europe, and one of the most famous mountains in the world. The snow-dome summit is the top of a spectacular massif stretching 60 miles by 20 miles, arguably the most magnificent mountain scenery in Europe. The trail (105 miles, 168km) that circumnavigates the massif, passing through France, Italy and Switzerland, is the most popular long distance walk in Europe. Includes Chamonix and Courmayeur guides.

The Walker's Haute Route – Mt Blanc to the Matterhorn
Alexander Stewart, 1st edn, 256pp, 60 maps, 30 colour photos
ISBN 978-1-905864-08-9, £12.99

From Mont Blanc to the Matterhorn, Chamonix to Zermatt, the 180km (113-mile) walkers' Haute Route traverses one of the finest stretches of the Pennine Alps – the range between Valais in Switzerland and Piedmont and Aosta Valley in Italy. Includes Chamonix and Zermatt guides.

Corsica Trekking – GR20 David Abram
1st edition, 208pp, 32 maps, 30 colour photos
ISBN 978-1-873756-98-0, £11.99

Slicing diagonally across Corsica's jagged spine, the legendary red-and-white waymarks of the GR20 guide trekkers across a succession of snow-streaked passes, Alpine meadows, massive boulder fields and pristine forests of pine and oak – often within sight of the sea. Physically demanding from start to finish, it's a superlative 170km, two-week trek. Includes guides to gateway towns: Ajaccio, Bastia, Calvi, Corte and Porto-Vecchio.   *'Indispensible'. The Independent*
'Excellent guide'. The Sunday Times

New Zealand – The Great Walks Alexander Stewart
2nd edition, 272pp, 60 maps, 40 colour photos
ISBN 978-1-905864-11-9, £12.99

New Zealand is a wilderness paradise of incredibly beautiful land-scapes. There is no better way to experience it than on one of the nine designated Great Walks, the country's premier walking tracks which provide outstanding hiking opportunities for people at all levels of fitness. Also includes detailed guides to Auckland, Wellington, National Park Village, Taumarunui, Nelson, Queenstown, Te Anau and Oban.

Inca Trail, Cusco & Machu Picchu
Alexander Stewart, 4th edition, 352pp, 74 maps, 40 photos
ISBN 978-1-905864-15-7, £12.99

The **Inca Trail**, from Cusco to Machu Picchu, is South America's most popular trek. Practical guide including detailed trail maps, plans of Inca sites, plus guides to Cusco and Machu Picchu. Route guides to other trails in the area: the **Santa Teresa Trek** and the **Choquequirao Trek** as well as the **Vilcabamba Trail** plus the routes linking them. This entirely rewalked and rewritten fourth edition includes a new history of the Incas by Hugh Thomson.

Trekking in the Everest Region *Jamie McGuinness*
5th edition, 320pp, 30 maps, 30 colour photos
ISBN 978-1-873756-99-7, £12.99

Fifth edition of this popular guide to the Everest region, the world's most famous trekking region. Includes planning, preparation and getting to Nepal; detailed route guides – with 30 route maps and 50 village plans; Kathmandu city guide – where to stay, where to eat, what to see. Written by a professional trekking and mountaineering leader.

Trekking in the Annapurna Region *Bryn Thomas*
4th edition, 288pp, 55 maps, 28 colour photos
ISBN 978-1-873756-68-3, £11.99

Guide to the most popular walking region in the Himalaya. Includes route guides, Kathmandu and Pokhara city guides and getting to Nepal. *'Good guides read like a novel and have you packing in no time. Two from Trailblazer Publications which fall into this category are Trekking in the Annapurna Region and Silk Route by Rail'. Today*

Trekking in Ladakh *Charlie Loram*
3rd edition, 288pp, 72 maps, 24 colour photos
ISBN 978-1-873756-75-1, £12.99

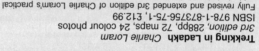

Fully revised and extended 3rd edition of Charlie Loram's practical guide. Includes 72 detailed walking maps, guides to Leh, Manali and Delhi plus information on getting to Ladakh. *'Extensive...and well researched'. Climber Magazine 'Were it not for this book we might still be blundering about...' The Independent on Sunday*

Dolomites Trekking Alta Via 1 & Alta Via 2 *Henry Stedman*
2nd edn, 192pp, 52 trail maps, 7 town plans, 38 colour photos
ISBN 978-1-873756-83-6, £11.99

AV1 (9-13 days) & AV2 (10-16 days) are the most popular long-distance hikes in the Dolomites. Numerous shorter walks also included. Places to stay, walking times and points of interest, plus detailed guides to Cortina and six other towns.

Kilimanjaro: the trekking guide to Africa's highest mountain
Henry Stedman, 2nd edition, 320pp, 40 maps, 30 photos
ISBN 978-1-873756-91-1, £11.99

At 19,341ft the world's tallest freestanding mountain, Kilimanjaro is one of the most popular destinations for hikers visiting Africa. It's possible to walk up to the summit: no technical skills are necessary. Includes town guides to Nairobi and Dar-Es-Salaam, excursions in the region and a detailed colour guide to flora and fauna. **Includes Mount Meru.** *'Stedman's wonderfully down-to-earth, practical guide to the mountain'. Longitude Books*

TRAILBLAZER'S LONG-DISTANCE PATH (LDP) WALKING GUIDES

We've applied to destinations which are closer to home Trailblazer's proven formula for publishing definitive practical route guides for adventurous travellers. Britain's network of long-distance trails enables the walker to explore some of the finest land-scapes in the country's best walking areas. These are guides that are user-friendly, practical, informative and environmentally sensitive.

● **Unique mapping features** In many walking guidebooks the reader has to read a route description then try to relate it to the map. Our guides are much easier to use because walking directions, tricky junctions, places to stay and eat, points of inter-est and walking times are all written onto the maps themselves in the places to which they apply. With their uncluttered clarity, these are not general-purpose maps but fully edited maps drawn by walkers for walkers.

● **Largest-scale walking maps** At a scale of just under 1:20,000 (8cm or 3¹/₈ inches to one mile) the maps in these guides are bigger than even the most detailed British walking maps currently available in the shops.

● **Not just a trail guide – includes where to stay, where to eat and public transport** Our guidebooks cover the complete walking experience, not just the route. Accommodation options for all budgets are provided (pubs, hotels, B&Bs, campsites, bunkhouses, hostels) as well as places to eat. Detailed public transport information for all access points to each trail means that there are itineraries for all walkers, for hiking the entire route as well as for day or weekend walks.

Coast to Coast *Henry Stedman* ISBN 978-1-905864-09-6, £9.99
3rd edition, 240pp, 109 maps & town plans, 40 colour photos

Cornwall Coast Path *Edith Schofield* ISBN 978-1-905864-19-5, £9.99
3rd edition, 256pp, 112 maps & town plans, 40 colour photos

Cotswold Way *Tricia & Bob Hayne* ISBN 978-1-905864-16-4, £9.99
1st edition, 192pp, 60 maps & town plans, 40 colour photos

Hadrian's Wall Path *Henry Stedman* ISBN 978-1-905864-14-0, £9.99
2nd edition, 208pp, 60 maps & town plans, 40 colour photos

Offa's Dyke Path *Keith Carter* ISBN 978-1-905864-06-5, £9.99
2nd edition, 208pp, 88 maps & town plans, 40 colour photos

North Downs Way *John Curtin* ISBN 978-1-873756-96-6, £9.99
1st edition, 192pp, 60 maps & town plans, 40 colour photos

Peddars Way & Norfolk Coast Path *Alexander Stewart* £9.99
1st edition, 192pp, 60 maps & town plans, 40 colour photos   **Due mid 2010**

Pembrokeshire Coast Path *Jim Manthorpe* ISBN 978-1-905864-03-4, £9.99
2nd edition, 208pp, 96 maps & town plans, 40 colour photos

Pennine Way *Keith Carter & Chris Scott* ISBN 978-1-905864-02-7, £11.99
2nd edition, 272pp, 135 maps & town plans, 40 colour photos

The Ridgeway *Nick Hill* ISBN 978-1-905864-17-1, £9.99
2nd edition, 192pp, 53 maps & town plans, 40 colour photos

South Downs Way *Jim Manthorpe* ISBN 978-1-905864-18-8, £9.99
3rd edition, 192pp, 60 maps & town plans, 40 colour photos

West Highland Way *Charlie Loram* ISBN 978-1-905864-13-3, £9.99
3rd edition, 192pp, 53 maps, 10 town plans, 40 colour photos

'*The same attention to detail that distinguishes its other guides has been brought to bear here*'. **The Sunday Times**

Sunart to Knoydart (see map p175)
Beinn Resipol 845m
Sgurr Ghiubhsachain 849m &
Sgurr Craoch a'Chaorainn 775m
Sgurr nan Coireachan 956m & Sgurr Thuilm 963m
(The Corryhully Horseshoe)
Beinn Bhuidhe (Knoydart) 855m
Ladhar Bheinn 1020m
Sgurr a'Mhaoraich 1027m

Glen Shiel to Torridon & Fisherfield (see map p202)
Beinn Sgritheall 974m
The Saddle 1010m & Sgurr na Sgine 946m
Sgurr na Lapaich 1036m, Mam Sodhail 1181m
& Carn Eige 1183m
Beinn Eighe 1010m
Beinn an Eoin 855m
A'Mhaighdean 967m & Ruadh Stac Mor 918m
An Teallach 1062m

The Far North (see map p235)
Stac Pollaidh 613m
Suilven 731m
Quinag 808m
Ben Stack 721m
Arkle 787m
Ben Hope 927m
Ben Loyal 764m

The Islands (see map p261 unless stated otherwise)
Arran (see map p255) - Goatfell 874m
Mull (see map p258) - Beinn Talaidh 762m
Rum - Ainshval 781m & Askival 812m
Skye - Bla Bheinn 928m
Skye - Sgurr nan Gillean 964m
Skye - The Storr 719m
Skye - Glamaig 775m
South Uist - Beinn Mhor 620m, Ben Corodale 527m
& Hecla 606m
Harris - Ceapabhal 365m
Harris - Clisham 799m
Lewis - Suainebhal 429m

Loch Lomond & The Southern Highlands (see map p63)
Ben Ledi 879m
The Cobbler 884m
Ben Lomond 974m
Ben Vorlich 943m
Beinn Dorain 1076m & Beinn an Dothaidh 1004m
Stob Ghabhar 1090m & Stob a'Choire Odhair 945m

Glen Coe & Glen Nevis (see map p90)
Buachaille Etive Mor 1021m
Aonach Eagach 967m
Stob Coire Sgreamhach 1072m, Bidean nam Bian 1150m &
Stob Coire nan Lochan 1115m
Ballachulish Horseshoe 1024m
Stob Ban 999m & Mullach nan Coirean 939m
Carn Mor Dearg 1220m & Ben Nevis 1344m

Central Highlands (see map p117)
Beinn Ghlas 1103m & Ben Lawers 1214m
Schiehallion 1083m
Sgor Iutharn 1028m, Geal Charn 1132m & Carn Dearg 1034m
Creag Dhubh 757m
Creag Meagaidh 1128m
Stob Coire Easain 1115m & Stob a'Choire Mheadhoin 1105m

The Cairngorms & Eastern Highlands (see map p142)
Ben Vrackie 841m
Mayar 928m & Driesh 947m
Carn a'Choire Bhoidheach 1110m & Lochnagar 1155m
Derry Cairngorm 1155m, Ben Macdui 1309m & Cairn a'Mhaim 1037m
Braeriach 1296m, Sgor an Lochain Uaine 1258m,
Cairn Toul 1291m & The Devil's Point 1004m
Cairn Gorm 1244m
Meall a'Bhuachaille 810m

Map labels: Campbeltown, Brodick, Port Ellen, Arran, Islay, Jura, Scalasaig, Killichlanig, Rothesay, Mull, Tobermory, Coll, Tiree, Rum, Eigg, Barra, Castlebay, Lochboisdale, South Uist, North Uist, Lochmaddy, Harris, Tarbert, W Isles, Skye & Rum, Stornoway, Carloway, Port of Ness, EDINBURGH, GLASGOW, Kirkcaldy, St Andrews, Dundee, Forfar, Pitlochry, Blair Atholl, Dalwhinnie, Kingussie, Aviemore, Braemar, Aberdeen, Huntly, Peterhead, Fraserburgh, Inverness, Lossiemouth, Dornoch, Helmsdale, Wick, Thurso, John O'Groats, Durness, Tongue, Kinlochbervie, Kylesku, Ullapool, Ledmore, Gairloch, Dundonnell, Kinlochewe, Torridon, Shieldaig, Kyle of Lochalsh, Lochcarron, Portree, Uig, Sligachan, Broadford, Mallaig, Fort William, Inverie, Tomdoun, Corrour, Spean Bridge, Glencoe, Bridge of Orchy, Tyndrum, Crianlarich, Callander, Arrochar, Ardlui

Scale: 0 10 20 30 40 50 miles / 0 20 40 60 80km